Manchester Medieval Sources Series

series advisers Rosemary Horrox and Simon MacLean

This series aims to meet a growing need amongst students and teachers of medieval history for translations of key sources that are directly usable in students' own work. It provides texts central to medieval studies courses and focuses upon the diverse cultural and social as well as political conditions that affected the functioning of all levels of medieval society. The basic premise of the series is that translations must be accompanied by sufficient introductory and explanatory material and each volume therefore includes a comprehensive guide to the sources' interpretation, including discussion of critical linguistic problems and an assessment of the most recent research on the topics being covered.

also available in the series

Andrew Brown and Graeme Small *Court and civic society in the Burgundian Low Countries c. 1420–1520*

John H. Arnold and Pete Biller *Heresy and inquisition in France, 1200–1300*

Martin Heale *Monasticism in late medieval England, c.1300–1535*

David Jones *Friars' Tales: Thirteenth-century exempla from the British Isles*

Graham Loud *Roger II and the making of the Kingdom of Sicily*

T.J.H. McCarthy *Chronicles of the Investiture Contest: Frutolf of Michelsberg and his continuators*

A.K. McHardy *The reign of Richard II*

Simon MacLean *History and politics in late Carolingian and Ottonian Europe: The* Chronicle *of Regino of Prüm and Adalbert of Magdeburg*

Anthony Musson and Edward Powell *Crime, law and society in the later Middle Ages*

Andrew Rabin *The political writings of Archbishop Wulfstan of York*

I. S. Robinson *Eleventh-century Germany: The Swabian Chronicles*

I. S. Robinson *The Annals of Lampert of Hersfield*

Craig Taylor *Joan of Arc: La Pucelle*

Diana Webb *Saints and cities in medieval Italy*

for a full list of titles available in this series, please see www.manchesteruniversitypress.co.uk

TOWNS IN MEDIEVAL ENGLAND

MANCHESTER
1824
Manchester University Press

Medieval Sources*online*

Complementing the printed editions of the Medieval Sources series, Manchester University Press has developed a web-based learning resource which is now available on a yearly subscription basis.

Medieval Sources*online* brings quality history source material to the desktops of students and teachers and allows them open and unrestricted access throughout the entire college or university campus. Designed to be fully integrated with academic courses, this is a one-stop answer for many medieval history students, academics and researchers keeping thousands of pages of source material 'in print' over the Internet for research and teaching.

titles available now at Medieval Sourcesonline include

Trevor Dean *The towns of Italy in the later Middle Ages*

John Edwards *The Jews in Western Europe, 1400–1600*

Paul Fouracre and Richard A. Gerberding *Late Merovingian France: History and hagiography 640–720*

Chris Given-Wilson *Chronicles of the Revolution 1397–1400: The reign of Richard II*

P. J. P. Goldberg *Women in England, c. 1275–1525*

Janet Hamilton and Bernard Hamilton *Christian dualist heresies in the Byzantine world, c. 650–c. 1450*

Rosemary Horrox *The Black Death*

David Jones *Friars' Tales: Thirteenth-century exempla from the British Isles*

Graham A. Loud and Thomas Wiedemann *The history of the tyrants of Sicily by 'Hugo Falcandus', 1153–69*

A. K. McHardy *The reign of Richard II: From minority to tyranny 1377-97*

Simon MacLean *History and politics in late Carolingian and Ottonian Europe: The* Chronicle *of Regino of Prüm and Adalbert of Magdeburg*

Anthony Musson and Edward Powell *Crime, law and society in the later Middle Ages*

Janet L. Nelson *The Annals of St-Bertin: Ninth-century histories, volume I*

Timothy Reuter *The Annals of Fulda: Ninth-century histories, volume II*

R. N. Swanson *Catholic England: Faith, religion and observance before the Reformation*

Elisabeth van Houts *The Normans in Europe*

Jennifer Ward *Women of the English nobility and gentry 1066–1500*

Visit the site at www.medievalsources.co.uk for further information and subscription prices.

TOWNS IN MEDIEVAL ENGLAND

Selected sources

translated and annotated

by Gervase Rosser

Manchester University Press

Published by Manchester University Press
Altrincham Street, Manchester M1 7JA
www.manchesteruniversitypress.co.uk

British Library Cataloguing-in-Publication Data
A catalogue record for this book is available from the British Library

Library of Congress Cataloging-in-Publication Data applied for

ISBN 978 0 7190 4908 8 hardback
ISBN 978 0 7190 4909 5 paperback

First published 2016

Typeset in Monotype Bell by
Servis Filmsetting Ltd, Stockport, Cheshire
Printed in Great Britain by
Bell & Bain Ltd, Glasgow

CONTENTS

ACKNOWLEDGEMENTS

It is a pleasure to set on record my debt to Rosemary Horrox, who, after inviting me to assemble a collection of sources on English medieval towns, extended infinite patience and tact to sustain the project and to ensure its eventual realisation. I am grateful both for her kindness and for her shrewd editorial advice. A more extensive obligation is owed to generations of archivists who have preserved an invaluable treasury of medieval urban records, including those who perform this service today, in defiance of diminishing resources. Equally selfless and invaluable have been the labours of those earlier scholars who transcribed and edited many of the sources of which excerpts are included in the following pages. To them, also, my profound thanks are due. All historians know that nothing is more important than the preservation of the historical record, and that a society which loses the critical perspective to which history gives access is at grave risk. This book is dedicated to the present custodians of our medieval archives.

Every effort has been made to obtain permission to reproduce copyright material, and the publisher will be pleased to be informed of any errors and omissions for correction in future editions.

EDITORIAL NOTE

All medieval texts have been rendered into modern English. The original language of each text is indicated at the end of the introductory note. Where the immediate source is a manuscript or an untranslated modern edition, the editor is responsible for the translation (whether from Latin – the medium of the vast majority of the records in question – or French or Middle English). In the case of sources in modern printed editions with a translated text, the editor has adapted this where necessary to modernise spelling and syntax and to remove the fustian language of earlier versions (noted as 'revised by GR'). The glossary on pp. 286–90 has been added to the same end: an asterisk against a word indicates its inclusion in the glossary.

Abbreviations

CUHB D. Palliser (ed.), *The Cambridge Urban History of Britain*, i, *600–1540*, Cambridge, 2000

INTRODUCTION

The urbanised landscape of England in the twenty-first century is the heir to a medieval experiment. After the collapse of the city-based empire of Rome in the fifth century, the medieval town was a fresh initiative, created and shaped by the cultural and commercial currents of its time. Although this point of origin is partially obscured by the subsequent layers of industrial growth and of more recent, post-industrial adaptation, the historical roots of the modern city lie in the Middle Ages. The publication of this collection of written sources is intended to encourage and facilitate the study of that medieval phase in the evolution of our towns and cities. The reader who samples the texts in this volume will be struck by their diversity. In the period represented by these documents – from the eleventh to the sixteenth centuries – England was already urbanised, in the sense that the presence of towns was felt in all parts of the country, and touched every aspect of life. As a result, the traces of medieval urban experience are to be found in a great variety of historical sources. Each one of these classes of evidence presents its own particular problems of interpretation, which are highlighted in the section introductions and in the notes on individual sources, together with the potential rewards of casting the historian's net as widely as possible. Much that we should like to know remains difficult to discern in the record, but, if we take a multi-faceted approach, we find that the documentation is rich, and that it invites us to deepen our understanding of this crucial phase in the history of the city.

The material city

The student who engages with these written records, with a view to thinking critically about their analysis and interpretation, is contributing to a distinguished body of scholarship which reaches back to the antiquaries and local historians of the seventeenth and eighteenth centuries and to the amateur and professional historians of the nineteenth to the twenty-first. A new generation has fresh questions to ask of the past, and imaginative use of the available sources can yield answers which will add significantly to the field. To facilitate that task, this volume focuses on the wealth and variety of the textual evidence. But the researcher will not wish to ignore the further testimony of material traces of the medieval town, which circumstances have brought to our particular attention in recent decades, and on which a preliminary comment is called for here. To awaken our interest in the past, there is no stimulus so powerful as a period of destruction. After the end of the Second World War, the sites of bomb damage remained for years, for lack of resources, as testimony to the recent conflict. To some of these melancholy places there came, at the end of each working day, crowds of Londoners who queued to see, for a penny, the latest finds of the archaeologists. Picking their way over the rubble – scattered with the purple flowers of the rose-bay willow-herb – visitors found their hopes for the future reinforced by newly discovered images of their common past. The greatest sensation was caused by objects from the Roman period; but these excavations in advance of rebuilding multiplied immeasurably, in addition, the material evidence for London's history in the Middle Ages.[1] Phoenix-like, the city's complex past arose from the ruins of its conflagration. Conserved in the Guildhall Museum, these finds offered access to a previously inconceivable urban history. Fresh devastation was brought to other parts of London, as also to the centres of many provincial English towns, by the prosperous last decades of the twentieth century, when the feverish construction of offices and shopping-centres briefly opened archaeological windows on to the origins and sequence of urban development. In consequence the Museum of London, successor to the Guildhall Museum, and numerous sister institutions in the regions now house collections of material objects which can give substance to a medieval urban history unimaginable by earlier generations.[2] The contents of a late medieval musical instrument-maker's shop in Oxford; loaded dice used by fraudsters in fifteenth-century London; a pet monkey discovered in a fifteenth-century merchant's house at Southampton – these and countless other surviving objects have the potential, when properly contextualised, to illuminate town life in the medieval centuries.[3] Over the past half-century our understanding of medieval towns everywhere has been transformed more by archaeological discoveries –

1 W. F. Grimes, *The Excavation of Roman and Mediaeval London*, London, 1968.

2 J. Clark, *London 1100–1600: The Archaeology of the Capital City*, London, 2011.

3 Oxford: B. Durham, 'Archaeological investigations in St Aldates, Oxford', *Oxoniensia*, XLII, 1977, pp. 83–203, at pp. 163–6 (incl. fig. 39), 194–5, 198. London: Museum of London accession no. 84.136. Southampton: C. Platt, *Medieval Southampton: The Port and Trading Community, AD 1000–1600*, London, 1973, p. 104.

and by their careful interpretation – than by any other particular mode of research. The collateral effects of economic boom have granted us a new insight into our urban past.

For a longer period than this, of course, material traces of the urban past have engaged historical imaginations. When, in the aftermath of the French Revolution and its attendant iconoclastic devastation of monuments throughout France, Alexandre Lenoir made a collection of the remains and housed them in a new Musée des Monuments Français, visitors recorded a heady excitement in the presence of things which seemed, in the romantic culture of the era, to transport them back to 'those chivalric times': an age not only of knights and ladies but of the imagined glories of Paris and of the other 'bonnes villes' of medieval France. From the 1850s Nuremberg, even before the creation of the state of Germany, attracted thousands to the Germanische Nationalmuseum which, through displayed objects of all kinds, from baronial and civic banners to a cast of the bronze lion in the marketplace of Brunswick, aimed to inspire an as yet disunited population with these tangible images of a shared medieval past, most splendid in its cities, perceived as harbingers of a common freedom. The Musée de Cluny in Paris – in effect the successor to Lenoir's museum from the 1840s – retains to this day the atmosphere of those nineteenth-century collections which aimed, by immersing the visitor in the secular and sacred objects of a past culture, from tapestries to forks and from shoes to pilgrim badges, to conjure from these ingredients a certain empathy with the period.[4]

The 'material turn' – a recent call across a range of disciplines for the close study of material traces of past cultures – cannot, therefore, be said to be wholly original. What has been introduced by recent scholarship is a new degree of historical rigour in the interpretation of objects, supported by an equal grasp of textual sources.[5] The individual archaeological find cannot speak unaided: what is needed is a contextualised interpretation. Such an integrated approach has informed the best work of recent decades on English medieval towns. Pioneering

4 F. Haskell, *History and Its Images. Art and the Interpretation of the Past*, New Haven and London, 1993, pp. 236–52, 282–7.

5 A. Appadurai (ed.), *The Social Life of Things: Commodities in Cultural Perspective*, Cambridge, 1986; D. Miller (ed.), *Material Cultures: Why Some Things Matter*, London, 1998; T. Hamling and C. Richardson (eds), *Everyday Objects: Medieval and Early Modern Material Culture and Its Meanings*, Farnham, 2010; R. Gilchrist, *Medieval Life. Archaeology and the Life Course*, Woodbridge, 2012.

and exemplary in this respect has been the comprehensive survey of Winchester.[6] The potential of detailed topographical reconstruction of the physical shape of a medieval town and its constituent buildings and open spaces, drawing at once upon archaeological and documentary evidence, has been further demonstrated by the project on Cheapside in London before the Great Fire.[7] The city of York, whose medieval past has been no less dramatically brought into view by the revelations of archaeologists, has benefited from collaborative study using similar historical methods.[8] Urban geographers have convincingly emphasised the potential of historic maps to reveal distinct phases in a town's evolution.[9] New scholarship in the related fields of social history and the history of gender relations, economic history and the history of religion has also brought fresh evidence and new questions to the particular context of urban studies.[10] The study of medieval towns has become, of necessity, a multi-disciplinary undertaking. Within that project, the written documents which are sampled in this volume remain of fundamental importance.

The early medieval town

Only from about 1200 do we have written materials concerning towns created by townspeople themselves. Yet recent archaeological discoveries have made it abundantly clear that, by 1200, medieval urban life in this country was already old. Although the chronological focus of

6 See especially: D. Keene, *Survey of Medieval Winchester*, Winchester Studies, 2, 2 vols, Oxford, 1985. The survey began in 1961, and is ongoing. Significant precedents for the topographical work of this project were the model documentary studies of W. Urry, *Canterbury under the Angevin Kings*, London, 1967; and H. E. Salter, *Survey of Oxford*, 2 vols, Oxford, 1969.

7 D. Keene and V. Harding, *Historical Gazetteer of London before the Great Fire*, i, *Cheapside*, London, 1987.

8 S. Rees Jones, *York: The Making of a City 1086–1350*, Oxford, 2014; P. V. Addymann (ed.), *The British Atlas of Historic Towns*, vol. 5, *York*, 2015.

9 D. M. Palliser, T. R. Slater and E. P. Dennison, 'The topography of towns 600–1300', in *CUHB*, pp. 153–86; M. D. Lobel et al. (eds), *The British Atlas of Historic Towns*, London, 1969– .

10 C. Dyer, *Making a Living in the Middle Ages: The People of Britain 850–1520*, London, 2002; P. J. P. Goldberg, *Women, Work, and Life Cycle in a Medieval Economy: Women in York and Yorkshire c.1300–1520*, Oxford, 1992; D. M. Hadley (ed.), *Masculinity in Medieval Europe*, London, 1999; R. H. Britnell, 'The economy of British towns 1300–1540', in *CUHB*, pp. 313–33; N. P. Tanner, *The Church in Late Medieval Norwich 1370–1532*, Toronto, 1984; T. R. Slater and G. Rosser (eds), *The Church in the Medieval Town*, Aldershot, 1998.

this book is upon the period *c.*1200–1500, it is important to be aware that the physical plans of many towns still bear the traces of that earlier phase of growth, and that laws and customs recorded in the late medieval centuries may in some cases transmit practices of considerably greater antiquity. There were many discontinuities in the history of later medieval towns, whose distribution, forms and functions were altered by changing demographic and social circumstances. None the less, the student of towns in this later period should be aware of their past. The extent of Anglo-Saxon urbanisation has been a revelation of recent archaeology. References in Bede's early eighth-century *Ecclesiastical History* to Canterbury and London as *emporia* were once thought to be rhetorical exaggerations: the discovery by excavation in each case of a substantial middle Saxon settlement, marked by evidence of both industry and international trade, has changed our picture both of the economy of pre-Conquest England and of the relationship of emergent central places to political power. London was one of a number of English *wics* or trading centres at this period, which also included Ipswich and *Hamwic*, later to evolve as Southampton: material finds demonstrate their interconnections with similar places on the farther side of the North Sea.[11] How far these international marketplaces were actively developed by royal decree is still a matter for speculation, although royal grants of toll-rights in eighth-century London indicate commercial awareness, and in a number of laws the Saxon kings expressed a keen interest in towns (or *burhs*), whether as points for the collection of taxes or as means to implement control in the localities. The early tenth-century Burghal Hidage, which in the context of the Viking raids listed arrangements for the defence of royal centres (not all of which actually were or became towns) in the west midlands and the south-west, is a further indication of royal interest in the potential of such places. After the Norman Conquest, the royal Domesday Book of 1086 would reinforce these links, showing the crown's deep concern with the construction of urban castles and with the military obligations of strategically positioned towns [**9**], [**10**].[12] The fortifications imposed on many towns at this period were motivated not by a benign desire to protect urban populations but

11 G. Astill, 'General survey 600–1300'; D. M. Palliser, T. R. Slater and E. P. Dennison, 'The topography of towns 600–1300'; D. Keene, 'London from the post-Roman period to 1300', all in *CUHB*, pp. 27–49, 153–86, 187–216.

12 J. Campbell, 'Power and authority 600–1300', *CUHB*, pp. 51–78; S. Kelly, 'Trading privileges from eighth-century England', *Early Medieval Europe*, i, 1992, pp. 3–28.

by the determination to control them. Typically, the castle mound at Oxford, erected after the Conquest by its new Norman lord, rests on top of the crushed remains of earlier houses and shops.[13] The charged political connection between towns and royal power was close from the beginning, and would remain so throughout the Middle Ages and into modern times. The Anglo-Saxon nobility, also, whether motivated by economic or cultural reasons, manifested an active interest in towns, anticipating what would be a significant pattern of aristocratic urban patronage in the later medieval period.[14] Whatever the strength of economic forces, the character and pace of urbanisation would always be conditioned by its political context.

The other key to the pre-Conquest development of towns in England was the Church. The cities of the Roman hegemony had ceased to function by the fifth century, and, where certain of these were subsequently selected by bishops of the Roman Church to establish their sees, it may be inferred that their choice was in part an ideological one, motivated by the prestige which continued to attach to these largely abandoned yet monumental witnesses to a former power. The ecclesiastical presence alone, however, does not appear to have sufficed to trigger the urban regeneration of Canterbury, York or Gloucester: royal or aristocratic and commercial functions were rather to the fore in these and similar cases.[15] More substantially responsible for catalysing urban growth in the middle and late Saxon period were the new, strategically situated churches known as minsters. The material needs and pastoral functions of the small communities of minster priests, often established in the first instance by royal and aristocratic patrons, have been shown to have brought into being an extensive network of new marketplaces and centres of population, required in the first instance to sustain the churches themselves and subsequently taking on a partially independent urban life of their own. The topographical work which has established the existence of this substantial category of small late Saxon towns underlines the need for the historian to see the 'new' town developments of the twelfth and thirteenth centuries, which are recorded in

13 T. G. Hassall, 'Excavations at Oxford Castle, 1965–1973', *Oxoniensia*, XLI, 1976, pp. 232–308, at pp. 253–4.

14 R. Fleming, 'Rural elites and urban communities in late Saxon England', *Past and Present*, CXLI, 1993, pp. 3–26.

15 D. A. Hinton, 'The large towns 600–1300', in *CUHB*, pp. 217–43; N. Baker and R. Holt, *Urban Growth and the Medieval Church: Gloucester and Worcester*, Aldershot, 2003.

documents of a kind not available for the earlier period, as additions or overlays in a landscape already well endowed with urban – albeit for the most part small – central places.[16]

The late medieval town as a historical subject

The source materials gathered in this book, therefore, which range in date from the late eleventh century to the early sixteenth, tell a story with a significant prehistory. Although far less well-documented and still only partially understood, the Anglo-Saxon town, in its diverse forms, would persist as a presence and an influence upon its post-Conquest descendant. By the thirteenth century, when series of documents begin to survive which were generated by townspeople themselves, the post-Roman reinvention of urban life had already taken place. In the past generation we have come to realise that the half-millennium between 700 and 1200 witnessed one of the most experimental and creative periods in the history of the post-classical city. But the last medieval centuries of the English town, from 1200 to 1500, are also rich in interest; and it is an interest which in this period can be deepened not only by the finds of archaeology but in the new light of a great wealth of surviving documentation. It is the purpose of this book to present a range of that late medieval evidence, and to draw attention both to the challenges which it presents to interpretation and to the potential rewards of its study. The documents introduced here have been chosen both for the interest of their particular content and in order to exemplify some of these issues of historical analysis. The extracts which are reproduced on the following pages sketch in outline the history of the late medieval English town. Our principal concern, however, is to introduce the reader to the variety, the difficulties and the potential of the surviving written evidence. The history of medieval towns continues to attract researchers, and the subject is now impressively served by scholarly monographs on individual places and on particular civic themes. But an accessible collection of printed primary sources for the study of English towns in the period has been lacking.[17]

16 J. Blair, 'Small towns 600–1300', in *CUHB*, pp. 245–70; J. Blair, *The Church in Anglo-Saxon Society*, Oxford, 2005, ch. 5.

17 For a collection of Latin texts on early British urban history see S. Reynolds, W. de Boer and G. Mac Niocaill (eds), *Select Texts on British and Irish Urban History before the mid Thirteenth Century*, Elenchus Fontium Historiae Urbanae, vol. ii, part 2, Leiden, 1988. For a selection of documents on the medieval town in Western Europe as a whole, see M. Kowaleski (ed.), *Medieval Towns. A Reader*, New York, 2008.

A number of the texts included in this book are translated into modern English from manuscript sources. Many others were first edited in the publications of local and scholarly record societies. The point of gathering them here is to give them greater visibility and to present them in the wider context of a diverse collection, thereby provoking fresh questions about their value and meaning. Medieval towns have not lacked the attention of scholars; but their historical records have yet much more to reveal about the life experiences of their inhabitants.

The definition of a town with which historians work is a settlement characterised by a concentration of people, of whom the majority are dependent on non-agrarian activity for their living and in which a diversity of crafts and professions is practised. Its *raison d'être* as a central place will depend upon particular administrative, economic or military functions, or some combination of these. This is essentially a qualitative, not a quantitative definition, and it allows for a wide diversity of scale. While precise figures cannot be known, it is clear that the size of English urban populations in the late medieval period ranged from a narrow apex to a wide base. Only the metropolis of London, with a population in 1300 which has been most reliably estimated at eighty thousand or a little more, could be measured alongside the other great cities of Western Christendom, including comparable centres in the Low Countries, such as Arras and Ghent, with which London had economic ties. At the same period a small category of still larger cities was represented by Paris, Venice and Milan.[18] A considerable gap separated London, which by the thirteenth century had effectively established its claim to be the capital of the English kingdom, from Bristol and Norwich, each of which is likely to have contained upwards of twenty thousand townspeople in the early fourteenth century. A further dozen English towns numbered between about five thousand and ten thousand inhabitants at the same period.[19] By far the largest category was that of the small towns of fewer than two thousand people: it has been suggested that there were as many as seven hundred such places.[20] English medieval urbanisation – with the important exception

18 D. Keene, *Cheapside before the Great Fire*, London, 1985, pp. 19–20; D. Keene, 'Medieval London and Its region', *London Journal*, XIV, 1989, pp. 99–111; D. Keene in *CUHB*, pp. 195–6.

19 E. Rutledge, 'Immigration and population growth in early fourteenth-century Norwich: evidence from the Tithing Roll', *Urban History Yearbook*, 1988, pp. 15–30, proposed a population for Norwich in 1333 of 25,000.

20 C. Dyer, 'How urbanised was medieval England?', in J.-M. Duvosquel and E. Thoen (eds), *Peasants and Townsmen in Medieval Europe: Studies in Honorem Adriaan*

of the metropolis of London – was not so much highly concentrated as it was widely spread.

Legal and constitutional frameworks

Our understanding of our subject will be shaped by the evidence we choose to call to witness. The multi-faceted and pluralistic approach which is recommended by this book has not always been in favour. The first scholarly investigations into medieval towns drew primarily upon legal records, in order to clarify the distinctions of formal status which were taken to differentiate urban settlements. The approach was informed by assumptions about the role which had supposedly been played by towns in the historical development of personal liberties and collective representation. In the work of Charles Gross, Mary Bateson and others at the turn of the twentieth century, this approach was immensely productive, especially in the identification and edition of urban legal texts, many of which still invite closer study.[21] The work of these historians remains of fundamental importance, even though their convictions about the supposed historical evolution of democratic principles led them at times to accord an imaginary precision to particular legal terms in the documents.[22] To scholars of their epoch and formation, it was a natural assumption that what made a town in the first instance was its charter of liberties. There is, after all, some justification for this view in the evident concern of groups of townspeople to acquire such formal grants of privilege. The early Anglo-Norman kings made such concessions with great reluctance; but the financial needs of Richard I and John in the years around 1200 prompted them to issue no fewer than fifty urban charter grants [**12**]. Thereafter, Henry III and his immediate successors were wary of urban bids for freedom, until royal weakness in the fifteenth century again opened the door

Verhulst, Ghent, 1995, pp. 169–83; C. Dyer, 'Small towns 1270–1540', in *CUHB*, pp. 505–37.

21 C. Gross, *The Gild Merchant: A Contribution to British Municipal History*, Oxford, 1890; M. Bateson (ed.), *Borough Customs*, 2 vols, Selden Society, XVIII, 1904; A. Ballard and J. Tait (eds), *British Borough Charters 1216–1307*, Cambridge, 1923; M. Weinbaum, *The Incorporation of Boroughs*, Manchester, 1937; M. Weinbaum, *British Borough Charters 1307–1660*, Cambridge, 1943.

22 A dead end of legal analysis was reached in J. Tait, *The Medieval English Borough*, Manchester, 1936. See G. H. Martin, 'The English borough in the thirteenth century' [1963], repr. in R. Holt and G. Rosser (eds), *The Medieval Town*, London, 1990, pp. 29–48, at pp. 30–2; and S. Reynolds, *An Introduction to the History of English Medieval Towns*, Oxford, 1977, pp. 91–117.

to more substantial concessions. The default, at all periods, was strict royal control, which the Tudor monarchs, in their turn, would reapply with avidity. The local desire for a significant measure of autonomy was manifest not only in the laborious and expensive acquisition of the charters themselves but in such communal movements as those of London in the 1130s, the 1180s and the 1260s. However, the English crown was only too able to extinguish such expressions of resistance to royal power, and the effectively independent communes of northern Italy and the Low Countries found only distant echoes in this country.

No royal grant ever conceded complete self-government to a town, and one that showed itself rebellious was likely to have its privileges removed. Following its involvement in the rising of Simon de Montfort, London found itself taken into the king's hands, and its mayoralty suspended, between 1265 and 1270 and again between 1285 and 1299. But despite the difficulties, both London and many other cities were prepared to fight hard and to pay well for charters which, with often finely illuminated initials and impressive seals, would be displayed on formal occasions as the material embodiment of the political community [**11**].[23] With variations in detail, the common ambition of townsmen requesting a charter – and it is evident that each case of a grant originated in such a request, and perhaps a phase of negotiation with the king's legal advisers – was a measure of self-regulation, which might be secured through the right to hold a guild merchant: a gathering of leading traders to manage the secular affairs of the town. A guild of this kind commonly preceded the emergence in the thirteenth century of a more fully empowered city council, headed in the grander cases by an elected mayor [**16**]. A further request of petitioners for charters was for the right of the 'borough farm' (*firma burgi*), a compounded regular payment in lieu of miscellaneous dues and obligations owed to the crown. The desired rights also included a borough court for the local settlement of property and trade disputes. What were sought, in sum, were limited rights of 'self-government at the king's command'.

Earlier historians sometimes attributed excessive significance to these grants, which can often be shown to have done little more than to ratify existing practice. Behind every petition for rights there must have operated a pre-existing organisation in the form of a guild or

23 Campbell, 'Power and the state'; D. M. Palliser, 'Towns and the English state, 1066–1500', in J. R. Maddicott and D. M. Palliser (eds), *The Medieval State: Essays Presented to James Campbell*, London, 2000, pp. 127–45.

a proto-council. A close reading of the charter texts can discern the evidence of pre-legal organisation amongst the townspeople. Thus the political leaders of Oxford, successfully petitioning for a charter in 1191, already claimed to speak for 'all the citizens'.[24] A similar argument applies to the many late medieval royal charters of urban incorporation, which supposedly gave the recipient communities a special legal status, although many of the rights which they specified were owned by the towns already.[25] But notwithstanding this qualification, we should not dismiss the evidence of the charters, which were evidently desirable enough to be petitioned and paid for. The very process of their acquisition was a political education for townspeople. Recent studies have redirected our attention to the political culture of the towns, where the rhetorical language and the physical form of charters – no less significant evidence, for the attentive historian, than their constitutional content – helped to structure both the citizens' sense of identity and the discourse of public life.[26] Paradoxically, the very intrusiveness of the crown's control over the legal rights and fiscal obligations of the late medieval towns was a stimulus to the self-conscious identity and responsibility of the citizens. Self-government in the king's name could be experienced locally as an expression of civic pride. Questioned by royal justices in 1220–1, the citizens of London were round in their response: 'And besides, it is the lord's court, not the lord, who ought to make the judgement.'[27] The imposition of royal taxation called for local discussion about the status of those who should be required to contribute, and consequent reflection on what it meant to be a qualified citizen with rights but also with obligations.[28] There is something for the historian to learn, therefore,

24 R. H. C. Davis, 'An Oxford charter of 1191 and the beginnings of municipal freedom', *Oxoniensia*, XXXIII, 1968, pp. 53–65.

25 S. Reynolds, 'The history of the idea of incorporation or legal personality: a case of fallacious teleology', in her *Ideas and Solidarities of the Medieval Laity*, Aldershot, 1995, separately paginated.

26 C. Liddy, *War, Politics and Finance in Late Medieval English Towns. Bristol, York and the Crown, 1350–1400*, Woodbridge, 2005; L. Attreed, *The King's Towns. Identity and Survival in Late Medieval English Boroughs*, New York, 2001.

27 S. Reynolds, *Kingdoms and Communities in Western Europe, 900-1300*, 2nd edn, Oxford, 1997, p. 59.

28 C. Liddy, '"Bee war of gyle in borugh": taxation and political discourse in late medieval English towns', in A. Gamberini, J.–P. Genet and A. Zorzi (eds), *The Languages of Political Society: Western Europe, 14th–17th Centuries*, Rome, 2011, pp. 461–85; Liddy, *War, Politics and Finance*, p. 58; Reynolds, *Kingdoms and Communities*, p. 180.

not merely from the fact of fiscal burden but from the evidence in the records of taxation concerning the way in which neighbourhoods determined how and upon whom the levy should fall [**43**], [**44**]. The representation of towns in national assemblies was initiated for royal convenience, townsmen being summoned regularly to parliament from 1275 (separately from the county MPs until 1353). But viewed from another perspective, attendance gave opportunities for lobbying in the civic interest. Relations between the throne and the urban periphery could be imperious: Henry VII in 1495 summoned the mayor of York to Greenwich in order to inform him that, if he could not prevent rioting, 'I must and will put in other rulers that will rule and govern the city according to my laws.'[29] But when the common council of Exeter was at odds with the dean and chapter of the cathedral over jurisdictional rights in the mid-fifteenth century, it was natural that the mayor should ride to London in order to gain audience with the king's chancellor, at which he reported to his councillors that he was greeted 'with laughing cheer' and promises of support [**5**].[30] By adopting an eclectic approach to our sources, and by shifting the camera-angle to consider them in different lights, we stand to gain an enriched, more textured understanding of our historical subject.

The difficulties of the mayor of Exeter in dealing with the jealously guarded privileges of the cathedral were symptomatic of the universal jurisdictional fact that every town of any size was legally fragmented into the various territorial interests of its constituent lords. The charters of a city such as York gave a splendid outward appearance of unity which was belied by the internal maze of particular rights, and especially by those of the Church.[31] Ecclesiastical urban estates could be substantial, and built up with secular properties whose occupants claimed immunity from the laws and impositions of the town council [**54**]. The result was a continual wrangling over authority in the town – a condition which would persist in many cases until the Municipal Reform Act of 1835. Once again our interest in the documentary evidence of these jurisdictional disputes is justified by the facts that they occasioned debates on the theme of political identity, and that they

29 A. Raine (ed.), *York Civic Records*, ii, Yorkshire Archaeological Society Record Series, CIII, 1941, p. 115.

30 S. A. Moore (ed.), *Letters and Papers of John Shillingford, Mayor of Exeter 1447–50*, Camden Society, 2nd series, ii, 1881, pp. 36–9.

31 E. Miller, 'Medieval York', in *The Victoria County History of Yorkshire, The City of York*, London, 1961, pp. 25–116.

galvanised the active involvement not only of the elites but also of the unenfranchised.[32]

Economic functions of large and small towns

If the evidence of charters and urban law tends to give prominence to those qualities which separated a town from its surroundings, the sources for economic activity demonstrate, by contrast, the many ways in which urban society was integrated with its larger environment. Earlier historians appreciated that the town was not to be understood as autonomous. Marx knew this, and the father of English medieval urban history, F. W. Maitland, despite the legal bias of his interest in the subject, placed it firmly in a larger context of fields, rural landowners and the produce of agriculture.[33] Scholars have lately re-emphasised the need to set the medieval town within its region. The argument has implications not only for our understanding of the urban economy [**34**], [**75**], [**76**] but also for analysis of social relations in towns, which, although differently inflected, were characterised by the same issues of political hierarchy and class tension which pervaded the population at large. A monograph on Colchester by Richard Britnell and another on Exeter by Maryanne Kowaleski, together with the project 'Feeding London', have exploited the evidence of agrarian manors in order to comprehend the medieval town in its regional setting, identifying the hinterland as part of an urban economic area and positioning the towns themselves within a partially integrated network.[34] Such 'urban network analysis' has been undertaken for some time

32 G. Rosser, 'Conflict and political community in the medieval town: disputes between clergy and laity in Hereford', in T. R. Slater and G. Rosser (eds), *The Church in the Medieval Town*, Aldershot, 1998, pp. 20–42.

33 'By all means let us study the gilds and all that is commonly regarded as the constitutional side of burghal history. But proprietary rights in lands and houses are important; rights of pasture were very important.' F. W. Maitland, *Township and Borough*, Cambridge, 1898, p. 50.

34 R. H. Britnell, *Growth and Decline in Colchester, 1300–1525*, Cambridge, 1986; M. Kowaleski, *Local Markets and Regional Trade in Medieval Exeter*, Cambridge, 1995; B. M. S. Campbell, J. A. Galloway, D. Keene and M. Murphy, *A Medieval Capital and Its Grain Supply: Agrarian Production and Distribution in the London Region c.1300*, London, 1993; J. A. Galloway, 'One market or many? London and the grain trade of England', in J. A. Galloway (ed.), *Trade, Urban Hinterlands and Market Integration c.1300–1600*, London, 2000, pp. 23–42; R. H. Britnell, *The Commercialisation of English Society, 1000–1500*, 2nd edn, Manchester, 1996, p. 115; *CUHB*, part iv, 'Regional surveys'.

also by Dutch and Belgian historians of the Flemish medieval cities.[35] Northern Italy, which was the other most densely urbanised zone of late medieval Europe, invites similar study, although in that case the historiography has tended hitherto to remain more localised and fragmented.[36] Even rural records, therefore, may have things of importance to tell us about the magnetic pull of the city upon the human and material resources of the countryside.

The break with a restrictive constitutional model has enabled historians to bring into focus the numerous family of smaller towns, typically lacking in substantial legal rights, relatively poorly documented, and therefore unnoticed by previous scholarship [**15**]. The evidence for their existence lies typically not in civic archives but amongst the manorial records of the predominantly rural estates of secular and ecclesiastical landlords.[37] Many of these places were even smaller than the urbanised minster settlements of Anglo-Saxon origin, and their arrival on the scene made a marked difference to the landscape. Following upon initial studies by Eleanora Carus-Wilson and Rodney Hilton, Christopher Dyer and others have demonstrated the role of small towns in the economy as a whole, and the witness they bear to the penetration of the market into all parts of the English countryside by the thirteenth century.[38] An instance studied by Hilton is the west midlands market town of Halesowen, founded in the mid-thirteenth century on its land by a monastic community. Although comprising

35 W. Prevenier and W. Blockmans, *The Burgundian Netherlands*, Cambridge, 1986; P. Stabel, *Dwarfs among Giants: The Flemish Urban Network in the Late Middle Ages*, Louvain, 1997.

36 But see the comparative studies of R. H. Britnell, 'The towns of England and northern Italy in the early fourteenth century', *Economic History Review*, 2nd series, XLIV, 1991, pp. 21–35; and G. Chittolini, 'Urban population, urban territories, small towns: some problems of the history of urbanization in northern and central Italy (thirteenth-sixteenth centuries)', in P. C. M. Hoppenbrouwers, A. Janse and R. Stein (eds), *Power and Persuasion: Essays on the Art of State Building in Honour of W. P. Blockmans*, Turnhout, 2010, pp. 227–41.

37 For a critical introduction and selected examples of manorial records, see M. Bailey, *The English Manor. Selected Sources*, Manchester, 2002.

38 E. M. Carus-Wilson, 'The first half-century of the borough of Stratford-upon-Avon' [1965], repr. in R. Holt and G. Rosser (eds), *The Medieval Town*, London, 1990, pp. 49–70; R. H. Hilton, 'Small town society in England before the Black Death' [1984], repr., in ibid., pp. 71–96; R. H. Hilton, 'Medieval market towns and simple commodity production', *Past and Present*, CIX, 1985, pp. 3–23; E. Miller and J. Hatcher, *Medieval England. Towns, Commerce and Crafts*, London, 1995, p. 257; C. Dyer, 'Small places with large consequences: the importance of small towns in England, 1000–1540', *Historical Research*, LXXV, 2002, pp. 1–24.

only six hundred or so inhabitants, its court rolls from the late thirteenth and early fourteenth centuries reveal a diversity of crafts and services and a market which functioned as a centre of exchange for the surrounding countryside.[39] It is similarly from manorial account rolls that we learn about Buntingford, a small town in Hertfordshire promoted by its secular lords, who vested power in their tenants and enabled them to secure a royal market grant in 1360. Containing no more than about 350 inhabitants in the early sixteenth century, the place was none the less both urban and prosperous.[40] As many as half of all inhabitants of towns may have lived in such relatively modest centres of trade. The seigneurial boroughs and urban estates (that is, those directly subject to lay or ecclesiastical lords), precisely because they lacked the regulation and by-laws which would have been the consequence of a more independent legal status, paradoxically enjoyed a potential measure of liberty for economic initiative which they would otherwise have been denied. Birmingham and Manchester, both of which grew from medieval industrial origins to their prominence in the nineteenth century as manorial vills,* are dramatic instances of this large class of unchartered towns.[41]

Once we take account of the smaller towns, we are faced with the striking statistics that as many as one person in ten was a town-dweller in England in 1200, and double this proportion – one person in five – in 1300. The latter ratio may have dropped slightly by 1500; but, for the period as a whole, the generalisation may be allowed that, given the distribution of market centres, no part of the country was untouched by the urban element.[42] Recent work on local markets, on personal mobility and on communications in later medieval England suggests that, even if eighty per cent of people still lived on the land, this was already, to a marked degree, an urbanised society. The statement, however, calls for further clarification. This was not the urbanisation

39 Hilton, 'Small town society'.

40 M. Bailey, 'A tale of two towns: Buntingford and Standon in the later Middle Ages', *Journal of Medieval History*, XIX, 1993, pp. 351–71.

41 R. A. Holt, *The Early History of the Town of Birmingham*, Oxford, 1985; J. Tait, *Medieval Manchester*, Manchester, 1904; G. Rosser, 'The essence of medieval urban communities: the vill of Westminster, 1200–1540' [1984], repr. in R. Holt and G. Rosser (eds), *The Medieval Town*, London, 1990, pp. 216–37.

42 C. Dyer, 'A summing up', in J. A. Galloway (ed.), *Trade, Urban Hinterlands and Market Integration c.1300–1600*, London, 2000, pp. 103–9; Dyer, 'How urbanised was medieval England?'; R. H. Britnell, *Britain and Ireland 1050–1530. Economy and Society*, Oxford, 2004, pp. 348–50.

of central and north Italy in the period, characterised as these areas were by effectively autonomous cities enjoying extensive control and powers of exploitation over their respective hinterlands. Nor was it similar to Sicily, whose comparative deregulation gave effective licence to localised urban investment and industrial innovation.[43] The prosperity of the urban network in the late medieval Low Countries owed much to the relatively light hand of the Flemish counts and later of the Burgundian dukes.[44] In England, by contrast, the establishment before the Conquest of centralised royal power meant, as we have seen, that the towns would never acquire either the political liberties or the economic resources available to cities elsewhere. On the other hand, the ability of secular and ecclesiastical landlords to exploit their territorial resources as they pleased – a capacity strongly encouraged from the thirteenth century by increasingly insistent royal demands for taxation – made possible the proliferation of those small, seigneurial towns which, taken together with the rest, resulted in an urban presence which was felt throughout the country. The relative density of this small-scale urbanisation seems to have been a distinctive feature of central and southern England – the same level was not found in France, for example – and future research may bear out the suggestion that it was a significant precondition of the later Industrial Revolution.[45]

The quality of life

We should not, of course, blithely equate the multiplication of towns with the happiness and prosperity of their inhabitants. To say that living conditions during the three centuries from 1200 were unstable is a euphemism. This period of shifting fortunes hinges on the crisis-ridden fourteenth century. The years around 1300 marked the climax of medieval population growth in Europe. By this time the urban structure in England was in place: particular centres would flourish or decay, partly in response to regional shifts of the economy, but the distribution of towns in the landscape by the late thirteenth century was not to alter greatly before the Industrial Revolution. The twelfth

43 S. R. Epstein, 'Town and country: economy and institutions in late medieval Italy', *Economic History Review*, 2nd series, XLVI, 1993, pp. 453–77.

44 Prevenier and Blockmans, *The Burgundian Netherlands*; Stabel, *Dwarfs among Giants*.

45 R. H. Hilton, *English and French Towns in Feudal Society. A Comparative Study*, Cambridge, 1992.

and thirteenth centuries were a time of increasingly rapid expansion of both rural and urban settlements, building to a peak at which the limitations of agricultural technology and the unequal distribution of its produce caused mounting social tension (instances are presented in Sections II and VII). For some, this age of urban opportunity brought not only personal prosperity but the rewarding experience of contributing to collaborative public purposes in the civic sphere. To others, the period of town growth brought disillusionment and suffering. The custumals* of English towns in the twelfth and thirteenth centuries regularly note the arrangements for a burgess compelled by poverty to sell his town houses.[46] The majority, of course, never owned such property in the first place. As population mounted, food prices rose, and those without ready access to cash – a condition which all too readily befell the wage-labourers who made up a large proportion of urban society – found themselves crushed by debt and hunger. As the documentary record makes clear, this was a boom time for the foundation and enlargement of markets and towns – but (as has been the case in other periods of rapid economic expansion) this did not necessarily make these places comfortable for the majority of their inhabitants. Once more, the historian needs to consider the evidence from more than one vantage point.

The ensuing demographic downturn would also impinge sharply on the lives of the inhabitants of towns. Relatively crowded urban populations were especially vulnerable to famine and plague, both of which soon struck with horrific effect. The Great Famine of 1315–21 carried off an unknown but large proportion of town-dwellers.[47] The Black Death which arrived in 1348 is agreed to have killed between a third and a half of those living in towns.[48] The plague remained endemic throughout the rest of the medieval period, and this must be the principal reason that both global and urban population levels were kept stagnant until the turn of the sixteenth century brought indications of what would be a lasting recovery.[49] The variable but locally severe impact

46 Bateson (ed.), *Borough Customs*, ii, pp. 61–8.

47 B. Harvey, 'Introduction: the "crisis" of the early fourteenth century', in B. M. S. Campbell (ed.), *Before the Black Death: Studies in the 'Crisis' of the Early Fourteenth Century*, Manchester, 1991, pp. 1–24; W. C. Jordan, *The Great Famine: Northern Europe in the Early Fourteenth Century*, Princeton, 1996.

48 J. Hatcher, 'England in the aftermath of the Black Death', *Past and Present*, CXLIV, 1994, pp. 3–35.

49 For a critical review of the sources, see R. Horrox, *The Black Death*, Manchester, 1994.

of warfare; a fifteenth-century shortage of precious metal for coinage; and a late medieval period of cooler summers and sharper winters each contributed further to the difficulties of the towns, although no single generalisation can be made about the fortunes of all. Paradoxically, the first impact of the plague stimulated an unprecedented flood of migration to the towns on the part of those who sought to benefit from rising wage levels: the property records of most English towns between 1350 and the turn of the next century bear witness to this pressure of demand, evident in rising rents and speculative building [**66**]. But from early in the fifteenth century the same series of sources show that the growth could not be maintained: falling revenues and gaps in rentals tell an unequivocal story of a reduced and stagnant population. Civic petitions for relief from royal taxation, which were naturally exaggerated and must be read with due caution, tell a partly convincing story of decayed houses and failing industry. Archaeology and archives bear out the truth of at least some of these complaints. The petition of the citizens of Winchester in 1452 appears to round up the number of houses alleged to have been abandoned, but gives a fair impression of their distribution, and a 'remarkably accurate' list of seventeen ruined churches in the city [**77**].[50] There can be no easy generalisation about 'urban decline' in the late Middle Ages, and the problems of the period are best explored under different headings, as they are in this book. None the less, the halving of the national population between the early fourteenth century and the mid-fifteenth unquestionably reduced overall productivity.[51] The questions which should concern the historian who scans the late medieval evidence are how far adaptation to changing circumstances may have enabled some town-dwellers to exploit new opportunities for material gain; and what effect these changes in demography and economy may have had upon urban culture.

In very broad terms, the circumstances might seem on the face of things to have favoured the economic strength of the towns more in the years before 1300 than afterwards. Closer consideration of the

50 Keene, *Winchester*, i, pp. 97–8; *Calendar of Patent Rolls 1446–52*, p. 80; W. H. Stevenson (ed.), *Calendar of Records of the Corporation of Gloucester*, Gloucester, 1893, nos 58–9, cit. B. Dobson, 'Urban decline in late medieval England' [1977], repr. in R. Holt and G. Rosser (eds), *The Medieval Town*, London, 1990, pp. 265–86, at p. 276.

51 D. M. Palliser, 'Urban decay revisited', in J. A. F. Thomson (ed.), *Towns and Townspeople in the Fifteenth Century*, Gloucester, 1988, pp. 1–21; S. H. Rigby, 'Urban population in late medieval England: the evidence of the lay subsidies', *Economic History Review*, 2nd series, LXIII, 2010, pp. 393–417.

evidence may, however, lead us to question both this and indeed any such crude generalisation. The picture is varied, and significance lies in the detail of individual urban experiences. The economic consequences of urbanisation were, at any rate until the fifteenth century, more limited than might be expected. Certainly, these concentrated, dependent populations made their presence felt. The research on the sources of grain needed to supply the London market has shown the existence by 1300 of a metropolitan zone which affected agricultural systems even so far away as the east midlands. Evidence from Exeter and Newcastle suggests that provincial towns had, to this extent, their own more local spheres of economic influence.[52] But the economic evidence in general does not indicate that levels of consumption in English towns (most of these being small, as we have seen) sufficed by that date to bring about major changes in agrarian organisation. Nor did the age of major urban expansion, to 1300, see marked specialisation of urban crafts: there were regional differences of emphasis but, although larger towns had more crafts than others, the diversity of recorded trades is broadly similar across the range (see the examples in Section III). Before the fifteenth century, also, there is only very limited evidence of urban production of goods for distant markets or for significant profits. The export of cloth during the long thirteenth century made the personal fortunes of a mercantile elite. But for the most part the craftsmen and women of the earlier towns operated at a modest level of production, for low levels of return.[53] We should be careful, therefore, while recognising their micro-economic significance, not to exaggerate the difference which the towns made at the macro-economic level before 1300.

The fifteenth century, by contrast, would see at least a relatively greater differentiation of urban industry, especially in the cloth trade. The older cloth-producing towns adapted to contracting and shifting markets by concentrating on better-quality woollens: York would become known for its broadcloths, Norwich for its worsteds, Coventry for its blue woollen cloths and its caps. Some of these products were traded over long distances: russet cloth from Colchester found buyers in the towns of the Baltic and the Mediterranean. To follow such developments, the historian must consult the records of customs officials at the sea-ports, and the correspondence of agents working on behalf

52 Galloway, 'One market or many?'; Kowaleski, *Local Markets and Regional Trade*; M. Threlfall-Holmes, *Monks and Markets. Durham Cathedral Priory 1460–1520*, Oxford, 2005, p. 226.

53 Britnell, *Britain and Ireland*, pp. 151–2.

of international merchant companies [**35**], [**36**]. Newly emergent cloth towns in the West Riding (Halifax and Leeds), the south-west (Stroud and Mells) and East Anglia (Lavenham and Long Melford) can be cited as instances of commercial adaptation and technological advance. In these and other cases, the new centres of production, although initially rural in character, soon developed the characteristics (including the documentary records) of small towns. Both older and newer cloth-producing towns made some contribution during the long fifteenth century to the early stages of proto-industrialisation.[54] Yet even in this sector, there did not appear a class of merchant investors willing or able to make structural changes to the organisation of industry. For a variety of reasons, including the demographic slump and the reorientation of European trade, the most prominent merchants in fifteenth-century English towns struggled to expand their capital or to establish lasting dynasties.[55] It is possible that the economic dominance of the metropolis, to which it is noticeable that many provincial merchants migrated in the later Middle Ages, may have discouraged urban enterprise elsewhere.[56] London itself, however, although it boasted a more dazzling range of specialist crafts and shops than any other English city [**8**], continued to foster small-scale industrial production for largely local and regional consumption, while its merchant class showed, with individual exceptions, limited entrepreneurial flair. Although its importance in the distributive trade endured throughout the Middle Ages, local industry was principally responsive to London's diverse and relatively wealthy consumer market.[57]

If there was no English take-off to industrial development on a larger scale within the medieval period, this was partly for lack of a critical

54 Britnell, *Britain and Ireland*, p. 352; Britnell, *Colchester*, pp. 167–71; J. Munro, 'The symbiosis of towns and textiles: urban institutions and the changing fortunes of cloth manufacturing in the Low Countries and England, 1270–1570', *Journal of Early Modern History*, III, 1999, pp. 1–74.

55 J. Kermode, *Medieval Merchants. York, Beverley and Hull in the Later Middle Ages*, Cambridge, 1998, pp. 305–12; S. Thrupp, *The Merchant Class of Medieval London, 1300–1500*, Chicago, 1948.

56 R. H. Britnell, 'The English economy and the government, 1450–1550', in J. L. Watts (ed.), *The End of the Middle Ages?*, Stroud, 1998, pp. 89–116.

57 A. L. Beier, 'Engine of manufacture: the trades of London', in A. L. Beier and R. Finlay (eds), *London 1500–1700: The Making of the Metropolis*, London, 1986, pp. 141–67; C. M. Barron, 'London 1300–1540', in *CUHB*, pp. 395–440, at pp. 426–7; C. M. Barron, *London in the Later Middle Ages. Government and People 1200–1500*, Oxford, 2004, p. 76; A. Sutton, *The Mercery of London: Trade, Goods and People, 1130–1578*, Aldershot, 2005.

mass of demand for the products of industry. But it has been compellingly argued that, amongst the reduced population of both town and countryside in fifteenth-century England, there was emerging a relatively prosperous class of peasants and artisans who, if they could not amount to a mass market, none the less provided a stimulus for the diversification of production of material goods. For this economically successful minority, the reduced demographic pressure created new possibilities for financial investment and social self-advancement: a development noted with some irony by contemporaries [**46**]. With the reduction of demographic pressure, basic living costs (both food and rents) became lower, freeing cash for the purchase of small material luxuries beyond the reach of men and women of similar status in previous generations. The increased value of labour is evident in a broad increase in craftsmen's wages: to give an indication of this, whereas around 1300 a carpenter typically earned 4*d* a day, a century later, in the context of population decline, the rate was more commonly 6*d*. At both periods, 1*d* would suffice to keep a single individual for a day with a dish of meat or fish. It seems possible that the urban craftsmen and women of the fifteenth century who, as we learn from both written inventories and archaeology, manufactured belts with metal clasps, knives with elaborate handles, pewter vessels, glass for domestic windows or painted hangings for domestic decoration were able to profit from the increased spending power – and the social aspirations – of some of their neighbours. The great diversity of specialist shops in the late medieval capital speaks to this, and the contents of a particular London 'shop with haberdasher's ware' in 1486 can be used to illustrate the argument: buckles and horse tackle, thimbles, needles and pins, combs and hat-bands, diverse belts, beads and handkerchiefs, and spectacles – of which last item the owner had almost five hundred in stock.[58] It is important to emphasise that such an isolated example cannot prove the existence of a trend, and indeed the inventory of another London haberdasher from a century earlier reveals no less diverse and tempting a stock [**29**]. But cumulative archaeological evidence, including that for the fifteenth-century renewal of the housing stock in the smaller towns, together with domestic inventories from the period,

58 C. Dyer, *An Age of Transition? Economy and Society in England in the Later Middle Ages*, Oxford, 2005, pp. 148, 154; C. Dyer, *Standards of Living in the Later Middle Ages: Social Change in England c.1200–1520*, revised edn, Cambridge, 1998. For the appearance and proliferation from the late fourteenth century of one craft of importance in this connection, that of the pewterers (mainly citing evidence from York), see H. Swanson, *Medieval Artisans*, Oxford, 1989, pp. 76–8.

give at least some substance to the idea that, within the context of a reduced population and hence a restrained economy, a redistribution of resources in the fifteenth century saw modestly improved material conditions in some parts of the urban network. What individuals chose to do with the resources freed up by reduced economic pressure will, of course, have varied. The improvement of social standing by the acquisition of domestic goods may have been a priority for some, while others may have preferred to spend their money on the attractions of commercialised leisure, such as archery butts and tennis courts, which appear in the record from the mid- to late fifteenth century [**99**]. Others, again, may have patronised bookshops (and haberdashers, for spectacles) [**31**].[59]

Careful assessment of our evidence warns repeatedly against totalising generalisations. If some town-dwellers of the late Middle Ages could boast of clothes and dinner-services which would have impressed their grandparents, in the general conditions of the era most lives were at constant risk of illness, unemployment or debt, any of which could turn modest prosperity into indigence overnight. The quality of life, moreover, depended upon more than mere material sufficiency. The greatest challenge of the towns, throughout the length of our period (and indeed well beyond it), was to create a viable and satisfying human life for crowded communities of diverse origins and resources. A generalisation which can be ventured in this context is that no easy solution to the problem was found. Personal relationships were strained by life at close quarters; by unequal working relationships; by the selfish exploitation of their power by the citizen and mercantile elite. Each of these occasions for conflict was liable to trigger hostility between groups of diverse cultural background. Measures, both official and informal, were invented and refined in order to address the issues as they were perceived. Experimental and never more than partially effective though they were, these are amongst the most creative and lasting achievements of medieval urban populations.

Ideas and practice of the common good

Environmental and hygienic issues were the first to demand consideration at the level of public discourse and legislation, and thereby to enter the historical record [**62**]. The material conditions of life tended

59 G. Rosser, 'Urban culture and the Church 1300–1540', in *CUHB*, pp. 335–69, at pp. 365–7.

to compound the difficulties of adaptation to the town, especially in the overcrowded thirteenth century. With the exception of the grandest, patrician residences, which were adapted from the model of the rural aristocratic house, urban accommodation was broadly divided between two distinct categories. For those who could afford it, new timber-framing technology, first recorded in London around 1180 and spreading subsequently to other towns, brought into being the house of several rooms for diverse purposes: a structure within which it was possible at least partially to distinguish the workplace from the home, and where some measure of privacy could be enjoyed [**64**], [**65**]. Meanwhile the majority of town-dwellers – and not only the very poor – crowded into comparatively tiny houses of just one or two rooms, with no privy or kitchen and no privacy whatever.[60] Some inhabitants of shops with cramped living quarters on the High Street in Oxford in the later Middle Ages got by in no more than a few square feet.[61] Shops on Cheapside in London could be as little as six feet wide and ten or twelve feet deep.[62] In a central ward of Norwich in the early fourteenth century, seventy-five per cent of the population was living in accommodation rented from exploitative landlords, much of this densely occupied.[63] Such crowding on commercial frontages reflected a certain economic prosperity, but living conditions could be unpleasant. From as early as the twelfth century we have evidence of town

60 F. Riddy, 'Looking closely: authority and intimacy in the late medieval urban town house', in M. C. Erler and M. Kowaleski (eds), *Gendering the Master Narrative: Women and Power in the Middle Ages*, Ithaca and London, 2003, pp. 212–28; F. Riddy, '"Burgeis" domesticity in late-medieval England', in M. Kowaleski and P. J. P. Goldberg (eds), *Medieval Domesticity. Home, Housing and Household in Medieval England*, Cambridge, 2008, pp. 14–36; S. Rees Jones, 'Building domesticity in the city: English urban housing before the Black Death', in ibid., pp. 66–91; J. Schofield, *Medieval London Houses*, New Haven, 1995; S. Pearson, 'Medieval houses in English towns: form and location', *Vernacular Architecture*, XL, 2009, pp. 1–22.

61 A shop near the corner of the High Street and Cornmarket comprised a cellar (10 ft 6 in. square), a shop (12 ft 7 in. by 15 ft 6 in.) and a solar or upper room (13 ft 1 in. by 15 ft 4 in.). In 1515 the property was let to a goldsmith for the relatively substantial rate of 40*s* per annum. (The measurements were taken in the seventeenth century, but the building was essentially unaltered since the fourteenth century.) H. E. Salter, *Survey of Oxford*, 2 vols, Oxford Historical Society, new series, XIV, XX, 1960–69, i, pp. 99–100.

62 D. Keene, 'Shops and shopping in medieval London', in L. Grant (ed.), *Medieval Art, Architecture and Archaeology in London*, London, 1990, pp. 29–46; D. Keene, *Cheapside before the Great Fire*, London, 1985; D. Clark, 'The shop within? An analysis of the architectural evidence for medieval shops', *Architectural History*, XLIII, 2000, pp. 58–87.

63 E. Rutledge, 'Landlords and tenants: housing and the rented property market in early fourteenth century Norwich', *Urban History*, XXII, 1995, pp. 7–24.

communities establishing procedures to address the contentions which arose. In Northampton around 1190, whenever a dispute erupted over a party wall or a gutter, the bailiffs of the town, the jurors of the town court and the neighbours were together to assess the question and make a judgement.[64] London's assize* of nuisance, whose records begin in 1301 but which had earlier origins, tells a long and vivid narrative of dripping gutters and leaking cess-pits, to which the legal procedure offered some practical redress [**67**]. The general issue of sanitation was an inevitable catalyst of public debate, generating dedicated officers for overseeing the removal of waste and rubbish [**71**], [**73**].[65] The London assize of nuisance also documented a recurrent concern about the creation of windows which allowed people to see into their neighbours' properties, expressive of a heightened sensitivity concerning privacy in the urban context in which personal space was at a premium.[66] These sources record a sense of moral discretion which attempted to limit prying intrusion into the space of the household. We should be wary, however, of suggestions that medieval urban space was segregated between feminised interiors and a masculine outdoors. If there was ever a prevailing concept of the clearly separated female and domestic sphere – an ideological concept which had some currency in the nineteenth century but which, even then, was complicated by the realities of gendered experience – it was far from the medieval situation, in which labour and domesticity tended to be intermixed.[67]

The density and diversity of urban populations in the thirteenth century generated social tensions which in turn gave rise both to conflict and to an emergent concept of public responsibility. To see this, we need

64 Bateson (ed.), *Borough Customs*, i, p. 245.

65 E. L. Sabine, 'Latrines and cesspools of medieval London', *Speculum*, IX, 1934, pp. 303–21; E. L. Sabine, 'City cleaning in medieval London', *Speculum*, XII, 1937, pp. 19–43; D. J. Keene, 'Rubbish in medieval towns', in A. R. Hall and H. K. Kenward (eds), *Environmental Archaeology in an Urban Context*, Council for British Archaeology Research Reports, 43, 1982, pp. 26–30; Barron, *London*, pp. 261–2.

66 H. M. Chew and W. Kellaway (eds), *London Assize of Nuisance 1301–1431*, London Record Society, X, 1973, p. xii and *passim*.

67 P. J. P. Goldberg, 'The fashioning of bourgeois domesticity in later medieval England: a material culture perspective', in M. Kowaleski and P. J. P. Goldberg (eds), *Medieval Domesticity. Home, Housing and Household in Medieval England*, Cambridge, 2008, pp. 124–44; P. J. P. Goldberg, 'Space and gender in the later medieval English house', *Viator*, XLII, 2011, pp. 205–32; S. Rees Jones, 'Women's influence on the design of urban homes', in M. C. Erler and M. Kowaleski (eds), *Gendering the Master Narrative: Women and Power in the Middle Ages*, Ithaca and London, 2003, pp. 190–211; A. Vickery, 'Golden age to separate spheres? A review of the categories and chronology of English women's history', *Historical Journal*, XXXVI, 1993, pp. 383–414.

to attend not merely to the ostensible practical purposes served by the material and written evidence but to the language and resonance of its rhetoric. City walls are a case in point. The security of urban populations did not call so consistently for civic defences as it did in less effectively governed parts of Europe. But although their construction and maintenance was sometimes resented locally as a costly royal imposition, such walls did not have the same functions of local mastery as had the early Anglo-Norman royal castles, and town populations along the south coast or close to the Welsh or Scottish borders had occasion at diverse periods of the Welsh and Hundred Years Wars to be glad of them [**56**]. Moreover, they came to be seen as symbols of civic pride, being frequently represented on civic seals.[68] This is especially clear in such a case as that of Coventry, where the walls, which had no military function, were inaugurated by the mayor in 1356 and erected over a protracted period, as resources allowed, to be completed only in the 1530s. Many towns at a distance from the periphery of the country never had walls at all. But most were motivated to erect gates, as practical and even more as symbolic markers of the city's claim to monitor the passage of people and goods.[69] Town halls were no less the embodiment of political ambition on the part of the mercantile elites who dominated the councils held within these buildings, and yet they also contributed to the prestige and the civic pride of the larger urban population. The most splendid of all, the London Guildhall, was erected in the fifteenth century on the model of the recently renovated royal hall of Westminster.[70] Public works undertaken in the smaller towns tended to be less grandiose and to engage the active involvement of a larger proportion of the townspeople. The construction in the mid-fifteenth century of two new stone bridges across the Thames at Abingdon was the collaborative project of the secular population at large, all of whom stood to gain both from the consequent increase of trade and from the sense of personal moral worth which flowed from an enterprise that benefited rich and poor alike [**98**]. Careful attention to the documentary evidence reveals,

68 For examples, see G. Pedrick, *Civic Seals of the Gothic Period*, London, 1904. For discussion of the iconography of medieval urban seals, see B. Bedos Rezak, *When Ego Was Imago: Signs of Identity in the Middle Ages*, Leiden, 2010, pp. 238–42.

69 O. Creighton and R. Higham, *Medieval Town Walls. An Archaeology and Social History of Urban Defence*, Stroud, 2005, p. 32 and *passim*; H. L. Turner, *Town Defences in England and Wales*, London, 1970.

70 J. Schofield, *The Building of London from the Conquest to the Great Fire*, London, 1984, pp. 107–8; C. M. Barron, *The Medieval Guildhall of London*, London, 1974. On civic guildhalls or town halls in general, see R. Tittler, *Architecture and Power: The Town Hall and the English Urban Community, c.1500–1640*, Stanford, 2001.

once again, that a project of this nature, beyond its pragmatic purpose, could become the catalyst of shared experience and ideals amongst the urban population. Of universal concern was the safe provision of fresh water to all parts of the town, and this involved town assemblies in civil engineering projects for public fountains which could be both complex and expensive, yet at the same time prestigious expressions of civic ambition [**70**].[71] At Lichfield, another small town in the shadow of a powerful ecclesiastical interest in the form, in this case, of the cathedral, a group of five secular residents gave property in 1305 to endow a communal aqueduct. By the end of the Middle Ages and probably for a considerable time before, the civic water-supply was managed by the town guild, whose members included a wide range of the local population and which acted, in the absence of more formal municipal rights, as a surrogate town council. The former property of the guild, suppressed at the Reformation, continued to be used to fund the civil water works until modern times [**95**].[72] Here and elsewhere, the provision of clean water was an index of good government, evidence of the moral no less than the material worth of the town.

A further index of civic consciousness can be considered in arrangements made to care for the poor and the sick, of whom medieval towns knew only too many. It is impossible precisely to quantify the number of the indigent poor, but scattered evidence suggests that in the larger towns this figure may have represented as many as a third of the total population. The difficulty of establishing exact levels of mendicancy means that historians have had to approach the subject obliquely, through the evidence of personal and institutional charitable provision. The issue concerns not simply absolute needs and their provision but the variable perceptions of those who at different times defined themselves as poor and those who did not.[73] In addition to the permanently mendicant poor, those periodically in need of support included many artisans, whom a crisis could readily reduce to temporary or long-term penury and dependence. Their presence was a constant reminder of the inequality and lack of unity of urban society. Yet the measures instituted for their

71 J. S. Lee, 'Piped water supplies managed by civic bodies in medieval English towns', *Urban History*, XLI, 2014, pp. 369–93; Barron, *London*, pp. 255–61.

72 G. Rosser, 'The town and guild of Lichfield in the late Middle Ages', *Transactions of the South Staffordshire Archaeological and Historical Society*, XXVII, 1987 for 1985, pp. 39–47, at pp. 46–7.

73 M. Mollat, *The Poor in the Middle Ages*, transl. A. Goldhammer, New Haven and London, 1986, pp. 148–66, 173–7 and *passim*.

relief, however limited in their overall effect, deserve attention for what they can tell us about moral and civic attitudes. The grandest gestures emanated from great patrons, such as the bishop of Norwich who in 1256 founded the hospital of St Giles in that city, with thirty beds for poor sick people. Managed by leading townspeople, this hospice offered at least some relief to the indigent, the aged and the unwell, at the same time raising civic consciousness and consciences about the presence of the poor.[74] More modest foundations commonly originated with groups of neighbours or guilds, whose members would typically play a practical part in the provision of care [**107**]. Such was the almshouse in Stratford-upon-Avon, rebuilt at the start of the fifteenth century by the local guild of the Holy Cross. Poor people, not members of the guild, were taken in on request, including, in 1475–76, 'Agnes, a girl in the almshouse', and Robert Scot and John Dunseprowe, for whose attendance Margaret Myller received a reward from the guild.[75] Larger towns offered a range of provision: York at the same period contained five hospitals and eighteen small almshouses known as *maisonsdieu*.[76] The later Middle Ages saw such provision undertaken by certain town governments as a public responsibility.[77] The challenge of poverty could not be adequately met by the resources made available in medieval urban society, which thereby stands indicted.[78] But if we read the texts not merely with a view to quantifying the outcome in welfare terms but with sensitivity to what the sources can tell us about mutual collaboration, we may note how the various ways in which townsmen and women involved themselves in such measures of support as they knew – not least in the guilds, of which a great many were members [**94**], [**95**] – were schools of citizenship. Without idealising their goals, it is reasonable to suggest that these urban charities helped to cultivate in their participants a sense of moral responsibility for the larger body of the townspeople.[79]

74 C. Rawcliffe, *Medicine for the Soul. The Life, Death and Resurrection of an English Medieval Hospital*, Stroud, 1999.

75 Stratford-upon-Avon, Shakespeare Birthplace Trust, MS. BRT 1/3/88.

76 P. H. Cullum and P. J. P. Goldberg, 'Charitable provision in late medieval York: "To the praise of God and the use of the poor"', *Northern History*, XXIX, 1993, pp. 24–39.

77 S. Sweetinburgh, *The Role of the Hospital in Medieval England. Gift-Giving and the Spiritual Economy*, Dublin, 2004; N. Orme and M. Webster, *The English Hospital, 1070–1570*, London, 1995.

78 C. Dyer, 'Poverty and its relief in late medieval England', *Past and Present*, CCXVI, 2012, pp. 41–78.

79 G. Rosser, *The Art of Solidarity in the Middle Ages. Guilds in England 1250–1550*, Oxford, 2015, ch. 2.

While there were certainly different degrees of vulnerability, it is important to realise the extent to which everyone living in medieval towns was at risk. Because of relatively high urban mortality rates, town populations could sustain themselves only as a result of a constant influx from elsewhere: the majority of young men and women seeking work in the late medieval town were either first- or second-generation settlers. The larger the town, the greater was its attraction to hopeful migrants, who often left their native families and villages far behind them.[80] The newcomer might arrive with an introduction to a relative or former neighbour from his or her place of origin; but the primary challenge of settlement in the city was that of winning the acceptance and trust of others without which survival would be impossible. Few artisans owned all the necessary tools of their trade, and to find accommodation and work or to set up a shop required both social and financial credit to gain the support of landlords, employers, fellow workers and customers. A commonly employed means to establish the necessary degree of credit-worthiness was to join one of the many religious and social guilds which, although not exclusively urban, were particularly concentrated in the towns [**94**]. Most called for only modest financial contributions, but all set moral criteria for membership which lent to the men and women who joined a standing which could help them to make their way in the new environment. For many, enrolment in a guild marked the beginning of a new life in the town.[81]

Faith in the city

Hospitals and guilds apart, the records of other religious bodies also have much light to shed on our subject, although once again we need to be prepared to read the sources not merely as the imprint of particular institutions, with their respective possessions and legal privileges, but in order to discern the needs and aspirations expressed by those who animated them. The overwhelming impression conveyed by the evidence for urban religious life in the later Middle Ages is of its rich diversity (see Sections VIII and IX). For the most part within the scope of a Catholic orthodoxy which allowed for considerable variety of spiritual expression, the towns were distinguished from the countryside by the

80 P. McClure, 'Patterns of migration in the late Middle Ages', *Economic History Review*, 2nd series, XXXII, 1979, pp. 167–82.

81 G. Rosser, 'Crafts, guilds and the negotiation of work in the medieval town', *Past and Present*, CLIV, 1997, pp. 3–31; Rosser, *Art of Solidarity*, ch. 5 and *passim*.

choice which they offered in forms and objects of devotion. Some of the older towns presented the densest parochial provision, from London's one hundred parish churches, through Norwich's fifty and the thirty or more of York, to the ten of Gloucester, Worcester and Cambridge.[82] The numerous market towns, such as Ludlow in Shropshire on the Welsh March, Kendal in Cumbria or Banbury in Oxfordshire, were typically served in each case by a single parish church. The cathedrals and monastic churches added further variety of architecture, liturgical style and preaching.[83] The wills of townspeople confirm, in the range of their bequests, their appreciation of this diversity, which was itself the creation of secular patronage [**105**]. In the centre of Carlisle there was a chapel of St Alban, which was especially popular with the local population. In the mid-fourteenth century the bishop discovered that the building had never been consecrated, and ordered its closure. But the ban was ineffective, and bequests in the testaments of late medieval townspeople reveal its enduring status as a focus of civic religion.[84] Religious culture in the city was expressed in the potent language of the universal Church; but it was open to appropriation at the local level by townsmen and women even of the most humble status, who could invest it with particular meaning of their own.

City governors, too, clothed themselves in the reflected splendour of locally venerated saints and civic cults [**101**]. Yet these devotions were always more than political tools, or they would not and could not have been used in this way. The evidence tends to reveal, rather, a convergence of governmental strategy with popular devotion. An instance is the way in which the cult of Osmund, the popular protector of Salisbury venerated locally as an unauthenticated saint, was taken up by the secular rulers of the town who were prepared, even at considerable expense, to secure his official canonisation.[85] Similarly, the adoption of

82 M. D. Lobel (ed.), *The British Atlas of Historic Towns*, iii, *The City of London from Prehistoric Times to c.1520*, London, 1989, map of parishes *c.*1520; J. Finch, 'The churches', in C. Rawcliffe and R. Wilson (eds), *Medieval Norwich*, London, 2004, pp. 49–72; D. M. Palliser, *Medieval York 600–1540*, Oxford, 2014, p. 216; N. Baker and R. Holt, *Urban Growth and the Medieval Church: Gloucester and Worcester*, Aldershot, 2004, chs 4 and 7 and plans on pp. 103, 199; C. N. L. Brooke, 'The churches of medieval Cambridge', in D. Beales and G. Best (eds), *History, Society and the Churches: Essays in Honour of Owen Chadwick*, Cambridge, 1985, pp. 69–72.

83 For London, Norwich and York: C. M. Barron and M. P. Davies, *The Religious Houses of London and Middlesex*, London, 2007; Tanner, *Church in Late Medieval Norwich*; Miller, 'Medieval York'.

84 H. Summerson, *Medieval Carlisle*, 2 vols, Kendal, 1993, i, pp. 355–6, ii, p. 610.

85 A. R. Malden, *The Canonization of Saint Osmund*, Wiltshire Record Series, II, 1901.

the Virgin Mary as the official patroness of the city of Carlisle, where she appeared on the civic seal in addition to that of the cathedral priory, was inspired by a popular story that in 1385 she had saved the town from destruction by the Scots. Indeed, she was said to appear often to inhabitants of Carlisle, which further encouraged the civic officers to vie with the cathedral canons for the role of the Virgin's chief advocate in the city. In 1451 the canons, for their part, displayed a new image of the city's patron in order to satisfy 'the devotion of Christ's faithful people daily flocking there on pilgrimage'. This was described as 'an image of the Blessed Virgin covered with plates of silver and overlaid with gold, gems and precious stones'.[86] Our sources tend, in the way of much historical evidence at all periods, to record an elite perspective. That perspective was real: the hierarchical organisation of urban society was shored up by wealth and privilege, as well as by the trappings of political rhetoric and religious iconography. But if we read our sources against the grain, they tell us also about other visions of urban life.

What insights we may gain into our own urban lives by the study of these medieval sources remain to be seen. But as a matter of analytical method, their careful reading should sensitise us to the presence of diverse voices. Urban elites demand to be heard; but we do not need to confine our attention to them. Medieval towns were characterised by inequality and exploitation, and we should no longer expect to find that their populations were guided by modern democratic values. But their culture was neither rigid nor monolithic, and the creative, experimental quality of a number of its forms – such as the neighbourhood courts [**52**], [**53**], or the guilds [**94**], [**95**], or the universities [**40**], [**85**], or the civic drama of the 'mystery plays' [**114**], [**115**], [**116**] – remind us that towns, in the Middle Ages and at all periods, are made by people. The sense of powerlessness in the face of an impersonal force is a comprehensible reaction to the urban experience. Yet the very challenge of creating a modus vivendi with unfamiliar others is an invitation, as medieval townsmen and women knew, to step up to a shared responsibility.

Most of us live for a significant part of our lives in towns and cities. It would be vain to attempt to avoid them, in a world in which more

86 R. B. Dobson, 'Cathedral chapters and cathedral cities: York, Durham and Carlisle in the fifteenth century', *Northern History*, XIX, 1983, pp. 15–44, at pp. 41–2; G. H. Martin (ed.), *Knighton's Chronicle 1377–1396*, Oxford, 1995, p. 336; Summerson, *Carlisle*, i, p. 359.

than half of the earth's population lives in an urban area and in which all natural resources have been commandeered into the service of the megalopolis.[87] We learn the arts of survival in the city, adapt ourselves to its spaces and its rhythms, and we naturalise these capacities so that they appear to us to be the essence of human life. On the planet of the global city, it is impossible to find the distance and the vantage point from which our present condition of urbanisation may be observed and critiqued. We can only live on the inside; nowhere else exists. If we wish to comprehend the age in which we live, and to gain a critical perspective on its qualities, positive and negative as these may be, our sole recourse must be to history. The world in its time has seen diverse ages of great cities: so many different experiments in the organisation of human lives. Ours is one in this sequence, no less and no more. If, before the end of its cycle, we want to make the most of it, we need to understand how we have arrived at our present state of dependence upon our own particular, seemingly all-powerful, urban machine. The world city of today has diverse roots, and no single narrative can account for it. But a vital key to that lineage lies in medieval Europe. Following the collapse of the highly urbanised empire of Rome, in the context of what had reverted to become a predominantly rural society, new ventures in civilisation brought into being the towns and cities of the modern continent, and a model of urbanisation which empire and economy have more recently exported to the remainder of the globe. Our lives today are still conditioned by those first, medieval, steps in city-building. No historical subject has more claim on our attention than the medieval European town. The subject calls for continuing study, both for its intrinsic interest and as a place from which we may review with some detachment the character and values of the cities we inhabit today.

87 Since 2007 more than half of the world's population resides in urban areas, according to the World Health Organization: www.who.int/kobe_centre/measuring/en/.

I. HISTORY AND PRAISE

As much as it was a tangible construction of stone, wood and plaster, the medieval town was an idea in the minds of its inhabitants and of its visitors. Mythologised or romantic as they might be, ideas of the town's prestigious origins and present eminence influenced the ideals and actions of its population. The sources gathered in this section include examples of the currency and expression of such ideas. They also exemplify some of the ways in which a distinguished history and idealised image of the town circulated and became embedded in local culture. Stories told to children, rhymes and song, sermons delivered in honour of locally venerated saints, mythical tales of kings and giants, antiquarian researches by town clerks, all enriched the shared memories of townspeople and conditioned their actions.

The clerical authors of the three twelfth-century texts represented below each wrote with an agenda, although in each case the writer's purpose is not completely transparent. Geoffrey of Monmouth flattered the Angevin monarchs with the idea that they belonged to a regnal tradition which had seen their predecessors populate the country with fine cities [**1**]. At the same time he provided townspeople themselves with the materials to imagine the greatness of their origins. William fitz-Stephen contributed to a proliferating literature of praise for the martyred Thomas Becket, killed in front of the high altar of Canterbury cathedral in 1170 by soldiers of the crown, a text which underlined Thomas's London roots and celebrated the saint as a hero and protector of the metropolis no less than of Canterbury [**2**]. Liberally strewn with allusions to the antique world of Rome, fitz-Stephen's text joins Christian hagiography to a classicising emulation of pre-Christian writers in praise of cities. Lucian, the monk of Chester, combines a narrowly parochial focus on the pattern of his local streets with a universal vision: indeed, this paradox is resolved in the way in which Lucian finds the macrocosm mirrored or epitomised in the plan of his city [**3**].

At the end of the period the celebratory allusions to the history of Exeter and of Bristol come from civic officials: a mayor and a town clerk. The role of encomiast had passed by this time to secular figures with administrative functions within their respective cities. Exeter's mayor turned to convenient histories in vindication of his council's position in its battle over jurisdiction with the cathedral [**5**]. It fell in particular to clerks such as Robert Ricart of Bristol to combine the custody of urban records with the composition of glorificatory histories [**6**]. In other instances the business of compiling and ordering the records became a historically creative process in its own right. A case in point is that of John Carpenter, the common clerk of the city of London who around 1419 assembled the extensive records which he copied into the 'Liber Albus' or White Book, adding in the process some original writing of his own [**52**].[1] In William Worcester we encounter an early instance of a different figure: the antiquary. Like the officers of the town, Worcester had become used to finding historical precedents in his legal and administrative work for Sir John Fastolf. But with his retirement and more extensive travels, he became fascinated with the past for its own sake [**7**].

What was the relationship between each of these written accounts and the memories, traditions and legends which during the same centuries circulated amongst the wider population of the towns? On the one hand, these writers claimed authority: the power of spiritual, political or intellectual eminence. On the other, to the extent that they were not simply inventing the material of their histories, these authors were drawing inspiration from a wider, and largely oral, historical culture. When the town council of Colchester in the fifteenth century commissioned a set of civic annals which incorporated the legend of the city's foundation by King Cole, that story was already widely known. At Coventry, the tale of Lady Godiva and her naked ride through the town to win freedom from toll for the citizens from her husband was common knowledge. The town council in the late fourteenth century had an image of her placed in a window of the municipal church of St Michael. But on the other hand, in the following century the poor weavers of Coventry invoked Godiva in their cause against the town council's imposition of a new tax [**91**].[2] When in Henry VIII's reign the antiquary and royal topographer John Leland came to Stamford, he asked local people about the history of the town, and was shown buildings which had supposedly

1 C.M. Barron, *London in the Later Middle Ages. Government and People 1200–1500*, Oxford, 2004, pp. 186–8.

2 G. Rosser, 'Myth, image and social process in the English medieval town', *Urban History*, XXIII, 1996, pp. 5–25, at p. 8.

once housed the university that had briefly existed in the thirteenth century.[3] The holders of political power and learned writers did not have a monopoly on the creative use of history, and civic memory was available for anyone to invoke.

1. Legends of the origins of cities

Geoffrey of Monmouth compiled his pseudohistorical account of British history in *c.*1136. He was a scholar, and probably a canon of St George's chapel in Oxford castle. Beyond his debt to Bede and to the few known early Welsh historical writings, it is hard to know what proportion of his work was invented by the author. Geoffrey was criticised by some of his earliest readers as a writer of fiction, and no modern scholar would rely upon him for the early history of British towns.[4] But his work became a vital element in late medieval urban culture, being appropriated and reworked in history-writing [**6**], iconography and civic pageants [**61**].[5]

J. A. Giles and A. Thompson (ed. and transl.), *The British History of Geoffrey of Monmouth*, London: J. Bohn, 1842, pp. 1, 22–4, 29, 31. Latin, transl. by the editors.

Whilst occupied on many and various studies, I happened to light upon the History of the Kings of Britain, and wondered that in the account which Gildas[6] and Bede,[7] in their elegant treatises, had given of them, I found nothing said of those kings who lived here before the Incarnation of Christ, nor of Arthur and many others who succeeded after the Incarnation, though their actions both deserved immortal fame, and were also celebrated by many people in a pleasant manner and by heart,

3 L. T. Smith (ed.), *The Itinerary of John Leland in or about the Years 1535–1543*, 5 vols, London, 1906–10, iv, pp. 89–90; G. Rosser, 'Urban culture and the Church 1300–1540', *CUHB*, pp. 335–69, at p. 347.

4 M. Otter, *Inventiones: Fiction and Referentiality in Twelfth-Century English Historical Writing*, Chapel Hill, 1996; E. van Houts, 'Historical writing', in C. Harper-Bill and E. van Houts (eds), *A Companion to the Anglo-Norman World*, Woodbridge, 2002, pp. 103–21, esp. pp. 114–15.

5 On Geoffrey's mythical account, in the passage below, of the origins of London, see J. Clark, 'Trinovantum – the origin of a legend', *Journal of Medieval History*, VII, 1981, pp. 135–51.

6 The sixth-century clerical author of *On the Ruin and Conquest of Britain.*

7 Bede's *Ecclesiastical History of the English People* was completed *c.*730.

as if they had been written. Whilst I was intent upon these and such like thoughts, Walter, archdeacon of Oxford, a man of great eloquence, and learned in foreign histories, offered me a very ancient book in the British tongue, which, in a continued regular story and elegant style, related the actions of them all, from Brutus the first king of the Britons, down to Cadwallader the son of Cadwallo ...

[Brutus, of Trojan descent, after many adventures landed in England at Totnes.] The island was then called Albion, and was inhabited by none but a few giants. Notwithstanding this, the pleasant situation of the places, the plenty of the rivers abounding with fish, and the engaging prospect of its woods, made Brutus and his company very desirous to fix their habitation in it ... Brutus, having at last set eyes upon his kingdom, formed a design of building a city, and with this in view, travelled through the land to find out a convenient situation, and coming to the river Thames, he walked along the shore, and at last pitched upon a place very fit for his purpose. Here, therefore, he built a city, which he called New Troy; under which name it continued a long time after, till at last, by the corruption of the original word, it came to be called Trinovantum. But afterwards when Lud, the brother of Cassibellaun, who made war against Julius Caesar, obtained the government of the kingdom, he surrounded it with stately walls, and towers of admirable workmanship, and ordered it to be called after his name, Kaer-Lud, that is, the City of Lud.

Ebraucus was the first after Brutus who invaded Gaul with a fleet, and distressed its provinces by killing their men and laying waste their cities; and having by these means enriched himself with an infinite quantity of gold and silver, he returned victorious. After this he built a city on the other side of the Humber, which, from his own name, he called Kaerebrauc, that is, the city of Ebraucus [York], about the time that David reigned in Judaea, and Sylvius Latinus in Italy; and that Gad, Nathan, and Asaph prophesied in Israel.

[King Hudibras] built Kaerlem or Canterbury, Kaorguen or Winchester, and the town of Mount Paladur, now Shaftesbury. At this place an eagle spoke, while the wall of the town was being built; and indeed I should have transmitted the speech to posterity, had I thought it as true as the rest of the history.

2. Description of London *c.*1173

This rhetorical description of London in the time of Henry II is the prologue to William fitz-Stephen's Life of Thomas Becket. A Londoner like Becket himself, fitz-Stephen presented a double celebration of the city and its patron saint. Replete with classical allusions, the text advertises its artifice. An educated writer, who served the archbishop in the 1160s as a legal adviser, fitz-Stephen drew on his reading of ancient Roman texts in praise of cities in order to show twelfth-century London in a similar light. He was also able, by underlining the piety of its citizens and its association with Constantine, the first Christian emperor, to imply that its Christian identity made London superior to its classical predecessors. At the same time, the circumstantial detail of particular passages is evidently based on direct experience. In flowery language, fitz-Stephen gives concrete information about the social composition of the city (note the presence of rural aristocrats and peasant vendors, and the clerical population), its cosmopolitan trade, and its intellectual and sporting culture.[8] The text is therefore of value both for its descriptive content and for the claims implied by its rhetorical composition.

D. C. Douglas and G. W. Greenaway (eds), *English Historical Documents*, ii, *1042–1189*, 2nd edn (copyright © 1981), London: Eyre Methuen, 1981, pp. 1196–201. Latin, transl. by the editors. Reproduced by permission of Taylor and Francis Books UK.

Among the noble and celebrated cities of the world, that of London, the capital of the kingdom of the English, is one which extends its glory farther than all the others and sends its wealth and merchandise more widely into distant lands. Higher than all the rest does it lift its head. It is happy in the healthiness of its air; in its observance of Christian practice; in the strength of its fortifications; in its natural situation; in the honour of its citizens; and in the modesty of its matrons. It is cheerful in its sports, and the fruitful mother of noble men. Let us look into these things in turn.

If the mildness of the climate of this place softens the character of its inhabitants, it does not make them corrupt in following Venus, but rather prevents them from being fierce and bestial, making them liberal

8 For a comment see C. N. L. Brooke and G. Keir, *London 800–1216: The Shaping of a City*, London, 1975, pp. 112–21.

and kind. In the church of St Paul there is the episcopal seat. Once it was metropolitan, and some think it will again become so, if the citizens return to the island,[9] unless perhaps the archiepiscopal title of the blessed martyr, Thomas, and the presence of his body preserves that dignity for ever at Canterbury where it is at present. But as St Thomas has made both cities illustrious, London by his rising and Canterbury by his setting, each can claim advantage of the other with justice in respect of that saint. As regards the practice of Christian worship, there are in London and its suburbs thirteen greater conventual churches and, besides these, one hundred and twenty-six lesser parish churches.

It has on the east the Palatine castle [the Tower of London], very great and strong: the keep and walls rise from very deep foundations and are fixed with a mortar tempered by the blood of animals. On the west there are two castles very strongly fortified, and from these there runs a high and massive wall with seven double gates and with towers along the north at regular intervals. London was once also walled and turreted on the south, but the mighty Thames, so full of fish, has with the sea's ebb and flow washed against, loosened, and thrown down those walls in the course of time. Upstream to the west there is the royal palace [of Westminster] which is conspicuous above the river, a building incomparable in its ramparts and bulwarks. It is about two miles from the city and joined thereto by a populous suburb.

Everywhere outside the houses of those living in the suburbs, and adjacent to them, are the spacious and beautiful gardens of the citizens, and these are planted with trees. Also there are on the north side pastures and pleasant meadow lands through which flow streams wherein the turning of mill-wheels makes a cheerful sound. Very near lies a great forest with woodland pastures in which there are the lairs of wild animals: stags, fallow deer, wild boars and bulls. The tilled lands of the city are not of barren gravel, but fat Asian plains that yield luxuriant crops and fill the tillers' barns with the sheaves of Ceres. There are also outside London on the north side excellent suburban wells with sweet, wholesome and clear water that flows rippling over the bright stones. Among these are Holywell, Clerkenwell and St Clement's Well, which are all famous. These are frequented by great numbers and much visited by the students from the schools and by the young men of the city, when they go out for fresh air on summer evenings.

9 The phrase echoes the 'Prophecies of Merlin' as reported by Geoffrey of Monmouth in his *History* (see [1]). These alluded vaguely to a brave new world which would be inaugurated when 'citizens returned to the island'.

Good indeed is this city when it has a good lord! The city is honoured by her men, glorious in its arms, and so populous that during the terrible wars of King Stephen's reign the men going forth from it to battle were reckoned as twenty thousand armed horsemen and sixty thousand foot-soldiers, all equipped for war. The citizens of London are regarded as conspicuous above all others for their polished manners, for their dress and for the good tables which they keep. The inhabitants of other towns are called citizens, but those of London are called barons. And with them a solemn pledge is sufficient to end every dispute.

The matrons of this city are very Sabines.[10]

In London the three principal churches (that is to say, the episcopal church of St Paul, the church of the Holy Trinity, and the church of St Martin) have famous schools by special privilege and by virtue of their ancient dignity. But through the favour of some magnate, or through the presence of teachers who are notable or famous in philosophy, there are also other schools. On feast-days the masters hold meetings for their pupils in the church whose festival it is. The scholars dispute, some with oratory and some with argument; some recite enthymemes;* others excel in using perfect syllogisms. Some dispute for ostentation like wrestlers with opponents; others argue in order to establish the truth in its perfection. Sophists who speak paradoxes are praised for their torrent of words, while others seek to overthrow their opponents by using fallacious arguments. Now and then orators use rhetoric for persuasion, being careful to omit nothing essential to their art. Boys of different schools strive against each other in verses, or contend about the principles of grammar and the rules governing past and future tenses. Others use epigrams, rhythm and metre in the old trivial banter; they pull their comrades to pieces with scurrilous licence: mentioning no names, they dart abuse and gibes, and mock the faults of their comrades and sometimes even those of their elders, using Socratic wit and biting harder even than the tooth of Theon [a carping Roman grammarian] in daring dithyrambics. Their hearers, ready to enjoy the joke, wrinkle up their noses as they guffaw in applause.

10 According to ancient Roman historians, the greatness of Rome began with a union between the Romans and the women of the Sabines, a people who inhabited the centre of the Italian peninsula. The Sabine women were held to be wise, strong, and morally irreproachable. The allusion by fitz-Stephen makes a pointed analogy between London and Rome. See below, however, for the author's claim that London was the more ancient of the two.

Those engaged in business of various kinds, sellers of merchandise, hirers of labour, are distributed every morning into their several localities according to their trade. Besides, there is in London on the river bank, among the wines for sale in ships and in the cellars of the vintners, a public cook-shop. There daily you may find food according to the season, dishes of meat, roast, fried and boiled, large and small fish, coarser meats for the poor and more delicate for the rich, such as venison and big and small birds. If any of the citizens should unexpectedly receive visitors, weary from their journey, who would fain not wait until fresh food is bought and cooked, or until the servants have brought bread or water for washing, they hasten to the river bank and there find all they need. However great the multitude of soldiers and travellers entering the city, or preparing to go out of it, at any hour of the day or night – that these may not fast too long, and those may not go out supperless – they turn aside thither, if they please, where every man can refresh himself in his own way. Those who would cater for themselves fastidiously need not search to find sturgeon or the bird of Africa or the Ionian godwit. For this is a public kitchen, very convenient to the city, and part of its amenities. Hence the dictum in the Gorgias of Plato that the art of cookery is an imitation of medicine and decorates a quarter of civic life.

Immediately outside one of the gates there is a field which is smooth both in fact and in name [Smithfield]. On every sixth day of the week, unless it be a major feast-day, there takes place there a famous exhibition of fine horses for sale. Earls, barons and knights, who are in the town, and many citizens come out to see or to buy. It is pleasant to see the high-stepping palfreys with their gleaming coats, as they go through their paces, putting down their feet alternately on one side together. Next, one can see the horses suitable for esquires, moving faster though less smoothly, lifting and setting down, as it were, the opposite fore and hind feet: here are colts of fine breed, but not yet accustomed to the bit, stepping high with jaunty tread; there are the sumpter-horses,* powerful and spirited; and after them there are the war-horses, costly, elegant of form, noble of stature, with ears quickly tremulous, necks raised and large haunches. As these show their paces, the buyers first try those of gentler gait, then those of quicker pace whereby the fore and hind feet move in pairs together. When a race is about to begin among such chargers that are so powerful to carry and so swift to run, a shout is raised, and orders are given that the inferior animals should be led apart. Three jockeys who mount these flying steeds (or at times two, as may be agreed) prepare themselves for the contest; skilled in managing them, they curb their untamed mouths with bitted bridles. To get a good start in the race is their chief concern. Their mounts also enter into the spirit of the contest as they are able; their limbs tremble, and so impatient are they of delay that they cannot keep still. When the signal is given, they stretch their limbs to the uttermost, and dash down the course with courageous speed. The riders, covetous of applause and ardent for victory, plunge their spurs into the loose-reined horses, and urge them forward with their shouts and their whips. You would agree with Heraclitus that all things are in motion! You would know Zeno to be completely wrong when he said that there was no motion and no goal to be reached!

By themselves in another part of the field stand the goods of the countryfolk: implements of husbandry, swine with long flanks, cows with full udders, oxen of immense size, and woolly sheep. There also stand the mares fit for plough, some big with foal, and others with brisk young colts closely following them.

To this city from every nation under heaven merchants delight to bring their trade by sea. The Arabian sends gold; the Sabaean spice and incense. The Scythian brings arms, and from the rich, fat lands of Babylon comes oil of palms. The Nile sends precious stones; the men of Norway and Russia, furs and sables; nor is China absent with purple silk. The Gauls come with their wines.

London, as historians have shown, is a much older city than Rome, though it derives from the same Trojan ancestors. It was founded by Brutus before Rome was founded by Romulus and Remus. Wherefore they still have the same laws from their common origin. This city is like Rome divided into wards; it has annual sheriffs instead of consuls; it has its senatorial order and lower magistrates; it has drains and aqueducts in its streets; it has appointed places for the hearing of cases deliberative, demonstrative and judicial; it has its several courts, and its separate assemblies on appointed days.

I do not think there is a city with a better record for church-going, doing honour to God's ordinances, keeping feast-days, giving alms and hospitality to strangers, confirming betrothals, contracting marriages, celebrating weddings, providing feasts, entertaining guests, and also, it may be added, in care for funerals and for the burial of the dead. The only plagues of London are the immoderate drinking of fools and the frequency of fires.

To this it may be added that almost all the bishops, abbots and magnates of England are in a sense citizens and freemen of London, having their own splendid town-houses. In them they live, and spend largely, when they are summoned to great councils by the king or by their metropolitan, or drawn thither by their private affairs.

We now come to speak of the sports of the city, for it is not fitting that a city should be merely useful and serious-minded, unless it be also pleasant and cheerful. For this cause on the seals of the supreme pontiff, down to the time of the last Pope Leo (IX, 1048–54), on one side of the lead was engraved the figure of Peter the fisherman and above him a key, as it were, held out to him from heaven by the hand of God, and around it was inscribed the verse, 'For me didst thou leave the ship, receive now the key.' And on the other side was engraved a city with the inscription 'Golden Rome'. Moreover, it was said in honour of Augustus Caesar and Rome, 'It rains all night, games usher in the day; Caesar, thou dost divide dominion with Jove.' Instead of shows in the theatre and stage-plays, London provides plays of a more sacred character, wherein are presented the miracles worked by saintly confessors or the sufferings which made illustrious the constancy of martyrs. Furthermore, every year on the day called Carnival* – to begin with the sports of boys (for we were all boys once) – scholars from the different schools bring fighting-cocks to their masters, and the whole morning is set apart to watch their cocks do battle in the schools, for the boys are given a holiday that day. After dinner all the young men of the town go out into the fields in the suburbs to play ball. The scholars of the various schools have their own ball, and almost all the followers of each occupation theirs also. The seniors and the fathers and the wealthy magnates of the city come on horseback to watch the contests of the younger generation, and in their turn recover their lost youth: the motions of their natural heat seem to be stirred in them at the mere sight of such strenuous activity and by their participation in the joys of unbridled youth.

Every Sunday in Lent after dinner a fresh swarm of young men go out into the fields on war-horses, steeds foremost in the context, each of which is skilled and schooled to run in circles. From the gates there sallies forth a host of laymen, sons of citizens, equipped with lances and shields, the younger ones with spears forked at the top, but with the steel point removed. They make a pretence at war, carry out field-exercises and indulge in mimic combats. Thither too come many courtiers, when the king is in town, and from the households of bishops, earls and barons come youths and adolescents, not yet girt with the belt of knighthood, for the pleasure of engaging in combat with each other. Each is inflamed with the hope of victory. The fiery steeds neigh with tremulous limbs and champ their bits; impatient of delay they cannot stand still. When at last their trampling hooves ring on the ground in rapid flight, their boy riders divide their ranks; some pursue those immediately in front of them, but fail to catch up with them; others overtake their fellows, force them to dismount and fly past them.

At the Easter festival they play at a kind of naval warfare. A shield is firmly bound to a tree in mid-stream, and a small boat, swiftly impelled by many an oar and the current of the river, carries on the stern a youth armed with a lance with which to strike the shield. If he breaks the lance by striking the shield, and yet keeps his footing, he has achieved his aim and gratified his wish, but if he strikes the shield firmly and the lance remains unbroken, he is thrown overboard into the flowing river, and the boat, impelled by its own motion, rushes past him. There are, however, two other boats moored, one on each side of the target, with several youths on board to seize hold of the striker who has been engulfed by the stream, as soon as he comes into view or when he rises on the crest of the wave for the second time. On the bridge and the terraces fronting the river stand the spectators, ready to laugh their fill.

On feast-days throughout the summer the young men indulge in the sports of archery, running, jumping, wrestling, slinging the stone, hurling the javelin beyond a mark and fighting with the sword and buckler. Cytherea* leads the dance of the maidens, and until the moon rises, the earth is shaken with flying feet.

In winter on almost every feast-day before dinner either foaming boars, armed with lightning tusks, fight for their lives 'to save their bacon', or stout bulls with butting horns, or huge bears do battle with the hounds let loose upon them. When the great marsh that washes the north wall of the city is frozen over, swarms of young men issue forth to play games on the ice. Some, gaining speed in their run, with feet set well apart, slide sideways over a vast expanse of ice. Others make seats out of a large lump of ice, and while one sits thereon, others with linked hands run before and drag him along behind them. So swift is their sliding motion that sometimes their feet slip, and they all fall on their faces. Others, more skilled at winter sports, put on their feet the shinbones of animals, binding them firmly round their ankles, and, holding poles shod with iron in their hands, which they strike from time to time against the ice, they are propelled swift as a bird in flight or a bolt shot from an engine of war. Sometimes, by mutual consent, two of them run against each other in this way from a great distance, and, lifting their poles, each tilts against the other. Either one or both fall, not without some bodily injury, for, as they fall, they are carried along a great way beyond each other by the impetus of their run, and wherever the ice comes in contact with their heads, it scrapes off the skin utterly. Often a leg or an arm is broken, if the victim falls with it underneath him; but theirs is an age greedy of glory, youth yearns for victory, and exercises itself in mock combats in order to carry itself more bravely in real battles.

Many of the citizens take pleasure in sporting with birds of the air, with hawks, falcons and such-like, and with hounds that hunt their prey in the woods. The citizens have the rights of the chase in Middlesex, Hertfordshire, all the Chiltern country, and in Kent as far as the river Cray. The Londoners, who were then known as Trinobantes, drove back Julius Caesar, whose delight was to wade through paths steeped in blood. Whence Lucan wrote, 'To the Britons whom he had sought he turned his back in flight.'

The city of London has given birth to several men who have subdued many realms and even the Roman Empire to their dominion, and also many another whose valour has raised him to the gods as lord of the world, as was promised to Brutus by the oracle of Apollo. 'Brutus, beyond Gaul, beneath the setting sun, there lies an isle washed by the waves of the ocean. Thither direct thy course, for there shall be thy seat for ever. This shall be to thy sons a second Troy. Here from thy stem shall kings arise, and the whole world shall be subject to them.'

Afterwards in Christian times this city produced that noble emperor Constantine, son of the empress Helena, who bestowed the city of Rome and all the imperial insignia on God and St Peter and on Sylvester, the Roman pope [AD 314–35], to whom he dispensed the office of a groom,[11] no longer rejoicing to be called emperor but rather the defender of the holy Roman Church; and, lest the peace of the lord pope should be disturbed by the uproar of secular strife occasioned by his presence, he himself altogether abandoned the city which he had bestowed upon the lord pope, and built for himself the city of Byzantium. And in modern times also London has given birth to illustrious and noble monarchs,

11 I.e. the emperor walked before the pope, leading his horse in procession, as a mark of honour.

the empress Maud, King 'Henry III',[12] and the blessed Archbishop Thomas, that glorious martyr of Christ, than whom she bore no purer saint nor one more dear to all good men throughout the Latin world.

3. Chester's divine plan

The author of this celebration of Chester was a monk of the Benedictine abbey of St Werburgh (founded by Hugh d'Avranches, the earl at the time of Domesday Book [**9**]). Lucian wrote in *c.*1195. The translation omits some of the text's redundant repetitions. Like William fitz-Stephen [**2**], Lucian employed a rhetoric which elevated his subject. Yet he reveals some historical awareness by his allusion to the Roman Empire and to the exclusion of the Britons from the Roman culture of the city. This evidence of a twelfth-century memory (however confused) of the Roman past is precious, as is Lucian's precise indication of the commercial coordinates of a twelfth-century city of no mean importance.

M. V. Taylor (ed.), *Liber Luciani de laude Cestrie,* Lancashire and Cheshire Record Society, LXIV, 1912, pp. 45–7. Latin, transl. by GR.

First it is to be seen what Chester is, how it was built as a city, what aspect its position gives it. It was placed in the west of Britain as a place of rest and shelter for the legions who once came from far away and, guarding the border of the Roman Empire, to hold, as I might say, the keys to Ireland. For lying opposite the northern tip of Ireland, it opens a passage for ships and sailors bringing goods at all times. To the east its view extends not only to the Roman see and to the Empire, but to the whole world, such a sight being to the eyes as 'heroic deeds of the forefathers, a long series of exploits',[13] so that whatever occurs in the world may be seen, and the good known, the evil eschewed. From the four winds it has four gates: the east looks towards India, the west towards Ireland, the north towards Norway, the south towards Wales, which is the narrow corner left to the Britons by divine justice on account of their unnatural civil wars ... By God's provision our Chester has below the city walls a beautiful and fish-filled river, and a harbour on the south side into which ships arrive from Aquitaine, Spain, Scotland and Germany [with wine and other merchandise]. The

12 'Henry III' was 'the Young King', son of Henry II.

13 Virgil, *Aeneid,* I, l. 641.

waters now give fish to the population and a living to the fishermen… It has two straight and excellent streets which traverse the city in the form of the holy cross, each one beginning at one of the gates. By this it is seen mystically and wonderfully that the city has within it the grace of God, who showed in the four Gospels how his double law of the Old and New Testament was fulfilled in the holy cross … Nor in this interpretation do I fear the contradiction of a just judge, since it must be a solid truth, being passed down in written memory … It should also be understood that in the middle of the town, equitably positioned for all, is a market of copious goods, especially food, frequented by local people and outsiders who bring cash and return with provender. This is doubtless an image of the eternal bread which came from heaven to be born, as the prophets said, 'in the centre and umbilical knot of the earth', thereby appearing equally to all the nations of the world … If one stands in the middle of the marketplace and turns one's face to the rising sun, the churches are aligned in such a way that one sees St John the forerunner of Christ to the east, St Peter the Apostle to the west, St Werburgh the Virgin to the north and the Archangel Michael to the south. No truer thing has been written than that 'over your walls, O Jerusalem, I have placed guardians'.[14]

4. A poem in praise of Winchester *c.*1400

Local pride is expressed in concentrated form in these verses. While their survival depends upon their having been written down, they have the form and tone of an oral – and probably sung – tradition. For popular urban rhymes of a different kind, see [**91**].

C. Sisam (ed.), *The Oxford Book of Medieval English Verse*, Oxford: Clarendon Press, 1970, p. 374. English.

Me liketh ever the lengere the bet — *take more pleasure*
By Wingester, that joly cite:
The town is good and wel y-set; — *situated*
  The folk is comely on to see. — *to look at*
The air is good bothe inne and oute;
  The cité stont under an hille; — *stands*
The riveres renneth all aboute; — *run all around it*
  The town is rulèd upon skille. — *wisely*

14 Isaiah 62.6.

5. The mayor of Exeter appeals to history 1447–48

Locked in dispute over his jurisdiction with the cathedral and canons, the mayor of Exeter made, in the city's case before the royal chancellor, an appeal to history. Churches could always claim ancient foundation and supernatural sanction. To compete, civic rulers needed to be able to point to a no less prestigious past. Shillingford drew for political purposes on stories which may well have had popular currency. The example illustrates how conflict fostered appeals to (and the invention of) civic history.

S. A. Moore (ed.), *Letters and papers of John Shillingford, Mayor of Exeter 1447–50*, Camden Society, 2nd series, II, 1871, pp. 75–6. English, revised by GR.

The said mayor, bailiffs and commonalty say that the said city of Exeter of right old time is called *Penholtkeyre*, the most, or one of the most ancient cities of this land, of whose beginning no man can find nor read; the which city before the incarnation of Christ was a city walled, and having a suburb to the same, of most reputation, worship, defence and defensible of these parts, and yet is in time of need, and most favour and succour to all the king's people of the land, especially in time of war repairing thereto. The which city, upon the Passion of Christ, was by [Emperor] Vespasian besieged by time of eight days; the which obtained not the effect of his siege, and so went forth to Bordeaux and from Bordeaux to Rome and from Rome to Jerusalem, and there he with Titus besieged Jerusalem and obtained [it], and sold 30 Jews for a penny, as it appears by the Chronicles: and always the said city of Exeter [was] whole and undivided in worship as it is above said, unto the time of the coming thither of the bishop and canons.

6. History and civic pride in Bristol

Robert Ricart was town clerk of Bristol from 1479. He compiled his 'Kalendar', a collection of customary, historical and legal material about the city, while in office. He may have known William Worcester [**7**], who came to live in Bristol. Ricart's situation is comparable with that of John Carpenter, town clerk of London and author of the 'Liber Albus'. For his account of early British history, Ricart was indebted to Geoffrey of Monmouth [**1**], whose authority was, with one or two exceptions, largely unquestioned before the sixteenth century. Perhaps it was natural for a town clerk to interest himself in such matters, but Ricart held that it was 'right convenient and according to every burgess of the town of Bristol' to know these things. It is plausible to imagine a version of this narrative being read aloud at meetings of the town council.

L. Toulmin Smith (ed.), *The Maire of Bristowe is Kalendar*, Camden Society, 2nd series, V, 1872, pp. 8–10. English, revised by GR.

For as much as it is right convenient and according to every burgess of the town of Bristowe, especially those that be men of worship, for to know and understand the beginning and first foundation of the said worshipful town. Therefore let him read the old chronicles of Brutus, and he shall find how soon after that Brutus had set and built the city of New Troy, which now is London, in remembrance of the great Troy that he and all his lineage came from, then Brutus reigned 20 winters and more, and was buried in the New Troy. And he had 3 manly men to sons, Lotryn, Albanac and Kambor. Brute ordered Lotryn to be king of this land called the great Britain, Albanac king of Scotland, and Kambor king of Wales. And after the decease and occisioun [killing] of Lotryn and Albanac, reigned Madhan 30 years. And after Madhan, reigned Memprys 22 years. And after Memprys reigned his son Ebrac 60 years, a noble prince and a manly, which by his prowess and manhood and with the help of his Bretons conquered all France and got there great riches, so that when he came home he made and built a noble city and called it after his name Eborac, that now is Evirwyk, alias York. And also he built the castle of Maidens, which is Edinburgh in Scotland. And after this Ebrac reigned his son Brut Greeneshall 30 years. And after him reigned King Leil, which built the city of Carlisle, in whose time King Solomon reigned in Jerusalem, which built the Temple of Our Lord. And after this King Leil reigned his son Ludludubras 13 years, which built the cities of Winchester and of Canterbury. And after this King Ludludubras, reigned his son Bladud 21 years, a great necromancer, which built the city of Bath and devised there the hot baths. And after this King Bladud reigned his son Leire, which built the town of Leicester and called it after his name. And soon after this King Leir, by occasion of great wars the land was departed in four: that is to say, England to one Dowalyn, Scotland to one Scater, Wales to one Rudak, and Cornwall to one Cloton. This Cloton by just title was right heir to all these lands, and he had a son called Dondbaude. This

King Donebaude had 2 manly men to sons, that one Belin, and that other Brynne, which after the decrees of their father departed the land between them as their father had commanded and ordained. That is to say, Belin the eldest son had all the land on this side of the Humber, and Brynne had all the land beyond the Humber into Scotland. And for as much as Belin had the more part and the better part, Brynne waxed wroth and would have had more; but Belyn would not suffer him, so they began to war. But Brynne the younger brother had no force nor power against his brother Belin, so Brynne, by counsel of his people, voided [departed] into France and there abode a long time, and got there great lordships by marriage…

And then Brynne first founded and built this worshipful town of Bristut that now is Bristowe, and set it upon a little hill, that is to say, between St Nicholas' gate, St John's gate, St Leonard's gate, and the New gate. And no more was built until many years after.

7. William Worcester on the cities of England *c.*1480

While working for the Norfolk knight Sir John Fastolf, William Worcester developed a personal fascination with English history and topography, which he pursued through both reading and travel. The scholarly rhetoric of his text lends a spurious authority to a series of stories, part history and part myth, about the supposed origins of various towns. Its content and tone announce the antiquarian. But the fact that allusions to such legendary civic histories were incorporated into pageant performed on the occasion of royal visits shows that these ideas had a wider currency.[15]

J. H. Harvey (ed.), *William Worcestre: Itineraries,* Oxford: Clarendon Press, 1969, pp. 211, 273. Latin, transl. by the editor.

Of Norwich. Edward the Elder, son of King Alfred, a most victorious prince, among other noble works restored the *burh* which in Saxon was formerly called *Burghchester* and now Norwich, but which in the British tongue is named Kaergwelyn after King Gwytelinus who first founded that city with its castle, and gave it the name of 'the blanch flour castel' from its beauty.

15 G. Rosser, 'Myth, image and social process in the English medieval town', *Urban History,* XXIII, 1996, pp. 5–25.

Julius Caesar was not the first builder of that castle, but he caused various fortifications to be made there, as he did in every city whose name includes 'Chester', as one may suppose Chichester, Winchester, Rochester, and others.

Hampton [Southampton] was named by Arviragus, king of the Britons, who slew the Roman Hamon by the sea-shore in the place where the town of Hampton stands. On this account it was called Hampton in the time of Gwyder, king of the Britons, who refused to pay tribute to the Romans and who was afterwards slain by Claudius Caesar the Roman at Portchester town.

Cirencester town in the county of Gloucester. Grismond's Tower by the chapel of St Cecilia, where King Arthur was crowned, lies west of Cirencester town, which anciently was called the City of Sparrows.

8. An Italian visitor *c.*1500

A Venetian visitor to England focuses on the one metropolis, London, as worthy of comparison with Venice. Being used to Venetian society, dominated by a patrician class of ancient nobility, he is particularly struck by the absence from London of such an aristocratic elite. The concentration of goldsmiths' shops in Cheapside, next to St Paul's cathedral, and along the Strand (which to the visitor sounded like 'Strada', or 'the Street') which linked the city of London to the courtly suburb of Westminster, is documented in contemporary property records.[16]

C. A. Sneyd (ed.), *A Relation … of the Island of England*, Camden Society, XXXVII, London, 1897, pp. 41–3. Italian, transl. by the editor, revised by GR.

Eboracum (*Boraco*) was in ancient times the principal city of the island, and was adorned with many buildings by the Romans, in their elegant style; but, having been sacked and burnt in the reign of King William the Conqueror, she never afterwards could recover her former splendour; so that, at present, all the beauty of this island is confined to London. Which, although sixty miles distant from the sea, possesses all

16 D. Keene and V. Harding, *Historical Gazetteer of London before the Great Fire*, i, *Cheapside*, London, 1987.

the advantages to be desired in a maritime town; being situated on the river Thames, which is very much affected by the tide, for many miles (I do not know the exact number) above it; and London is so much benefited by this ebb and flow of the river, that vessels of 100 tons burden can come up to the city, and ships of any size to within five miles of it; yet the water in this river is fresh for twenty miles below London. Although this city has no buildings in the Italian style (*a l'usanza italiana*), but of timber or brick like the French, the Londoners live comfortably, and, it appears to me, that there are not fewer inhabitants than at Florence or Rome. It abounds with every article of luxury, as well as with the necessaries of life; but the most remarkable thing in London, is the wonderful quantity of wrought silver. I do not allude to that in private houses, although the landlord of the house in which the Milanese ambassador lived, had plate to the amount of 100 crowns, but to the shops of London. In one single street, named the Strand (*che si chiama la Strada*), leading to St Paul's, there are fifty-two goldsmiths' shops, so rich and full of silver vessels, great and small, that in all the shops in Milan, Rome, Venice, and Florence put together, I do not think there would be found so many of the magnificence that are to be seen in London. And these vessels are either salt cellars, or drinking cups, or basins to hold water for the hands; for they eat off that fine tin [pewter], which is little inferior to silver. These great riches of London are not occasioned by its inhabitants being noblemen or gentlemen; being all, on the contrary, persons of low degree, and artificers who have congregated there from all parts of the island, and from Flanders, and from every other place. No one can be mayor or alderman of London, who has not been an apprentice in his youth; that is, who has not passed the seven or nine years in that hard service … Still, the citizens of London are thought quite as highly of there, as the Venetian gentlemen are at Venice.

II. URBAN GROWTH

This collection of textual sources opens in the long twelfth century, but its earliest contributions make clear that the story of some English towns is much older. Regime change at the Norman Conquest produced unprecedented forms of documentation; but the findings of Anglo-Norman administrators, even while they express the shift of political power, at the same time underline continuities in urban life reaching back well before 1066. As is noted in the Introduction, archaeology has recently filled out the written record of Anglo-Saxon boroughs, to show that central and southern England were significantly urbanised well before the Norman invasion. The Domesday Book is not a simple source for the historian to use [**9**], [**10**]. It was drawn up not to provide a rounded description of English towns or society but to record the rights of the king. Much that we should like to know is therefore omitted. None the less this extraordinary record sheds at least a flickering light on the state of urbanisation at the time of the Conquest. We should be struck, in the first place, by the extent of royal involvement in the towns by this date. What mixture of political ambition and fiscal policy motivated that involvement? The financial value of royal rights was an evident priority of the officials; at the same time, the crown's dues were clearly also a matter of honour and prestige. Already in the late tenth century Chester's role as a theatrical stage for the ritual of royal power had been demonstrated by King Edgar 'the Peaceable'. In 973, following his coronation at Bath (another urban setting with its own particular distinction as a former Roman place and cult centre associated with the hot springs), Edgar sailed to Chester and held there a meeting with Celtic and Scandinavian rulers. Although accounts of this diplomatic gathering were elaborated later, scrutiny of the evidence confirms that the strategically significant port of Chester [**3**] had on this occasion been the setting for an international summit.[1] The use by English monarchs of their towns as frames for the spectacular display of royal power would have a long history [**59**], [**61**]. The different case of Bury St Edmunds exemplifies the potential of a monastic

1 D. E. Thornton, 'Edgar and the eight kings, AD 973: *textus et dramatis personae*', *Early Medieval History*, X, 2001, pp. 49–79.

establishment to act as a catalyst of urban growth [**10**]. Although the religious settlement probably originated as early as the seventh century, the foundation of the Benedictine monastery in 1020 created a substantial community of monks entirely dependent upon the services of others. That the religious were also endowed with extensive estates, the produce of which neeed to be brought to market, was an additional boost for the growing town at the monastery gates. The record's comparison between Bury as it had been before the Conquest and in 1086 gives a glimpse of the enterprise of the monastic landlords in a context of expanding demand and economic opportunity.

A further reflection of urban growth in the Anglo-Norman period are the bids by local groups of merchants for increased autonomy and scope to manage their affairs, free from the daily meddling of royal officials. By the charter which they were probably granted in the early 1130s by Henry I, the Londoners secured remarkably extensive rights of self-government [**11**].[2] The farm or annual payment of £300 into the king's exchequer which was agreed by the citizens must have seemed attractive to the royal treasurer at the time of the charter, but the inflationary period of population growth and rising prices which followed will soon have rendered this an economically unrealistic return – a bargain for the townspeople. That the leading townsmen were concerned to have confirmation of their hunting rights in the forests outside the city is a hint concerning the culture of the urban elite: as has been demonstrated for other towns in the period, it is likely that the leading investors in London's expanding trade included the owners of substantial rural estates. A charter of liberties distinguished a town from other places. None the less urban populations comprised both aristocrats and socially more modest immigrants who all shared roots in the country. The English kings did not tend naturally to extend the privileges which were enshrined in London's first charter; nor did they ever allow the development of fully independent communes such as were becoming familiar at this period in parts of the Italian and German territories.[3] But King John's financial weakness helps to explain the success of the burgesses of Ipswich in securing similar, if less extensive, rights [**12**]. In this instance we are able, in accompanying documentation, to witness the townspeople responding

2 See further C. N. L. Brooke, G. Keir and S. Reynolds, 'Henry I's charter for the City of London', *Journal of the Society of Archivists*, IV, 1970–73, pp. 558–78.

3 J. Tait, *The Medieval English Borough. Studies on Its Origins and Constitutional Growth*, Manchester, 1936, pp. 154–61.

to their new charter by instituting new civic officers and procedures. Also notable in the record is the evident appreciation of the symbolic value of the copy of the civic customs in what was, somewhat portentously, christened the 'Domesday' of the town, and of the splendid new seal of the community. As towns in this period became more bureaucratised in their government, they expressed their new-found identities in the very form of their official records.[4]

The documents which follow exemplify the variety of 'new town' developments which characterised the long thirteenth century.[5] By no means all such initiatives represented wholly new creations on green-field locations; but the period was unquestionably marked by the planned erection of thousands of houses and shops on previously unbuilt sites, and by the issuing of local charters to incentivise settlers. The latter, indeed, in return for marketing privileges, were largely expected to build their own homes on plots newly made available by enterprising landlords. A spectacular instance of urban promotion was the bishop of Salisbury's project to relocate both his cathedral and its surrounding city from the dramatic hilltop setting of 'Old Salisbury' to the foot of the escarpment, where advantage could be taken of a greatly superior water supply and – following the strategic realignment of roads in the vicinity – lines of communication [**13**]. While archaeology has revealed traces of earlier settlement on the site of 'New Salisbury', the grid-planned and partially fortified town laid out in the thirteenth century is a dramatic instance of ecclesiastical involvement in the urban expansion of the period.[6] By the time of the grant of the royal charter, it is evident from this text that much practical work had already been accomplished. The townspeople themselves, perceiving the economic advantage in the town's relocation, must be envisaged as willing collaborators in the project. With the passage of time and increased prosperity their collaboration might not always be so easy to secure. In 1217 the bishop had obtained from the crown the right to levy a 'reasonable aid' from the citizens of 'New Salisbury'

4 G. H. Martin, 'The English borough in the thirteenth century', repr. in R. Holt and G. Rosser (eds), *The Medieval Town. A Reader in English Urban History*, London, 1990, pp. 29–48; C. Liddy, *War, Politics and Finance in Late Medieval English Towns. Bristol, York and the Crown, 1350–1400*, Woodbridge, 2005, pp. 56–7.

5 In general see M. Beresford, *The New Towns of the Middle Ages*, Leicester, 1967.

6 K. H. Rogers. 'Salisbury', in M. D. Lobel (ed.), *Atlas of Historic Towns*, i, London, 1969, pp. 1–5; Royal Commission on the Historical Monuments of England, *Salisbury. The Houses of the Close*, London, 1993, pp. 1–6; RCHM, *Ancient and Historical Monuments in the City of Salisbury*, London, 1980–.

whenever the king tallaged his domains. This right was enshrined in the 1228 charter. When, however, the bishop later, in 1305, attempted to raise such a tax from his citizens, they revolted, and forced him to renounce the right. According to the frustrated lord, the townspeople had 'grown wanton with fatness'.[7]

Edward I's new town foundations were often shaped by military and strategic considerations, whether along the south coast, in north Wales or on the border with Scotland. But the writ quoted here refers also to an intention to benefit trade [**14**]. The same document implies the emergence, in the context of multiple ventures of the kind, of specialists in the arts of town foundation. All lords were reviewing their estates and considering their potential for urban development.[8] The monks of Eynsham in Oxfordshire, by designating certain fields for building and offering attractive terms to settlers, created a new street of houses and workshops [**15**].[9] Whereas many small town foundations of the period were located on virgin sites – for example, the new borough of Stratford-upon-Avon, created around 1220 by the bishop of Worcester[10] – this initiative at Eynsham represented an early thirteenth-century addition to an existing borough around a marketplace (the Sunday market is first recorded in the time of King Stephen; Henry II added two annual fairs), which had probably first grown up prior to the Norman Conquest before the gates of the abbey. A survey of 1366 records thirty-one houses in Newland. Newland Street still exists, and a map of 1782 shows the houses evenly spaced along its length, each with a garden extending for 110 yards, as described in the charter. Unlike the cathedral town of Salisbury, Eynsham was more typical of ecclesiastical new towns [**10**] in having a primary function of serving as a market for the produce of the monastic estates, with the result that it would never grow beyond modest proportions. But it appears from the distinct court rolls for Newland that the inhabitants elected their own reeve; and the charter itself already refers to the 'commune'

7 *Rotuli parliamentorum*, 6 vols, London, 1832, i, pp. 174–5; J. S. Davies (ed.), *The Tropenell Cartulary*, 2 vols, Devizes, 1908, i, pp. 189–98.

8 For a regional study focused on Wales and the Marches, see R. A. Griffiths, 'Urban colonisation in England and Wales in the later Middle Ages: examples and implications', in M. Boone and P. Stabel (eds), *Shaping Urban Identity in Late Medieval Europe*, Leuven-Apeldoorn, 2000, pp. 221–34.

9 J. Blair, 'Small towns 600–1270', in *CUHB*, pp. 245–70, fig. 11.4.

10 E. M. Carus-Wilson, 'The first half-century of the borough of Stratford-upon-Avon', repr. in R. Holt and G. Rosser (eds), *The Medieval Town. A Reader in English Urban History*, London, 1990, pp. 49–70.

of those inhabitants. The need for a communal organisation was evident in the towns of this period not only with respect to the keeping of order within the walls, but to repel jealous lords. In the case of High Wycombe, a town growing up on this secular estate had already by the late twelfth century been effectively granted into the hands of the townspeople. Yet a later lord resented the commune's autonomy and denied the merchant guild its right to exist [**16**]. In this case the eventual outcome was a victory for the burgesses, but their experience underlines the fragility of communal rights in the presence of aristocratic power. The final text in this section is an informal and personal list of the reputations of many different towns in thirteenth-century England [**17**]. It records a contemporary impression that this was a land of many towns, markedly diverse one from another: 'marble of Corfe, cattle of Nottingham …'. If some of the noted associations seem less grounded in economic realities and more likely to be the trace of personal experience – 'girls of Hereford, beggars of Chichester' – we should acknowledge that such impressions were no less real for being personal.

9. Chester in 1086

Domesday Book is a problematic source, not least for the urban historian.[11] Ostensibly a full description of the material resources of the kingdom ruled by the new Anglo-Norman monarchy, its perspective in reality was limited. Its compilers were primarily concerned with Crown rights, and, despite the Conqueror's extensive views of these, much escaped the royal inventory. A peculiar challenge is caused by the treatment of lordship under distinct headings, with the result that the rights of diverse lords in a particular town may appear on widely separated pages of the Domesday Book. For all its difficulties, however, this extraordinary source contains valuable evidence of urban life. Chester's Domesday Book entry is unusual in recording a set of pre-Conquest customs in use in the city. Chester's obligation for tax on land outside the city indicates that estates had previously been assigned for the maintenance (whether in food or military defence) of the town. We should note not only the crown's entitlement to the proceeds of urban

11 G. H. Martin, 'The Domesday boroughs', in P. H. Sawyer (ed.), *Domesday Book: A Reassessment*, London, 1985, pp. 143–63; S. Reynolds, 'The Domesday town', in J. C. Holt (ed.), *Domesday Studies*, Woodbridge, 1987, pp. 295–310.

commerce but also the extent of royal control over other aspects of life in the town, including violence and moral behaviour. While cataloguing, as its main purpose, the dues owed to the king, the text also refers to separate rights of the bishop and the earl.

P. Morgan (ed.), *Domesday Book: Cheshire*, C, Chichester: Phillimore, 1978. Latin, transl. by A. Morgan and the editor.

The city of Chester paid tax on 50 hides* before 1066. 3½ hides which are outside the city, that is 1½ hides beyond the bridge and 2 hides in Newton and 'Redcliff' and in the Bishop's Borough, these paid tax with the city.

Before 1066 there were 431 houses in the city paying tax, and besides these the bishop had 56 houses paying tax. This city then paid 10½ silver marks;* two parts were the king's, the third the earl's.

These were the laws there.

If the peace given by the king's hand, or by his writ or his commissioner, were broken by anyone, the king had 100*s* thereby. But if the king's peace, given by the earl or on his orders, were broken, the earl had the third penny [one-third of the sum] of the 100*s* which were given for it; and if the peace given by the king's reeve or the earl's officer were broken, the fine was 40*s* and the third penny was the earl's.

If a free man, breaking the peace given by the king, killed a man in a house, his land and all his goods were the king's, and he became an outlaw himself. The earl had the same [right], but only over his own man who paid this penalty. But no one could restore peace to any outlaw except the king.

Whoever shed blood between Monday morning and Saturday noon was fined 10*s*; but from Saturday noon to Monday morning the fine for bloodshed was 20*s*. Similarly, whoever did so in the Twelve Days of Christmas, on Candlemas Day [2 February], on the first day of Easter, on the first day of Whitsun [the seventh Sunday after Easter], on Ascension Day [the fortieth day after Easter], on the day of the Assumption [15 August] or of the Nativity of St Mary [8 September], or on All Saints' Day [1 November], paid 20*s*.

Whoever killed a man on these holy days was fined £4; on other days, 40*s*. Similarly, whoever committed breaking and entering or highway robbery on these holidays and on a Sunday paid out a fine of £4; on other days 40*s*.

Whoever committed collusion with a thief in the city gave up 10*s*; but if a reeve of the king or the earl incurred this penalty, he paid 20*s*.

Whoever committed robbery or theft or did violence to a woman in a house was fined 40*s* for each of these [offences].

If a widow had intercourse with anyone unlawfully, she was fined 20*s*, but a girl 10*s* for such an offence.

Whoever took possession of another's land in the city, and could not prove it to be his own, was fined 40*s*; likewise whoever made a claim thereto, if he could not prove that it should be his.

Whoever wished to enter possession of his own, or his kinsman's land paid 10*s*. But if he could not or would not, the reeve received his land into the king's hand.

Whoever did not pay tribute at the due term was fined 10*s*.

If a fire burnt the city, the man from whose house it came was fined 3 ora* of pence and gave 2*s* to his next door neighbour.

Two parts of all sums forfeit were the king's, the third part the earl's.

If ships arrived at the city port or left port without the king's permission, the king and the earl had 40*s* from each man in the ships.

If a ship arrived against the king's peace and despite his prohibition, the king and the earl had both the ship itself and the crew, together with everything in it.

But if it came with the king's peace and permission, those in it sold what they had without interference. But when it left the king and the earl had 4*d* from each cargo; if the king's reeve instructed those who had marten-skins not to sell to anyone until they were first shown to him and he had made his purchase, whoever did not observe this instruction was fined 40*s*.

Any man or woman who gave false measure in the city was fined 4*s* when caught; similarly anyone who made bad beer was either put in the dung-stool [cucking-stool]* or paid 4*s* to the reeves. The officer of the king or the earl received this fine in the city, on whoever's land it was, whether the bishop's or any other man's. Similarly with the toll; if anyone withheld it for more than three nights, he was fined 40*s*.

Before 1066 there were 7 moneyers in the city, who paid £7 to the king and the earl, additional to the revenue, when the coinage was changed.

There were then 12 judges in the city; they were from the king's, the bishop's and the earl's men. If any of them stayed away from the hundred* on a day when it sat without plain excuse, he was fined 10*s*, [shared] between the king and the earl.

For the repair of the city wall and the bridge, the reeve used to call out one man to come from each hide in the county. The lord of any man who did not come paid a fine of 40*s* to the king and the earl. The fine was additional to the revenue.

This city then paid in revenue £45 and 3 timbers* of marten-skins.* The third part was the earl's and two parts the king's.

When Earl Hugh [d'Avranches] acquired it [in 1071], its value was only £30, for it was thoroughly devastated; there were 205 houses less than before 1066. Now there are as many as he found there.

Mundret held this city from the earl for £70 and 1 gold mark.

10. Bury St Edmunds in 1086

The Domesday Book entry for Bury, although brief, is unusually detailed, yielding a rich characterisation of this expanding monastic borough. Significant comparisons are made between the situation prior to the Conquest and in 1086. At this period the local economy appears to have been dominated by the service trades required by the Benedictine community: clergy, administration, retailing and clothing. As, over the course of the following two centuries, the cloth trade of this Suffolk market town acquired a more than local significance, tensions would arise with the monastic lords, whose tutelage came to be resented by the townspeople [**79**].

A. Rumble (ed.), *Domesday Book: Suffolk*, 2 vols, Chichester: Phillimore, 1986, i, 14.167. Latin, transl. by the editor.

In [Bury St Edmunds], the town where St Edmund the glorious king and martyr lies buried, Abbot B[aldwin] held 118 men before 1066 for the monks' supplies. They could grant and sell their land. Under them, 52 smallholders (*bordars*) from whom the abbot could have a certain [amount of] aid. 54 free [men], somewhat poor (*satis inopes*); 43 almsmen; each of them has one smallholder. Now 2 mills; 2 ponds or fish ponds. Value of this town then £10; now £20.

It has 1½ leagues in length and as much in width. When the hundred* pays £1 in tax, then 60*d* goes from here for the monks' supplies; but this is from the town as [it was] before 1066 and yet it is the same now although it is enclosed in a larger circuit of land which then was ploughed and sown [but] where [now] there are 30 priests, deacons and clerics, and 28 nuns and poor persons, who pray daily for the king and all Christian people. [Also] 75 bakers, brewers, tailors, washers, shoemakers, robemakers, cooks, porters, bursars; all these daily serve St Edmund's, the abbot and the brethren. Besides these, there are 13 reeves in charge of the land who have their houses in the same town; under them, 5 smallholders. [Also] now 34 men-at-arms, including French and English; under them, 22 smallholders. Now in all [there are] 342 houses in lordship on land [which was] St Edmund's arable before 1066.

11. Charter of Henry I in favour of the citizens of London

As a historical source, this charter is problematic. Charters could institute new rights and practices, but they were often motivated by a primary desire to describe and defend the *status quo.* Consequently the historian needs to be sensitive not only to the contents of these documents but also to the value placed by contemporaries on their physical form, their visual iconography and their verbal rhetoric. Like many royal charters issued in the decades following the Norman Conquest, this one is replete with references to older practices which local interest is anxious to protect in the context of the new regime – and in a new world in which the defence of privilege was coming to depend increasingly upon the ability to produce written evidence of its origin. This charter probably dates from between 1130 and 1133. Some doubt has been cast on its authenticity, partly because of the generosity of its provisions. However, most of the rights granted here were included in a (certainly genuine) confirmatory charter issued by Henry II in *c.*1155. In any case, the one reproduced here dates from the mid-twelfth century, and encapsulates the written privileges which groups of leading townsmen, in London and elsewhere, increasingly sought from the crown. Amongst many points of interest, we should notice the protection of 'sokes' or islands of private, secular jurisdiction within the city. The hunting rights of the urban elite are a reminder of their important landed connections (see also [**2**]).

D. C. Douglas and G. W. Greenaway (eds), *English Historical Documents 1042–1189*, 2nd edn (copyright © 1981), London: Eyre Methuen, 1981, pp. 1012–13. Latin, transl. by the editors. Reproduced by permission of Taylor and Francis Books UK.

Henry, by the grace of God king of the English, to the archbishop of Canterbury, and to the bishops and abbots, and earls and barons and justices and sheriffs, and to all his liegemen, both French and English, of the whole of England, greeting. Know that I have granted to my citizens of London that they shall hold Middlesex at farm for £300 at the account[12] for themselves and their heirs from me and my heirs, so that the citizens shall appoint as sheriff from themselves whomsoever they may choose, and shall appoint from among themselves as justice whomsoever they choose to look after the pleas of my crown and the pleadings which arise in connection with them. No other shall be justice over the men of London. And the citizens shall not plead outside the walls of the city in respect of any plea; and they shall be quit of scot* and Danegeld* and the murder-fine.* Nor shall any of them be compelled to offer trial by battle. And if any one of the citizens shall be impleaded* in respect of the pleas of the crown, let him prove himself to be a man of London by an oath which shall be judged in the city. Let no one be billeted within the walls of the city, either of my household, or by the force of anyone else. And let all the men of London and their property be quit and free from toll and passage* and lastage* and from all other customs throughout all England and at the seaports. And let the churches and barons and citizens hold and have well and in peace their sokes,* with all their customs, so that those who dwell in these sokes shall pay no customs except to him who possesses the soke, or to the steward whom he has placed there. And a man of London shall not be fined at mercy except according to his *were*,[13] that is to say, up to 100 shillings: this applies to an offence which can be punished by a fine. And there shall no longer be miskenning* in the husting court,* nor in the folk-moot,* nor in other pleas within the city. And the husting court shall sit once a week, that is, on Monday. I will cause my citizens to have their lands and pledges and debts within the city and outside it. And in respect of the lands

12 This was the 'farm of the borough': the right, in return for a regular payment to the royal exchequer, to govern legal and financial affairs within the town and its hinterland.

13 Not to be fined at discretion, and only at the level of his blood-price (a principle of Anglo-Saxon justice).

about which they make claim to me, I will do them right according to the law of the city. And if anyone has taken toll or custom from the citizens of London, then the citizens of London may take from the borough or village where toll or custom has been levied as much as the man of London gave for toll, and more also may be taken for a penalty. And let all debtors to the citizens of London discharge their debts, or prove in London that they do not owe them; and if they refuse either to pay or to come and make such proof, then the citizens to whom the debts are due may take pledges within the city either from the borough or from the village or from the county in which the debtor lives. And the citizens shall have their hunting chases, as well and fully as had their predecessors, namely, in Chiltern and Middlesex and Surrey. Given at Westminster.

12. The liberties and customs of Ipswich 1200

On occasion the grant of a charter can be shown to have had practical and immediate consequences. King John's grant of a first charter of liberties to the town of Ipswich (a) was promptly followed by meetings to appoint urban officials and to issue the first civic ordinances (b). As in other such cases, the securing of the charter indicates prior organisation on the part of the townspeople, embodied in this instance in a merchant guild. As a marker of the town's new status, the charter's dissemination by public reading throughout neighbouring counties is notable, as is the creation of a civic seal and a 'Domesday' roll in which to preserve the rights of the community.

S. Reynolds, W. de Boer and G. Mac Niocaill (eds), *Elenchus fontium historiae urbanae*, ii (2), Leiden: Brill, 1988, pp. 101–2 (a), 103–7 (b). Latin, transl. by GR.

(a) 25 May 1200. By John, by the grace of God king of England. Know that we have confirmed by this charter to our burgesses of Ipswich our town of Ipswich with all its possessions, liberties and customs, to be held by them and by their heirs from us and our heirs, paying annually at Michaelmas into our exchequer 100*s.*

We grant that all burgesses of Ipswich should be free of toll, stallage,* lastage,* pontage,* passage* and all other customary dues throughout our lands and at the ports.

We grant that none of them shall be made to plead* outside the borough of Ipswich; that they shall have their merchant guild with its privileges (*gildam mercatoriam et hansam suam*); that no one can be billeted by force within the town ...

We desire and firmly prescribe that the said burgesses shall hold these liberties and free customs in peace, just as they are held by the burgesses of our other free boroughs in England, saving in all things the liberties and free customs owned by our citizens of London.

(b) On the procedure for electing bailiffs and coroners* in Ipswich, according to the charter of King John. On Thursday after the feast of the Nativity of St John the Baptist [24 June] 1200, the whole township of the borough of Ipswich gathered (*congregata est tota villata burgi Gippeswici*) in the cemetery of St Mary at the Tower in order to elect two bailiffs and four coroners, in accordance with the charter which the king recently granted. They elected two law-worthy men of their town, John the son of Norman and William de Belines, who were sworn to guard the goods of the town and that they would treat faithfully and well both rich and poor. They also elected on the same day four coroners, John the son of Norman, William de Belines, Philip of the gate and Roger Lew, who were sworn to hold the pleas of the crown and to do whatever pertained to the royal interest within the town, and to ensure that the bailiffs dealt justly with both rich and poor.

On the same day it was agreed by common consent of the township that there should henceforward be in the town twelve chief 'portmen' (*capitales portmenni jurati*), as they are called in other free English boroughs, who will have full authority to govern and maintain the town ... And the bailiffs and coroners said that the whole township should come to the cemetery on Sunday after the feast of St Peter and St Paul [29 June] to elect these twelve chief portmen. On that day, the whole township of Ipswich being congregated in the presence of the bailiffs and coroners, the latter by the assent of the township chose four worthy and legal men from each parish of the town, who were sworn to elect twelve chief portmen from among the best and most discreet and substantial (*potencioribus*) men of the town. And the jurors of the parishes came and chose John son of Norman, William de Belines, Philip of the gate, Roger Lew, Peter Everard, William Goscalk,

Amisius Bolle, John of St George, John le Mayster, Sayer the son of Thurstan, Robert Parys and Andrew Peper. They swore before the whole township that they would protect and rule the borough of Ipswich and would maintain to the limits of their power all the liberties which the burgesses of the town had recently received by the king's charter ...

On Thursday after the feast of the Translation of St Thomas the Martyr [7 July] 1200 the bailiffs, coroners and other chief portmen met to direct the state of the town of Ipswich ... They ordained that there should be two bedels* sworn to make arrests and to carry out the orders of the bailiffs, coroners and chief portmen; and that one of the bedels should be in charge of the prisons. They ordained that by common counsel of the township there should be made a common seal in the borough, to be used in major negotiations touching the community of the town. They ordained that a suitable man should be elected as alderman of the merchant guild; and that he should have four worthy men of the town as his associates. They ordained that the new charter should be sent throughout the counties of Suffolk and Norfolk, and that it should be read in public, so that the liberties contained in the charter should be openly and publicly known everywhere in both counties ...

On Thursday after the feast of St Faith [6 October] 1200 the bailiffs and coroners, the rest of the chief portmen and the whole community (*tota communitas*) met together in the church of St Mary at the Tower. The bailiffs showed the common seal of the town which had been newly made ... An alderman was elected by the common counsel of the township, William Gosscalk; and four to be associated with him, Peter Everard, John le Mayster, Roger Lew and John of St George ... The twelve chief portmen were granted, in return for their labour for the community, the meadow of Odenholm for their horses. It was agreed by the whole community that the laws and free customs of the town should be placed in a roll called the Domesday; and that this roll should be for ever kept in the custody of the bailiffs, so that they should know how to carry out their office. Also that all the statutes of the guild merchant* should be placed in another roll, as is done elsewhere in towns and boroughs which have a guild merchant; and that the alderman should keep this always with him, so that he should know how to conduct his office.

13. The foundation of New Salisbury 1228

This royal charter ratifies the creation of a new town. With royal approval, Bishop Richard le Poore removed both his cathedral and the town which surrounded it from its previous hilltop location to a new, low-lying site. Notwithstanding the earlier Investiture Contest, following which ecclesiastical appointments were supposed to be free of secular interference, the king is explicit about his continuing claim to influence episcopal elections. In the royal perspective, both the city and the see were the king's possessions. There is no consideration given, in such a document as this, to the practical agency of the secular community of townspeople. Yet the latter must have played a significant role in the making of the new town. Albeit not formally recognised at this date, we should envisage some kind of political organisation among the inhabitants.

W. D. Macray (ed.), *Charters and Documents illustrating the History of the Cathedral, City, and Diocese of Salisbury, in the twelfth and thirteenth centuries*, Rolls Series, London: Eyre and Spottiswood, 1891, pp. 175–8. Latin, transl. by GR.

Henry [III], by the grace of God king of England, etc., to his archbishops, bishops, ministers, etc., sends greeting: Know that we, out of reverence for God and the Blessed Mary ever Virgin, and for our salvation and that of our ancestors and successors, have granted and by the present charter confirm to God and to the church of the blessed Mary – whose translation from our castle of Salisbury to a lower site was ordained by ourselves, and in the foundation of whose church we laid the first stone – and to the venerable father Richard, bishop of that place, and to his successors, and to the canons of the same church and their men, all the liberties and free customs which they had in the time of our forebears, the kings of England, throughout our kingdom, by virtue of charters either of our predecessors or of others of our realm granted to the said church, bishops and canons, as the charters of our predecessors and of other donors reasonably bear witness.

In addition, we desire and grant, for ourselves and our heirs, that the place called New Salisbury shall for ever be a free city (*libera civitas*), enclosed by ditches as is noted below; and that the citizens living in that city shall be quit of toll, pontage,* passage,* pavage,* lastage,* stallage,* carriage* and all other customs throughout all our land, with respect to all goods which they shall carry by land or water. And we forbid that anyone should vex or disturb them, or their possessions, or their lands or servants, contrary to the liberty of our charter, on pain of forfeit to us. And we grant that the said citizens shall have in perpetuity all other liberties and quittances throughout our kingdom which our citizens of Winchester hold.

We grant to the said bishop and his successors that, for fear of brigands, they may enclose the city of New Salisbury with sufficient ditches and keep these in perpetuity as their own domain. We reserve the right of ourselves and our heirs in the appointment of the bishop and during a vacancy, such as we rightly have during vacancies in other cathedral churches of our realm. It shall not be lawful for the citizens to give, sell or misappropriate the burgages* or tenements which they hold in the same city to churches or religious men, without the licence of the bishop and his successors.

In addition, we grant to the bishop and to his successors that, for the need of themselves and their church, they may levy a reasonable tallage* or aid from their citizens, whenever we or our heirs make a tallage in our domains.

We grant, moreover, to the bishop and his heirs that, for the improvement of the same city, they may alter and redirect the roads and bridges leading to it, as they see fit, saving the rights of others.

Furthermore, we grant to the bishop and his heirs that they may have each year for ever a fair in the said city of New Salisbury, lasting from the eve of the Assumption of the Blessed Mary [14 August] until the morrow of the octave of the same feast [23 August]; and each week a market there on Tuesday, with all liberties and free customs belonging to such fairs and markets. We also desire and direct that all merchants of our lands and of others at peace with us, coming and staying with their merchandise in the same city and then leaving it, should be free of any intervention by our bailiffs or others, whether on land or water, and should have free passage in and out of our lands, provided they render due customs.

All of these things we grant to the bishop and his heirs, the canons and the citizens, saving the liberties of our city of London. Given by the hand of Ralph, bishop of Chichester, our chancellor, at Westminster, 13 January 1228.

14. Royal foundation of a new town

This royal writ probably dates from the mid-1290s. Edward I's known involvement in the planning of towns extended to the Scottish border, into Wales and along the south coast of England.[14] Here, specialists in the art are summoned to attend on the crown for a fresh venture of the kind, in a location which is not specified and which had, perhaps, at the time of the meeting, yet to be identified with the aid of this commission of Londoners. The document gives a glimpse of the practical challenges and procedures surrounding the foundation of a new town, and of the emergence of a body of practical experience in the field.

H. T. Riley (ed.), *Liber Albus, Liber Custumarum, et Liber Horn*, 3 vols, Rolls Series, London: Longman, Brown, Green, Longmans and Roberts, 1859–62, ii (1), pp. 77–8, ii (2), p. 535. Latin, transl. by the editor, revised by GR.

Edward, by the grace of God, etc., to his faithful and loyal John le Bretoun, his warden of the city of London, and to the good people of the said city, greeting. We strictly command that you cause to be chosen four worthy men of the same city, of the most experienced and most sufficient, who may best know how to devise, ordain and array a new town, most to the profit of ourselves and of merchants. Let these persons be with us at Bury Saint Edmunds on the morrow of All Souls [2 November] next to come, ready and prepared to go elsewhere upon this business, where we shall enjoin them. Given under our Privy Seal, at *Tuggehale*, 21 September [apparently in the 24th year of Edward I, 1296].

15. A monastic new town: Eynsham 1215

The small monastic borough of Eynsham was an extension of a pre-existing market development at the abbey gates. The reference in the abbot's charter, printed here, to the liberties of the nearby county town of Oxford (granted by royal charter in 1191)[15] is of interest, as is the use of the word 'commune' to describe the small body of tenants of the

14 M. Beresford, *The New Towns of the Middle Ages*, Leicester, 1967; H. Colvin et al., *The History of the King's Works*, 6 vols, London, 1963–82.

15 See Introduction, p. 24.

new burgages. The rhetoric of such a monastic charter as this presents the abbot in the creative role of urban promoter. But while the monastic licence was necessary, and the rents were set by the lord at a level designed to attract settlers, it is implicit that it was the latter who, having taken up leases on the plots, would undertake to build on them.

H. E. Salter (ed.), *Eynsham Cartulary*, 2 vols, Oxford: Clarendon Press, 1907–8, i, pp. 60–1. Latin, transl. by GR.

To all those children of holy mother Church to whom the present writing shall come, A[dam], by the grace of God Abbot of Eynsham, and the convent of that place send greeting in the Lord. Know that we, for the utility and advancement of our house, have, by the advice of our friends, let all the lands which belonged to our demesne* outside the vill* of Eynsham, that is between that vill and the main street towards the Cassington bridge to the south, and similarly all that land which belonged to our demesne towards the north (extending for twenty perches* in length from the same street towards the north), on this condition: that whoever shall hold one acre of those lands shall pay us 4*s* annually ... and who shall hold three-quarters of an acre, shall pay us 3*s* annually at the same terms; and who shall hold half an acre, shall pay us 2*s* at the same terms. And whoever accepts any portion of these lands shall hold it without contradiction for the service named, by right of their own inheritance and that of their heirs in perpetuity, in ways and paths, entrances and exits within the aforesaid limits of the lands assigned, freely and quit of all [further] service and exaction belonging to ourselves; and they shall remain as free and quit of all service to other lords as our demesne in Eynsham. And if the tenants shall desire to give or to sell their tenement to any secular person, they shall do this freely: in such fashion, however, that the seller shall give us 2*d*, and the buyer 4*d*, in recognition of our lordship. But the tenants shall have free choice as to who should do fealty* [for the land] to both themselves and us. And if anyone shall forfeit that land, or be sued by another [over it], then the suit of that tenement shall be held. And if by judgement he is put in mercy [convicted], he shall make good his transgression, according to the degree of the crime, by the view of his equals, such that the fine shall not exceed 10*s*. And if one of the burgesses (*burgencium*) should die having made division of his goods within this lordship, then that division shall stand. If, however, he should die without making a division, his goods shall be divided into three parts: one for the child, another for the widow, the third to be divided by the nearest relatives for the soul of the deceased. We grant and confirm to [the burgesses] these liberties and all other good customs which we are able to give them in imitation of the liberties of the burgesses of Oxford, and of those other free tenants in the county of Oxfordshire. And in witness of this, we hand over to the commune (*commune*) of those who shall hold the said tenements this charter, furnished with the impression of our seal. Done in the year of the Incarnate Word 1215; witnessed by the chapter.

16. Dispute over a guild merchant at High Wycombe 1223–24

The evidence of legal conflict concerning control over a developing town can be a valuable indicator of its growing importance in the eyes of contemporaries. The record of verbal testimonies in this case draws attention to the increasing significance, at this period, of written titles to authority. It was a conspicuous weakness of the townspeople's position that they were forced to claim to have had a charter which had been lost in a fire. The men of Wycombe were already paying £4 per annum to maintain the liberties of their borough in the 1180s, so a charter of some kind predated that time. Those who, in these records, invoked their right to a guild merchant* were a narrow group of leading traders. The challenge to the townsmen's autonomy recorded in the text below came from a new lord who had received Wycombe by a royal grant – a third son with limited resources and every incentive to exploit the town if he could. The eventual decision of the court in the 1220s was, however, in favour of the townspeople, who retained control of their borough and its market, in return for a substantial annual rent payable to Basset of £30.[16]

A. E. Bland, P. A. Brown and R. H. Tawney (eds), *English Economic History: Select Documents,* London: G. Bell & Sons, 1914, pp. 123–4. Latin, transl. by the editors.

[Records of the Curia Regis before the king's justices, 1224] Buckingham. Alan Basset[17] was summoned to answer the burgesses of

16 L. J. Ashford, *The History of the Borough of High Wycombe from Its Origins to 1880,* London, 1960, pp. 11–13, 15–20.

17 Alan Basset (d. 1232) had been one of the closest counsellors of King John, from whom he had received a grant of part of the manor of Wycombe.

Wycombe as to why he does not permit them to have their guild merchant with its appurtenances, as they used to have it in the time of the lord King John, when he had that manor in his hand; concerning which the burgesses say that in the time when the lord King John had that manor in his hand, and when the lord the king gave it to the same Alan, they had a guild merchant and a liberty which the same Alan has taken away from them, by which they are much injured, for by that guild merchant they had this liberty, that no merchant within their town could sell cloths at retail, neither linens nor woollens, unless he were in the guild merchant or by licence of the bailiffs of the burgesses who were in the guild merchant, and furthermore in the same way could not sell fells* or wood or broom or such merchandise, unless he were in the guild, or by licence. And the same Alan contravened this liberty and granted to all merchants and others that they might sell cloths at retail and fells* and such wares as they please, and takes *3d* toll. And they used to give for the farm of the lord the king[18] *6s 8d* per annum to have that liberty; and because he has taken away that liberty from them, they are injured and suffer damage to the value of £26 *13s 4d*, and they bring a charge on this count, and if this does not suffice, they offer to prove that they had such seisin by the evidence of witnesses (*per vivam vocem*), if that is required, or by the body of a man,[19] or by the country,[20] and they offer £13 *6s 8d* to have an inquisition.

And Alan comes and defends force and tort [claims right of ownership] and says that he has taken no liberties from them, but will speak the truth. The lord king John gave him that manor with all its appurtenances for his homage and service for £20 a year and for the service of one knight, so that never afterwards did they have a guild merchant, although they often sued for it and murmured among themselves, so that he often asked of them their warrant, if they had any, and they show him none. And the town is amended in that merchants and others can sell their merchandise; and so they ought to have no guild.

And the burgesses say that his statement is contrary to right, because after his time, when he had that manor, they had that liberty, both before his time and after, and they offer as before £13 *6s 8d* to have an inquisition. Touching their warrant, they say that they had a charter of King Henry, grandfather of the lord the king, and it was deposited

18 The right to the independent control of their affairs.

19 Trial by battle.

20 Trial by jury.

in the church of Wycombe, and there in the time of war[21] was burned in the church, and of the truth of this they submit themselves to a jury.

And Alan defends that they had no charter of this kind nor any warrant, nor ever had seisin* of that guild in his time, nor can he admit nor will he admit any inquisition without the lord the king; but indeed it may be true that when they had the manor of the king at farm, then they did what they pleased.

A day is given to them on the morrow of Martinmas to hear their judgement.

17. Towns and their associations in the thirteenth century

This source is one of a kind. The text appears to be the idle jotting of a bureaucrat, and does not claim any more serious or definitive status. None the less it captures loose impressions current in the later thirteenth century. Its underlying premise, that towns differed markedly from one another in character, is as worthy of note as are the particular features ascribed to individual places.

H. Rothwell (ed.), *English Historical Documents*, iii, *1189–1327* (copyright © 1975), London: Routledge, 1975, pp. 881–4. French, transl. by the editor. Reproduced by permission of Taylor and Francis Books UK.

The Baronage of London	Regrating[22] of York	Sanctuary of Canterbury
Relics of Westminster	Prostitutes of Charing	The Pardon of St Paul's[23]
Sauce of Fleet[24]	Deer of Bury St Edmunds	School of Oxford
Scarlet of Lincoln	Hauberge[25] of Stamford	Blanket of Blyth
Burnet of Beverley	Russet of Colchester	Thieves of Grantham
Murderers of Royston	Knives of Thaxted	Sleeves[26] of Durham
Shears of Huntingdon	Needles of Wilton	Razors of Leicester

21 Presumably a reference to the civil war in the closing months of the reign of King John, in 1216.

22 Buying up goods before they come to market, in order to raise the price.

23 The Pardon Churchyard at St Paul's church in London, where indulgences were available.

24 Possibly ironic, referring to the pollution of this river in London.

25 A cloth, as others in the following entries.

26 *Maunches*: possibly *manches*, sleeves or alternatively metal points.

Butchers of Winchester	Bachelery[27] of Northampton	Eels of Cambridge
Iron of Gloucester	Plains of Salisbury	Cloister of Lichfield
The bath of Bath	The marvel of Stonehenge	Merchants of Lynn
Herring of Yarmouth	Plaice of Winchelsea	Merling of Rye
Dace of Kingston	Loches of Weybridge[28]	Barbels of St Ives
Salmon of Berwick	Ruffs of Bedford	The crossing of Chelmsford
Simnel[29] of Wycombe	Wastel[30] of Hungerford	Treet[31] of Newbury
Coverchief of Shaftesbury	Wimple of Lewes	Skins of Shrewsbury
The ferry of Tilbury	Archers of Wales	Robbers of Alton
Empyrean of Meldon[32]	Marble of Corfe	Plaster of Nower[33]
Pottery of Henham[34]	Cattle of Nottingham	Linen cloth of Aylesham
Cord of Warwick	Cambrick of Bridport	'Chalons' of Guildford[35]
Rymers[36] of Worcester	Fur of Chester	Shipping of Southampton
The warren of Walton	Quilts of Clare	Town of Bures[37]
Jousters of Yardley	Tourneyers of Blyth	Tilters of Ipswich
Mills of Dunwich	Priory of Waltham	Bread of St Albans
The harbour of Norwich	Mead of Hitchin	Bever[38] of Banbury
Ale of Ely	Cod of Grimsby	Covert of Sherwood
Chase of Englewood	Forest of Windsor	Horn of Carlisle
Saddlery of Ogerston[39]	Palfrey of Ripon	Colt of Rievaulx
Cheese of Jervaulx[40]	Scurvey[41] of Fountains	Soap of Coventry
Lodging of Dunstable	Scoffers of Elstow	[?] of Dunmow
Leather of Bristol	Girls of Hereford	Cord of Bridport

27 Young men.

28 *Loches* may have been a kind of stockfish; and Weybridge could be Weybourn, about five miles from the fish fair of Blakeney in Norfolk.

29 White bread of the finest flour.

30 Inferior bread.

31 Bread of coarse brown flour.

32 Meaning uncertain.

33 Nore Down, Purbeck, a source of gypsum for plaster of Paris.

34 In Essex.

35 See L. F. Salzman, *English Industries of the Middle Ages*, Oxford, 1923, pp. 199–200.

36 Reamers bored holes in metal.

37 Identification uncertain.

38 A drink.

39 Now a mere hamlet, between Huntingdon and Stamford.

40 Now known after Wensley, in the same dale.

41 Reading uncertain.

Pewter[42] of Exeter	Beggars of Chichester	The market of Pontefract
Tin of Cornwall	Hose of Tickhill	Gloves of Haverhill
Villeins of Tamworth[43]	Cingles[44] of Doncaster	Cake of Stamford
The manor of Woodstock	Hardihood of the Cinque Ports	The castle of Dover
The pride of Peterborough	The marsh of Ramsey	Tiles of Reading
Parish of Spalding[45]	Mules [or mullet] of Dengie	The entrance to Thorney[46]

There's plenty of places
But too much to drink
And much more to say
But my wits are away.[47]

42 Reading uncertain.

43 An ironic reference to the burgesses of this small town.

44 Horse-saddlery.

45 An exceptionally large parish.

46 Thorney Abbey.

47 Rothwell's rendition of: 'Asetz iad des viles / Mes trop iad des g'les [*gilles*: measures of wine] / Emoud plus a dire / Mess en ne put suffire.'

III. ECONOMIC LIFE

Medieval sources inform us, first and foremost, about the concerns of those who made them. To discover the things we should most like to know, we must read them across the grain. The ordinances of York from 1301 [**18**] give only a partial and oblique account of the trades and economy of the city, their primary motivation being to serve the interest of the king. The collaboration of royal and civic officers in the compilation of these regulations typifies the political situation of the medieval English towns, which did not enjoy the autonomy of cities in some other parts of contemporary Europe. To the monarch, York was a vital strategic and military base, and the civic issues uppermost in the minds of his officials concerned the provision of hospitality, food supply, the decency of the streets and the limitation of distractions for courtiers and soldiers: hence the curious pairing in the ordinances of pigs and prostitutes. Registers of admissions to the freedom (or citizenship) of a town can also beguile us, if we do not question the motives of their compilers. The York freemen's register [**19**] ostensibly gives, year by year, a statistical account of the presence and relative importance of the diverse listed crafts of the citizens. The realisation that admission required a cash payment, however, alerts us to the likelihood that fluctuations in the total numbers of freemen were influenced by the fiscal policy of the city government. The case of London, where after 1312 new freemen were compelled to find sponsors among existing London merchants or practitioners of the trade they wished to set up, underlines the need to weigh such evidence carefully before drawing clear economic conclusions from simple totals of freemen admissions.[1] This said, the York register does give a valuable impression of the diverse aspects of the urban economy. As we sharpen our focus to examine the organisation of industry at the level of individual trades, it is natural that we should draw upon the regulations compiled for particular crafts [**20**], [**21**]. Yet here again, our first question must concern the function of these documents. Their point of origin, and the reason for their preservation in collections of civic records, was usually the city government, whose

1 C. M. Barron, *London in the Later Middle Ages. Government and People 1200–1500*, Oxford, 2004, p. 205.

interest lay in the maintenance of good order. Having once established that the crafts were responsible for electing their own officers to ensure the quality of their products and the disciplined behaviour of their fellow workers, town councils tended to leave the detail of manufacture to its practitioners. For this reason we should be wary of taking craft ordinances as a full description: the picture they give is both simplified and idealised.[2] Yet these sources contain much of interest, not least in their insistence upon an ordered hierarchy of craft master, journeyman and apprentice: the very repetition of the legislation may suggest to us that reality was not always so tidy. And where we can find them, complementary records can amplify the picture by showing the application of craft regulations in practice [**22**].

A long tradition has seen the medieval urban craft worker as an isolated figure, and as one who was tightly regulated by what has sometimes been called the 'structure' of the crafts. Modern economic thought, influenced in this respect both by Adam Smith and by Karl Marx, has tended to accept that, in order for a breakthrough to entrepreneurial industrial production to take place, it was necessary for the 'craft system' to be dismantled.[3] The flaws in this argument include not only the fact (just noted) that the medieval 'system' was less systematic than it may appear but also that master craftsmen and women, in order to manufacture the many complex products which were sold in the urban marketplace, necessarily collaborated in multifarious ways which are not reflected in the records of any individual craft. Even a relatively simple object such as a painted candlestick was the product of both the wood-turner's and the painter's art. Enterprise on a larger scale – the construction of a cathedral, for example – entailed multiple and carefully negotiated collaboration between the masters of many crafts. Privately contracted arrangements between masters, whether of the same or of different crafts, must have been common, even if on occasion the relationship turned sour [**23**]. The anxiety expressed in many sets of craft ordinances, that individual masters were stealing a march on their peers by extending their workforce, is the clearest evidence that this was in fact the case [**24**].

2 H. Swanson, 'The illusion of economic structure: craft guilds in late medieval English towns', *Past and Present*, CXXI, 1988, pp. 29–48; G. Rosser, 'Crafts, guilds, and the negotiation of work in the medieval town', *Past and Present*, CLIV, 1997, pp. 3–31.

3 A. Smith, *The Theory of Moral Sentiments* [1759], ed. D. D. Raphael and A. L. McFie, New York and Oxford, 1976, pp. 139–44; Robert C. Tucker (ed.), *The Marx–Engels Reader*, 2nd edn, New York, 1978, pp. 182–6, 396–7.

The usual route into a trade throughout the period was by apprenticeship [**25**]. Young women were bound apprentices as well as men, and indeed women are found across the entire spectrum of the medieval urban economy, although it is hard to assess their relative prominence in any particular area.[4] Small numbers of women are found being admitted to the freedom of diverse towns in their own right, while a larger number would gain mediated rights to trade by virtue of marriage to a freeman. Many more, however, were licensed by the year to trade: at Norwich this was so regularised as to appear to have been an official system [**53**]. A woman might well simultaneously assist her husband in his own trade and undertake another, such as weaving or brewing, on her own part, while at the same time taking care of children.[5] Because medieval officialdom preferred to deal with male heads of household, women are severely under-represented in the record, yet their role in the economy was no less significant than that of the men.[6] London custom, which appears to have had an influence on that of other English towns, permitted a single woman or a widow to conduct a business in her own right, as a *femme sole* [**26**]: a marked degree of independence, by contrast, for example, with the townswomen of Italy.[7] Those, both men and women, without the resources to set up a shop of their own necessarily sought other masters for whom to work, whether on long-term or short-term contracts. The many who worked by the day began early, assembling at designated hiring-places in the hope of finding an employer [**27**]. Women were especially visible in the marketplace, where stalls of herbs, flowers and dairy products were their particular domain [**28**].[8] But they were active also in almost

4 P. J. P. Goldberg, *Women, Work, and Life Cycle in a Medieval Economy: Women in York and Yorkshire c.1300–1520*, Oxford, 1992, esp. pp. 27–31; M. Kowaleski and J. M. Bennett, 'Crafts, gilds, and women in the Middle Ages: fifty years after Marion K. Dale', in J. M. Bennett et al. (eds), *Sisters and Workers in the Middle Ages*, Chicago, 1988, pp. 11–38.

5 Swanson, 'The illusion of economic structure'; Rosser, 'Crafts, guilds and the negotiation of work'.

6 K. Reyerson, 'Urban economies', in J. Bennett and R. M. Karras (eds), *The Oxford Handbook of Women and Gender in Medieval Europe*, Oxford, 2013, pp. 295–307.

7 C. M. Barron and A. Sutton (eds), *Medieval London Widows 1300–1500*, London, 1994; M. K. McIntosh, 'The benefits and drawbacks of *femme sole* status in England, 1300–1630', *Journal of British Studies*, XLIV, 2005, pp. 410–38; B. A. Hanawalt, *The Wealth of Wives: Women, Law, and Economy in Late Medieval London*, Oxford, 2007, esp. p. 215.

8 R. H. Hilton, 'Women traders in medieval England', in his *Class Conflict and the Crisis of Feudalism: Essays in Medieval Social History*, London, 1983, pp. 205–15; M. K. McIntosh, *Working Women in English Society, 1300–1620*, Cambridge, 2005, pp. 128–32.

all other sectors, including the luxury trades in which delicate work was called for. When Queen Philippa needed three new counterpanes as part of the ceremonial for the celebration of the birth of the Black Prince in 1330, the commission was handled by the queen's tailor, William de London, who employed – evidently in London – seventy men (earning a high rate of 4½*d* a day) and forty-two women (earning 3¼*d* a day: less, as usual, than the men, yet still more than the pay of an unskilled man) to carry out the embroidery.[9] A conspectus of the stock-in-trade of two high-end London shopkeepers [**29**] gives an impression of the diversity and sophistication of the wares on offer in the greater towns, to those who could afford them. The commercial pre-eminence of the capital, already marked by 1300 and even more evident by 1500, was apparent in the extraordinary concentration of goldsmiths' and other luxury shops along Cheapside [**8**].[10] The craftsmen working in the Nottingham alabaster industry found a profitable outlet through the shops of London [**30(b)**];[11] and here, strategically poised between the mercantile class of the city and the courtiers of Westminster, William Caxton in 1476 set up the first English printing press, and his bookshop 'at the sign of the red pale' [**31**].[12] For the many to whom such goods were beyond purchase, there operated an extensive marginal economy of hawkers, who carried their miscellaneous wares on their backs from house to house [**32**], and 'evening markets' of dubious reputation [**33**].

The infrastructure of external and internal trade which supported these old and new industries and this endlessly beguiling urban market is illuminated by accounts of tolls on goods in transit. The records of Southampton offer a unique perspective on internal traffic, and give an impression of the scale of transportation inland of imported wine, dyes and other goods [**34**]. Loaded on to carts, these rumbled their way to the cloth-making centres of Salisbury and Winchester, and occasionally continued as far as Coventry. Tax on international trade, meanwhile, gives us records of goods coming into the major ports. The range of merchandise entering Hull in the cargo of a single ship from the Baltic in 1483 gives a small insight into the material culture of a world in which purchasers were anticipated not only for quan-

9 K. Staniland, *Medieval Craftsmen: Embroiderers*, London, 1991, pp. 23, 28.

10 D. Keene, *Cheapside before the Great Fire*, London, 1985.

11 N. Ramsay, 'Alabaster', in J. Blair and N. Ramsay (eds), *English Medieval Industries*, London, 1991, pp. 29–40.

12 L. Hellinga, *William Caxton and Early Printing in England*, London, 2010.

tities of wood, iron and steel, but also for gaming tables, lutes and a spinet [**35**]. The network of correspondence and constantly updated information which underpinned the international trade of a mercantile enterprise such as that of the Cely family is illustrated by the final document in this section, which shows how merchants adapted their strategies of markets and investments to the shifting alliances and outright warfare of late medieval northern Europe [**36**]. They took risks, and (contrary to what is sometimes thought to be the business mentality) could not be said to be consistently rational in their commercial decisions. But the Celys grew rich on the urban markets they supplied.[13]

18. York civic ordinances 1301

Ordinances or by-laws are statements of ideals: we should not assume that they were easy to implement in practice. Yet their specific concerns and timing can be revealing to the historian. These particular ordinances were agreed jointly by the city authorities of York and the king's council. The crown took a particular interest in York at this period, both as a military base and as an administrative headquarters and occasional capital city. Hence the focus of these regulations on hospitality and the provision of food and drink. The ordinances agreed in 1301 were to a degree idealistic, and some difficulty was encountered in their imposition. However, the text is a valuable testimony to some of the pressing concerns of civic rulers around 1300.

M. Prestwich (ed.), *York Civic Ordinances 1301*, York: Borthwick Institute, 1976. Latin, transl. by the editor.

For the remedy and relief of those coming to York, and staying in the city, both on the king's business and on that of others, who complain of the extortions and oppressions imposed by the citizens, both by failing to observe the assize* of bread and ale, and by the intolerable cost of other victuals and necessities agreed between the citizens. The people have been compelled to leave the city, leaving their affairs unfinished. On the feast of [the Decollation of] St John the Baptist [29 August] 1301, the mayor, bailiffs and citizens were called before the king's

13 A. Hanham, *The Celys and Their World: An English Merchant Family of the Fifteenth Century*, Cambridge, 1985.

council, then at York, and by ordinance of the council, with the assent of the citizens, the following was decreed and ordained.

Firstly, that to assist the mayor and bailiffs ten law-worthy and discreet citizens should be elected, together with four men from each of the liberties in the city with their bailiffs, who should be sworn in the presence of justices appointed for this purpose, and assigned to keep and maintain the king's assize* in all particulars, so that the assize which is kept elsewhere shall be maintained in the city, both within and without the liberties, with only one ell, one measure of weight, one of grain, and one of wine and ale, as elsewhere in the kingdom. They shall prosecute and punish well and faithfully those who go against the assize.

[There follow regulations for the making of bread and ale, according to the royal assize for these products.]

Taverners, wine sellers and sauce makers shall not keep bad or putrid wine or vinegar in their houses.

Anyone buying an ox, a cow, a pig, a sheep, a calf or a goat, shall have two of those sworn to keep these ordinances come to his house before he kills it, and he shall swear as to the price for which he bought it, and they with two neighbouring butchers shall set a price for the labour involved, which shall be enrolled, so that he shall not sell the animal for a higher price than they assign. Any butcher convicted of doing otherwise shall be fined *6s 8d* for the first offence, for the second *13s 4d*, and for the third *20s*. He shall then abjure his calling for ever. Butchers shall not sell measly meat, or fresh meat which has lain, either whole or in pieces, in the sun on their stall for more than one day, unless it has been well cleaned and salted. No butcher shall buy meat from others who have brought it for sale to the city, nor shall they sell meat that they have not slaughtered themselves. If convicted, any measly meat shall go to the lepers, and fresh meat kept for sale for more than a day, and meat bought from others for resale shall be sold, the money going to the common profit of the city. Notwithstanding, the butcher shall be imprisoned for forty days.

No cook shall buy fresh meat which has been on sale for more than a day in summer, nor shall he use meat or fish that is not good, sound and healthy. Roast chicken or chicken in bread is not to be sold for more than *2d*, roast goose for more than *4d*, other food is to be sold at reasonable prices.

It is agreed that hostellers who take in strangers, and those who rent out houses, rooms, stalls or other accommodation, shall not take more than ½*d* for stabling a horse for a night. If the guest has no horse, the hosteller shall be content with 1*d* a night for his bed and a room, but this is not to apply to boys and other poor people who cannot pay.

No one shall keep pigs which go in the streets by day or night, nor shall any prostitutes stay in the city. If anyone finds a pig in the streets he may kill it, and may at his choice cut off its trotters, or the bailiff of York may let him have 4*d* for them, if it happens that a pig escapes from someone's custody. If any prostitute keeps a brothel and resides in the city, she is to be taken and imprisoned for a day and a night. The bailiff who takes her shall have the roof timbers and the door of the building in which she lodged [shall make the building uninhabitable and sell the materials]. Nonetheless he who rents out houses to prostitutes shall lose the rent of such a house for one term.

19. Admissions to the freedom of York in the fourteenth century

By a process which still remains obscure, the early method of admitting a burgess to the community of traders in a town, on the basis of his ownership of a burgage property, was succeeded in the course of the thirteenth century by enrolment following an application and, unless the applicant was the son of a freeman, payment of a fee. The fiscal aspect of this process makes the records of admissions to the freedom unreliable guides to the quantities of those actually eligible for the privilege.[14] Freedom brought the right to trade in the market; but it also carried the responsibility to hold civic office, which some preferred to eschew. The option of living in one of the city's religious franchises* and so evading civic regulation was attractive to many. A list of freemen is therefore not equivalent to a register of householders or traders in a town. With this caveat, however, the York freemen's register may be considered as a uniquely extensive list of this kind, extending from the late thirteenth century to the end of the Middle Ages and beyond. Although the fourteenth-century entries appear not to include admissions by patrimony (granted to sons of freemen), they give a valuable impression of the range and importance of trades practised in the city.

14 R. B. Dobson, 'Admissions to the freedom of the city of York in the later Middle Ages', *Economic History Review*, 2nd series, XXVI, 1973, pp. 1–22.

Sample years have been taken from the early fourteenth century and from fifty years later (at which latter period the city council appears to have been increasing the numbers of admissions, at least in part for financial reasons). Placenames, which here have been given modern spellings, indicate the geographical origins of the individuals named: prior to the late fourteenth century, from which period the tendency was towards fixed surnames, a locative byname is a fairly reliable indicator of an individual's previous place of residence (or that of their parents).[15] In this case those places were most commonly outside York yet within the county of Yorkshire, but in some cases well beyond.

F. Collins (ed.), *Register of the Freemen of the City of York*, 2 vols, Selden Society, XCVI, CII, Durham: Andrews & Company, 1897–99, i, pp. 13–14, 54–5. Latin, transl. by GR.

Admissions to the freedom in 1310–11

Robert de *Sunderlawyk*, tanner
Adam de Kingston, cutler
Robert de Walmgate, tailor
Walter de Sutton, leather-worker
William de Rigton, lorimer*
Thomas de Sutton, belt-maker
Richard Kokerell, barber
Thomas de Strensall, mason
John le Long de Doncaster, mercer*
William Brown de Rudston, cook
Richard le Horner, baker
William de Skelton, fisherman
William de Settrington, 'wayder'[16]
Robert de Duffield, butcher
Alan de Grafton, salter
Thomas de *Pontebelli*
Peter de Wadworth, saddler
Henry de Steresby, cook
William de Hereford, goldsmith
Geoffrey de Ampleforth, ironmonger
Nicholas de Carlisle, goldsmith
Eleanor de *Angrom*
William Arkill, tawyer*
Andrew de Doncaster, tawyer
John de Appleton, smith
Nicholas de Steresby, mason
Alan de *Haunsard*, taverner
Henry de Burton, tailor
Nicholas Foukes, fisherman
Peter de Wilberfoss, potter*
Jordan de Harlethorpe
William de Tadcaster, sailor
Adam de Ilkley, merchant
Thomas de Hoton, tanner
Adam de Newton, cooper
Richard de Rickle, tanner
Roger de Stitenham, tailor
Adam de Fimber, potter
Richard de Warthill, girdler*
Robert de Bridlington, mason
Thomas Bele de Stillington, saddler
Adam de Beverley, bowyer

15 P. McClure, 'Patterns of migration in the late Middle Ages', *Economic History Review*, 2nd series, XXXII, 1979, pp. 167–82.

16 Possibly 'woader', a dyer with woad.

Geoffrey, forester of Torksey
William de Wistow, fishmonger
Alan de Pickering at the bridge, mercer
Thomas de Newcastle, furbisher*
Robert de Askham, fishmonger
John de Malton, mason
John de Barnby, mercer
Henry de Corbridge, merchant

Admissions to the freedom in 1311–12

Nicholas de Cologne (*Coln'*), merchant
Richard de Huntingdon, merchant
Henry the lacer
Roger the marshal*
John de Pontefract, skinner
Roger de *Ile*, tanner
Thomas de Bilham, sailor
John Page de Haxby, leather-worker
William de Monkton, tailor
William Skot, cook
Andrew de Stoke, cook
John de Catton, brother of Ralph de Catton
William de Duffield, mercer
William de Taunton, merchant
Richard de Burton, merchant
William de Foston, cook
William de Newton, cook
John de Cologne, merchant
Peter the young of Brandsby
Gilbert Kokerell, tailor
Walter de Harlington, mercer
William le Walche, girdler
Simon de Chilton, fisherman
Robert de Dunstable, skinner
Adam, servant of Ralph Wiles
Walter of St Nicholas (York), leather-worker

Henry de Brampton, hatter
Michael de Lincoln, cutler
William de Lincoln, cutler
Alan Segode, tailor
Thomas de Hornby, leather-worker
William de *Ile*, tailor
Henry, son of Alan de Copmanthorpe
Robert de Stainton, skinner
William de Thaxted, cutler
William de Malton, cutler
John, son of Doraunt de Moreby
Robert de Catton
Thomas de Copmanthorpe, hosier
Robert Palmer, butcher
Robert le Batour, butcher
Richard de Raskelf

Admissions in 1361–62

Adam de Cawood, currier*
Nicholas de Strensall, cutler
Laurence Sampson, glover
William Deyntez, glover
William Lax, mercer
Thomas de Driffield, mercer
John de Batley, arrowsmith
Adam Fetheler, mercer
Robert de Burton, bowyer
Thomas de Scrayingham, glover
Thomas le stringer
Adam de Tunstall
Thomas de Brampton, founder[17]
William Rayner, mercer
Robert de Killingwick, de *Huoum*, mercer
John Hemynge, baker
Richard de Thornton, bowyer
Thomas de Brigg carpenter

17 This seems the likely reading of the word transcribed by the editor as 'tounder'.

John Duke, de Beeston, chapman*
John Taite, tailor
William de Paris, mariner
William de Hessle, tailor
William de Hillum, bowyer
Robert de Middleton, spicer
William de Thornton, weaver
Adam Tredemond de Burton Agnes
William del Castell, mercer
Walter de Thirsk, tanner
William de Grimston, saucer
John de Killingwick, tanner
William de Brune, tanner
Robert Paw, riveter
John de Hornby, saddler
Richard Watermon, butcher
William de Newton, baker
Adam de Helperby, weaver
William de Harewood, weaver
Robert de Heminbrough, walker*
John de Stillington, chapman
Thomas Jordan, painter
John le clerk, nailer
Thomas son of John the smith, de Bulmer
Richard Tredemond de Burton Agnes
Richard de Bengley, leather-worker
Matthew de Thornton, leather-worker
Thomas de Burton, tanner
William de Hollym, mercer
William de Garsdale, draper
Adam Scraggy, pinner
Nicholas de Croxby, barber
John de Scarborough, painter
Robert de *Anelagy* (?Anlaby), dyer
John de *Ereghthorn*, tailor
Robert de Whitwell, tailor
John de Braithwaite, draper
Thomas Legheles, de *Dyvelyn*, mercer
Thomas del More, bowl-maker
Henry de Plena, goldsmith
John de Newton, baker
William Parcour de Helmsley, merchant
Edward de Brackenholme, painter
Thomas de Killingwick, tanner
Robert de Chester, tanner
Thomas de Whorlton, tanner
Adam del Hall weaver
John Gerveux, riveter
Henry de *Dyvelyn*, mercer
Walter de Linton, tanner
William de Catton, weaver
William de Arkendale, weaver
John de Newham, leather-worker
William de Wistow, potter
Adam de *Proshow*, tailor
Michael de Weatherall, butcher
William Paynott or Donington, butcher
John Archer, glazier
Alan de Askham, carpenter
Gilbert de Bamborough, skinner
John de Skipton, leather-worker
Robert de Linton, de Wetherby
Robert de Seacroft, lorimer
Adam de Beswick, cardmaker*
Thomas de *Touthorop*, pinner
John de Clifton, joiner
William de Brompton, dyer
Peter le gray, water-leader*

20. Craft ordinances of the tailors of York 1386–87

These ordinances of the York tailors can be paralleled in many other urban crafts of the period. They describe the period and process of apprenticeship, the requirements for setting up shop as an independent master, and the employment of contracted assistants. Like all rules, these draw attention to the reality of their infringement. It is notable, in these as in all such ordinances, that most of the technical details of the craft were omitted from the legislation. How to cut and sew material were skills understood within the tailoring community, and passed down within the workshop without being committed to writing. The reference to a pageant at Corpus Christi is an allusion to the series of religious plays presented at certain festivals by the various crafts of York (see further [**114**], [**115**], [**116**]). The function of a craft organisation such as this one was to regulate the professional practices of its respective trade. Members might also combine to form a related fraternity or guild, with a religious dedication and a range of social, devotional and charitable purposes. Some such guilds were dominated by the practitioners of a particular craft, but the majority were diverse in their membership (see further [**93**], [**94**], [**95**], [**96**], [**97**]).

M. Sellers (ed.), *York Memorandum Book*, Surtees Society, CXX, CXXV, Durham: Andrews & Company, 1912–15, i, pp. 94–100. French, transl. by the editor.

These are the ordinances made by the assent and advice of the master tailors listed below and of all the craft, in the time of William de Selby, mayor, 1386–7 [128 names of masters listed].

First it is ordained and established amongst the master tailors of the said city, that each year on the day of St James the Apostle [25 July] four good and loyal men of the same art should be elected to search, oversee and examine the craft, and to present any faults of its practitioners to the mayor of the said city, and upon his advice and theirs duly to punish such faults according to their severity. And any master failing to come to the election of these officers or to any other assembly touching the governance of the craft (without reasonable excuse allowed by the searchers) shall pay 6*d* or 1 lb of wax to the four searchers.

The four searchers shall gather annually the contribution from each master towards the craft's pageant at Corpus Christi, and shall bear all the costs and expenses to sustain and maintain the said pageant, rendering account for the same on the third Sunday after Corpus Christi, on pain of 10*s*, half to [the craft] and half to the council chamber on Ouse bridge.

It is ordered that no master tailor should hire the servant of another master until he has left on the full completion of his covenanted term with the same master. Nor should any master set up his stall to practise the craft before he has paid *6s 8d* as is customary. Any breach of this rule by a master of the craft shall be punished with a 40*d* fine on the first occasion, *6s 8d* on the second, and on the third the stall is to be taken down.

Those apprentices who have loyally served their masters to the end of their agreed terms shall pay no more than 40*d* when they first set up their stalls, notwithstanding any other ordinance.

That no master tailor shall deliver any garment or cloth to be worked or sewn by the servant of another master. And that no master tailor shall keep any cutters or servants in chambers, privily or openly, without informing the four searchers, on pain of 40*d*. And that no master tailor should hire any servant, on his first coming to the city, to cut or sew, for less than a full year, on pain of the same fine, unless by grant and licence of the same searchers.

That no master tailor shall take an apprentice as his servant for less than seven years, on pain of *6s* 8d payable to the searchers and 2 lbs of wax to the mystery* of tailors; and that no master shall do any cutting (*face nul coturer*) in the same mystery before his inspection and just examination by the said four searchers, on pain of 40*d*.

If any complaint be made concerning any garment, and brought before the searchers together with the maker, and it can be amended with the same material, he shall take it back to mend it, provided he can give the searchers surety for it.

If any master tailor detains the salary of his servant beyond the day accorded between them for payment, and will not agree to pay, if the servant advise the four searchers, they will have the servant paid on pain of a fine of 2*s* payable by the said master.

Anyone interfering with the searchers in the performance of their duty shall pay a fine of 40*d*.

That no servant [journeyman]* of the said craft shall hire another servant to work for him in the same craft, so long as he is a servant or of the degree of a servant, on pain of 40*d*.

That no stranger or servant of the said craft shall be in any place except only in the shop of a master tailor in the city, on pain of 40*d*.

21. Ordinances for crafts at Bristol

Ordinances of urban crafts were made not with a view to describing the trades in full but in order to address particular problems. The historian who makes use of these texts needs to bear such motivation in mind. By (a) the Bristol fullers, whose job was to clean woven cloth in troughs with soap and water, attempted to regulate the supply, often by women, of raw wool and spun thread prior to the weaving process. The civic measures for ale-sellers in (b) and for metal-workers in (f) underline the importance, in the civic sphere, of ensuring that trade was practised in public ('commune') places, where it could be regulated. That for the bakers (c) points to the role of ambulant salesmen and saleswomen in distribution for the victualling trades. The limits imposed in (d) were probably motivated both by a concern to maintain quality and by a desire to restrain individuals who sought, by enlarging the scale of their operations, to gain business at the expense of other masters. A limit on the size of a master's workforce appears again in (e). Here the altered circumstances of the post-Black Death period are evidenced in the effort to prevent masters from offering increased financial incentives to secure workers.

F. B. Bickley (ed.), *The Little Red Book of Bristol*, 2 vols, Bristol: W. Crofton Hemmons, 1900, ii, pp. 9 (a), 30 (b), 32–3 (c), 38–40 (d), 41–4 (e), 182–4 (f). Latin and French, transl. by the editor, revised by GR.

(a) Ordinance for the fullers* (mid-fourteenth-century)
That no tranter* or huckster* or any other person of the town receive oiled wool or woollen thread for sale, purchase or pledge, on pain of forfeiting what is found in their possession. And if any such thread be borne by the owner or by a porteress (*porteresse*), that it be borne on Friday and on no other day.

If any porteress be found bearing oiled wool or woollen thread for sale on other days than Friday, or putting it in windows for sale, that the goods be forfeited. On the third offence, the said porteress shall forswear her office for ever.

(b) Note concerning tapsters (mid-fourteenth-century)
It is ordained that every brewer and brewster who has ale to sell shall have their ale on sale in a public (*commune*) place, and not in solars, chambers, or other secret places, and that the sign of that

ale be at the door of the house where that ale will be sold all the time that the said ale is on sale.

(c) Ordinance for the bakers (*c.*1340s)

It is ordained by the bakers that no baker henceforth give to any huckster* selling his bread but 1*d* over and above 12*d*[18] and no more; and if any one shall give more under any pretence, either in the price of any goods or in repayment of any money on the receipt of the money for the aforesaid bread sold, and is convicted, he shall give to the commonalty 40*d.* Also it is ordained that no baker shall deliver to any huckster more bread than can be sold for the day's consumption (*pro dieta*), and if any one shall have taken more it shall be at the peril of the buyer. And if any baker adulterate any bread after it has been standing in his window for sale and is convicted, he shall likewise give to the commonalty 40*d.*

(d) Note for the dyers (*c.*1350s)

Recently grievous losses and damages have happened to a number of people of the town of Bristol for their woad* which has been put in working by certain dyers roving through the town, who have used this woad in various vats in several places at once, with the result that the dyer cannot give his attention to all at the same time, and so through want of care the woad has been lost. It is therefore ordained by Richard Lespicer then mayor, with the assent of all the good people of the same, that no dyer who has put one vat of woad in working should undertake to put any other in working within the franchise* of the town so long as the vat which he has put in working is open or full. And if anyone do so and is convicted, let him pay to the commonalty 6*s* 8*d* for each conviction. Also it is ordained that if a dyer of the town undertake to work in his own house the woad of another [dyer] after it has been assayed, the woad must be forfeited, the dyer bound to restore to the owner as much as the woad cost, and the money be levied from the goods and chattels of the dyer by coercion and distress of the mayor and his officers. Also that no dyer undertake to put [in working] any woad within the franchise of the town until it has been assayed by the assayers.

18 One penny loaf for every dozen taken for resale by the huckster.

(e) Ordinance of the cobblers (1364)

These are the ordinances made before Robert Cheddre, mayor of Bristol, Monday next after the Epiphany [6 January], 1364, for the relief of the estates of the masters of the craft of cobblers of the town of Bristol, who are now virtually impoverished by the excessive price of their servants of the aforesaid craft who are loath to apply themselves to the craft unless they have too outrageous and excessive salary, contrary to the statutes of our lord the king[19] and the usages of the said town.

First, that no master of the said craft pay any servant for sewing and yarking [preparing, working the leather] shoes, well and fitly, any more than 6*d* per dozen: that is to say for sewing 3*d* and for yarking 3*d*. And if anyone do so and is convicted he shall pay for each occasion, to the use of the commonalty of Bristol, 6*s* 8*d*, and to the contribution of the said craft 40*d*, without any pardon. Also for making a pair of boots entirely 3*d*, that is to say for cutting 1*d* and for sewing and yarking 2*d* and no more on pain of the same penalty. Also for cutting a dozen pairs of shoes 2*d*: that is to say for the overleathers 1*d* and for the soles 1*d* and no more on the same penalty. Also for lasting [shaping] the dozen shoes 1*d* and no more on the same penalty.

Also that every master shall keep one servant called a 'covenant-hire' and no more, on pain of the same penalty, and he must be one who knows well how to cut and sew and to serve people of this craft. His pay will be 18*d* a week, and each year 8 pairs of shoes. No one is to pay more, on the said penalty. Every other servant, that is to say those who serve at piece work (*ceux qe servent a taxe*), shall take as stated above, and according to their status in the craft.

Also that no master may employ any other servant within the term agreed upon between them, nor another servant taken away or procured from another's service, and if he does so and is convicted, let him incur the same penalty above and he shall make satisfaction to the injured party.

And the men of the craft pray that two good men may be elected every year to survey the defaults of the craft, and be sworn to present loyally the defaults which they find. On which the mayor and good men, having regard to the evils which may

19 The statute of wages of 1350, 23 Edward III c.5.

arise to the said town if suitable remedy be not ordained for them, have ratified and confirmed all these ordinances.[20]

(f) Ordinances for the farriers, smiths, cutlers and lockyers (1403–4)

These be the ordinances made and enrolled in the guildhall of Bristow by the wise men of the crafts of farriers, smiths, cutlers and lockyers in the time of John Barstaple, mayor of the said town, in 1403–4.

In the first they be assented and accorded that no person of the four crafts aforesaid should practise or in any manner work in their halls or in their shops or in any other place within the franchises of Bristow until they be burgesses and sworn to the franchise of the same town.

Also that no smith called [an] arrowsmith of the town of Bristow nor any of their servants [bear] not through the town any manner of ironwork to sell in their arms nor upon their heads in any sacks, privy or open, but that [unless] they have an open place beside the high cross of Bristow or in their house openly, and nowhere else, upon pain to pay to the use of the community of Bristow 20*d* sterling, and the same to the masters of the aforesaid 4 crafts in their common box in sustenance of their alms and other expenses.

And that all strangers that come to the same town with any pennyworths called 'smithware' to sell, that they shall stand in a place beside the high cross of Bristow openly so that the defaults, if any be, of the said 'smithware' may be overseen by the masters of the said crafts and in no other place nor nowhere else upon certain pains by the discretion of the mayor of Bristow and of his ministers.

And also they be assented and accorded that no man of the aforesaid four crafts [should] occupy [employ] any servant in the said crafts but he be not [unless] by covenant of a whole year or half a year at the least without reasonable cause, and that upon pains aforesaid.

And that no other master of the said crafts [should] occupy the servant of another within the term betwixt them accorded, nor [the work] of another servant slokke [entice] or procure,

20 At an uncertain later date, these ordinances for the cobblers were crossed out in the register.

and if he do and thereof be attainted [then he should incur] the pains aforesaid and over that make gree [amends] to him that be so aggrieved.

And upon these ordinances and articles the good folk of the said four crafts pray that four masters now be chosen by the said crafts every year for to survey the defaults of the said crafts, and sworn before the mayor truly to present to the mayor and to his ministers of the said town all the defaults that they may find.

22. Application of the regulations of a merchant guild

The practical implementation of craft rules is not often recorded in surviving documents. However, the rolls of the merchant guild* of Leicester record the application of regulations instituted for the cloth trade.

M. Bateson (ed.), *Records of the Borough of Leicester*, i, London: C. J. Clay, 1899, pp. 68–9. Latin, transl. by the editor.

[Merchant guild roll] On Wednesday before the Conversion of St Paul [25 January], 1254, Roger Aldith, John's son, was charged because he twice offended against the commune of the guild: that is, in that he made a blanket and it was in the first part of good woof and elsewhere in many places of bad woof, and again because he caused a poor and bad vermilion cloth to be sewed to another good vermilion cloth, at Lynn. He swore that in future he will not offend against the guild and that if he should be convicted again for any infidelity or for any trespass against the commune of the guild, he will lose the guild; and he pledged a cask of ale and before that another because of the first offence. Roger Aldith was convicted a third time concerning a certain vermilion cloth made against guild rules, that is with the woof in the middle poorer and worse than at the ends, together with another vermilion cloth on which he had sewed a border contrary to guild rules. He was cut off from the guild and separated from the community of the guild in 1258–9.

23. Partnership between two metalworkers 1380s

The rules drawn up for particular crafts give a false impression of their separation from one another. To a greater degree than is made clear by sets of craft ordinances, opportunities were open to craftsmen and women to join forces, either in order to create complex products requiring diverse techniques or in order to increase their turnover and profits.

W. H. Stevenson (ed.), *Records of the Borough of Nottingham*, 3 vols, London: Quaritch, 1882–85, i, pp. 235–7. Latin, transl. by the editor.

Geoffrey the lorimer* of Lenton brings a case against John the lorimer of Nottingham, on a plea of debt, alleging that he owes him 10*d* for a hammer sold to him in 1380–1; also for a bridle, a pair of stirrups, and a hammer, 6*d*; and for a bridle and stirrups, 4*d*, after they had agreed with each other to work for their profit (*sibi convenerunt invicem ad operandum pro eorum profiguo*), whereby Geoffrey should always receive half of the gain and John the other half. Despite this, Geoffrey has received nothing of his share. John received 4*d* from John of London for a pair of stirrups, of which Geoffrey should have had 2*d* for his share. And John received 10*d* from the wife of Thomas Breton of Annesley, for the binding of a chest, and for the key to the chest; from Matilda Fishlake of Lenton, for binding a chest and its key, four flagons of ale to the value of 4*d*; from William de Halam, 4*d* or a hammer for making a bridle; from Friar John de Coventry, 4*d* for making a 'clicket-key' (*klyketkey*); from the wife of Robert Saddler of Nottingham, 5*d* for a lock and key … from Thomas Passenham, 12*d* for a pair of spurs. But Geoffrey says he has received nothing.

24. Relations between masters and servants in the cloth trade at Worcester

Civic legislation often strengthened the hand of employers. On occasion, however, either a rift amongst employers themselves or the petition of an organised body of workers could precipitate regulation of shop-owners and at least partial protection of wage-labourers. At the end of the fifteenth century the civil government of Worcester retained the old name and form of a guild merchant. This extract is taken from a lengthy compilation of city customs drawn up by the guild in 1467. Two concerns are at issue. One is the payment of workers in kind, rather than in cash. The other is the masters' employment (by the 'putting out' of raw materials to be worked locally) of unregistered, cheap labour found on or beyond the margins of the city. The text illustrates the difficulty of enforcing regulations on master craftsmen. At the same time, the ordinance implies that lesser workers in the cloth trade also had a political voice.

J. Toulmin Smith and L. Toulmin Smith (eds), *English Gilds*, Early English Text Society, original series, XL, London: N. Trübner, 1870, p. 383. English, revised by GR.

Where it is used and accustomed great cloth-making to be had within the said city and suburbs of the same, and so occupied by a great part of the people there dwelling, that is to say spinners, weavers, dyers, shearmen and other labourers or artificers appertaining to the same, as now of late right and practice has been used, i.e. that to these artificers, by masters and makers of cloth, they should in no other way be contented or paid but in mercery, victuals or by other means, and not in silver, that has grown to a great hurt on the part of the all the artificers, labourers and all the poor commonalty.

It is ordained from henceforth, by this present guild, that no artificers, labourer, or any other person of the said city, against his assent, will or agreement, be compelled or charged to receive anything in chaffer [in kind], but in gold and silver, of any makers, chapmen, or sellers of cloth. And he or they that presume to do the contrary, as often as they be found in default, to pay 20*s*, the one half to the bailiff of the city and the other half to the commons of the city.

And that no manner of citizen, tenant or inhabitant within the said city, because of this act of common custom, put out any wool in hurting of the said city, or in hindering of the poor commonalty of the same, where [when] there be persons enough and people to do the same, to dye, card,* or spin, weave or cloth-walk [do the work of a walker*], within the said city, to every manner [of] person or persons foreign, unless it be to men or women dwelling within the said city or suburbs of the same.

25. Apprenticeship

Given that young people were commonly apprenticed to a trade in their early teens, the related agreements with masters are naturally concerned with the moral behaviour of the former and the pastoral responsibility of the latter. Like craft regulations [**20**], [**21**], bonds of apprenticeship tend not to enter into the technical details of the craft in question, which it was assumed would be learned through practice in the workshop. Apprenticeship records are of value to the historian, however, for what they can reveal about recruitment to the labour force and the social organisation of the crafts. The four indentures reproduced here record apprentices enrolled with the same master and mistress, to learn and practise the craft of tanning leather, in the Somerset town of Bridgwater between 1424 and 1437. The diverse lengths of the terms of these particular apprenticeships, and the overlap in time between them, reflect the facts that more than one apprentice could be retained at once (although craft regulations often imposed a limit on the number as a check on competition) and that apprentices occasionally changed master in the course of their training (the contract sometimes being sold on to the new master).

T. B. Dilks (ed.), *Bridgwater Borough Archives 1400–1445*, Somerset: Somerset Record Society, LVIII, 1945, nos. 616 (a), 628 (b), 655 (c), 673 (d). Latin, transl. by the editor, checked against the originals and corrected by Andrew Butcher.

(a) This indenture made at Bridgwater on Saturday the feast of St Martin the bishop [11 November] 1424 between John Davy of Bridgwater, tanner, and his wife Joan on the one part, and Michael Laleye, son of John Laleye, of Ireland, on the other part, witnesses that the said Michael has placed himself as servant and apprentice to the said John and Joan according to the use and custom of the city of London from the day written above to the end of ten years to be fully completed. During which term the said apprentice shall serve his master and mistress in all things well and faithfully, shall keep their secrets and counsel, and shall gladly do all their honest commands. He shall not absent himself from his service by day or night. He shall do them no damage or dishonour, nor allow others to do so in so far as he can prevent it or forewarn his master and mistress. He shall not waste their goods, nor lend them to anyone without their leave or special mandate. And he shall give a good and faithful account of all goods and chattels of his master and mistress which are in his care to guard, whenever required to do so. He shall not contract matrimony with any woman within the said term without licence of his master and mistress. He shall not commit fornication or adultery on or off their premises with any domestic of theirs; but if he do so and is convicted of it, he shall double his service, or shall make reasonable amends to his master and mistress according to the decision of trustworthy men chosen by the parties. And if it should happen that the apprentice should quit his service within the said term, then he wills that his master and mistress or their agent may seek him in whosesoever service he may be found and bring him back again to his former service without contradiction. And the said master and mistress, John Davy and Joan, will practise, teach and instruct the said apprentice Michael as best they can in the arts and goods they use, finding him meat and drink, clothing linen and woollen and all other things necessary for him as is suitable to be found for such an apprentice during the said term, paying the said apprentice moreover at the end of the said term 6*s* 8*d*. In witness of which indenture the seals of both parties are appended.

(b) This indenture made at Bridgwater on Tuesday after the feast of St Matthew [24 September] 1426 between John Davy of Bridgwater, tanner, and his wife Joan, on one part, and John Taylour son of Thomas Taylour of Swansea in Wales, on the other, witnesses that the said John Taylour places himself as a servant and apprentice to the said John Davy and Joan from Michaelmas next until the completion of three years. [The rest more or less as in the indenture above.]

(c) This indenture made at Bridgwater on the feast of All Saints [1 November] 1432 between John Davy, tanner, and Joan his wife on the one part, and John Benet the younger, son of John Benet, on the other, witnesses that the said John Benet has placed himself as a servant and apprentice to the said John Davy and Joan from this day until the completion of seven years. At the end of the term he is to receive 13*s* 4*d*, a coverlet, two blankets and a pair of sheets for his stipend. [The rest as above.]

(d) This indenture made at Bridgwater on 29 June 1437 between John Davy, tanner, and Joan his wife, on the one part, and William Baker son of John Baker of Taunton, on the other, witnesses that the said William Baker has placed himself as a servant and apprentice to the said John Davy and Joan from this day until the completion of seven years. At the end of the term he is to receive a bed coverlet, a pair of sheets and a pair of blankets for his stipend. [The rest as above.]

26. Women's rights to conduct a business

Recorded in the early fifteenth century, this statement of London custom originates in the fourteenth century. A married woman could practise a craft independently of her husband, trading as what was called a *femme sole.* A widow who did not remarry could enjoy still greater economic opportunity, since she could be a freewoman of the city.[21] These privileges differentiated London women from those of southern European cities, who enjoyed no such rights.

H. T. Riley (ed.), *Liber Albus,* Rolls Series, 3 vols, London: Longman, Brown, Green, Longmans and Roberts, 1859–62, i, pp. 204–5; iii, p. 38. French, transl. by the editor, revised by GR.

And when a woman who has a husband follows any craft within the said city by herself apart, with which the husband in no way interferes, such a woman shall be bound as a single woman as to all that concerns her said craft. And if the husband and wife are impleaded,* in such case, the wife shall plead* as a single woman in a court of record, and shall have her law and other advantages by way of plea just as a single woman. And if she is condemned, she shall be committed to prison until she have made satisfaction; and neither the husband nor his goods shall in such case be charged or impeached.

27. Women as dealers in the marketplace

Urban court-rolls are dense with the records of petty offences against market laws. These can shed light not only on the trade in question but on the gendered nature of the economy, and on modes of co-ordination between practitioners. Women were prominent in the sale of cheese, herbs, fish and petty goods from urban market-stalls. As these records show, their stock-in-trade could be quite diverse. The documents also hint at a significant degree of collaboration and organisation amongst the women traders.

I. H. Jeayes (ed.), *Court Rolls of the Borough of Colchester 1310–1379,* 3 vols, Colchester, 1921–41, i, p. 29 (a); H. T. Riley (ed.), *Memorials*

21 C. Barron, 'Introduction: the widow's world in late medieval London', in C. M. Barron and A. F. Sutton (eds), *Medieval London Widows, 1300–1500,* London, 1994, pp. xiii–xxxiv, at pp. xxvii–xxviii.

of London and London Life in the XIIIth, XIVth, and XVth Centuries, London: Longman, Green & Co., 1868, p. 435 (b); W. H. Stevenson (ed.), *Records of the Borough of Nottingham*, 3 vols, London: Quaritch, 1882–85, i, pp. 271, 277 (c). Latin, transl. by the editors.

(a) [Colchester 1311] John Kelye was charged that he procured some stinking fish called ray and sent it for sale to the market. He acknowledges it and asks for the court's favour, which is granted and he pays the fine. Adam Body was similarly charged. Petronilla Potes, Petronilla Dounyng, Sibil Belcher, Sibil her daughter, and Nota Godwyf were charged with obtaining and carrying into market the same stinking fish. They say that it was sweet when they obtained it, but owing to the mass of it, it took heat and lost its sweetness. They ask for the court's favour and are fined 15*d*, that is, 3*d* each.

(b) [London 1379] Be it remembered that the stations about the high cross of Cheap in London were let by John Phelipot, mayor, and John Ussher, chamberlain, on 5 September 1379, to diverse persons underwritten, to hold from the feast of St Michael [29 September] next, at the will of the city, they paying yearly to the chamberlain, to the use of the commonalty, 13*s* 4*d* each: Joanna Hernest, Cecily Eyr, Johanna Suttone, Johanna Staunford, Matilda Olyver, Cristina atte Forde, Johanna Coulee, Cristina Walwayn, Agnes Bromwyche, Johanna Holdernesse, Elena Hempier.

(c) [Nottingham 1395] The jurors say that all the female poulterers of Nottingham sell garlic, flour, salt, tallow candles, butter, cheeses, and suchlike things too dearly against the statute, and that each of them makes candles without putting a wick in them to the deception of the people, and is a common forestaller* of such victuals aforesaid coming to be sold in the town of Nottingham, standing at street openings where such victuals come to be sold.

Also they say that Isabel de Belton, Alice Anker, Anne Hukkester, Maud Okkebrok, Alan Culchi's wife, Katherine, the wife of Richard Byrford, mason, Ibot, the wife John Albayne, Margaret Glover, Maud Skynner, Isabel, the wife of John Hakkenay, Robert Ostiler, and Henry de Hykkeling are common forestallers of geese, capons, hens, poultry, doves, and such victuals before the due hour.

28. Labour for hire

A high proportion of work in the medieval town was performed by wage labour. Not all of this was contracted over long periods; working people in large numbers hired themselves by the day. Typical in this respect of all towns and of earlier periods, the council (known as 'the guild') of Worcester in 1467 recorded this ordinance for the hiring of daily labour in the city.

J. Toulmin Smith and L. Toulmin Smith (eds), *English Gilds*, Early English Text Society, original series, XL, London: N. Trübner, 1870, p. 395. English, revised by GR.

Also it is ordained by this present guild, that all manner [of] labourers that will be hired within the city, that they stand daily at the Grass Cross on the workdays within the said city, there ready to all persons such as will hire them to their certain labour, for reasonable sums: in the summer season at 5 of the bell in the morning, and in winter season at 6. And that proclamation be made at four places assigned, two times a quarter, by the bedeman* of the city.

29. Contents of shops in London 1378, 1382

Inventories of commercial premises have not survived in large numbers from the Middle Ages. They cannot easily be used to build a larger economic picture or to discern trends. They are principally of value as a snapshot, from a given moment, of what met the eye of a customer entering a particular shop. The first of these lists is the post mortem inventory of a shopkeeper; the second a tally compiled following a burglary. One concerns a haberdasher, the other a goldsmith. The variety and sophistication of the stock in both cases is striking.

H. T. Riley (ed.), *Memorials of London and London Life in the XIIIth, XIVth, and XVth Centuries*, London: Longmans, Green & Co., 1868, pp. 422–3 (a), 470–1 (b). Latin, transl. by the editor, revised by GR.

(a) Articles that were in the shop of Thomas Trew, haberdasher* of London, in the parish of St Ewen, in the ward of Faringdon Within, in the month of July 1378. 2 dozen laces of red leather, value 8*d*; one gross of tagged laces (*points*) of red leather, 18*d*; one dozen of 'cradilbowes' [presumably for infants' cradles], made of wool and flax, 18*d*; 3 'cradilbowes' made of wool and flax, 3*d*; one dozen caps, half of which are red and half green, 2*s* 8*d*; one dozen white caps called 'nightcaps', 2*s* 3*d*; 2 dozen woollen caps of diverse colours, 16*s*; 6 caps of black wool, 4*s*; 5 blue caps and one of russet colour, 2*s* 6*d*; 5 children's caps, red and blue, 2*s* 1*d*; one dozen black hures [caps], 4*s*; one black hure, 4*d*; two hair camises [light coats of camlet, a soft cloth], 12*d*; one red cap, 7*d*; one other cap of russet, 7*d*; one hat of russet, 6*d*; one white hat, 3*d*; 2 papers covered with red leather, 12*d*; 2 other papers, one of them covered with black leather, and the other with red, 8*d*; one purse, called 'hamondeys' ['almond-eyes'?], of sea-green colour, 6*d*; 4 pairs of spurs, 2*s*; one double chain of iron, 10*d*, and one other iron chain, 6*d*; one wooden gaming-table, with a set of men, 6*d*; 2 'permis' [jewel-cases?], 2*s*; one cloth painted with the Crucified, and other figures, 2*s* 4*d*; 8 white chains of iron for ferrets, 8*d*; a set of beads of black alabaster, 4*d*; three sets of beads of wood, 3*d*; two pairs of pencases, with [ink-]horns, 8*d*; one pair of children's boots of white woollen cloth, 2*d*; one osculatory,* called a 'pax-bred', 3*d*; 2 sets of wooden beads, called 'knottes', 4*d*; 4 articles called combs of box-wood, 4*d*; 2 wooden boxes, 3*d*; 2 wooden pepper querns [grinders], 3*d*; 2 pounds of linen thread, green and blue, 2s; 2 wooden[-framed] cushions, 2d; 6 purses of red leather, 4*d*; 4 *specularia* [lenses for reading?], 2*d*; 18 horns called inkhorns, 18*d*; 2 pencases, 6*d*; one black girdle [belt] of woollen thread, 2*d*; 13 quires of paper, 6*s* 8*d*; other paper, damaged, 6*d*; one hat of russet, 6*d*; 2 wooden coffers, 8*d*; 2 gaming-tables with the men, 16*d*; one wooden block for shaping caps, 2*d*; 6 skins of parchment, called 'soylepeles', 6*d*; one wooden whistle, 2*d*; 7 leaves of paper, 1*d*; and 3 pieces of whipcord, 3*d*.

(b) Delivery of infangthief,* in the guildhall of London, before John of Northampton, mayor, and the aldermen and sheriffs, and John Charneye, coroner, on Friday after the Assumption of the Blessed Virgin Mary [15 August], 1382.

Walter atte Watre, goldsmith, and Nicholas Somerset, of Norton St Philip in the county of Somerset, were taken at the suit of John Frensshe of London, goldsmith, with the mainour [stolen goods] of various of his possessions: namely 2 silver girdles, with red silk braids, value 46*s*; one silver girdle, with a blue braid, 30*s*; one other small silver girdle, with a green braid, 16*s*; one chain of silver gilt, 40*s*; one other small silver chain, 5*s*; one girdle of red silk, with a buckle, and studded with silver gilt, 16*s*; one silver chalice, with paten, 38*s*; 2 sets of phials of silver, their necks gilt, 20*s*; one osculatory* of silver gilt, 20*s*; 2 mazer* cups, bound with silver gilt, 33*s* 4*d*; 6 silver spoons, 14*s*; 2 gold rings, with 2 diamonds, £15; one gold ring with a balas ruby, 26*s* 8*d*; 3 strings of pearls, 70*s*; 6 gold necklaces, £5; and other goods and silver gilt, 16*s*; one silver chalice and paten, 38*s*; 2 sets of phials* of silver, with gilt chattels such as fermails [clasps and settings for jewels] and silver-gilt rings, broken silver, girdles set with silver, buckles and pendants for girdles, and rosaries of silver and pearls, to the value of £40. Which goods and chattels the same Walter atte Watre and Nicholas Somerset, on Wednesday after the feast of the Assumption of the Blessed Virgin Mary, in the year named, feloniously stole by night at the corner of Friday Street in West Cheap, in the parish of St Matthew in the ward of Faringdon Within, in London, and there criminally broke into John Frensshe's shop.

And also the same Walter atte Watre and Nicholas Somerset were taken at the suit of Thomas Stoke of London, goldsmith, with the mainour of goods and chattels of him, Thomas Stoke: namely with one mazer cup, bound with silver gilt, value 10*s*; one other small mazer cup, bound with silver gilt, 5*s*; 3 buckles with 3 pendants, for silver girdles, 15*s*; one other buckle and one silver girdle, 6*s* 8*d*; and one knife called a 'cut-throat' with the scabbard ends of silver, 6*s* 8*d*; by them stolen at night on the Wednesday stated, from the shop of John Frensshe, goldsmith, in the place, ward and parish aforesaid.

And the jury declared upon their oath the said Walter atte Watre and Nicholas Somerset to be guilty of these felonies. And because the said Walter atte Watre and Nicholas Somerset were clerks [i.e. could read and so claim benefit of clergy, the right to be tried in a church court], and judgement could not lawfully be proceeded to without the ordinary [ecclesiastical authority], they were committed to the prison of Newgate, there to be kept in safe custody. They had no possessions.

30. A specialist industry: Nottingham alabaster

While the normative records of craft ordinances [**20**], [**21**] tend to give a static and idealised impression of industrial practice, a different light on economic realities is shed by the evidence of litigation. In the following cases, brought to a borough court, concerning the manufacture and sale of alabaster reliefs, we learn about the distinct roles of those who supplied the raw material, the carver and the painter, and the distributor of the products. The relative softness of alabaster lends itself to detailed carving, while its sheen and its rarity gave it, in late medieval Europe, a precious quality. Local availability of the raw material led to the development of Nottingham during the later Middle Ages as a centre for the production of carved alabaster for local and foreign sale. Workshops made a variety of products, often displaying religious themes and frequently intended as objects of devotion for parish churches. Of images made for domestic use, that of the head of St John the Baptist on a dish became a 'signature' work of Nottingham manufacture.

W. H. Stevenson (ed.), *Records of the Borough of Nottingham*, 3 vols, London: Quaritch, 1885, iii, pp. 18–21, 28–9, 180–3. Latin, transl. by the editor.

(a) 31 October 1491. Nicholas Hill makes a plea against William Bott, that he render him his reasonable account of the time when he was receiver of Nicholas's money. Nicholas complains that whereas he, on 10 July 1491, here at Nottingham, delivered to William fifty-eight heads of Saint John the Baptist, part of them in tabernacles and in niches, to sell and to render his reasonable account to the aforesaid Nicholas of the money received for them; and although the same William has been often asked to render account, he has hitherto delayed to render that account, and still delays, to Nicholas's grievous damage to the value of £3 6*s* 8*d*. And William comes, and prays leave to imparl [delay] until Wednesday next after the feast of All Hallows [1 November] next to come. The same day and place is given to Nicholas. On which day William comes, and he says that he never was the receiver of the moneys of the said Nicholas, nor is he bound to render him any account of the same moneys, as he has complained against him. Both appeal to a jury.

14 December 1491. Nicholas Hill complains of William Bott of a plea that he render him 10*d*, which he owes and unjustly detains. The plaintiff complains that the defendant, on 9 June 1491, agreed that he would pay to the plaintiff 10*d* for painting and gilding three alabaster salt-cellars, with two images painted

and gilded: whereby he has damages of *2d.* And the defendant comes in his own person and defends himself.

(b) 7 January 1495. Robert Tull, husbandman, complains of Nicholas Hill, alabaster-man, in a plea of debt of *12d*, which he owes and unjustly detains. The plaintiff complains of Nicholas, who is in the care and charge of the sheriffs, that whereas the defendant on 6 June 1493 hired the aforesaid plaintiff to carry diverse images and heads of St John the Baptist from Nottingham to London for wages of *3s*, he only paid the plaintiff *2s*, and so there remain *12d* unpaid and now demanded; and although often requested he has not yet paid: whereby he says that he is injured and has damage of *4d.*

(c) 27 May 1530. John Nicholson, stainer [painter], complains of John Cottingham, image-maker, of a plea that he render him a head of St John the Baptist and half a quarter of gold, price *10s*, which he unjustly withholds from him, as he says. The plaintiff complains that whereas he, on Monday after the feast of St Andrew the Apostle [30 November] 1506, here at Nottingham, delivered to John Cottingham the aforesaid head of St John to paint before Christmas then next following, and then to redeliver it to the aforesaid John Nicholson: nevertheless John Cottingham, although often requested, has not yet done so, to the plaintiff's damage of *40d*; and therefore he brings suit. And John Cottingham comes, and defends himself; and he says that he does not withhold the aforesaid head from the aforesaid plaintiff. Both appeal to a jury.

(d) 28 June 1530. William Walsh of Chellaston complains of John Nicholson, stainer, of a plea of debt of *18d* which he owes to him and unjustly detains, as he says; that is, for carriage of a cartload of alabaster-stone from Chellaston to Nottingham, which money he should have paid to him. And John comes, and defends himself; and he says that he owes him nothing. Both appeal to a jury.

31. Advertising a new commodity in London *c.*1479

The advertisement of products for sale in the medieval town was effected largely through the medium of street cries. But handwritten and posted bills may also have been employed. The advent of printing introduced the possibility of readily reproduced announcements to promote merchandise. This notice was printed by William Caxton at Westminster. The Sarum Ordinal (also known as a Pye from its black and white appearance, like a magpie's) was a calendar. It is clear from Caxton's publicity for his product that he anticipated lay as well as clerical customers for this useful volume. He used the advertisement to demonstrate the typeface used in the book ('after the form of the present letter'). He had recently (in 1476) established the first English printing-press at Westminster, where by the time of publishing the Ordinal he was not only renting a house and workshop in the Almonry at the sign of the red pale but also leasing a small shop at the other end of the Abbey, close to the king's court and the houses of parliament. In the same period Caxton published an edition of Chaucer's *Canterbury Tales* (1478), a manual for learning French (1480) and the romance of *Godfrey of Boloyne* (1481).

G. D. Painter, *William Caxton*, Edinburgh: Chatto and Windus, 1976, pp. 98–9. English and Latin.

If it please any man spiritual or temporal to buy any Pyes of two or three commemorations of Salisbury use emprinted after the form of the present letter which be well and truly correct, let him come to Westminster into the Almonry at the Red Pale and he shall have them good cheap. Please do not remove this handbill (*Supplico stet cedula*).

32. Hawkers of goods at Winchester

Ordinances which sought to suppress door-to-door salesmen were part of a (certainly vain) attempt by magistrates to subject all trade to common procedures of quality control and taxation. The records of civic legislation are full of attempts to ensure that all economic transactions took place in the public view. Petty door-to-door tradesmen subverted that aspiration.

W. H. B. Bird (ed.), *The Black Book of Winchester*, Winchester: Warren and Son, 1925, p. 16. Latin, transl. by the editor.

At the borough moot held at Winchester on Monday after the feast of St Ambrose the Bishop [4 April], that is Hock Monday 1409, in the presence of John Bailly, mayor, Thomas Sutton and Edmund Danvers, bailiffs, it was ordered by the mayor and his fellows and the community of the city that no traders, known as hawkers, wherever they come from, carrying goods on their backs, shall go from door to door through the city nor into any of the streets of Winchester to proffer their wares for sale, on payment of a fine of 6*s* 8*d* at the first offence, and double and three times this rate on subsequent occasions. Instead, if they wish to sell, they must stand twice in the week, on Wednesday and Friday, in the established place, that is, on the east side of the town next to the gate of St Thomas by St Swithun's cemetery.

33. Unofficial markets in London

Occasional regulations such as these reveal a glimpse of what was doubtless an extensive unofficial, 'black' economy. The difficulty of imposing effective restrictions on this marginal economy is evident from the terms of the by-laws themselves. To the historian such legislation is also revealing of the official prejudice against unknown and unregistered outsiders who ventured to trade in the city.

H. T. Riley (ed.), *Memorials of London and London Life in the XIIIth, XIVth, and XVth Centuries*, London: Longmans, Green & Co., 1868, pp. 33, 339. Latin, transl. by the editor, revised by GR.

(a) On Thursday before the feast of Pentecost, 1297, it was ordered, in the presence of Sir John le Bretun, warden of the City of London, and certain of the aldermen, that on account of the fights and murders arising between persons known and unknown, the gathering together of thieves in the market, and of cutpurses and other criminals, in a certain market which had been lately held after dinner in Soper Lane,[22] and which was called 'the new fair'; that it should be abolished, and not be held any more, on pain of confiscation of the wares both bought and sold there: the market having been established by strangers, foreigners, and beggars, living three or four leagues from London.

(b) [Order of the mayor, 1369] Many disorders have been caused in the past by the 'Evynchepynge' [evening market] which is

22 Off Cheapside, by St Mary le Bow church.

held so late in the night upon Cornhill. Old clothes that have been renewed have been often sold there for new clothes … and various things stolen in diverse places are there sold in secret, to the great scandal and damage of the city; and many brawls and disputes have often broken out there. We therefore command, on behalf of our lord the king, that no man or woman be so bold as to carry clothes or any other things to sell on Cornhill after the bell has rung that hangs upon the Tun [prison] there, which bell is rung at sunset, on pain of forfeiture of all clothes and other things carried there for sale after that time.

34. Internal trade: Southampton in the mid-fifteenth century

By contrast with foreign trade [**35**], the domestic traffic in goods and raw materials is poorly documented in the medieval record. However, the records of Southampton give a rare glimpse of the detail of internal trade. Goods carried either into or out of the north gate, the Bargate, of the town were from 1430 onwards subject to three possible tolls, known as customs, brokage* and pontage.*[23] Vessels coming into the port with goods included local fishing-boats, wine-carrying ships from Bordeaux and the galleys of Genoa and Venice which, in the former case, had been coming annually to Southampton since 1277 or before. These laconic entries do not supply the precise motives for the shipments between Southampton and other towns, but these may partly be inferred by the historian.

O. Coleman (ed.), *The Brokage Book of Southampton 1443–1444*, 2 vols, Southampton Records Series, IV, VI, Southampton: University of Southampton, 1960–61, i, pp. 8–111. Latin, transl. by the editor.

	C	B	P
Saturday 5 October [1443]			
From Roger Woldynge going to Salisbury with 5 barrels of tar of John Hall	*5d*	*2½d*	*1d*

23 The source is the basis of an online project, 'People, places and commodities 1430–1540. The overland trade of Southampton with southern and midland England from the Southampton brokage books': www.overlandtrade.org. See further M. Hicks (ed.), *English Inland Trade 1430–1540: Southampton and Its Region*, Oxford, 2015.

	C	B	P
From John Walton going to Salisbury with 2 butts* of wine of William Hore	4*d*	4*d*	1*d*
From John Basset going to Romsey with 8 half-bales of woad* of Simon Long	8*d*	1*d*	1*d*
From William Potter going to Salisbury with 120 heads of garlic of Richard Bele	free	2½*d*	1*d*
From Roger Marow going to Salisbury with 5 barrels of tar of John Hall	5*d*	2½*d*	1*d*
From John Cook going to Salisbury with 60 heads of garlic and ¼ hundredweight of fish of Richard Bele	free	2*d*	1*d*
From John Chavon going to Salisbury with 8 barrels of black soap[24] of William Warwyke	8*d*	4*d*	1*d*
From Henry Chavon going to Salisbury with 1 tun of oil of William Hore	8*d*		
and 1 hundredweight of wax	1*d*	4*d*	1*d*
From Ralph Stride going to Salisbury with 4 barrels of soap of William Warwyke	4*d*	2*d*	1*d*
From Edward Granncell going to Salisbury with 2 barrels of tar and 21 bunches of garlic of John Hall	3*d*	2*d*	1*d*
From John Rownde going to Salisbury with 180 heads of garlic of Richard Bele	free	4*d*	1*d*
From Henry Curlynge for 1 hundredweight of wheat			2*d*
From Thomas Hayward for 2 quarters of malt	1*d*		
From John Harpor for 2 quarters of malt	1*d*		
From Stephen Cook going to Salisbury with 6 bales of woad of William Wyther	6*d*		
and 1 bale of alum* of John Noyle of Taunton	free	4*d*	1*d*
Sunday 6 October			
From Isabel Wexcombe for her stall at the Friars Minor for 2 days	2*d*		
From William Bocher for his stall at the Friars Minor for 1 day	1*d*		
From John Bocher for his stall at the Friars Minor for 2 days	2*d*		

24 Used in cloth manufacture; generally from Spain.

Monday 7 October

	C	B	P
From Yngram Hewet entering with lambskins			1*d*
and leaving for London with 9 bales of dates of Simon Spenell	*per mare*[25]	8*d*	1*d*
From John Loder leaving with 5 horses with alum of John Gryffyn of Ludlow	10*d*	5*d*	
From John Mathew going to Salisbury with 5 bales of woad of Thomas Cook of London	free	2*d*	1*d*
From John Waryn going to Salisbury with 7 bales of woad of Thomas Cook of London	free	3*d*	1*d*
From Stephen Kyng going to Salisbury with 9 barrels of black soap of Thomas Pakker	9*d*	4*d*	1*d*
From Walter Cabbyll going to Romsey with 2 bales of madder* of Gregory Dyer	4*d*	½*d*	1*d*
From Richard Gonnor entering with wool and leaving for London with 2 chests of Gregory Cattanei [of Genoa] with diverse things for his household	nil	8*d*	1*d*
From William Laurence going to Coventry with 9 bales of woad of John Goold	free	8*d*	1*d*
From Ingram Twynham entering with wool and leaving for Coventry with 3 bales of madder and 1 bale of alum and 2 bales of woad of William Rastell	free	8*d*	1*d*
From Thomas Hewet entering with lambskins and leaving for Coventry with 6 bales of woad and 2 bales of madder of William Per'	free	8*d*	1*d*
From Thomas White going to Stoneham [Hants] with 3½ quarters of coal of William Smyth	1*d*	nil	1*d*
From Robert Hyde for 3 oxhides	1½*d*		
From William Watersale for 1 oxhide	½*d*		
From John Ber' going to London with 6 bales of woad and 3 bales of dates of Simon Spenell	*per mare*	8*d*	1*d*

Tuesday 8 October

From Thomas Dene going to Winchester with 1 butt of Rumney [wine] and 3 barrels of tar of Laurence Trygg	free	1½*d*	1*d*

25 'By sea.'

	C	B	P
From John Dyper entering with biscuit and leaving for Winchester with 4 bales of woad of Richard Lucays	free		
and 4 inferior bales of woad of the bailiff of the soke*	free	nil	1*d*
From John Pynhorn going to Salisbury with 2 pipes* of wine of John Halsted	4*d*	4*d*	1*d*
From Richard Lang going to Alton [Hants] with 7 bales of woad and 1 bale of alum of Robert Dyer	9*d*	4*d*	1*d*
From Walter Cabbyll going to Romsey with 6 bales of woad of John Brond	6*d*	1*d*	1*d*
From Thomas Leef going to Romsey with 1 bale of madder and 3 bales of woad of John Brond	5*d*	1*d*	1*d*
From John Hygon entering with wool and leaving for Coventry with 9 bales of woad of Thomas Rastell	free	8*d*	1*d*
From Henry Laurence for 4 quarters of malt	2*d*		
From Richard Paysegood for 4 quarters of malt	2*d*		
From Henry Curlyng for 5 quarters of malt	2½*d*		
From William Hawtot for 5 quarters of malt	2½*d*		
Monday 23 December			
From William Mafay going to Winchester with 1 hundredweight of paving tiles for the abbot of Hyde	free	1*d*	1*d*
From John Pynhorn going to Salisbury with 5 bales of alum of William Swayn	5*d*	4*d*	1*d*
From William Smyth going to Romsey with 7 bales of woad of John Brond	7*d*	1*d*	1*d*
From William Hayward going to Salisbury with 1 butt of wine of Thomas Whyte	free	2*d*	1*d*
From John Mathow going to Salisbury with 1 butt of wine of Thomas Whyte	free	2*d*	1*d*
From Jenyn Glover leaving with 100 woolfells*	3*d*		
From John Shopper for 1 hundredweight of canvas	2*d*		
From John Hayward entering with cloth of Gabriel Corbet and Edward Cattanei [of Genoa]	1*d*		
and going to Romsey with 1½ hundredweight of almonds of John	2*d*		
Bole and 3 barrels of herrings of John Medmor	6*d*	½*d*	1*d*
Friday 14 February [1444]			
From John Crokker going to Winchester with 2 pipes* of wine of John Wodecok	free	2*d*	1*d*

	C	B	P
From John Mathew going to Salisbury with 2 barrels of salmon and 2 kilderkins* of herrings of Richard Bele	free	2½*d*	1*d*
From Richard Walton going to Winchester with 1 butt of wine of Laurence Trygg	free	1*d*	1*d*
From Walter Cabbyll going to Romsey with 2 barrels of salmon, 2 barrels of herrings, 4 casks of herrings and 2 bushels* of onions of Richard Bele	free	1*d*	1*d*
From Nicholas Couper leaving with 1 barrel of herrings and 2 hundredweight of iron in his own cart	3*d*		1*d*
and entering with 3 quarters of wheat	1½*d*		
From John Style going to Winchester with 2 pipes of wine of John Wodecok	free	nil	1*d*
From Richard Gorman leaving with 5 horses with 5 bales of woad of John Trever	5*d*		
1 bale of alum on 2 horses of the said John Trever	4*d*	5*d*	
From Stephen Mychell going to Salisbury with 1 butt of wine of John Lydford	4*d*		
1 chest with diverse haberdashery and 17 hats of Henry van Oye	*per mare*	2*d*	1*d*
From John Palmer going to Salisbury with 1 butt of inferior wine of John Helyer	2*d*		
and 1 hundredweight of rosin		1*d*	
and 1 package of iron pans			
and 1 chest of haberdashery of William van Gyldre	*per mare*	3*d*	1*d*
From Hugh Hancok entering with 2 quarters of malt	1*d*		
50 hake	1*d*		
1 quarter of salt fish	½*d*		
1 barrel of onions	½*d*		
3 casks of herrings	1½*d*		
600 coarse herrings	1½*d*		
on 5 of his own horses			
From William Rabayne going to Salisbury with 1 tun of oil of Richard at Well of Glastonbury	16*d*	4*d*	1*d*
From John Rowde going to Salisbury with 2 pipes of inferior wine of John Helyer	4*d*	4*d*	1*d*

	C	B	P
From Ingram Hewet going to Oxford with 1 bale of alum of Richard Spraget, 5 baskets of raisins, 3 bales of rice, 1 bale of dates, 3 baskets of almonds, and 4 measures of figs, of Thomas Tanfeylde	free	8*d*	1*d*
From John Bole entering with wool and leaving for Oxford with 6 measures of fruit, 1 bale of dates, 1 bale of rice, and 1 bale of cotton of William Hayll and William Dagvyle	free	8*d*	1*d*

35. International trade: Hull in the fifteenth century

This text is taken from the account of the collectors of customs for Hull and nearby ports between 9 April and Michaelmas 1483. About sixty or seventy ships entered Hull from foreign ports each year during the later Middle Ages. The officers' inventories of their cargoes provide an extensive catalogue of the goods and materials which subsequently found their way (by internal distribution along lines exemplified in [**34**]) to local and more distant English urban markets. To give an idea of the scale and range of materials imported, this extract lists the contents of a single ship. The collectors recorded the values of goods entering the port but in the source the Hansards, traders from the Hanseatic towns of the Baltic coast who took shares of the cargo, paid no dues, thanks to an Anglo-Hanseatic treaty of 1474.

W. R. Childs (ed.), *The Customs Accounts of Hull 1453–1490*, Yorkshire Archaeological Society Record Series, CXLIV, 1984, pp. 192–4. Latin, transl. by the editor.

The ship of Andreas Hartwych[26] called the *Trinity* of Danzig moored [at Kingston upon Hull] on 16 July [1483].

The same Andreas [Hartwych], Hansard:*
2 nests of counters;[27] 1 double counter; 10 pairs of playing tables;[28] 2 shocks[29] of trenchers;* 1 small counter; 5 pairs of playing tables; 6 barrels of tar; 1 bowstaff; 3 sack hoops; 6 bunches of wire; 300 wainscots;

26 The master, rather than the owner, of the ship.

27 Counting boards for reckoning accounts.

28 Games tables.

29 A shock was 60 pieces. A trencher is a wooden plate.

360 clapholts;[30] 1 shock of wooden troughs; 6 barrels of potash*; 5 barrels of osmunds.*
£25 6*s* 8*d*

Herman Overkampe, Hansard:
8 bundles of iron from Butow; 5½ lasts and 15 bundles of flax; 27 barrels of osmunds; 14 eighths of eels; 6½ timbers of redwork;[31] 1 small piece of wax weighing 56 lbs; 14 pieces of hyndorlance[32] containing 6 ells; 14 barrels of tar; 3 pieces of linen cloth.
£62 3*s* 4*d*

Hans Molner, Hansard:
3½ lasts and 30 bundles of flax; 1 last of osmunds.
£62 3*s* 4*d*

Jost Eller, Hansard:
1½ lasts of osmunds; 8 nests of counters; 8 nests of boxes; 1 dozen lutes; 2 shocks of lutestrings; 3 double counters with 2 shocks of white playing tables.
£52 6*s* 8*d*

Peter Eckstede, Hansard:
7 lasts and 60 bundles of flax; 1½ straw of wax containing 3 pieces of wax weighing 1400 lbs; 2 barrels of train-oil:* 6 barrels of osmunds; 5 barrels of tar.
£118 0*s* 0*d*

Hans Stagnet, Hansard:
3 barrels of osmunds; 2972 bowstaves; 5 lasts and 65 bundles of flax; 1 barrel of train-oil; 1 straw of wax containing 10 pieces of wax weighing 1250 lbs; 4 nests of coffers; 8 shocks of trenchers.
£140 0*s* 0*d*

Gerard Lesebern, Hansard:
2 lasts and 60 bundles of flax; 15 barrels of train-oil; 1 roll of wax containing 6 pieces of wax weighing 750 lbs; 1 chest with 7 dickers of buckskins;[33] 5 shocks of trenchers.
£42 10*s* 0*d*

30 Small split timbers for barrel staves or panelling.

31 Parcels of squirrel skins.

32 Flax or linen.

33 Dicker: ten.

Hans Droye, Hansard:
2 barrels of potash; 3 lasts and 90 bundles of flax; 1 barrel of tar; 1 barrel of pitch; 2 nests of counters; 13 shocks of trenchers; 1 chest with 3 bunches of linen yarn and 13 bundles of flax.
£29 6*s* 8*d*

Tobias Stenvech, Hansard:
8 lasts and 90 bundles of flax; 2 barrels of tar; 1 barrel of osmunds; 4 furs of redwork; 1 shock of winding.[34]
£61 0*s* 0*d*

Mathew Pepersack, Hansard:
2½ lasts and 18 bundles of flax; 2 barrels of tar.
£17 0*s* 0*d*

Paul Auekynck, Hansard:
5 lasts of flax; 1 barrel of osmunds; ½ barrel of train-oil; 2 nests of counters; 2 nests of coffers; 1 chest with 5 small pieces of wax; 2 small pieces of wax without a chest weighing 250 lbs; 1 pair of clavysymballes;[35] 23 shocks of lutestrings.
£48 0*s* 0*d*

Andreas Klepper, Hansard:
1½ lasts of flax and candlewick; 1 barrel of tar; ½ barrel of osmunds; 14 eighths of eels; 1 chest with 2 nests of coffers; 20 bunches of winding.
£15 0*s* 0*d*

George Plaman, Hansard:
20 barrels of osmunds; 1 barrel of tar; 5 barrels and 16 bundles of flax; 8 nests of counters; 8 nests of coffers.
£45 0*s* 0*d*

Michael Wittenbarch, Hansard:
1 last and 30 bundles of flax; 1½ barrels of osmunds; 1 barrel with 3 pieces of wax weighing 200 lbs.
£17 10*s* 0*d*

Herman Overkampe, Hansard:
1½ lasts and 45 bundles of flax.
£11 5*s* 0*d*

34 Probably ropes.

35 A form of harpsichord or spinet.

Peter Bedeker and Peter Nyggebur, Hansards:
1 nest of chests; 2 shocks of trenchers; 1 chest with 4 bundles of flax; 2 barrels of tar; 6 painted platters; 6 buckets; 1 bowstaff; ½ barrel of tar; 1 chest with 18 bundles of flax; 4 shocks of trenchers; 1 lb of amber beads; 3 nests of chests; 30 shocks of trenchers; 1 small counter; 1 barrel of tar; 3 nests of coffers; 2 dickers of buckskins; 5 shocks of trenchers; 1 small counter; 1 chest with 10 bundles of wax; 1 dozen troughs; 1 dozen shoemaker's boards; 1 chest with 6 bundles of flax; 1 stone of candlewick; 10 boards; 8 pieces of bast;* 20 painted platters; 50 bunches of bristles; 1 chest; 1 coffer; 3 stone of candlewick; 32 pieces of bast; 1 chest with 6 shocks of trenchers; 20 pieces of bast; 1 chest with 6 bundles of flax; 1 coffer; 1 lectern; 1 chest with 12 bundles of flax; 20 painted platters; 20 pairs of pepper-grinders; 70 bundles of flax; 2 barrels of tar; 1 barrel of pitch; 2 nests of counters; 2 nests of coffers; 7 barrels of train-oil; 1 chest with 5 lutes; 3 pieces of bast.
£31 10*s* 0*d*

36. The business of the merchant: William Cely 1487

To the medieval merchant, accurate information was as valuable a resource as the goods in which he traded. In their letters, where these survive, the historian can observe the eager exchange of news regarding markets, economic competitors, and the larger context of diplomacy and war. The foreign agent or factor of a firm was naturally concerned to present his efforts on behalf of his employers in the best light. The Cely clan was one of the mercantile dynasties of London which in the later Middle Ages built up substantial commercial and financial networks in the Low Countries, primarily via the Calais Staple* through which English wool exports were channelled. At the time of this letter, however, the instability of Burgundy under the Emperor Maximilian was disrupting patterns of trade and financial markets, encouraging the Cely family to diversify into importing dyes and other goods to London. The brothers Richard and George were the senior partners at this date; William, who seems not to have been a relation, came to the firm as an apprentice and took, as was not uncommon in such circumstances, the family name.

A. Hanham (ed.), *The Cely Letters 1472–1488*, Oxford: Oxford University Press, 1975, pp. 237–8. English. Reproduced by permission of Oxford University Press.

William Cely at Calais to Richard and George Cely at London, 19 November 1487.

Right worshipful sirs and my reverend masters, after all due recommendation preceding I lowly recommend myself unto your masterships. Furthermore, please it your masterships to understand that I am come to Calais in safety, thanked be Almighty God, for I was never in so great jeopardy coming out of Flanders in my life, for men of war [enemy ships] lying by the way waiting for Englishmen; and also I and my company was arrested [for] two days at Dunkirk, but for Sir James Tyrrell's[36] sake we were let go. And so, sir, the world goes marvellously in Flanders now, for it is open war between Ghent and the king of the Romans, etc. Sir, as for making over of your money, since this trouble began[37] I could not make over a penny, saving £18 sterling, whereof I shall send you the bill at the next passage. But sir[s], John Delopys showed me at my departing that I should write unto your masterships to understand whether there shall be any jeopardy to bring wares out of the east parts into England now from henceforth, or not, as he supposes that that act of the contrary shall be put in suspense for diverse causes; wherefore, sir, he advises you to bestow your money in gross wares[38] now betimes at this Bergen-op-Zoom market: in such wares as your masterships think will be best at London, whether it be in madder,* wax or fustians, but I trow madder be best. And so be that you will, Gomes de Soria[39] shall buy it for your masterships and ship it in Spanish ships in his own name, for John Delopys and he are purposed to buy much madder to send into England. And if so be that it fall to peace, there will be good done upon madder if it be bought betimes, and John Delopys says, if your masterships will, he will bestow your money as well as his own, and he says that that is the best way to make over your money, for the exchange[40] is right nought, etc. No more unto your masterships at this time, but Almighty Jesus preserve you. Written at Calais the 19th day of November.

By your servant,

William Cely

36 An English ambassador to the emperor.

37 Evidently a reference to restrictions on trade between England and the Low Countries.

38 Goods sold by the hundredweight.

39 A merchant of Spain and Bruges. John Delopys (de Lopez) was another.

40 I.e. of currency.

IV. SOCIAL DEVELOPMENT

Urban society in the Middle Ages was in some important ways very like that of the countryside. Notwithstanding the old fable that 'town air makes free', the peasant who escaped dependence upon a rural landlord and found her or his way to the city was vulnerable to exploition in analogous ways to the villeins and cottagers they had left behind. Their employer, normally a workshop-owner, a merchant or an ecclesiastical corporation, had similar material interests to the landowning gentry and aristocracy. This was the less surprising in that, in the centuries which followed the first investment in the expanding urban sector by the Anglo-Saxon landed elite, economic ties at this level between town and country remained strong, and, while landowning aristocrats and gentry continued to maintain substantial town houses, some (if only a minority) of those who made fortunes in the city repaid the compliment by purchasing landed estates.[1] The urban man of business might see himself in a different light from the rural aristocrat, and it is perhaps significant that a wealthy Londoner of the late fourteenth century chose to have himself depicted on his tomb brass not in the trappings of a gentleman but as a merchant [**37**].[2] None the less, the merchant of the town shared a certain class interest with the country landowner.

This said, the social experience of the town differed from that of its rural surroundings by virtue of its concentrated diversity and its fluidity. Both before and after the plague, urban populations depended, in order to remain buoyant, upon a constant influx from the countryside (not until recent times have improvements in health provision enabled

1 R. Fleming, 'Rural elites and urban communities in late Saxon England', *Past and Present*, CXLI, 1993, pp. 3–26; S. Reynolds, 'The rulers of London in the twelfth century', *History*, LVII, 1972, pp. 337–57; C. M. Barron, 'Centres of conspicuous consumption: the aristocratic town house in London 1200–1500', *London Journal*, XX, 1995, pp. 1–16; R. Horrox, 'The urban gentry in the fifteenth century', in J. A. F. Thomson (ed.), *Towns and Townspeople in the Fifteenth Century*, Gloucester, 1988, pp. 22–44.

2 C. M. Barron, 'Chivalry, pageantry and merchant culture in medieval London', in P. Coss and M. Keen (eds), *Heraldry, Pageantry and Social Display in Medieval England*, Woodbridge, 2002, pp. 218–41.

some cities to contain what had previously been a relatively high level of mortality). Because surnames became fixed only from around 1350, the study of placenames in personal names, such as 'Margaret of Devizes', has made it possible to map the magnetic range of early fourteenth-century towns of diverse sizes: the larger the urban centre, the longer the pull. A new small town of the thirteenth century such as Stratford-upon-Avon drew most of its settlers from within a radius of sixteen miles, while a quarter of recorded names in Bristol indicated origins more than sixty miles away.[3] Our sources, however, tend to prioritise those who, having come to town, made good sufficiently to acquire property and so to enter the written record.[4] The poor migrant tended only too often to stay beneath the radar [**38**], [**39**]. The narratives of poor criminals interviewed in Paris in the late fourteenth century record both seasonal migration and, in some cases, quite lengthy personal trajectories.[5]

Immigrants were attracted to towns not only for commercial reasons but in order to acquire practical knowledge, professional qualifications and – in a few cases – learning in its own right. In 1200 a number of cathedral towns offered schools at the higher level with teaching in diverse fields; but the long thirteenth century saw the two university centres of Oxford and Cambridge emerge pre-eminent and, in consequence, attract to themselves a substantial national and international population of young men [**40**]. The university was a creation of the medieval town, and the two bodies remained interdependent, even if the cuckoo seemed at times to crowd the nest, and the clerical privileges of the students regularly drove the city magistrates to distraction [**85**].[6] Although the university towns were by definition somewhat peculiar places, they were at the same time typical in their experience of a fluctuating body of strangers, compelled to find ways to live

3 P. McClure, 'Patterns of migration in the late Middle Ages: the evidence of English surnames', *Economic History Review*, 2nd series, XXXII, 1979, pp. 167–72; E. M. Carus-Wilson, 'The first half-century of the borough of Stratford-upon-Avon', repr. in R. Holt and G. Rosser (eds), *The Medieval Town*, London, 1990, pp. 49–70; S. Penn, 'The origins of Bristol migrants in the early fourteenth century: the surname evidence', *Transactions of the Bristol and Gloucestershire Archaeological Society*, CI, 1983, pp. 123–30; G. Rosser, *Medieval Westminster 1200–1540*, Oxford, 1989, pp. 183–90.

4 R. Holt, 'Society and population 600–1300', in *CUHB*, pp. 79–104, at p. 103.

5 B. Geremek, *The Margins of Society in Late Medieval Paris*, transl. J. Birrell, Cambridge, 1987.

6 A. Cobban, *The Medieval English Universities: Oxford and Cambridge to c.1500*, Aldershot, 1988; Cobban, *English University Life in the Middle Ages*, London, 1999.

together with one another (one solution was the creation of 'nations' – of the Welsh, of the Scots and so on – and another, the gathering of fellow students in common halls) and with the more permanently resident townsmen.

Another element in the urban population prior to the end of the thirteenth century, the history of which was both tragically unique and yet absolutely characteristic, were the Jews [**41**], [**42**]. Following the Norman Conquest, Jewish settlers scattered themselves through sixty English towns.[7] The fiscal interest of the crown led to these being formed into official communities, but these were not ghettos, and Jewish families lived in the same streets as Christians. In the twelfth century the area of London known as 'the Jewry' was inhabited also by Christian families.[8] The city of Bristol preserves the remains of a Jewish bath used for purification, while the Jewish cemetery in York which was discovered and excavated in the 1980s lay on the edge of, and by no means hidden away from, the town.[9] Anti-Jewish feeling in certain quarters was manifest in the terrible Christian attack on Jews in York in 1190, and continued to be fed thereafter by some inflammatory stories and preaching; but the expulsion of all Jews from England in 1290 was primarily a royal act and not the inevitable outcome of popular intolerance.[10]

From well before the Conquest, English towns were home to long-term and short-term settlers from all other parts of Christendom; but it is a small index of the increasing reach of the monarchy in the later Middle Ages that national surveys were undertaken in the fifteenth century of the foreigners (or in contemporary language, 'aliens') living in the cities [**49**]. At this point and thanks to these records, therefore, we can appreciate the scale of their presence.[11] From the lists compiled

7 A. S. Abulafia, *Christian–Jewish Relations, 1000–1300: Jews in the Service of Medieval Christendom*, Harlow, 2011, pp. 88–108; P. Hyams, 'The Jewish minority in mediaeval England, 1066–1290', *Journal of Jewish Studies*, 25, 1974, pp. 270–93.

8 J. Hillaby, 'The London Jewry: William I to John', *Jewish Historical Studies*, XXXIII, 1992–94, pp. 1–44.

9 R. R. Emmanuel and M. W. Ponsford, 'Jacob's Well, Bristol, Britain's only known medieval Jewish ritual bath (*Mikveh*)', *Transactions of the Bristol and Gloucestershire Archaeological Society*, CXII, 1994, pp. 73–86; J. Lilley (ed.), *The Jewish Burial Ground at Jewbury*, York Archaeological Trust, 1994; P. Skinner (ed.), *Jews in Medieval Britain: Historical, Literary and Archaeological Perspectives*, Woodbridge, 2003, pp. 102–3 and *passim*.

10 B. Dobson, 'The medieval York Jewry reconsidered', in Skinner (ed.), *Jews in Medieval Britain*, pp. 145–56.

11 S. Thrupp, 'A survey of the alien population of England in 1440', *Speculum*, XXXII, 1957, pp. 262–73; Thrupp, 'Aliens in and around London', in A. E. Hollaender and

for taxation at this period we can also get a sense of the differing status of the prosperous Baltic or north Italian merchant and of the often far more precariously situated Flemish craftsmen and -women who, while their command of unfamiliar and respected techniques such as tile- and glass-making earned them a certain economic status, tended to seek out one another's company, to continue to speak their native language and periodically to find themselves at risk of attack from resentful neighbours who on such occasions chose to identify them as 'aliens'.[12] In the 1460s, a trade recession and the unpopular Anglo-Burgundian alliance triggered widespread expression of anti-'Flemish' feeling. The fifteenth century shows the potential for the anti-foreigner riots of Evil May Day in London in 1517. The listing from Lynn in 1440 reveals a significant presence of Flemish workers from across the North Sea, many involved in shoemaking. The 1483 subsidy rolls for London and its suburbs, together with complementary records, indicate the presence of some 2700 alien men and women over the age of twelve in the metropolis – in an estimated total city population of around fifty thousand at this period. Their distribution, however, was very uneven, being concentrated especially in certain areas, notably the suburban districts of Southwark and Westminster (where aliens may have made up as much as 10 per cent of the local population). Their social range was also significant, and is indicated by their differential assessment for tax. Non-householders (servants) were required to pay 2*s*; householders 6*s* 8*d*; masters of brewhouses 20*s*; and resident merchants £2. The overwhelming majority of aliens recorded in the capital were 'Germans', which at the period loosely indicated an origin in Dutch- or German-speaking territories from Flanders to Prussia. Much of this human movement will have been temporary or seasonal migration. Many who came were skilled and brought particular talents. The adjacent wards of Langbourn, Limestreet, Cornhill and Bishopsgate, in the north-east part of the city, attracted a number of wealthy Italian merchants and workers in a variety of trades. The Byzantine ('Greek') goldwiredrawer was symptomatic of London's luxury market.[13] No crudely optimistic picture can be drawn of harmonious coexistence in the towns of medieval England. Perceived differences, often latent but

W. Kellaway (eds), *Studies in London History presented to P. E. Jones*, London, 1969, pp. 251–72; J. L. Bolton (ed.), *The Alien Communities of London in the Fifteenth Century. The Subsidy Rolls of 1440 and 1483–4*, Stamford, 1998.

12 M. Carlin, *Medieval Southwark*, London, 1996, pp. 149–67.

13 J. Harris, 'Two Byzantine craftsmen in fifteenth century London', *Journal of Medieval History*, XXI, 1995, pp. 387–403.

suppressed, had the potential to find voice in persecution when industrial competition or labour shortage applied the spur [**56**]. Yet some evidence also exists of intermarriage, of business partnerships and of association in the context of parish or guild.[14] Medieval history offers no simple ideal to hold up to the challenges of the modern city with its multiple diasporic populations, but it does offer relevant experience.

More or less sharp distinctions thus ran through urban society, separating Christian and Jew, native and alien, freeman and 'foreigner' (a non-citizen), layman and cleric, female and male. Certainly, too, there existed a hierarchy of wealth and poverty, which assessments of belongings for tax purposes reveal with stark clarity [**43**], [**44**].[15] The list for King's Lynn shows as near neighbours the merchant with goods valued at almost £250 and the huckster of bread whose few belongings the assessors rated at less than £1. And by definition such records omit altogether those, unquestionably present in significant number, with nothing. Of all the fault-lines which are evident in our sources, it is not easy to identify a single one which had primacy in determining social development. It is hard, not only because the lines of tension were so diverse but because the life-course of an individual might cross – and recross – the boundaries of wealth and status. Most workshop masters had begun their working lives as servants to others – and not a few, given the hazards of trade, subsequently reverted to that state. In so far as the wealth and status of a particular elite became identified with a town's political regime, as the members of the inner group formed the civic council, those – the great majority of the urban population – who were excluded from the franchise and yet compelled to obey the laws and pay the taxes imposed by government had every reason to feel the resentment of the exploited. The political control by the citizen elite over the disempowered majority may be seen as a conflict of classes.[16] At least some participants in civic disturbances during the period did see their interests in these class terms.[17] At the same time, the dominant groups in the towns were not homogeneous: they tended to include craftsmen alongside the general traders designated

14 See Section VIII.

15 For comparison with the evidence of archaeology, see R. Gilchrist, *Medieval Life: Archaeology and the Life Course*, Woodbridge, 2012.

16 R. H. Hilton, 'Status and class in the medieval town', in T. R. Slater and G. Rosser (eds), *The Church in the Medieval Town*, Aldershot, 1998, pp. 9–19; Hilton, *English and French Towns in Feudal Society*, Cambridge, 1992.

17 See Section VII.

as 'merchants', and their particular profile changed with time. What united all townspeople was the common challenge of how, in a constantly shifting social environment, one could establish the personal reputation which was the vital basis of trust, and in turn of all life in the city. Whether relatively rich or poor, every townsman and woman was in need of the trust which depended upon a good reputation. If damaged, it had to be defended at all costs [**45**].

Late medieval observers often declared that they were looking at significant social change in the form of inferior artisans and their wives who affected the manners and dress of their betters. Both the reality and the observation are perennial; but the demographic impact of the Black Death certainly enabled some craftsmen, benefiting from lower rents and higher wages, to sport clothes and household goods which annoyed conservative critics. Chaucer's attitude, as expressed in his lines on the fictional guildsmen on the road to Canterbury, captures something of this hostile satire, yet perhaps reserves judgement [**46**]. After all, the son of a vintner seeking aristocratic patronage for his writing may not have set himself wholly against social change. The poet's account in the same work of a rich merchant, however, raises sharper moral questions about the damage the love of money can do to human relationships [**47**]. In her autobiographical writing, Margery Kempe gives an account, inflected by the morality of her devotional models, of the insidious attractions of material gain motivated by the desire to acquire yet more splendid dresses [**48**]. Although cast in the penitential tone which was expected of a pious woman, Margery's book, in its explicit reflection on social aspirations in the town, sheds light on a prominent contemporary debate.[18] It was only too clear, both to those with resources and to those without, that this was a society in which status was determined, above all other distinctions, by wealth. The poor London Lickpenny has the last word: 'For want of money I might not speed' [**50**].

18 S. Rees Jones, '"A peler of Holy Cherch": Margery Kempe and the bishops', in J. Wogan-Browne (ed.), *Medieval Women. Texts and Contexts in Late Medieval Britain*, Turnhout, 2000, pp. 377–91; A. Goodman, *Margery Kempe and Her World*, London, 2002; J. Arnold and K. Lewis (eds), *A Companion to the Book of Margery Kempe*, Cambridge, 2004.

37. A fourteenth-century merchant depicted on his tomb

As much as a painted portrait in later times, an image made for a tomb in a fourteenth-century city church was an artificial creation: an idealised celebration of the deceased. For those with the means to pay for such an enduring representation, this was an opportunity to show the ideals which had guided the subject in life. Richard Lyons, buried in the church of St James Garlickhithe in London, came from obscure, possibly Flemish and probably socially humble, origins. He began trading in London in the 1340s, rising later to prominence with a share in a monopoly of the sweet wine trade. He eventually arrived at civic office, as an alderman and sheriff, and he held in addition a number of royal appointments, concerning which he was convicted of corruption. His unpopularity probably explains his murder by the rebels in Cheapside during the Peasants' Revolt on 14 June 1381.[19] Stow's record was made at the end of the sixteenth century.

John Stow, *A Survey of London*, ed. C. L. Kingsford, 2 vols, Oxford: Clarendon Press, 1908, i, p. 249. English, revised by GR.

Richard Lions … a famous merchant of wines … sometime one of the sheriffs, beheaded in Cheap by Wat Tiler, and other rebels, in the year 1381; his picture on his gravestone very fair and large, is with his hair rounded by his ears, and curled, a little beard forked, a gown girt to him down to his feet, of branched damask wrought with the likeness of flowers, a large purse on his right side, hanging in a belt from his left shoulder, a plain hood about his neck, covering his shoulders, and hanging back behind him.

38. Two beggars die in London 1253

What is unusual about the deaths of these obscure paupers is that they happen to be recorded. Such occurrences must have been extremely common. As is revealed in (a), the neighbours of the ward were supposed to know and to take responsibility for a beggar in the vicinity. These two cases were recorded during a periodic inquest by the sheriff of London, to whom were reported issues unresolved at the local level of the wards.

19 R. L. Axworthy, 'Richard Lyons (d. 1381)', *Oxford Dictionary of National Biography*, Oxford, 2004.

M. Weinbaum (ed.), *The London Eyre of 1276*, London Record Society, XII, 1976, pp. 8 (a), 9 (b). Latin, transl. by the editor.

(a) On the feast day of St Urban [25 May] an unknown beggar was found dead, apparently from hunger, in the ward of John de Blakethorn (Aldersgate Ward) outside Aldersgate. Nicholas de Herlauwe and Roger de Celario, neighbours, do not come and are not suspected … No one else is suspected. Judgment: misadventure … Because the mayor and aldermen testify that the beggar was living among them in the ward, and the men of the ward made no mention of his name at the inquest held before the chamberlain and they do not even yet know what he is called, the ward is judged at fault.

(b) Robert Bord, a beggar suffering from the falling sickness, suddenly fell down dead in the ward of John Horn (Bridge Ward). No one is suspected. Judgment: misadventure.

39. Child-stealing to aid a beggar 1373

The poor woman and outsider – Alice de Salesbury had probably come to London from Salisbury in Wiltshire – who was driven to stealing a child in order to elicit charity earned her place in the record as her crime was referred to the mayor's court.

H. T. Riley (ed.), *Memorials of London and London Life in the XIIIth, XIVth, and XVth Centuries*, London, 1868, p. 368. Latin, transl. by the editor.

[21 March 1373] Alice de Salesbury, a beggar, was condemned to the pillory called the thewe* ordained for women, by award of the mayor and aldermen, there to stand for one hour in the day, because on the previous Sunday, she had taken Margaret, daughter of John Oxwyke, grocer, in the Ropery in London, and had carried her away, and stripped her of her clothes, so that she might not be recognised by her family, and so that she might go begging with the same Alice, and gain might be made thereby. As to which, Alice was convicted before the mayor and aldermen.

40. The life of the student

The passage comes from an English thirteenth-century set of model letters. It was usual practice in the Middle Ages, when writing a letter, to make use of standard forms, which were taught from generic letter collections. These included compilations prepared for students, from one of which the following is a sample. The expression is consequently conventional, but the detail is true to life.

C. H. Haskins, 'Letters of medieval students', in his *Studies in Mediaeval Culture*, Oxford: Clarendon Press, 1929, p. 10. Latin, transl. by the editor.

B. to his venerable master A., greeting. This is to inform you that I am studying at Oxford with the greatest diligence, but the matter of money stands greatly in the way of my promotion, as it is now two months since I spent the last of what you sent me. The city is expensive and makes many demands; I have to rent lodgings, buy necessaries, and provide for many other things which I cannot now specify. Wherefore I respectfully beg your paternity that by the promptings of divine pity you may assist me, so that I may be able to complete what I have well begun. For you must know that without Ceres and Bacchus Apollo grows cold.

41. The Jewish communities and the crown

Introduced after the Norman Conquest, the Jewish population in England was concentrated in the towns until its expulsion from the kingdom in 1290. Of particular utility to the crown as a source of financial loans, the local Jewish communities were protected by royal decree until their role could be supplied by others, notably the Italian merchant-bankers whose presence in London and certain provincial towns became evident from around 1300. The ambiguities of Christian monarchy are apparent in this royal writ which, because of the fastidiousness of the queen mother, removed the Jews from her towns to others.

J. M. Rigg (ed.), *Select Pleas, Starrs, and Other Records from the Rolls of the Exchequer of the Jews: A.D. 1220–1284*, Selden Society, XV, London: Quaritch, 1902, p. 85. Latin, transl. by the editor.

By writ of the lord the king [Edward I] directed to the justices: Whereas by our letters patent we have granted to our dearest mother, Eleanor, Queen of England, that no Jew shall dwell or stay in any towns which she holds in dower by assignment of the lord King Henry [III], our father, and of our self, within our realm, so long as the same towns be in her hand; and for this cause we have provided that the Jews of Marlborough be transferred to our town of Devizes, the Jews of Gloucester to our town of Bristol, the Jews of Worcester to our town of Hereford, and the Jews of Cambridge to our city of Norwich, with their chirograph* chests, and with all their goods, and that from now on they live in these towns among the rest of our Jews. Witness myself at Clarendon on 16 January 1275. The sheriffs of these counties and the constables are ordered to cause those Jews to be transferred to the places named.

42. The Jews of Oxford

The first of these texts records an inscription on a stone cross, erected in 1269 in Oxford, in the square of St John's church near Merton College. This was one of two crosses which the Jews of Oxford were compelled to pay for, following an incident in which an unknown Jew allegedly damaged a crucifix during a procession through the city. The second, an inquisition into the property held by Jews in the city in 1290, was one of the concluding acts of the tragic process by which the Jews were expelled from England in that year. They had ceased to be vital to royal finance, and were increasingly a religious embarrassment in the context of ecclesiastical criticism. The list reflects a great reduction in the size and importance of the community compared to earlier generations.[20] It gives, however, some indication of the substantial extent to which the Jewish community had been embedded in Oxford, principally in St Aldate's parish immediately to the south of Carfax, the market cross at the centre of the city.

H. Anstey (ed.), *Munimenta Academica*, 2 vols, Rolls Series, London: Longmans, Green, Reader and Dyer, 1868, i, p. 37 (a); H. E. Salter (ed.), *Cartulary of the Hospital of St. John the Baptist*, ii, Oxford Historical Society, LXVIII, Oxford: Clarendon Press, 1915, pp. 152–4 (b). Latin, transl. by the editors.

20 See also C. Roth, *The Jews of Medieval Oxford*, Oxford Historical Society, new series, 9, 1951, pp. 151–4.

(a) Who was my author? The Jews. How? By tax.
Who ordered me? The king. Who procured me? The masters.
Why? For a broken wooden cross. When? In the feast
Of the Lord's Ascension. Where did this happen? Here where I stand.

(b) Inquisition made at Oxford before Peter de Leycester and William de Greynville sheriff of Oxford on Wednesday the morrow of St Peter ad Vincula [2 August] 1290 on the oath of Henry Owayn, Andrew de Pyrie, Robert de Wermenhale, John Wyth, John de Arderne, Ralph de Stoke, Nicholas de Overtone and Thomas de Durham, Christians, and Vives le Chapeleyn, Bonef' de Crickelade, Moses de Stanford and Jacob de Wycombe, Jews, sworn to enquire about the houses and rents of the Jews of Oxford, what they are and what they are worth in all outgoings, apart from service to the lords of the fee and apart from the cost of maintenance of the houses; who, sworn, say on their oath that Bonefey son of Lumbard of Cricklade the Jew holds a messuage with a shop adjacent in the parish of St Martin, paying nothing for it, and it is worth 26*s* 8*d* per annum; Flora the widow holds a messuage in the parish of St Aldate (of the brothers of St Bartholemew's Hospital outside Oxford) of Thomas de Henxey, and she pays 18*d* to the brothers and 12*d* to Thomas, so it is worth 13*s* 6*d* clear per annum; Sarah the widow of Benedict le Eveske holds one messuage with four shops in the parish of St Aldate of the king and she pays to the crown 10*s* which are assigned to the converted Jews of London, and so it is worth 43*s* 4*d* clear per annum; Samuel de Berchamstede holds a messuage in the parish of St Aldate of the king, paying 4¼*d* landgable* yearly towards the farm of the town of Oxford, so that it is worth 9*s* 7¾*d* clear per annum; Pya, the widow of Benedict de Caus holds a messuage in the parish of St Aldate of the king, paying 4¼*d* landgable so that it is worth 9*s* 7¾*d* clear per annum; Avegaye, daughter of Benedict de Wynton holds in the parish of St Aldate two messuages of the abbot of Abingdon, paying 12*d* to the said abbot, so they are worth 25*s* 8*d* clear per annum; Benedict de le Corner holds a messuage with a cellar in the parish of St Aldate from the heirs of Walter Fateplace, paying them 3*s* 4*d*, so it is worth 20*s* 8*d* clear per annum; Moses son of Jacob de London holds a messuage in the parish of St Aldate of John le Orfevere, paying him 15*d*, so it is worth 13*s* 9*d* clear per annum; the whole community of the

Jews of Oxford holds a house in the town called their schools, for which they pay John le Orfevere 15*d*, so they are worth 18*s* 9*d* clear per annum; Margalicia the widow of Uines de Glovernia holds a messuage with a shop of John le Orfevere in the parish of St Aldate, paying him 15*d*, so it is worth 25*s* 5*d* clear per annum.

43. Moveable goods of inhabitants of King's Lynn *c.*1285–90

The material culture of the medieval urban household is partially recorded in inventories. The most common occasion for the preparation of a list of material goods was the death of a person who left no will. Such inventories are not very common at this period, but, where they survive, they give a vivid impression of the furnishings in the houses of townspeople of diverse social status. For two inventories of London shops, see [**29**]. These inventories of an innkeeper, a merchant and a retailer of bread at King's Lynn were made as the basis for a royal tax of a fifteenth of the worth of goods. The barley owned by the innkeeper's wife will have been used by her for brewing ale.

D. M. Owen (ed.), *The Making of King's Lynn*, Records of Economic and Social History, new series, IX, Oxford: Oxford University Press for the British Academy, 1984, pp. 242 (a), 247–8 (b), (c). Latin, transl. by the editor. Reproduced by permission of the British Academy.

(a) Thomas de Holbeach, taverner

Coin 70*s*; silver £10; 17 silver cups £17 10*s* 4*d*; 1 bowl of maplewood 6*s* 8*d*; 12 silver spoons 11*s* 8*d*; 102 lbs of brass dishes; trivets, fire-dogs, etc. 4*s*; 2 carcases and 4 legs of beef in the larder 17*s* 9*d*; 5 barrels and 1 pipe of wine £40; 2 table-cloths, 6 towels, and 8 canvas cloths 4*s*; 11 blankets 18*s*; 12 sheets 10*s*; 3 feather quilts 10*s*; a cupboard 13*s* 4*d*; an oven etc. 3*s*; 2 lamps 3*s*; 1 woman's cap 7*s*; fire-wood and turves 20*s*; 4 chests 8*s*; 1 hand-mill 18*d*; wooden dishes, cutlery, etc. 16*s* 4*d*; his wife's goods: 34 quarters of barley 8½ marks; 28 quarters of barley £6 6*s*; he has 110*s* belonging to the guild of St Mary. Total £58 8*s* 5*d*; 15th 77*s* 10¾*d*.

(b) Philip de Bek

Money owed to him £6 6*s* 8*d*; 1 bowl of maplewood 15*s* 8*d*; 1 silver bowl 52*s* 8*d*; 1 ship called a cog with all its gear £40; the fourth part of a ship called a cog with its gear £10; 1 ship called a hulk £13 6*s* 8*d*; 2 lasts of herrings £6; silver spoons 12*s* 5*d*; 2 lasts of less good herrings 52*s*; dried fish 10*s*; brass dishes 13*s* 6*d*; 104 quarters of wheat £28 12*s*; 24 quarters of barley 66*s* 8*d*; 40 quarters of malt; 3 cows 13*s* 9*d*; 6 pigs 10*s*; 2 pigs 6*s*; 1 horse 30*s*; 1 saddle 2*s*; goods and mercery in the said ships £43; 2 quarters of Bay salt 4*s* 8*d*; 2 barrels of tar 4*s* 6*d*; 1 bag of tallow; 20 boards 20*s*; provisions in the larder 13*s* 4*d*; 3 barrels and 1 pipe of wine £8 3*s* 4*d*; 3 hand-mills 2*s* 8*d*; 1 robe 26*s* 8*d*; lead 16*s* 6*d*; wooden dishes 21*s*; trivets, fire-dogs, etc. 12s; 8 blankets and 1 cushion 41s; 15 sheets 12s; 4 table-cloths and 8 towels 18*s* 2*d*; 2 woman's robes 47*s*; 4 chests 13*s*; 50 lbs of [wax] candles 5*s* 2½*d*; 1 lamp 2*s*; armour 10*s*; tables, chairs, benches and stools 2*s* 8½*d*; half a dozen gloves 4½*d*. Total £246 8*s* 1½*d*; 15th £16 8*s* 6½*d*.

(c) Agnes de Swaffham staying in the house of Edmund Taverner 1 robe 8*s*; 1 table-cloth and 1 towel 12*d*; 1 chest 18*d*; baked bread and other things pertaining to regraters* 7*s*. Total 17*s* 6*d*; 15th 14*d*.

44. Tax assessment at Shrewsbury 1316

This document, like the extracts in [**43**], is an assessment for a tax on goods. In Shrewsbury as elsewhere, such appraisals were carried out by appointed fellow citizens and neighbours of those assessed. In this case the crown had imposed a tax of one-fifteenth of the value of the goods of everyone living in towns. The detail of the record enables the historian to gain an impression of the character of the local economy (the butchering and leather trades are prominent) and of the wide diversity of material resources and social status amongst the townspeople.

D. Cromarty and R. Cromarty (eds), *The Wealth of Shrewsbury in the Early Fourteenth Century: Six Local Subsidy Rolls 1297 to 1322*, Shropshire Archaeological and Historical Society, 1993, pp. 118–22. Latin, transl. by the editors.

[Illegible; probably Adam le Dier:] woad* 8*s*; lead vat 5*s*; vessels and household utensils 2*s* 6*d*. Sum 15*s* 6*d*; 15th 1*s* 0½*d*.
William Whelwruyghte: 1 affer* 7*s* 6*d*; 1 cart 3*s*; timber 2*s* 6*d*; 1 piglet [. . .]; household utensils 12*d*. Sum 15*s*; 15th 12*d*.

[… probably Richard] le Hopere: in goods 15*s*. Sum 15*s*; 15th 12*d*.
Juliana, widow of William le Potter:* brass/brassware 7*s* 6*d*; clay moulds 6*s* 6*d*; malt 8*s* … household utensils 16*d*. Sum 30*s*; 15th 2*s*.
[… probably John] le Barbur: 1 horse 20*s*; malt 1 mark; clothes 10*s*; […]; brassware 10*s*; jewelry […]; firewood 30*s*; household utensils 6*s*. Sum 100*s*; 15th 6*s* 8*d*.
Hugh, son of Robert le Dunfowe: 1 horse 20*s*; 2 cows 13*s* 4*d*; in money 20*s*; malt 20*s*; […] 20*s*; meat 10*s* 8*d*; 6 silver spoons 6*s* 8*d*; […] *s* 4*d*; household utensils 16*s* 8*d*. Sum £7 10*s*; 15th 10*s*.
[… probably Andrew] le Barbur: malt 30*s*; […] 10*s*; firewood 20*s*; clothes 10*s*; brassware 6*s* 8*d*; household utensils 3*s* 4*d*. Sum £4; 15th 5*s* 4*d*.
[… probably Richard] de Hulton, merchant: in merchandise £15; 15th 20*s*.
[… probably Thomas He]rdmon: in goods 15*s*. Sum 15*s*; 15th 12*d*.
Thomas Lawe: tanned hides 30*s*; tanning bark 20*s*; shoes and thigh boots 16*s* 8*d*; meat 10*s*; household utensils 3*s* 4*d*. Sum £4; 15th 5*s* 4*d*.
Ellen, widow of Richard Sullelont: in goods 15*s*. Sum 15*s*; 15th 12*d*.
John de Lake, dyer: woad, lead vats and brassware 15*s*. Sum 15*s*; 15th 12*d*.
Richard de Upton, smith: iron, coal/charcoal and household utensils 45*s*. Sum 45*s*; 15th 3*s*.
Hugh de Wygan, apothecary: 1 horse 20*s*; spices, ointments and a brass mortar 60*s*. Sum £4; 15th 5*s* 4*d*.
Nicholas le Spicer: goods to the value 30*s*. Sum 30*s*; 15th 2*s*.
William Godyer: 2 horses 20*s*; malt of wheat and oats 40*s*; firewood 13*s* 4*d*; household utensils 6*s* 8*d*. Sum £4; 15th 5*s* 4*d*.
William de Sutton: goods to the value 40*s*. Sum 40*s*; 15th 2*s* 8*d*.
Thomas le Dissher: 1 affer* 10*s*; dishes, platters, cups and wood 27*s* 6*d*. Sum 37*s* 6*d*; 15th 2*s* 6*d*.
Cecily, widow of Richard de Besford: 3 affers and 1 cart with harness 20*s*; malt of wheat and oats 20*s*; firewood 6*s* 8*d*; clothes 10*s*; household utensils 3*s* 4*d*. Sum 60*s*; 15th 4*s*.
John de Westbury: cloth £4. Sum £4; 15th 5*s* 4*d*.
William de Wilderdehope: ox and pig meat 100*s*. Sum 100*s*; 15th 6*s* 8*d*.
John Russel: 2 affers 10*s*; 1 cart with harness 4*s*; hay and fodder 6*s*. Sum 20*s*; 15th 16*d*.
Richard le Taillor: cloth 20*s*. Sum 20*s*; 15th 16*d*.
William de Sutton: in goods to the value 15*s*. Sum 15*s*; 15th 12*d*.
William Lace: in goods 20*s*. Sum 20*s*; 15th 16*d*.

Roger le Monck: 1 horse 13*s* 4*d*; 1 cow 8*s*; meat 3*s* 8*d*; brassware 3*s*; household utensils 2*s*. Sum 30*s*; 15th 2*s*.
Ralph le Dene: in goods 20*s*. Sum 20*s*; 15th 16*d*.
Nicholas de Grymesby: dried fish and herring 15*s*. Sum 15*s*; 15th 12*d*.
John de Burleton: 2 affers 20*s*; 1 cart with harness 6*s*; meat 8*s*; 1 heifer 20*d*; brassware 16*s*; firewood 6*s*; household utensils 2*s* 4*d*. Sum 60*s*; 15th 4*s*.
Ralph de Cobbeleye: 1 horse 20*s*; malt of wheat and oats 24*s*; meat 13*s* 4*d*; firewood 10*s*; clothes 9*s*; brassware 3*s*; household utensils 8*d*. Sum £4; 15th 5*s* 4*d*.
William de Wrocwardyn: in merchandise to the value 26*s* 8*d*. Sum 26*s* 8*d*; 15th 21½ *d*.
Richard Madyn: in goods 20*s*; 15th 16*d*.
Philip Molendarius: 1 horse 10*s*; 6 bushels* wheat 12*s*; 2 bushels rye 3*s*; 2 pigs 3*s* 4*d*; household utensils 20*d*. Sum 30*s*; 15th 2*s*.
Richard de Cantelop: in merchandise and his goods to the value 30*s*. Sum 30*s*; 15th 2*s*.
Henry de Sutton: 1 horse 10*s*; 6 bushels wheat 12*s*; 2 bushels rye 3*s*; 2 pigs 3*s* 4*d*; household utensils 20*s*. Sum 30*s*; 15th 2*s*.
Richard de Foryate: in goods 20*s*. Sum 20*s*; 15th 16*d*.
William, son of Richard le Parmenter: in money £10; cloth/clothes £10; jewellery £10; household utensils £7 10*s*. Sum £37 10*s*; 15th 50*s*.
Roger de Muridon: in goods to the value 40*s*. Sum 40*s*; 15th 2*s* 8*d*.
William le Barbur: in goods to the value 60*s*. Sum 60*s*; 15th 4*s*.
Henry, son of William Charite: 1 horse 20*s*; ox meat 20*s*; firewood 10*s*; brassware 6*s*; household utensils 4*s*. Sum 60*s*; 15th 4*s*.
Thomas Vaghan: in money £20; cloth/clothes £20; meat 100*s*; jewellery £12; firewood 60*s*; 2 horses £7; brassware 60*s*; household utensils 100*s*. Sum £75 0*s* 7*d*; 15th 100*s* ½*d*.
Ralph de London: shoes and thighboots 20*s*; tanning bark 20*s*; tanned hides 20*s*; wood and lead vats 13*s* 4*d*; tan-liquor 6*s* 8*d*. Sum £4; 15th 5*s* 4*d*.
Richard Beget: 1 horse 26*s* 8*d*; 3 oxen 48*s*; 20 pigs 40*s*; ox and pig meat 60*s*; firewood 20*s*; brassware and household utensils 5*s* 4*d*. Sum £10; 15th 13*s* 4*d*.
William le Cheser: in goods 15*s*; 15th 12*d*.
Nicholas le Deyer: 1 horse 20*s*; woad 30*s*; vats 6*s*; firewood 3*s*; household utensils 12*d*. Sum 60*s*; 15th 4*s*.
Thomas Hildebront: 2 oxen 20*s*; ox and pig meat 22*s*; clothes 12*s*; brassware 13*s* 4*d*; firewood 10*s*; household utensils 2*s* 8*d*. Sum £4; 15th 5*s* 4*d*.

Roger Hotales: 1 horse 20*s*; 6 bushels wheat 12*s*; 1 quarter rye 12*s*; 1 heifer 4*s*; clothes 10*s*; household utensils 2*s*. Sum 60*s*; 15th 4*s*.
Edith, widow of Alan Atteyate: malt 10*s*; 3 pigs 6*s*; clothes 5*s*; brassware 2*s*; meat 2*s* 6*d*; firewood 2*s*; household utensils 2*s* 6*d*. Sum 30*s*; 15th 2*s*.
Robert de Whitemor: tanned hides, vats and tan-liquor 52*s*. Sum 52*s*; 15th 3*s* 6*d*.
Richard de Wenlok: in merchandise 25*s*. Sum 25*s*; 15th 20*d*.
Thomas Lumbard: 1 horse 10*s*; cloth 13*s*; brassware 6*s*; firewood 12*s*; meat 4*s*; household utensils 20*d*. Sum 46*s* 8*d*; 15th 3*s* 1¾*d*.
Cecily, widow of Roger le Longe: 2 pigs 13*s* 4*d*; malt 20*s*; clothes 8*s*; brassware 6*s* 8*d*; household utensils 2*s*. Sum 50*s*; 15th 3*s* 4*d*.
Prior of the Hospital of St John, Shrewsbury: 3 affers 9*s*; 1 cart with harness 4*s*; 4 bushels wheat 8*s*; 4 bushels rye 6*s*; hay and fodder 3*s*. Sum 30*s*; 15th 2*s*.
Reginald de Calverhale: in goods 15*s*. Sum 15*s*; 15th 12*d*.
Roger Michel: wool-fells,* salted hides, honey and wax £4. Sum £4; 15th 5*s* 4*d*.
Lucy, widow of William de Nesse: 2 affers 10*s*; 1 cart with harness 6*s* 8*d*; clothes 8*s*; household utensils 5*s* 4*d*. Sum 30*s*; 15th 2*s*.
Alice, widow of Richard le Vileyn: malt 10*s*; 2 pigs 6*s* 8*d*; clothes 8*s*; firewood 3*s*; household utensils 2*s* 4*d*. Sum 30*s*; 15th 2*s*.
Simon Colle: in merchandise 50*s*. Sum 50*s*; 15th 3*s* 4*d*.
Alice, widow of John de Chestre: in goods 60*s*. Sum 60*s*; 15th 4*s*.
Edward le Mustarder: iron and steel, tallow, nails and candles of Paris 15*s*. Sum 15*s*; 15th 12*d*.
Hugh Lewe: 1 horse 10*s*; iron and steel 16*s*; tallow 6*s*; nails 3*s* 4*d*; candles of Paris 2*s* 7*d*; household utensils 2*s*. Sum 40*s* [39*s* 11*d*]; 15th 2*s* 8*d*.
Thomas Colle: 1 horse 20*s*; clothes 20*s*; meat 20*s*; jewellery 13*s* 4*d*; firewood 7*s*; brassware 6*s* 8*d*; household utensils 13*s*. Sum 100*s*; 15th 6*s* 8*d*.
John de Oswaldestre, tanner: tanned hides, tanning bark and vats 20*s*. Sum 20*s*. 15th 16*d*.
Walter Geffrey: in money 100*s*; 1 horse 40*s*; meat 30*s*; jewellery 30*s*; clothes 53*s* 4*d*; firewood 26*s* 8*d*; vessels and household utensils 20*s*. Sum £15; 15th 20*s*.
Parnel, widow of William Balle: tanned hides, tanning bark, vats and tan liquor 40*s*. Sum 40*s*; 15th 2*s* 8*d*.
Robert de Wych, shoemaker: shoes, tanned hides, tanning bark, vats and tan-liquor 45*s*. Sum 45*s*; 15th 3*s*.
Adam Gilemin, shoemaker: tanned hides 20*s*; shoes and thighboots 13*s*

4*d*; tanning bark 6*s* 8*d*; wood and lead vats 13*s* 4*d*; household utensils 6*s* 8*d*. Sum 60*s*; 15th 4*s*.

John le Sadeler: saddles, bridles and stirrups 100*s*. Sum 100*s*; 15th 6*s* 8*d*.

Roger Moldesonne, butcher: ox and pig meat 45s. Sum 45*s*; 15th 3*s*.

Roger Atteyate: wool-fells,* lamb, goat and rabbit skins 45*s*. Sum 45*s*; 15th 3*s*.

Walter de le Clyve, tanner: tan-liquor, tanning bark, vats and hides in the tannery £6. Sum £6; 15th 8*s*.

Adam de Stretton, butcher: ox and pig meat £4. Sum £4; 15th 5*s* 4d.

Robert de Prees, tanner: tanned hides, tanning bark and vats 100*s*. Sum 100*s*; 15th 6*s* 8*d*.

William de Wilverstone: shoes and thighboots 16*s* 3d. Sum 16*s* 3*d*; 15th 13*d*.

Alan de Worcester: tanned hides, tanning bark, shoes, tan-liquor and vats £4. Sum £4; 15th 5*s* 4*d*.

William de Hulton, tanner: leather in the tannery, and vats 20*s*. Sum 20*s*; 15th 16*d*.

Thomas Willesone: in goods to the value 15*s*. Sum 15*s*; 15th 12*d*.

Richard de Wemme: in goods 37*s* 6*d*. Sum 37*s* 6*d*; 15th 2*s* 6*d*.

Agnes, widow of John le Blak, butcher: ox and pig meat 40*s*; household utensils 10*s*. Sum 50*s*; 15th 3*s* 4*d*.

Roger de Wythiford: in merchandise 100*s*. Sum 100*s*; 15th 6*s* 8*d*.

Richard de Shoplatch: shoes, thighboots and tanned hides 22*s* 6*d*. Sum 22*s* 6*d*; 15th 18*d*.

Adam de Routon: in the tannery 31*s* 3*d*. Sum 31*s* 3*d*; 15th 2*s* 1*d*.

Alan Dawe: in goods to the value 20*s*. Sum 20*s*; 15th 16*d*.

Isabel Borrey: cloth/clothes 40*s*; 2 mazer* cups 10*s*; 2 silver cups 13*s* 4*d*; 10 spoons 10*s*; jewellery 13*s* 4*d*; household utensils 13*s* 4*d*. Sum 100*s*; 15th 6*s* 8*d*.

Adinet Cissor [i.e. tailor]: goods to the value 10*s*. Sum 10*s*; 15th 8*d*.

Henry Crok: saddles and bridles 10*s*. Sum 10*s*; 15th 8*d*.

Richard Bercar [shepherd] de Edeneston: 8 sheep 8*s*; skins 7*s*. Sum 15*s*; 15th 12*d*.

Edith la White: 1 cow 6*s* 8*d*; 6 pigs 6*s*; 1 calf 2*s* 4*d*; household utensils 20*d*. Sum 20*s* [16*s* 8*d*]; 15th 16*d*.

Richard Bernard: goods to the value £5. Sum 100*s*; 15th 6*s* 8*d*.

Nicholas in le Dich: 7*s* 6*d* in goods. Sum 7*s* 6*d*; 15th 6*d*.

Richard de Hadenhale: 15*s* in goods. Sum 15*s*; 15th 12*d*.

William le Trumpour: 3 affers 20*s*; 1 cart with harness 9*s*; 1 cow and calf 6*s* 8*d*; 4 bushels wheat 8*s*; 6 bus rye 9*s*; firewood 4*s*; brassware 2*s* 4*d*; household utensils 2*s*. Sum 50*s* [51*s*]; 15th 3*s* 4*d*.

Richard le Gaunter: in goods to the value 15*s*. Sum 15*s*; 15th 12*d*.
John le Tipper: gloves 11*s*; wool-fells and horse hides 20*s*; 1½ quarters of wheat 24*s*; 1 quarter rye 12*s*; malt 13*s*; brassware 6*s* 8*d*; firewood 6*s* 8*d*; household utensils 6*s* 8*d*. Sum 100*s*; 15th 6*s* 8*d*.
John le Fissher: in goods 10*s*. Sum 10*s*; 15th 8*d*.
Matilda, widow of William le Frensche: 1 affer 10*s*; malt 13*s* 4*d*; 1 heifer 40*d*; 1 pan 12*d*; household utensils 2*s* 4*d*. Sum 30*s*; 15th 2*s*.
Roger le Mareschal: iron, horse shoes and coal/charcoal 15*s*. Sum 15*s*; 15th 12*d*.
Roger, son of Roger atte Shupene: 1 cow 6*s* 8*d*; 2 bullocks 6*s* 8*d*; 10 sheep 10*s*; hay and fodder 6*s* 8*d*. Sum 30*s*; 15th 2*s*.
Alan le Glovere: wool-fells 10*s*; gloves 6*s*; malt 8*s*; firewood 10*s*; clothes 7*s*; meat 6*s*; brassware 4*s*; jewellery 8*s*; household utensils 15*d*. Sum 60*s* 3*d*; 15th 4*s* 0¼*d*.
Ralph de Ellesmere: in goods to the value 15*s*. Sum 15*s*; 15th 12*d*.
Roger atte Shupene: 40 sheep 40*s*; wool-fells 13*s* 4*d*; hay and fodder 6*s* 8*d*. Sum 60*s*; 15th 4*s*.
Richard Mile: 4 sheep 4*s*; 4 pigs 3*s*; firewood 3*s*; timber 7*s*; household utensils 6*d*. Sum 17*s* 6*d*; 15th 14*d*.
William le Colier: shoes 9*s*; tanned hides 7*s*; tanning bark and vat 4*s*. Sum 20*s*; 15th 16*d*.
Adam le Mareschal: iron and coal/charcoal 8s 4*d*; 1 cow 6*s* 8*d*; 1 sow with piglets 4*s* 4*d*; 2 bushels wheat 4*s*; horse shoes and nails 6*s* 8*d*. Sum 30*s*; 15th 2*s*.
William le Pety, skinner: goat, hare and fox skins 25*s*; lamb and rabbit furs 25*s*. Sum 50*s*; 15th 40*d*.
Philip de Benethale: in merchandise 60*s*. Sum 60*s*; 15th 4*s*.
John Bayeson: cloth 30*s* 4*d*. Sum 30*s* 4*d*; 15th 2*s* 0¼*d*.
William de Mudle [Myddle]: iron, coal/charcoal and horse shoes 10*s*. Sum 10*s*; 15th 8*d*.
Henry de Prestecote: malt 32*s*; firewood 26*s*; meat 5*s*; brassware 8*s*; household utensils 4*s*. Sum 75*s*; 15th 5*s*.
Anota de Kent: in goods to the value 10*s*. Sum 10*s*; 15th 8*d*.
John le Wayte, baker: 1 affer 8*s*; 6 bushels wheat 12*s*; household utensils 2*s* 6*d*. Sum 22*s* 6*d*; 15th 18*d*.
Reginald Gravegos: in goods 10*s*. Sum 10*s*; 15th 8*d*.
Henry de Lidleye: 1 horse 13*s* 4*d*; malt of wheat and oats 20*s*; 1 quarter wheat 16*s*; firewood 20*s*; meat 6*s* 8*d*; brassware 13*s* 4*d*; household utensils 10*s* 8*d*. Sum 100*s*; 15th 6*s* 8*d*.
Richard de Ellesmere: 1 affer 10*s*; iron and steel, knives and daggers, silk and muslin 20*s*. Sum 30*s*; 15th 2*s*.

Walter Piscator [Fisher]: 1 affer 10*s*; dried fish and herring 40*s*. Sum 50*s*; 15th 40*d*.
Agnes le Roo: in goods 15*s*. Sum 15*s*; 15th 12*d*.
Thomas de Ondeslowe: 1 horse 20*s*; cloth £4. Sum 100*s*; 15th 6*s* 8*d*.
Peter Cox: in goods 20*s*. Sum 20*s*; 15th 16*d*.
Peter Gerard: cloth 60*s*; dried fish 40*s*. Sum 100*s*; 15th 6*s* 8*d*.
Richard de Colnham: 1 horse 20*s*; 1 cow 6*s* 8*d*; meat 13*s* 4*d*; timber 13*s* 4*d*; household utensils 6*s* 8*d*. Sum 60*s*; 15th 4*s*.
John Reyner: in merchandise 45*s*. Sum 45*s*; 15th 3*s*.
Aline le Cok: in goods to the value 15*s*. Sum 15*s*; 15th 12*d*.
Thomas le Frerecokes: in goods to the value 16*s* 6*d*. Sum 16*s* 6*d*; 15th 13*d*.
Adam le Parminter: furs, wool-fells, fox and hare skins 45*s*. Sum 45*s*; 15th 3*s*.
William le Hayward, miller: 2 horses 20*s*; malt 20*s*; hay and fodder 10*s*. Sum 50*s*; 15th 3*s* 4*d*.
Henry Mether, parmenter:* furs 40*s*; goat, fox, hare, lamb and rabbit skins 40*s*. Sum £4; 15th 5*s* 4*d*.
Hugh Andreu: in goods to the value 16*s*. Sum 16*s*; 15th 13*d*.
John Baldewyne: in money £10; clothes £6; 2 horses 40*s*; jewellery 40*s*; vessels and household utensils 50*s*. Sum £22 10*s*; 15th 30*s*.
Alan Clement: in goods 45*s*. Sum 45*s*; 15th 3*s*.
Thomas de la Clyve: in merchandise 100*s*. Sum 100*s*; 15th 6*s* 8*d*.
Richard Stury: in money £10; clothes £6; 2 horses 40*s*; household utensils 50*s*. Sum £22 10*s*; 15th 30*s*.

45. The importance of reputation and trust

In the context of the medieval urban economy, reputation was a vital material resource. Legal cases such as these reveal the importance attached to personal standing in the community, and the perceived loss if this were damaged (b). The extract in (a) exemplifies the strategies sometimes used by local traders to marginalise those coming from outside the town or to limit their ability to compete in the market. The trustworthiness – real or apparent – of local knowledge was a potent resource. A significant strategy for the creation of a trustworthy reputation, which could help to secure economic advantage in addition to moral status, was to join a fraternity [**94**], [**95**].

I. H. Jeayes (ed.), *Court Rolls of the Borough of Colchester 1310–1379*, 3 vols, Colchester, 1921–41, i, p. 84 (a); J. S. Furnivall (ed.), *Town Life in the XIV Century as seen in the court rolls of Winchester City*, Winchester: Warren and Son, n.d., pp. 148–9 (b). Latin, transl. by the editors, revised by GR.

(a) [Colchester 1312] John Proffete was charged by the bailiffs that when a certain stranger came to the Colchester market and exposed for sale herrings at eight-a-penny, the said John reproved him, saying that he should have sold them at four-a-penny, thereby disturbing the market, to the great scandal of the town. And that he has been accustomed to do the same thing with various other merchandise coming to the market. John pleads* not guilty and asks for an enquiry, which is made and finds him guilty, and he is cautioned not to offend in this way again.

(b) [Winchester 1373] William Inge and Margery, his wife, presented themselves against William Coterengham on a plea of trespass ... And he makes plaint hereon that on the first Sunday in Lent 1373 the said William [Coterengham] came to the house of William Inge with force and arms, namely, cudgel and knife, and there assaulted Margery, his wife, calling her false, untrustworthy and unfaithful (*falsam, incredulem et infedelem*), whereby she has lost credit (*pro quod amisit credenciam*), and has inflicted other illegalities on her, finding fault with the red and white herring which are their merchandise, whereby they have lost repute (*per quod deteriorati sunt*) and suffer damage to the amount of one hundred shillings; and on this account they bring suit. And William acknowledged the trespass, on account of which the sentence of the court is that the said William Inge and Margery, his wife, recover the said hundred shillings, and the said William Coterengham is in amercement for trespass, and in default of security for the said moneys he must remain in custody until (he pay or produce security).

46. Social pretensions of the late fourteenth-century townsman and woman

The *Canterbury Tales* do not, of course, provide an objective account of fourteenth-century social types. But, as an inhabitant of London,

Geoffrey Chaucer forged his characters from a commingling of the books he had read and the social world he knew. The poet's characterisation of the Canterbury pilgrims is full of sharply observed and ironic references to the social mores and pretensions of his day. The five London tradesmen introduced in these lines are representative of the 'lesser' crafts of the city, whose commerce and government tended to be dominated by the interests of merchants. Very few artisans were ever elected to be aldermen. In the late fourteenth century, however – at the time of the composition of the *Canterbury Tales* – the social and political upheavals which followed the arrival of the Black Death saw the prevailing order challenged by craftsmen who aped the clothes and manners of their social superiors, and who even, for a short time, forced a widening of the city government to include a broader representation of ordinary townspeople. The five different craftsmen in the tale derive social confidence from their membership of 'a solemn and a great fraternity': one of the many religious brotherhoods maintained in London as in other towns, to which the practitioners of diverse crafts were drawn for a variety of motives, including that of the status afforded to the members of so morally respectable an organisation. The cool tone of Chaucer's nicely observed portrait perhaps indicates his deprecation of these ambitions.[21]

Geoffrey Chaucer, *General Prologue to the Canterbury Tales*, ll. 361–78, in F. N. Robinson (ed.), *The Works of Geoffrey Chaucer*, 2nd edn, London: Oxford University Press, 1957, p. 20. English.

An Haberdasshere and a Carpenter,
A Webbe, a Dyere and a Tapycer, – *weaver; tapestry-maker*
And they were clothed alle in o lyveree *one costume*
Of a solempne and a greet fraternitee.
Ful fresh and newe hir geere apiked was; *clothes; adorned*
Her knyves were chaped noght with bras *mounted*
But al with silver; wroght ful clene and weel
Hire girdles and hir pouches everydeel. *belts; bags; altogether*
Wel semed ech of hem a fair burgeys
To sitten in a yeldehalle on a deys. *guildhall; dais*
Everich, for the wisdom that he kan, *knew*
Was shaply for to been an alderman. *suitable*
For catel hadde they ynogh and rente, *goods; enough*
And eek hir wyves wolde it wel assente; *also; agree*

21 G. Rosser, 'The five guildsmen', in S. Rigby and A. Minnis (eds), *Historians on Chaucer: The 'General Prologue' to the Canterbury Tales*, Oxford, 2014, pp. 247–61.

And elles certeyn were they to blame.
It is ful fair to been ycleped 'madame', *called*
And goon to vigils al before, *services for the dead*
And have a mantel roialliche ybore. *cloak; carried* [i.e. the train]

47. Material values of a fictional merchant *c.*1390

The image of society recorded in the *Canterbury Tales* is refracted through the satire and irony of the poet. Yet the critical perspective of the literary text itself formed part of contemporary social debate, and the historian who reads with care has much to learn from such a source. The artful evocation of the merchant in *The Shipman's Tale* conveys a critical view of his class and values which itself formed part of the cultural context in which real merchants pored over their accounts, worried about their gains and, on occasion, neglected their wives. To the merchant in the tale (who lives at St Denis, which may indicate that Chaucer's literary source was a French *fabliau*), the cost of his abstraction is great. For his wife, desirous of new clothes – she too is caught up in the value-system of the marketplace – exploits his absence on business to secure money, in return for sexual favours, from a lecherous monk, Dom John – who, to complete the circle, raises the cash as a loan from the poor merchant himself. It is a significant detail that the merchant of the tale is anonymous. Read with due sensitivity to its literary art and its moral perspective, such a text as this can reveal something about the contemporary perception and critique of late medieval mercantile and urban values.

Geoffrey Chaucer, *The Shipman's Tale*, ll. 212–38, in F. N. Robinson (ed.), *The Works of Geoffrey Chaucer*, 2nd edn, London: Oxford University Press, 1957, p. 158. English.

Up to hir housbonde is this wyf ygon,
And knokketh at his countour boldely.
'*Quy la?* quod he. 'Peter! It am I,'
Quod she; 'what, sire, how longe wol ye faste?
How longe tyme wol ye rekene and caste
Youre sommes, and youre bookes, and youre thynges?
The devel have part on alle swiche rekenynges!
Ye have ynough, pardee, of Goddes sonde; *by God; gift*
Com doun to-day, and lat youre bagges stonde.
Ne be ye nat ashamed that daun John
Shal fasting al this day alenge goon? *miserable*

What! lat us heere a messe, and go we dyne.' *hear a mass*
'Wyf', quod this man, 'litel kanstow devyne *can you*
The curious bisyness that we have. *full of care*
For of us chapmen, also God me save, *merchants; as God preserve me*
And by that lord that clepid is Seint Yve, *called; St Ive/Ivo*
Scarsly amonges twelve tweye shul thryve *two*
Continuelly, lastynge unto oure age.
We may wel make chiere and good visage, *put a good face on it*
And dryve forth the world as it may be,
And kepen oure estaat in pryvetee,
Til we be deed, or elles that we pleye *take a holiday*
A pilgrimage, or goon out of the weye.
And therefore have I greet necessitee
Upon this queynte world t'avyse me; *elaborate*
For evermoore we moote stond in drede
Of hap and fortune in oure chapmanhede.' *merchandising*

48. Material desire and spiritual values *c.*1400

Margery Kempe (*c.*1373 – *c.*1439) was born to prosperous parents in the town of Bishop's Lynn (now part of King's Lynn) in Norfolk, where her father was five times mayor. She was illiterate, and her words were dictated in the 1430s, many years after the events they describe, to a priest. The time of her life referred to in this passage fell in the 1390s. Thanks both to the internal evidence of the text and to fragmentary external sources, we know something about Margery Kempe, her marriage, her pilgrimages, her particular devotion and her visionary experiences. There is some evidence that, while not all responses to her demonstrative religiosity were positive, she acquired a following in her life and after her death. The single extant manuscript copy of the book was made, a decade or so after the lost original, in or near Norwich, possibly in a religious house. That the book was first made with the help of a cleric should alert the historian: these are not Margery's unmediated words and thoughts. The stories which characterise the book, of her humiliation and mockery by others, and of her public testimony of her spiritual experiences, are suggestive of analogies between her life and that of Christ. However, this is not a text written to claim Margery's status as a saint (nor do we know that anybody attributed miracles to her). Although eccentric in certain ways, the life which is indirectly recorded in this book was formed in response to circumstances which we can recognise as common to Margery's contemporaries: the material possibilities and attractions of life in the city (especially to one born into substantial means); the example of a life lived, by contrast, according to non-material values; and the vision of human life as a pilgrimage, an arduous, periodically frustrated, but spiritually rewarded struggle to move from the first to the second ideal. In these contemporary currents of thought Margery Kempe, notwithstanding social conventions regarding the appropriate behaviour of women, found strength to negotiate the terms on which she lived with her husband, to travel independently and to speak out with remarkable boldness in the presence of ecclesiastical authority.

A. Bale (ed.), *The Book of Margery Kempe*, Oxford: Oxford University Press, 2015, pp. 13–14. English, revised by the editor. Reproduced by permission of Oxford University Press.

So when this creature had thus through grace come back to her right mind she thought she was bound to God and that she would be His servant. Nevertheless, she would not put aside either her pride or her pretentious costumes that she had been used to, neither for her husband nor on any other person's advice. And yet she knew full well that they said a great many insulting things about her, for she wore gold piping on her headdress [a fashionable arrangement using gold wire] and her hoods were dagged with tippets [slashed to allow a different coloured material to show through, and with long, narrow strips of material attached]. Her cloaks were also dagged and lined with many colours between the dags, so that it would be more striking to people's eyes and she herself should be more admired.

But when her husband wanted to speak to her about leaving aside her pride, she answered sharply and shortly, and said that she came from worthy kin – he never seemed a likely man to have married her – for her father had once been mayor of the town of N. and afterwards he was alderman of the high Guild of the Trinity in N.[22] And therefore she would uphold the honour of her kin, whatever anybody said.

She was hugely envious of her neighbours, that they were dressed as stylishly as she. Her every desire was that she should be honoured by the people. She would neither learn her lesson from one chastisement[23] nor be content (as her husband was) with the goods that God had sent

22 'N.' is King's Lynn. The guild of the Trinity was the most prestigious of the town's guilds.

23 After the birth of her child, Margery Kempe had suffered for a period from a severe mental illness.

her but always desired more and more. And then, out of pure covetousness and in order to maintain her pride, she began to brew and was one of the greatest brewers in the town of N. for three or four years until she lost a lot of money, as she did not have experience of doing this.[24] For, although she had ever such good servants and knowledge of brewing, things would not go successfully for them. For, when the ale had as fine a head on it as could be seen, suddenly the head would fall away, and all the ale would be lost one brew after another, so her servants were ashamed and did not wish to stay with her. Then this creature thought of how God had punished her before, and she could not take heed, and now again through the loss of her money; and then she left off and brewed no more.

49. Foreigners in English towns 1440, 1483

Foreigners in late medieval English towns were known as 'aliens'. ('Foreigns', meanwhile, were inhabitants of or visitors to a town who were not enrolled in the local lists of residents and who consequently lacked the rights enjoyed by the registered population.) The introduction by the crown of occasional taxation of aliens generated lists which survive from a number of towns. The records give some indication (if only in the name) of the place of origin and of the economic activity pursued by these migrants. A striking proportion of the substantial community of craftsmen of Flemish origin working in the east-coast town of Lynn were involved in shoemaking. Their mutual interconnections stand out, as they do also in the lists from London. In the metropolis there appears a significantly greater diversity of traders of foreign extraction.

D. M. Owen (ed.), *The Making of King's Lynn*, Oxford: Oxford University Press for the British Academy, 1984, pp. 457–9 (a), reproduced by permission of the British Academy; J. L. Bolton (ed.), *The Alien Communities of London in the Fifteenth Century*, Stamford: Paul Watkins for Richard III and Yorkist History Trust, 1998, pp. 66–70 (b). Latin, transl. by the editors.

24 Brewing was a common occupation for medieval women. See J. Bennett, *Ale, Beer, and Brewsters in England: Women's Work in a Changing World 1300–1600*, Oxford, 1999.

(a) Return of aliens resident in Lynn and its immediate neighbourhood and liable to pay the aliens' subsidy granted to the crown for sea defences in 1440.

Hundred* of Freebridge. Inquest made at Lynn in the county of Norfolk on Tuesday after the feast of St Barnabas the Apostle [11 June], 1440, before Miles Stapleton, sheriff of the same county, in virtue of the king's commission addressed to the sheriff, by the oath of the jurors, who say on their oath that none of the persons listed below were born in England, but that they are householders within the hundred of Freebridge, that is:

William Combe souter* of Bishop's Lynn, Peryn Otelemaker of the same, Deryk Ducheman, tenant of William Waynflete, of the same, John Boteler of Bishop's Lynn, shipman, Richard Peterson of the same, patten*-maker, John Byrste of the same, turner, Ioceus shoemaker, Dutchman, of Bishop's Lynn, John Mundesson of the same, tailor, Margaret Selander of the same, widow, James Ducheman of the same, souter, Herman Chapman, tenant of John Gebon' in Purfleet Street, Thomas Bowen of Bishop's Lynn, cordwainer,* William Brouns of the same, shoemaker, Deryk Claus of the same, shoemaker, Philip Johnson of the same, ferryman, Claus Smyth, tenant of Robert Hamond, chaplain, Peter Ducheman, tenant of Margaret Frank, Nicholas Tailiour, tenant of Richard Cosyn, John Taylour staying at Northend, Nicholas Swete, tenant of John Nicollasson, Isabella Duchewoman staying in Hobhorse Lane, John Sadiller, Dutchman, of Bishop's Lynn, Hugo Tyler staying in Braunche rents, Nicholas Irysshman of Bishop's Lynn, tailor, Ianyn Tyler staying in Northend, John Wryght of Geywode, Henry Houndesburgh of Ayleswythorp, John Clerk of Great Massingham, Nowell Adam of Gayton, William Goldsmyth of South Lynn, William Slynglond of the same, John Webster of Terrington Fen End, John Bernard of Hardwik.

And that none of the persons listed below was born in England, nor are they householders within the hundred of Freebridge, that is:

Richard Slynglond of South Lynn, labourer, John Berebrewer of the same, labourer, Joan, servant of Edward Goldyng of South Lynn, Margaret, servant of William Sweyn of Dersingham, Robert Hoberd, servant of John Waryn of Tilney, Thomas, servant of William Walton of East Walton, John, servant of John Stonham of Tilney, Richard, servant of William Kellowe of Bishop's Lynn, Henry Frese, servant of William Combe of the same, John Byrte, servant of Thomas Spicer of

Bishop's Lynn, Henry patten-maker and Matthew patten-maker, servants of Richard patten-maker of Bishop's Lynn, Gerard Grabo, servant of William Johnson, John Mathew, servant of John Depyng of Bishop's Lynn, James, servant of Robert Pynder of Bishop's Lynn, John, servant of William Wade of Bishop's Lynn, Hugo Man, servant of William Nayler, Richard Pers, servant of James shoemaker, John, servant of William Brons, cobbler, Deryk Symondesson, servant of Deryk Clays at the 'Ape' in Bishop's Lynn, John, servant of Peter Ducheman of Bishop's Lynn, Paul, servant of John Taylour in Northend, Simon, servant of William Mollesworth of Bishop's Lynn, William, servant of John Sadiller in Grassmarket, William, servant of Hugh Tyler of Bishop's Lynn.

(b) Foreign-born residents of London aged over twelve years listed for the alien subsidy in June 1483

Langbourn Ward

...				
Gaunt	Giles van	German	currier*	6*s* 8*d*
[Gaunt]	Elizabeth van	German	wife of Giles van Gaunt	2*s*
...				
Caren	Dederic van	German	currier	6*s* 8*d*
[Caren]	Elizabeth van	German	wife of Dederic van Caren	2*s*
Yevan	Daniel	German	capper	2*s*
...				
Frankenbury	Henry	German	bookprinter[25]	6*s* 8*d*
[blank]	Bernard	German	bookprinter	6*s* 8*d*
Ree	Stephen	German	servant to Henry Frankenbury	2*s*
Groce	Herman	German	servant to Henry Frankenbury	2*s*
Derikson	Dederic	German	servant to Henry Frankenbury	2*s*
Derykson	Adrian	German	servant to Henry Frankenbury	2*s*
...				
[blank]	Peter	German	goldsmith	2*s*
...				
[blank]	Ambrose	Lombard*	broker	2*s*
Justinian	John	Lombard	broker[26]	2*s*
...				

25 Identified in other records not as a printer but as a merchant of printed books, collaborating with Bernard van Stondo, who is presumably the person listed next.

26 Possibly Giovanni Giustiniani, of a Genoese merchant family of this name.

[blank]	Littil John	German	servant of Pancracius Justynyan[27]	2*s*
Pemontes	James	German	servant of Pancracius Justynyan	2*s*
Pemontes	Pancracius	German	servant of Pancracius Justynyan	2*s*
[blank]	Paul	Lombard	servant of Pancracius Justynyan	2*s*
[blank]	Simon	Lombard	servant of Pancracius Justynyan	2*s*
[blank]	Godfrey	German	servant of Pancracius Justynyan	2*s*
[blank]	Nicholas	Lombard	servant of Pancracius Justynyan	2*s*
Gaoloto	Mark	Lombard	servant of Pancracius Justynyan	2*s*

Limestreet Ward

...

Effamato	Alexander	Greek	goldwiredrawer	6*s* 8*d*
...				
Castomala	Anthony	German	servant of Cosine Spinell[28]	2*s*
Gamoff	Benedict	German	servant of Cosine Spinell	2*s*
Stepman	Bokyn	German	servant of Cosine Spinell	2*s*
Maromarius	Batyn	German	servant of Cosine Spinell	2*s*

...

Cornhill Ward

...

Milborn	Nicholas	German	cobbler	6*s* 8*d*
Jerbray	Mariona	German	silkwoman, widow	6*s* 8*d*
Symond	Margareta	German	servant of Mariona Jerbray	2*s*
Trumpet	Nichodeus	Roman	[not given][29]	2*s*
[blank]	Cornelius	German	servant of Nichodeus Trumpet	2*s*

Bishopsgate Ward

Legge	Philip de	German	servant of John Ambrose de Nigrono[30]	2*s*
[blank]	Henry	German	servant of John Ambrose de Nigrono	2*s*
...				
[blank]	Matthew	Greek	[not given]	2*s*
[blank]	Johanna	German	wife of Matthew the Greek	2*s*
Broun	John	Scottish	sheath maker	6*s* 8*d*

27 Pancrazio Giustiniani, a member of the Genoese merchant family.

28 Cosimo Spinola, a member of another Genoese merchant family.

29 Italian trumpeter who played at the coronation of Richard III.

30 Giovanni di Ambrogio di Negro was another Genose merchant operating in London.

Calaman	Benedict	Indian	[not given][31]	2*s*
Calaman	Antonia	Indian	wife of Benedict Calaman	2*s*
...				
Loy	John de	German	organ maker	6*s* 8*d*
Brokenhowt	Peter van	[blank]	servant to John de Loye	2*s*

50. A poor suitor at Westminster and London

This poem dates from the early fifteenth century. It describes the misfortunes of a peasant from Kent who visits the law-courts of Westminster in the vain hope of finding justice in a case, but who finds himself powerless because of his lack of money. In addition to the courts, the poem evokes a more inclusive image of the streets of London and its western suburb.[32] The text is a passionate critique of the city by a man of the country, of the late medieval social hierarchy by a peasant, and of a legal system perceived as accessible only to those with money by a poor suitor.

J. M. Dean (ed.), *Medieval English Political Writings*, Kalamazoo: Western Michigan University, 1996, pp. 222–5. English.

In London there I was bent, *where; hastening*
I saw my-self, where trouthe shuld be ateynte; *achieved*
Fast to Westminstar-ward I went
To a man of law, to make my complaint.
I sayd, 'For Marys love, that holy seynt, *Mary's*
Have pity on the powre, that would procede. *poor; litigate*
I would gyve sylvar, but my purs is faynt.' *silver; light*
For lacke of money, I may not spede. *succeed*

As I thrast thrughe-out the thronge *pushed; crowd*
Amonge them all, my hode was gonn; *hood; gone [stolen]*
Netheles I let not longe, *did not hesitate*
To kyngs benche tyll I come. *to King's Bench*
Before a juge I kneled anon;
I prayd hym for Gods sake he would take hede.
Full rewfully to hym I gan make my mone; *complaint*
For lacke of money I may not spede.

Benethe hym sat clerks, a great rowt; *company*
Fast they writen by one assent.

31 Perhaps from the Christian community in Kerala in south India.

32 For the context see G. Rosser, *Medieval Westminster 1200–1540*, Oxford, 1989.

There stode up one, and cryed round about
'Richard, Robert, and one of Kent!'
I wist not wele what he ment
He cried so thike there in dede; *quickly*
There were stronge theves shamed and shent, *powerful thieves; ruined?*
But they that lacked money mowght not spede. *might*

Unto the Comon Place I yowde thoo *Common Pleas; went then*
Where sat one with a silken houde.
I dyd hym reverence as me ought to do;
I told hym my case, as well as I coulde,
And seyd all my goods, by nowrd and by sowde, *north; south*
I am defraudyd with great falshed; *falsehood*
He would not geve me a momme of his mouthe. *the slightest word*
For lake of money, I may not spede.

Then I went me unto the Rollis *court of Rolls*
Before the clerks of the Chauncerie.
There were many *qui tollis*, *summons to plaintiffs*
But I herd no man speke of me.
Before them I knelyd upon my kne,
Shewyd them myne evidence and they began to reade.
They seyde trewer things might there nevar be,
But for lacke of money I may not spede.

In Westminster Hall I found one
Went in a longe gowne of ray. *striped cloth*
I crowched, I kneled before them anon;
For Marys love, of helpe I gan them pray.
As he had be wrothe, he voyded away
Bakward, his hand he gan me byd. *he offered me*
'I wot not what thou menest', gan he say. *know not*
'Ley downe sylvar, or here thow may not spede.'

In all Westminstar Hall I could find nevar a one
That for me would do, thowghe I shuld dye.
Without the dores were Flemings grete woon; *in a large number*
Upon me fast they gan to cry
And sayd, 'Mastar, what will ye copen or by – *barter or buy*
Fine felt hatts, spectacles for to rede
Of this gay gere?' – a great cause why
For lack of money I might not spede.

Then to Westminster gate I went
When the sone was at highe prime. *nine o'clock*
Cokes to me, they toke good entent,
Called me nere, for to dyne,

And proferyd me good brede, ale, and wyne.
A fayre clothe they began to sprede,
Rybbes of befe, both fat and fine;
But for lacke of money I might not spede.

In to London I gan me hye; *hasten*
Of all the lond it bearethe the prise. *is the best*
'Hot pescods!' one gan cry,
'Strabery rype, and chery in the ryse!' *branch*
One bad me come nere and by some spice;
Pepar and saffron they gan me bede, *offer*
Clove, grayns, and flowre of rise. *branch*
For lacke of money I might not spede.

Then into Chepe I gan me drawne, *Cheapside; went*
Where I saw stond moche people.
One bad me come nere, and by fine cloth of lawne, *linen*
Paris thred, coton, and umple. *fine gauze*
I seyde there-upon I could no skyle, *knew nothing about it*
I am not wont there-to in dede.
One bad me by an hewre, my hed to hele: *cap; cover*
For lake of money I might not spede.

Then went I forth by London Stone
Thrwghe-out all Canwike street. *Candlewick*
Drapers to me they called anon;
Grete chepe of clothe, they gan me hete; *bargains in cloth; offer*
Then come there one, and cried 'Hot shepes fete!' *sheep's feet*
'Risshes faire and grene', an othar began to grete; *rushes; another*
Both melwell and makarell I gan mete, *mulvel (cod)*
But for lacke of money I myght not spede.

Then I hied me into Estchepe. *Eastcheap*
One cried, 'Ribes of befe, and many a pie!'
Pewtar potts they clatteryd on a heape.
Ther was harpe, pipe and sawtry. *psaltery*
'Ye by Cokke!' 'Nay by Cokke!' some began to cry;
Some sange of Jenken and Julian, to get themselvs mede. *reward*
Full fayne I wold had of that mynstralsie,
But for lacke of money I cowld not spede.

Into Cornhill anon I yode *went*
Where is moche stolne gere amonge. *stolen goods*
I saw wher henge myne owne hode *hung*
That I had lost in Westminstar amonge the throng.
Then I beheld it with lokes full longe;
I kenned it as well as I dyd my Crede.

To be myne owne hode agayne, me thought it wrong, — *buy*
But for lacke of money I might not spede.

Then came the taverner, and toke me by the sleve,
And seyd, 'Ser, a pint of wyn would yow assay?'
'Syr', quod I, 'it may not greve; — *it cannot hurt*
For a peny may do no more then it may.'
I dranke a pint, and therefore gan pay;
Sore a-hungred away I yede; — *went*
For well London Lykke-peny for ones and eye, — *for once and for all*
For lake of money I may not spede.

Then I hyed me to Byllingesgate, — *Billingsgate*
And cried 'Wagge, wagge yow hens!' — *move; hence*
I prayed a barge man, for Gods sake,
That they would spare me myn expens.
He sayde, 'Ryse up, man, and get the hens. — *thee hence*
What wenist thow I will do on the my almes-dede? — *Do you think; charity*
Here skapethe no man, by-nethe ii. pens!' — *for less than twopence*
For lacke of money I myght not spede.

Then I conveyed me into Kent,
For of the law would I medle no more;
By-caus no man to me would take entent,
I dight me to the plowe, even as I ded before. — *set myself*
Jhesus save London, that in Bethlehem was bore,
And every trew man of law, God graunt hym souls med; — *his soul's reward*
And they that be other, God theyr state restore: –
For he that lackethe money, with them he shall not spede!

V. URBAN GOVERNMENT

Political power in the borough derived its authority from two principal sources. From above, it depended upon the concession of royal rights, more or less extensively granted in the form of a charter. Regal powers might be conceded directly or mediated by lords who were themselves dependent upon the crown. Royal grants were precious, not only for the right to regulate the market and to hold a court of justice but also for the protection of trading members of the urban community when they travelled to other towns [**51**]. Monarchs under financial duress were the more willing to delegate powers for a financial return; but no civic corporation under the aegis of the medieval English monarchy was allowed to forget that it exercised delegated authority on suffrance, and might at any time be compelled to yield it back to the giver. The county towns, as an elite class of regional centres which was largely defined by about 1100, would always be seen from the point of view of royal government as means for the expression and assertion of central authority.[1] Meanwhile, a second and no less significant basis of urban rule lay in customary practices of self-regulation in the neighbourhoods which made up the town. The implementation of civic administration called for the engagement of the townspeople themselves, and this was typically realised by means of local systems of policing and self-assessment which in many cases, having originated long before, became enshrined in the structure of civic government. The wards of London are one case in point, the leets of Norwich another: in both instances the neighbourhood body has the appearance of having predated (and perhaps by a long period) the more or less systematic organisation of the urban constitution in the thirteenth century [**52**], [**53**]. Even after their incorporation within the civic structure, these elements of street and neighbourhood culture would continue to have great importance both for their participants and for the everyday running of the town.

The body which acquired and claimed to exercise administrative powers in the town might be a collectivity of property-owners like the

1 D. Palliser, 'Towns and the crown in England: the counties and the county towns', in D. Palliser, *Towns and Local Communities in Medieval and Early Modern England*, Aldershot, 2006, separately paginated.

universitas of townspeople in twelfth-century Oxford; a group of traders such as the 'merchant guild' of Leicester in the thirteenth century; or, most grandly, a common council with an elected mayor exemplified in fourteenth-century York. The rhetoric of urban government emphasised the ideal of unity under the crown: several town councils claimed that their respective city was 'the king's chamber'.[2] None the less, in whatever terms civic government presented itself as a unitary authority, power in the borough was always in practice refracted through a diversity of jurisdictions by which the hierarchical character of urban politics was complicated and at times subverted. In the eleventh and twelfth centuries, the sokes of powerful secular lords continued to function as islands of legal privilege within the town. Subsequently it was rather the ecclesiastical bodies whose significant territorial presence within the urban fabric endured as an archipelago of jurisdictional immunities in the lake of municipal government. To the constant frustration of mayors and corporations throughout the land, the prosperous artisan or wealthy merchant who chose to inhabit a part of the town owned by a monastic body or cathedral chapter could enjoy many of the privileges of urban life without undertaking any of its public burdens of tax or office.[3] In addition the custom of sanctuary, which allowed the person accused of serious crime to take refuge in any church for forty days prior to handing themselves over to royal justice or to abjuring the realm, was in a small number of towns extended to a permanent protection. In the sanctuary towns, which included Durham and Westminster, both the wealthy tax evader and the poor criminal found a comfortable haven [**54**].[4] Lawyers and sheriffs might shake their heads over the fragmentation of authority within the towns; but this was a condition which remained broadly unchanged to the end of the medieval period and even well beyond. The issue was a part of the even larger challenge of convincing all townspeople of means to contribute to the smooth running of the community. Petitions for exemp-

2 C. Liddy, 'The rhetoric of the royal chamber in late medieval London, York and Coventry', *Urban History*, XXIX, 2002, pp. 323–49.

3 E. Miller, 'Medieval York', in *The Victoria County History of Yorkshire: The City of York*, London, 1961, pp. 25–116, at pp. 38–40; D. M. Palliser, 'The birth of York's civic liberties, *c.*1200–1354', in S. Rees Jones (ed.), *The Government of Medieval York*, York, 1997, pp. 88–107; G. Rosser, 'Conflict and political community in the medieval town: disputes between clergy and laity in Hereford', in T. R. Slater and G. Rosser (eds), *The Church in the Medieval Town*, Aldershot, 1998, pp. 20–42.

4 G. Rosser, 'Sanctuary and social negotiation in medieval England', in J. Blair and B. Golding (eds), *The Cloister and the World: Essays in Medieval History in Honour of Barbara Harvey*, Oxford, 1996, pp. 57–79.

tion from the duty to hold office, on grounds both of its expense and of the time it detracted from personal business, are symptomatic of the recurrent difficulty of persuading all in a position to do so to shoulder a share of the communal burden [**55**].[5]

Only a small minority of the urban population enjoyed the right to hold civic office and to participate in town government. Women were universally excluded. The privileged body comprised a variable proportion of male householders. About a half of this group became freemen in late fourteenth-century York [**19**]; only between a fifth and a third in the case of Exeter.[6] The admission of individuals to the freedom, or full citizenship, was influenced by the fiscal policies of town councils which collected fees from those admitted. The pattern in detail therefore varied between towns and over time, making it difficult or impossible to perceive general trends. Urban government towards the end of the Middle Ages tended to become more narrowly concentrated in a few hands. The evidence, however, qualifies this generalisation. The underlying principle of citizenship was that full rights to participate in the economic opportunities of urban life also carried a responsibility to share in its regulation through office-holding and to bear its costs by contribution to civic taxes. The need for both time and money to sustain this role confined citizenship to those owning real estate in the town. The assumptions behind medieval government were far from any modern principle of democracy. But they were regularly debated, as at Norwich in the early fifteenth century when the bailiffs and the council of twenty-four were challenged by the assertion that their ordinances were invalid without 'the assent of the commonalty', and later at Coventry where the weavers protested at the fixing of taxes by the elite [**91**].[7]

In return for recognition of its right to rule, the town council undertook in the first place to guarantee the safety and security of the urban

5 J. I. Kermode, 'Urban decline? The flight from office in late medieval York', *Economic History Review*, 2nd series, XXXV, 1982, pp. 179–98. As Kermode points out, civil government on occasion succeeded in extracting fines for exemption from office-holding from townsmen who would never have been in a position to take up public posts; so the fines are not an exact guide to evasion.

6 M. Kowaleski, *Local Markets and Regional Trade in Exeter*, Cambridge, 1995, p. 96.

7 S. Reynolds, 'Medieval urban history and the history of political thought', *Urban History Yearbook*, 1982, pp. 14–23; S. H. Rigby, 'Urban "oligarchy" in late medieval England', in J. A. F. Thomson (ed.), *Towns and Townspeople in the Fifteenth Century*, Gloucester, 1988, pp. 62–86; S. H. Rigby and E. Ewan, 'Government, power and authority 1300–1540', *CUHB*, pp 291–312; C. Liddy, *War, Politics and Finance in Late Medieval English Towns: Bristol, York and the Crown 1350–1400*, Woodbridge, 2005, pp. 213–14.

population, and beyond this to promote its economic interests. These policies were pursued both through practical measures and by means of no less significant symbolic rituals. Town walls, although in practical terms of neither universal nor continuous utility, were erected and maintained in part as a potent image of the protective role of urban government [**56**].[8] Beside any other purpose, the city was constructed as a theatre for the representation of power: a significant urban function in its own right. By staging public executions, civic authorities demonstrated their collaboration with the officers of the crown and implied their own command over the lives of the urban population [**57**]. The accounts of the late medieval mayor of Leicester show that officer working hard on behalf of his constituents, controlling the measures for use in the market, pressing forward the construction of a bridge, liaising with the town's member of parliament, and hosting officers of the crown [**58**]. External relations, both with other cities and with the royal court, were a constant diplomatic concern [**59**], [**60**].[9] While an individual town might carry relatively little weight in national politics, close and strategic communication between cities meant that on occasion an urban lobby could command sway in the royal council.[10] The perceived importance of the king's favour was demonstrated most dramatically in the staging of royal entries, in which the town arrayed itself to present a microcosm of the kingdom [**61**].

51. Customs of Newcastle-upon-Tyne in the time of Henry I

The acquisition of a charter was an important milestone for a body of townsmen. The purpose of the charter being to enshrine what were perceived as existing rights or good practices, the document was typically conservative in content, and the historian should be careful not to overestimate its transformative effect. Many small medieval towns found means to organise local affairs and to create a sense of collective identity without ever enjoying the formal dignity of a charter.[11] However, those who did lobby for a charter of rights attached great

8 See Introduction, p. 25.

9 R. Horrox, 'Urban patronage and patrons in the fifteenth century', in R. A. Griffiths (ed.), *Patronage, the Crown and the Provinces in Later Medieval England*, Gloucester, 1981, pp. 145–66.

10 E. Hartrich, 'Town, crown, and urban system: the position of towns in the English polity, 1413–71', University of Oxford D.Phil. thesis, 2014.

11 G. Rosser, *Medieval Westminster 1200–1540*, Oxford, 1989, pp. 226–48.

importance to the privilege. Close reading of the terms of such a collection of royally approved customs as this one from Newcastle-upon-Tyne is revealing of the conversation, which must have preceded its compilation, between the burgesses of the town and officers of the king: each was careful to reserve their respective spheres of competence. It is evident that townspeople could be organised and politically astute even before the acquisition of the formal entitlement to act in this way (which is one reason why not all towns bothered to press for a charter at all). The concessions enshrined in the Newcastle customs were typical of civic charters of the period. As in other cases, they include two particularly remarkable clauses. One declared that the villein arriving from the countryside who remained in the town as a property-owning burgess for a year and a day would enjoy in perpetuity the rights of citizenship. The number of rural tenants able to escape service to their lords and to accumulate sufficient means to pay for a burgage in town can never have been large. Yet the principle expresses a contemporary perception of the town as a potential agent of social change. This perception also underlies the declaration – the second especially noteworthy clause here – that the rights of a free burgess were inheritable by his son. For comparison of the customs enshrined in diverse urban charters, the work of Mary Bateson remains valuable.[12] The unique copy of this text was made apparently under Henry II to record customs in the time of his grandfather.

D. C. Douglas and G. W. Greenaway (eds), *English Historical Documents 1042–1189*, 2nd edn, London: Eyre Methuen, 1981, pp. 1222–3; with S. Reynolds, W. de Boer and G. Mac Niocaill (eds), *Elenchus Fontium Historiae Urbanae*, Leiden: Brill, 1988, pp. 53–4. Latin, transl. by Douglas.

These are the laws and customs which the burgesses of Newcastle-upon-Tyne had in the time of Henry, king of England, and which they still have by right:

i. The burgesses may distrain* foreigners within their market and without, and within their houses and without, and within their borough and without, and they may do this without permission of the reeve, unless the courts are being held within the borough, or unless they are in the field on army service, or are doing castle-guard.

12 M. Bateson, *Borough Customs*, 2 vols, Selden Society, XVIII, 1904.

ii. A burgess may not distrain on another burgess without the permission of the reeve.

iii. If a burgess shall lend anything in the borough to someone dwelling outside, the debtor shall pay back the debt if he admit it, or otherwise do right in the court of the borough.

iv. Pleas which arise in the borough shall there be held and concluded except those which belong to the king's crown.

v. If a burgess shall be sued in respect of any plaint he shall not plead* outside the borough except for defect of court; nor need he answer, except at a stated time and place, unless he has already made a foolish answer, or unless the case concerns matters pertaining to the crown.

vi. If a ship comes to the Tyne and wishes to unload, it shall be permitted to the burgesses to purchase what they please.

vii. And if a dispute arises between a burgess and a merchant, it shall be settled before the third tide.

viii. Whatever merchandise a ship brings by sea must be brought to the land; except salt and herring which must be sold on board ship.

ix. If anyone has held land in burgage for a year and a day justly and without challenge, he need not answer any claimant, unless the claimant is outside the kingdom of England, or unless he be a boy not having the power of pleading.

x. If a burgess has a son in his house and at his table, his son shall have the same liberty as his father.

xi. If a villein (*rusticus*) comes to reside in the borough, and shall remain as a burgess in the borough for a year and a day, he shall thereafter always remain there, unless there was a previous agreement between him and his lord for him to remain there for a fixed time.

xii. If a burgess sues anyone concerning anything, he cannot force the burgess to trial by battle, but the burgess must defend himself by his oath, except in a charge of treason when the burgess must defend himself by battle. Nor shall a burgess offer battle against a villein unless he has first quitted his burgage.

xiii. No merchant except a burgess can buy wool or hides or other merchandise outside the town, nor shall he buy them within the town except from burgesses.

xiv. If a burgess incur forfeiture he shall give 6 oras* to the reeve.

xv. In the borough there is no merchet* nor heriot* nor bloodwite* nor stengesdint.*

xvi. Any burgess may have his own oven and handmill if he wishes, saving always the rights of the king's oven.

xvii. If a woman incurs a forfeiture concerning bread or ale, none shall concern himself with it except the reeve. If she offend twice she shall be punished by forfeiture. If she offend thrice justice shall take its course.

xviii. No one except a burgess may buy cloth for dyeing or make or cut it.

xix. A burgess can give or sell his land as he wishes, and go where he will, freely and quietly, unless his claim to the land is challenged.

52. The wardmotes of London

The two dozen wards of London originated, probably before the Conquest, in the private sokes of rich residents. In the thirteenth century they were still known by the names of their respective aldermen. The records of the medieval wards have not survived, but in 1419 the city's common clerk, John Carpenter, transcribed into the Liber Albus or White Book the mode of holding a wardmote and its principal business.

H. T. Riley (ed.), *Liber Albus: the White Book of the City of London*, London: Richard Griffin, 1861, pp. 32–5, 287–92; with H. T. Riley (ed.),

Liber Albus, Rolls Series, London, 1859, pp. 332–6. Latin, transl. by the editor, revised by GR.

(a) The wardmote is so called as being a meeting together by summons of all the inhabitants of a ward, in the presence of its head, the alderman, or else his deputy, for the correction of faults, the removal of nuisances and the promotion of the well-being of the ward … The aldermen were in the habit also, by virtue of warrants issued by the mayor, to hold their wardmotes at least twice, or more often, in the year, on which occasions enquiry used to be made as to the condition and tranquillity of the ward, and such faults as were presented were corrected by the alderman, as will be shown below.

The process of holding a wardmote in London has customarily been as follows. The alderman, after receipt of the warrant, is to command his bedel* to summon all such men as are householders, as well as all hired servants, in his ward, to appear before him at a certain day and hour on the morrow of such summons, in a certain place within the same ward, for the purpose of holding such a wardmote. These names, after the persons have been duly summoned, the bedel is to have entered in a certain roll, that is those of the freemen of the city who dwell in that ward, and a separate list of the hired servants and non-freemen. And when at the hour appointed they have duly met together, the alderman having taken his seat with the more opulent men of the ward, each in his proper place, the clerk of the alderman is to enjoin the bedel, on the alderman's behalf, to command attention. It is then the clerk's duty to read aloud the warrant and then to read to the bedel the names that are entered on the roll; while the bedel in his turn proclaims aloud that every person who shall not, there present, answer to his name, and shall make default, shall be noted down and fined at least 4*d.* After this, the bedel is to present to the alderman a panel, arrayed by the constables of the ward, of those reputable men of the ward by whom inquisition should be made; which array, if the alderman shall deem it expedient, he shall be at liberty to amend. This done, the jurors are to have read to them all the articles touching the wardmote. After this a certain day for making their presentment is given by the alderman to the jurors. On which day the jurors are to present their verdict on an indenture,* one part of it to remain in possession of the alderman and the other with the ward. It is also the duty of the alderman to present his part to the mayor, at the next sitting of his general court, so that after it has been seen, and enquiry made if there is any matter the correction of which pertains to the mayor and city, the indenture may be redelivered to him, to be acted upon in other respects.

And at the wardmote there ought to be elected, by the alderman, the reputable men of the ward and the jurors, the scavagers [supervisors of street-cleaning], ale-conners [tasters of ale for quality control], bedel, and other officials, who at the mayor's general court take the oaths befitting their respective offices.

The alderman also used to be specially certified by the bedel as to the names of such hostelers, brewers, bakers, cooks, victuallers and sellers as lived in the ward. Bakers were also to have their stamps there, the impressions of which were to be entered upon the alderman's paper ... It was customary also for the alderman to seal the measures and weights in their respective wards, and to condemn such as were not sealed ...

At such a wardmote also, those persons who are not free of the city, and who have not been previously sworn in this way, ought to be put in frankpledge,* even if they had already been sworn into frankpledge in another ward.

(b) It is the first responsibility of the wardmote to keep the peace of God and Holy Church, and the peace of his lordship the king, between clerks and laymen, rich and poor, in common.

Of strangers. That no person be resident or harboured within the ward if he be not of good repute and under frankpledge charged before the alderman of the ward, even if he has been in under frankpledge in another ward.

Of the same. That no one receive a stranger in his house beyond a day and a night, unless he is willing to be responsible for presenting him at his trial, if it so happen that he offends.

Of prostitutes. That no woman of immoral life (*de fole vye*), prostitute or common scold* (*tenseresse*), be resident in the ward, but be immediately removed by the alderman and driven out of the ward, or else to be brought by the constables and bedel to the counter prison [of one of the two London sheriffs], there to remain in the manner provided in the article as to the peace.

Of erecting furnaces. That no man or woman erect any furnace or furnaces, or place any hearth beneath where they are, or any reredos [tiled back to a fireplace] where a fire is made for preparing bread or ale, or for cooking meat, near to partitions, laths or boards, above or in a solar, or elsewhere, by which a fire could be caused. And if there be any, that the scavagers cause them immediately to be removed or destroyed; for doing which the scavagers shall have 4*d* for every such nuisance so removed or destroyed.

Of chimneys. That no chimney be made except of stone, tiles, or plaster, and not of timber, on pain of being pulled down.

Of rebellious persons. If there be any one whether foreigner or denizen, who is not willing to be amenable to the officers of the city, who have the peace of his lordship the king to keep, all persons belonging to the peace shall be ready and prepared to come in aid of the officers, for arresting and bringing to justice such disobedient persons, as the law demands.

Of scotale.* That no person of the ward make scotale in the ward, or in any other place within the franchise* [of London], under pain of imprisonment.

Of labourers. That no one hire or pay masons, carpenters, daubers,* tilers or any other labourers whatsoever, otherwise [i.e. more] than according to the assize [by-law] on this ordained by the common council of the city, under pain of paying to the chamber double the amount of the excess.

Of ladders. That all persons who live in large houses within the ward should have a ladder or two, ready and prepared to help their neighbours in case of fire.

Of barrels filled with water. That all who occupy such houses should in summer time, and especially between Pentecost [the fiftieth day after Easter] and St Bartholemew [24 August], have before their doors a barrel full of water for quenching a fire, if the house does not have a well (*fountaigne*) of its own.

Of carpentry work in houses. That no house within the liberties [of London] be covered otherwise than with lead, tile, or stone. If there be any, they should at once be rased by the constables and scavagers, they taking for their trouble as was stated earlier.

Of iron crooks. That the reputable men of the ward, with the alderman, provide a strong crook of iron with a wooden handle, together with two chains and two strong cords; and that the bedel have a good horn, and loudly sounding.[13]

13 These items were also intended for fire-fighting.

Of dirt. That no-one throw straw, dust, dung, sawdust or other refuse into the streets or lanes, but cause the same to be taken by the rakers or others to the places ordained for such rubbish, under penalty of two shillings payable to the chamber.

Of rakers. That they have sufficient rakers for cleansing the wards of all kinds of rubbish, and order the constables, with the bedel, to help them to collect their salary from the people of the ward.

Of pigs and cows. That no person should rear swine, oxen or cows in their houses, on pain of forfeiture of the animals to the chamber.

Of sealed measures. That all who sell by measure within the ward, that is to say, by gallon, pottle and quart, quarter, bushel,* half-bushel and peck, show all their measures four times a year to the alderman … and they shall there be sealed with the alderman's seal (if not already sealed with the seal of the city chamber) … And if any measures be, on assay by the alderman, smaller than they ought to be, they shall be burnt at once in the principal street of the ward, so that they may not serve another time, and the name of him who has used them shall be presented by the bedel to the chamberlain, and the person fined accordingly. And if it be found that the bedel has put the mark on a false measure, he shall be sentenced to the pillory.

Of stalls. That no stalls be beyond the house of greater breadth than two feet and a half, and they are to be moveable and flexible, at the discretion of the alderman, according to the breadth of the streets or lanes.

Of pentices. That pentices* be sufficiently high that people may easily go and ride beneath them. If there be any lower than they ought to be, they should be altered within fifteen days after notice is given by the constables, scavagers, or bedel; or otherwise, these officers are to demolish them, taking for their trouble 4*d* as above.

Inquisitions at the wardmotes. You shall present if the peace of his lordship the king has been broken, or any affray made within the ward since the last wardmote, and by what person or persons; or if any conspiracy (*covyne*) or assembly against the king's peace has been made.

You shall also present if there is any one resident or harboured within the ward who is not a lawful person, or not of good fame, or not under frankpledge;

if there is any huckster* in the ward;

if there is any leper resident in the ward;

if any bargain of usury has been made within the ward since the last wardmote;

if any baker of *tourte* bread [the coarsest brown bread] bakes white bread, or the converse;

if anyone is in the habit of wandering in the ward after forbidden hours, and in a manner forbidden by the common council of the city;

if any officer of the city has made extortion or affray within the ward under cover of his office, to the wrong or detriment of any person;

if the ale-stake [sign] of any tavern is longer or extends further than is ordained.

53. Local jurisdiction in Norwich

The four 'leets' or areas of jurisdiction into which Norwich was divided for administrative purposes in the thirteenth and fourteenth centuries had significantly older origins, probably antedating the Conquest. These principal districts of the city were subdivided so that householders reported to the courts by neighbourhood. The system was an adaptation of that used in rural manors for the regulation of behaviour by groups of householders. Only in the fifteenth century did Norwich's leets, then renamed 'wards', cede place to the developing system of central municipal courts. The 'chief pledges' of the leets were responsible for discovering offences and made their presentments to the four bailiffs of the city (in existence from 1223) in the tollhouse (on the site of the later guildhall). Prior to the city's charter of incorporation of 1404, the bailiffs represented the king's interest in a town which belonged to him. Major crimes were the responsibility not of the leets but of the king's sheriff or coroner. But the records of the leet courts give some insights into the everyday life of particular urban neighbourhoods. One of the motifs to emerge from these records is collaboration amongst townspeople, who are sometimes said to have sought for economic advantage by forming unlicensed guilds.

W. Hudson (ed.), *Leet Jurisdiction in the City of Norwich during the XIIIth and XIVth Centuries*, Selden Society, V, London: Quaritch, 1891, pp. 5–6, 8, 10, 14, 39, 42–3, 52, 55, 66, 70–1. Latin, transl. by the editor, revised by GR.

1287–88

The chief pledges present that Henry de Campesse is a thief and they hold him in suspicion and say that he is against the peace and dresses well but nobody knows how, and is always roving about by night … Thomas the leather-dresser, lodging over against Trowse bridge, buys corn ahead of the market [in order to raise the price]; and three others similarly … Thomas Gerveys, fripperer,* and Walter Hee have fullers'* blocks for working up old clothes in a fraudulent manner. Walter Hee also has a measure not sealed so that those measures make one gallon … The men of Sprowston knowingly buy measly pigs, and they make and sell their sausages and puddings, unfit for human consumption, in Norwich market … Adam Cabel sells whelks with good and bad mixed together, and is in the habit of doing so … John the bleacher and Ralph the fishmonger rode out to Brundall[14] to meet a boat laden with oysters and bought them, so raising the price in the Norwich market.

1290–91

The chief pledges present Richard de Stalham because he makes fraud in his work by tanning his hides with bark of ash (and this is called *Stalsitelether*) and because they have a guild hurtful to the lord the king in buying hides, and because they correct transgressions which ought to be pleaded before the bailiffs; fined 13*s* 4*d*. 42 other tanners likewise.

1292–93

The cobblers fined 20*s* because they have a guild contrary to the prohibition of the lord king,[15] whereby they take of their apprentices 2*s*, and those who carry on the business of a cobbler on their own account give 10*s* to the same guild. The saddlers fined 13*s* 4*d* because they similarly have a guild hurtful to the king. The fullers 6*s* 8*d* for the same.

1299–1300

Fine imposed upon all the chandlers for making an agreement amongst themselves, that is, that none of them should sell 1 lb of candle at less than another (8 chandlers fined).

14 About eight miles down-river on the way to Yarmouth.

15 A charter of Henry III (1256) had forbidden the formation of craft organisations, as compromising the authority of the king's bailiffs.

1312–13

The jurors present Rose, the daughter of William Gerberge of Chedgrave, because she buys corn and sells malt like a fellow-citizen and is not of the freedom: fined 12*d.* Also Margery, sister of the same Rose, for the same: 12*d.*

1374–75

John the silkman buys and sells and has an apprentice, and is not a citizen (*non est civis*: is not enrolled in a tithing, as a member of the frankpledge); fined 2*s.* Alice the wigmaker similarly buys and sells, and is not a citizen; fined 2*s.* Agnes the bookbinder similarly, and is not a citizen; fined 12*d.* Andrew the lantern-maker similarly; fined 40*d.* Richard Clerk, cardmaker,* has done the same; 6*d.* Edmund de Metton, weaver, the same 18*d.*

1390–91

A maidservant of Nicholas Fastolf, parish clerk of St Stephen, entered the garden of William Ides twice by night, and there stole his apples and pears and carried them off, and the said Nicholas received her with the apples and pears, knowing she had stolen them ... Robert the cook is a common re-heater (*recalefactor*) of all kinds of food, and he sold to Friar Thomas Walsham a re-cooked goose, to the peril of his life; fined 40*d.*

54. Sanctuary in the borough

All churches could provide short-term sanctuary to the person fleeing the law of the land. One who claimed sanctuary might remain for up to forty days unharmed in a church (the local community having responsibility for preventing his escape), at the end of which period he was obliged to hand himself over to the law or otherwise to be declared an outlaw and abjure the realm, leaving the kingdom under the sheriff's orders without right of return. This was not an exclusively urban phenomenon, but with the development of civic authorities the persistence of sanctuary rights became one of the distinctive complications of jurisdiction in the towns. A few centres, including Beverley, Durham and Westminster, boasted much more extensive sanctuary rights, with the result that they developed into havens for substantial resident communities of the disenfranchised. The records concerning the operation of sanctuary privileges shed light, not only on crime in the city but also on the duty and agency of urban neighbourhoods in the identification of and response to social offences.

H. T. Riley (ed.), *Memorials of London and London Life in the XIIIth, XIVth, and XVth Centuries*, London, 1868, p. 17 (a); A. F. Leach (ed.), *Beverley Town Documents*, Selden Society, XIV, London: Longmans, Green & Co., 1900, p. 20 (b); J. Raine (ed.), *Sanctuarium dunelmense et sanctuarium beverlacense*, Surtees Society, V, London: Quaritch, 1887, p. 27 (c). Latin, transl. by the editors, revised by GR.

(a) On Thursday the feast of St Dunstan [19 May], 1278, the chamberlain and sheriffs [of London] were given to understand that one Henry de Lanfare was lying dead in the house of Sibil le Feron ('the ironmonger') in the ward of Cheap, in the parish of [St Mary] Colechurch … having called together the good men of that ward, and of the ward of John de Blakethorn [Aldersgate ward] and the ward of Henry de Frowyk [Cripplegate ward], diligent inquisition was made thereon.

Who say that one Richard de Codesfold having fled to the church of St Mary Staining Lane in London, because of a certain robbery being by one William de London, cutler, imputed to him, and the same William pursuing him on his flight thereto; it so happened that on the night following the Day of the Invention of the Holy Cross [3 May], in the present year, there being many persons watching about the church aforesaid, to take him, in case he should come out, a certain Henry de Lanfare, ironmonger, one of the persons on the watch, hearing a noise in the church, and so fearing that the same Richard was about to get out by another part of the church, and so escape through a breach that there was in a particular glass window, went to examine it. The said Richard and one Thomas, the then clerk of that church, perceiving this, Thomas, seizing a lance, without an iron head, struck at Henry through the hole in the window, and wounded him between the nose and the eye, penetrating almost to the brain. From the effects of this wound he languished until the day of St Dunstan [19 May], when he died, at about the third hour. They say also, that both Richard and Thomas are guilty of the felony, seeing that Richard was consenting to it.

And Thomas was taken, and imprisoned in Newgate, and afterwards delivered before Hamon Haweteyn, justiciar of Newgate. Meanwhile Richard still keeps himself within the church. Being asked if they hold any more persons suspected as to that death, they say they do not. They have no lands or chattels. And the body was viewed, upon which no other injury or wound was found except the wound aforesaid. And the two neighbours nearest to the spot where he was wounded, were attached;* and the two neighbours nearest to the place where he died; and the said Sibil was attached, in whose house he died.

(b) The community of the town of Beverley assembled together in the Guildhall on Tuesday 16 March 1429 for a certain letter to the twelve keepers or governors of the town of Beverley named below in the name of Sir Henry Broomfleet, knight, and Master John Ellerker; the contents or purport of which letter was this, that for the respect due to their worships and at their request, the twelve keepers or governors of the town should admit William Gelle, fisherman, and make him a burgess. This being shown to the community, they with one consent said that the said William Gelle is a sanctuary man, and that inasmuch as it was ordered and decreed before that day that they would make no sanctuary man a burgess, therefore he should not be admitted to that freedom, nor any other sanctuary man for ever.

And it was ordered and decreed the same day that no burgess of the town of Beverley who is a sanctuary man should for offence against the common people or against the peace of the lord king henceforward carry on him a knife or dagger, except with blunted points, nor any club or sword in the town of Beverley, on pain of forfeiture of the same to the archbishop, and forfeiture of his burgess-ship to the community of the town of Beverley for ever.

(c) Thomas Coke of Bridgwater in Somerset came to the cathedral church of Durham on 6 February 1485, and at once sought immunity – the bells being rung, as was customary – on account of the fact that he had lately attacked one David, servant to Lord Audeley, wounding him and cutting off his right hand. Because of this, Thomas, greatly fearful both of that powerful lord and of the friends of the said David, fled away on the horse of Master John Drew, his master – or rather, a horse which Master Drew had hired at York. Fearing due punishment for these actions, he craves sanctuary.

55. Exemptions from holding office in York 1476–78

It was a principle of communal government in the medieval town that those property owners who enjoyed its privileges should share the burden of its responsibilities. To enforce this principle, however, was not always easy. Some preferred to pay a fine rather than hold public office. Some of those recorded as paying such fines may never have been able to take up office: in these instances the process was a merely fiscal device employed by cash-strapped civic rulers.

L. C. Attreed (ed.), *The York House Books 1461–1490*, 2 vols, Stroud: Alan Sutton for Richard III and Yorkist History Trust, 1991, pp. 61 (a), 137 (b). Latin, transl. by the editor.

(a) Meeting of the mayor's council, 21 September 1476. The same day, presence and place it was agreed by all that William Ward, draper, for considerations reasonable and for £10 paying to the common use of this city … and also considering the great age and sickness of the said William Ward, that he from that time forth for the said sum of £10 be discharged of bearing of any manner of office within the said city.

(b) Meeting of the mayor's council, January 1478. The same day it was agreed by a whole consent and assent that Brian Conyers shall not be called to the office of sheriff within this city of York within the space of eight years, unless he by the grace of God within the said eight years may grow in goods and riches to have the said office, then he to be elected and accepted to the same office by the discretion of the council.

56. Defence of the city: the walls of Hereford

Internal evidence, including several references to the bailiff John Gaunter, dates this version of the customs of Hereford to the third quarter of the fourteenth century. After this period, the chief officer of the town acquired the title of mayor. Several of the provisions relate to

Hereford's situation on the internally troubled border with Wales. By the mid-fourteenth century, however, sieges had ceased to be a normal concern; the passage below has its origins in less peaceful times. A recurrent motif in urban legislation are the status and obligations of those living in houses belonging to one or another 'liberty' – in the case of Hereford, many occupied the 'bishop's fee' – and thereby claimed to be free of any obligation to the civic authority. There was a perceived injustice in those who enjoyed the benefits of the town while finding excuses to avoid the common burdens of its maintenance and defence. The authors of the civic customs were, meanwhile, insouciant about the further injustice of the exclusion from the city's protection in time of war of poor cottagers living in the surrounding countryside.

Hereford Public Library, Hill MSS, vol. iv (sixteenth-century copy of a fourteenth-century original). Latin, transl. by GR.

When the town is besieged by the king's enemies, or if the city walls are in great need of repair or rebuilding, then the bailiff, in the king's name and for the safety of the city, uses all means to compel the men of the city and suburb to assist: the stronger and healthier, to watch by night, and all others to be made to contribute from their goods and chattels, without respect to anyone's liberty or to ecclesiastical possessions within the city … And he should receive [for safety within the walls] those citizens living outside the gates – except the cottagers [*cottars*] – to come with their goods and chattels to stay for the time within the city, and should allocate to them empty houses for their temporary residence.

57. The town as a political stage: public executions *c.*1400

This chronicle was written by a member of the Franciscan house at London during the reign of Henry VIII. Although the notices of events before his own time are laconic, they reveal the interests of the townsman no less than the friar. The annals reflect the mendicants' keen awareness of, and occasional direct involvement in, secular public affairs.[16] The public execution of declared traitors and the exposure of their remains to public view was a regular utility of urban space to the

16 See in general J. Röhrkasten, *The Mendicant Houses of Medieval London, 1221–1539*, Münster, 2004.

monarch, such as the violent usurper Henry Bolingbroke, unsure of his public support.

J. G. Nichols (ed.), *Chronicle of the Grey Friars of London*, Camden Society, LIII, 1852, pp. 9–11. English, revised by GR.

The first year of [Henry IV's] reign was beheaded at Cirencester the earl of Salisbury and the earl of Kent, and at Oxford Sir Thomas Blount, Sir Benet Ely [? *recte* Sely], knights, Thomas Wynter [*recte* Wintercell or Wintershall] esquire, and Sir John Holland, earl of Huntingdon, was beheaded at Pleshy in Essex, and their heads set on London Bridge, and Sir Bernard Brocas knight was beheaded at London in Cheapside, and Sir Thomas Shelley knight, Maudlyne and Feryby clerks, were hanged at Tyburn.

5th year [of Henry IV, 1403–4]. This year the bishop of York, Scrope, and Mowbray, the earl marshal [were] beheaded. And three men of the king's chamber hanged, and the prior of Launde, Sir Robert Clarendon knight, and eight friars minor [Franciscans] were hanged at Tyburn. And this year was the battle of Shrewsbury, in the which was slain Henry Percy and Thomas Percy taken, and two days kept, and after was hanged and beheaded and his head with one quarter of Henry Percy set on London Bridge ... And William Serle that was chief yeoman with King Richard was drawn and hanged and beheaded at Tyburn, and the quarters salted.

8th year [of Henry IV, 1406–7]. This year the earl of Northumberland and the lord Bardolf was beheaded in the north, and the earl's head with one of his quarters ... were set on London Bridge.

58. Expenses of the mayor of Leicester

Urban accounts roll together petty expenses with the funding of substantial projects. All can be revealing of the concerns and strategies of civic officers. Alongside the practical undertakings of mayoral government, also notable in these accounts are a variety of hospitality and gifts evidently intended to cultivate good relations with the crown and its agents.

M. Bateson (ed.), *Records of the Borough of Leicester*, ii, London: C. J. Clay, 1901, pp. 7–8. Latin, transl. by the editor.

(a) Account of John Alsy, mayor, 1327–8. Expenses. He accounts for the expenses of the king's marshal and of his servants (staying four days in December: bread, wine, beer, large meat bought, roast meat bought) ... hay for ten horses for four days and three nights *3s* ... total £2 *4s 10½d.* He accounts for £6 paid to the marshal for the fine of the whole town ... He accounts for a gift sent to the king and queen at that time in bread *11s 8d* and in a tun of wine £4 *13s 4d.* In two carcases of beef *32s.* In five pigs' carcases *18s 4d.* In porterage of this gift to the castle *10d* ... In a gift sent to the taxers of the twentieth [a royal tax granted for the war against the Scots], viz. to Sir Hugh of Prestwold, one of them (bread and wine), to Roger of Belgrave his fellow (bread and wine), to Sir Robert de Malmesthorp, Sir Walter of Friskney, justices of the lord king assigned after Hockday [after Easter] (bread and wine). To Sir Roger of Gildesborough at that time (bread and wine). In a present sent to Sir Robert Burdet coming through the lord (earl of Leicester) to enquire of misdeeds done to the servants of the lady Queen [Isabella] and Le Mortimer [the earl of Leicester] (bread and wine) ...

Three cartloads of stone from Swannington bought for the north bridge *1s 6d.* For carriage of the same with three hired carts *3s 3d.* In two cartloads of limestone bought for the same *2s 4d.* In a cart hired for two days for carrying hard stone and sand to the same *2s.* In the wages of two masons hired for one week for the same *3s 4d.* In the wages of a groom hired to serve them during that time *9d.* In the wages of a paver [working] on the bridge *3d.* In the wages of a woman helping them to collect stones out of the water and this for one day *1d.* Total *13s 6d.*

(b) Account of John le Marewe, mayor, 1332–3. Expenses ... For the expenses of the king's marshal coming to Leicester at Michaelmas and staying for three days £1 *10s* ... In a present sent to the earl at Lady Day [2 February] in bread *15s* and in a tun of wine £4 *13s 4d* ...

A piece of iron bought for making the seal for sealing measures *3½d,* and in making the same *3d.* In the repair of a chest for keeping and placing the muniments and charters of the community, and in nails and boards bought for the same *1s.* In the expenses of the mayor, John Alsy and other honest men of the community, treating and discussing the business of the community at the tavern after the departure of the justices that is to say of Sir

Richard Willoughby, in wine, 10*d.* Given to Henry of Winchester for having his aid in speaking good to the lord earl and to his son for diverse causes 6*s* 8*d* and a pair of gauntlets for 2*d* ... In 9 lb of mixed metal bought for [making] a standard gallon 1*s* 6*d*, and in making the same 9*d.* In beer given for making the same 2*d* ... To John of Knighton coming to parliament and bearing his writ for his expenses arising from the community, a pair of hose ...

59. The city of Coventry cultivates royal patronage 1451

The public encounter between sovereign and city, such as is described in this record, was choreographed in advance and carefully staged, to secure and enhance the dignity of each. The historian must imagine the conversation and negotiation between the mayor's and the king's officers which preceded and prepared the events recorded in the text (see [**61**]).[17]

M. D. Harris (ed.), *The Coventry Leet Book: or Mayor's Register*, 4 vols, London: Oxford University Press, 1907–13, pp. 263–4. English, revised by GR.

Receiving the king

Memorandum that the 21st day of September, the year of our sovereign lord afore rehearsed [1451], the king our sovereign lord came from Leicester towards Coventry, the mayor being then, that is to say, Richard Boys and his worthy brethren arrayed in scarlet and all the commonalty clad in green gowns and red hoods in Hazelwood beyond the broad oak on horseback attended the coming of our sovereign lord. And as soon as they had sight of our sovereign lord's presence, the mayor and his peers alighted on foot, and meekly thrice kneeling on their knees did unto our sovereign lord their due obeisance, the mayor saying to him these words: 'Most highest and gracious king, you are welcome to your true liege men with all our hearts.' At which the mayor, by advice of counsel, had no mace in his hand, but his sergeant attending upon the mayor, the words afore rehearsed said, put the

17 See further C. Kipling, *Enter the King. Theatre, Liturgy, and Ritual in the Medieval Civic Triumph*, Oxford, 1998; H. Carrel, 'The rituals of town–crown relations in post-Black Death England', in F. Andrews (ed.), *Ritual and Space in the Middle Ages*, Donington, 2011, pp. 148–64.

mace in the mayor's hand, and the mayor kissing the mace offered it to the king. The king, tarrying and hearkening to the mayor's speech in favourable wise, said these words: 'Well said, Sir Mayor, take your horse.' The mayor then rode forth afore the king, bearing his mace in his hand, with the knight constable next afore with the king's sword, the bailiffs of this city riding afore the mayor with their maces in their hands making way and room for the king's coming. And so they rode afore the king till the king came to the outer gate of the priory. The king then forthwith sent for the mayor and his brethren by a knight to come to his presence, and to speak with him in his chamber, and the mayor and his peers according to the king's commandment came into his chamber and thrice there kneeling did their obeisance. Thomas Lytelton, then recorder, said unto the king such words as was to his thinking most pleasant, our sovereign lord saying again these words: 'Sirs, I thank you of your good rule and demesne [i.e. lordship or government], and in special for your good rule the last year past, for the best ruled people then within my realm. And also I thank you for the present that you now gave to us.' The which was a tun of wine and 20 great fat oxen. The king then moreover gave them in commandment to govern well his city and to see his peace be well kept, as it has been afore-time, saying then to them he would be their good lord. And so the mayor and his peers departed.

60. Diplomatic relations: Hull 1464–65

Presents from the mayor of Hull found their way to a significant list of royal officials and peers of the realm, whose support for the city was clearly perceived to be vital. Some of these gifts were doubtless intended to oil the wheels in particular current controversies; others, which recur in the chamberlains' accounts on an annual basis, demonstrate the conviction that it was always worthwhile to cultivate amicable relations with the royal family and with the clerical and lay nobility.

R. Horrox (ed.), *Selected Rentals and Accounts of Medieval Hull, 1293–1528*, Yorkshire Archaeological Society Record Series, CXLI, 1983, pp. 96–7. Latin, transl. by the editor.

Extract from the account roll of the chamberlains of Kingston upon Hull, Michaelmas 1464 – Michaelmas 1465.

... And the same seek allowance in their account for various payments made by them on the orders of the mayor this year ... paid for four gallons of wine given to Robert Constable, knight, John Barneby, Nicholas Portyngton[18] and others on the mayor's orders *2s 8d* ... And for two pikes, two tenches and other fish given to the king's commissioner in the port of the aforesaid town to have his favour in the payment of £40 granted to the burgesses of the aforesaid town by the king *10s 6d*. And paid to William Mabson for his expenses in going to London with the king's letters patent for the said forty pounds *20s*. And paid to Richard Doughty for his expenses in going to London to labour to have allowance of the said £40 in the account of the said customer in the king's exchequer this year *40s*. And paid for three pikes, two tenches and other fish given to the earl of Northumberland and his wife the countess when they dined in the town, on the orders of the mayor *24s 7d*. And paid for one gallon of sweet wine given to the said countess *12d*. And paid for one hogshead of wine given to the said countess on the orders of the mayor *26s 8d*. And paid for two and a half dozen gallons of ale given to the said countess on the orders of the mayor *5s*. And paid to John Berker, servant of the said countess, as a reward when he brought two bucks sent to the burgesses of the aforesaid town by the said countess, on the orders of the mayor *13s 4d*. And paid for the expenses of the said mayor and the other burgesses present when the said bucks were eaten at the last collection of taxes *7s*. And paid for a tun of wine given to the chancellor of England, the archbishop of York, on the orders of the mayor £6. And paid for the carriage of the said tun of wine to Cawode on the orders of the mayor *2s 6d*. And paid for a tun of wine given to the duke of Suffolk, the duchess his wife and the duchess his mother, on the orders of the mayor £6. And paid for the carriage of the said cask to the place of the said duke on the orders of the mayor *12d*.

Total: £20 *16s 1d*.

61. Preparations for a royal visit to York 1483

In the second of these documents, the secretary of King Richard III writes to urge the rulers of York to provide a splendid and flattering show for an impending royal visit. Such a hastily written letter – an

18 These were all powerful men in the region. Sir Robert Constable was a constable of Flamborough; John Barnby was associated with the constables of Burton Constable; Nicholas Portington was the son of a judge.

urgent word of advice from the royal secretary to the governors of York – is an unusual survival, preserved in this case because copied into the civic records. The first record reveals that the mayoral council already planned just such a 'sight to be made at the king's coming'. A number of priests are identified as advisers for the invention of pageants, or staged spectacles, to greet the monarch.

L. C. Attreed (ed.), *The York House Books 1461–1490*, 2 vols, Stroud: Alan Sutton for Richard III and Yorkist History Trust, 1991, pp. 288 (a), 713 (b).

(a) Meeting of the mayoral council 4 August 1483. At the which day it was agreed that my lord the mayor and all my masters his brethren the aldermen in scarlet and all my masters of the twenty-four and the chamberlains and all those that have been chamberlains and also all those that will have bought out their charges of all offices in this city, shall in red gowns on horseback meet our most dread liege lord the king at Brekles Mills, and over this that the bridgemasters and all others that have been bridgemasters and all other honest men of the city shall be in red, upon the pain of 20*s* to be forfeit and paid to the commonalty of this city by every man doing the contrary … (their servants shall be in blue) and that all other persons of every occupation in blue, violet and musterdevil [yellow] shall on foot meet our said sovereign lord at St James's church.

Memorandum to send for Sir Henry Hudson [priest], Richard Burgess, parish clerk of St Crux church, Richard Standish, parish clerk of Christ's church, William Hewet, parish clerk of All Hallows' church, William Gylmyn, parish clerk of All Hallows' Belfry, and George Lovell, esquire, of St Mary's Abbey, to have their advice for a sight [spectacle] to be made at the king's coming at Micklegate Bar, Ouse Bridge and Stonegate.

(b) To my good masters the mayor, recorder, aldermen and sheriffs of the city of York:

Right worshipful sirs, I recommend me unto you as heartily as I can, and thanked be Jesus the king's grace is in good health, and in like wise the queen's grace, and in all their progress have been worshipfully received with pageants and other etc., and his lords and judges in every place sitting, determining the complaints of poor folks with due punishment of offenders [against] his laws. The cause I write to you now is for so much as I verily know the king's mind and entire affection that his grace bears towards you and your worshipful city, for manifold your kind and loving deservings to his grace shown heretofore, which his grace will never forget, and intends therefore so to do unto you that all the kings that ever reigned upon you did never so much, doubt not hereof, nor make no manner [of] petition of desire of anything by his highness to you to be granted, but this I advise you, as honourably as your wisdoms can imagine, to receive him and the queen at their coming, dispose you to do as well pageants with such good speeches as can goodly, this short warning considered, be devised, and under such form as Master Lancaster of the king's council, this [letter's] bringer, shall somewhat advertise you of my mind in that behalf, as in hanging the streets through which the king's grace shall come with cloths of Arras, tapestry-work and other, for there come many southern lords and men of worship with them, which will mark greatly your receiving their graces. Me needeth not to advise you, for I doubt not ye have provided therefore better than I can advise you, how be it on my faith I show you thus of good heart, and for the singular zeal and love that I bear to you and your city, afore all others, ye shall well know that I shall not forbear calling on his grace for your weals nor unremember it, as Master Lancaster shall show you, which in part heard the king's grace speak herein, to whom touching the premises it may like you [to] give credence. Scribbled in haste the 23rd day of August [1483] at Nottingham with the hand of your servant and hearty lover, John Kendale, secretary.

VI. THE ENVIRONMENT AND QUALITY OF LIFE

Life at close quarters, industrial sounds and at the same time a pervasive flavour of the farmyard characterised the streets of the medieval town. Communal spaces, together with a larger idea of the public realm, had to be won from the persistent residue of private sokes and ecclesiastical franchises, and tended to remain at constant risk of reappropriation for personal and exclusive use. Large-scale planning of the townscape was rendered almost impossible by the congeries of local and particular rights. None the less, the records sampled in this section demonstrate the partially successful attempts of urban councils and officials to establish and to implement norms of good practice for building [**62**], and in the process to foster a more inclusive sense of collective responsibility for public spaces, for common interests in food supply, water and health, and for the quality of life in the town.

It is illuminating to consider the range of urban and environmental matters for which city rulers were willing and even anxious to take responsibility. An instance of communal urban planning on a relatively grand scale is the city of Bristol's extension of its harbour, for evident economic reasons, in the 1240s [**63**].[1] Major civic works largely comprised walls and gates which were ostensibly provided for security but which, in many cases and for much of the time, rather served to define an image of the town as contained, coherent and controlled.[2] The scale and texture of the townscape was also conditioned by ecclesiastical building, to which in various ways the secular community might contribute.[3]

Beyond singular and very expensive projects, town councils from the thirteenth or fourteenth centuries are found, on an increasingly regular basis, legislating for the communal supply of clean water to public fountains and for the clearance of rubbish [**68**], [**70**], [**71**], [**73**]. Complaints about the neighbour with a leaking gutter, noisy industrial

1 On the topography of the medieval port see M. D. Lobel and E. M. Carus-Wilson, 'Bristol', in M. D. Lobel (ed.), *Atlas of Historic Towns*, ii, London, 1975.

2 See Introduction, p. 25.

3 See further Section IX.

equipment or an antisocially sited privy arose early in the history of the medieval towns, and such parochial issues gave rise to some of the first discussions concerning the identity and purpose of the city as a public body. In the process of negotiating the boundaries of domestic and communal space, urban governments contributed to evolving ideas, on the one hand, of personal identity and, on the other, of civic duty and decorum [**67**]. The street was contested territory [**71**], [**72**], [**73**], [**74**], although by the end of the period a number of towns had recently sought and obtained parliamentary permission to impose upon individual residents to pay for the paving of the principal thoroughfares, if not yet (or for centuries to come) the side-streets [**78**]. The provision of a town cross, often connected to provision for market stalls, was another public work with both practical and symbolic purpose.[4] These and the efforts to provide uncontaminated water (many would continue throughout and for long after this period to depend upon street water-vendors [**69**]) were significant contributions by town councils to the enhancement of the quality of life.

The regulation of food supply, which was an equally pressing concern of the magistrates, led them to attend to the fields and pastures of the immediate hinterland. The town herd of cattle emblemised this fundamental and enduring bond between the city and the country [**75**]. The more or less uncontrolled population of animals and fowl kept by private citizens for butchering and for their eggs expressed the same tie, and generated another occasion for the council to legislate in the interests of communal safety [**72**]. Fuel, too, was a limited and precious resource, the supply of which from the surrounding woods and hedgerows called for municipal scrutiny [**76**].

The smallest dwellings of medieval townspeople had no fireplaces and little opportunity for cooking or heating beyond small stoves.[5] Many will have had recourse to the ovens of bakers, or else to the suppliers of ready-cooked food [**2**], [**50**].[6] The homes of more prospering artisans and merchants could be relatively comfortable, offering the advantages not only of warm fires and draught-excluding windows

4 See in general G. T. Salusbury-Jones, *Street Life in Medieval England*, 2nd edn, Oxford, 1948; T. Scrase, 'Crosses, conduits and other street furniture in the south west of England', in M. Boone and P. Stabel (eds), *Shaping Urban Identity in Late Medieval Europe*, Leuven-Apeldoorn, 2000, pp. 201–19.

5 See Introduction, p. 23.

6 M. Carlin, 'Fast food and urban living standards in medieval England', in M. Carlin and J. Rosenthal (eds), *Food and Eating in Medieval Europe*, London, 1998, pp. 27–52.

(which by the fifteenth century might even be glazed) but also of degrees of segregation of activities and personal privacy denied to humbler classes [**64**], [**65**].[7]

The question of the quality of life in this context calls for careful assessment. It is evident that some townspeople lived not only prosperously but well. At the same time, contemporaries were aware that money was not everything, and the view is recorded that even the rich could suffer in human and spiritual ways for their enslavement to material gain [**47**]. Individual cases of personal business success and social advancement can be identified at all times across the period. It is harder to be certain whether the conditions of life for the generality of the late medieval urban population were improving or otherwise. When the owners of urban estates thought it worthwhile to build new rows of shops, it is evident that commerce, at least, was perceived to be flourishing [**66**]. On the other hand, we are invited to consider the claims made by a number of urban governments in the mid-fifteenth century that the loss of population was causing an uncontrollable decline both in the economic power and in the civic spirit of the towns [**77**]. The larger question of the quality of life needs to be considered in the light of a wide range of sources, and in view not merely of material criteria but of the opportunities for personal fulfilment open to townspeople of diverse social class and status.[8]

62. Building regulations in twelfth-century London

These ordinances, the first of their kind to be recorded, were included in an 'assize of buildings' issued in 1189 by the mayor of London, Henry fitz-Ailwin. The reference to a major fire in the city during the reign of Stephen is an indication that the vulnerability of wooden buildings and the need to build in stone had been debated in earlier periods, and indeed such fires must have generated collective discussion of the common interest long before the twelfth century. The implementation of some of these and related ordinances in the city is recorded from 1300 in the 'assize* of nuisance' [**67**].

H. T. Riley (ed.), *Liber Albus: The White Book of the City of London*, London: Richard Griffin, 1861, pp. 278–85; with, for the Latin text,

7 A. Quiney, *Town Houses of Medieval Britain*, New Haven and London, 2003; J. Schofield, *Medieval London Houses*, New Haven and London, 1994.

8 See also Sections VIII and IX.

H. T. Riley (ed.), *Liber Albus*, London: Longmans, Brown, Green, Longmans and Roberts, 1859, pp. 321–9. Latin, transl. by the editor, revised by GR.

i. If anyone wishes to build in stone, and his neighbour on account of poverty is unable, or is unwilling, then the latter must give the other three feet of his own land, on which he can make a wall, at his own cost, 3 feet thick and 16 feet high. He who gives the land shall have one clear half of the wall, and may place his timber [joists] upon it for building. And they shall make a gutter to receive and carry off the water falling from their houses at their joint expense.

ii. Concerning privies in the houses of citizens, it is ordained that if the pit made in such a chamber be lined with stone, the mouth of the pit shall be 2½ feet distant from the neighbour's land. But if not lined with stone, it should be 3½ feet distant from the neighbour's land.

iii. If any person has windows looking onto his neighbour's land, although he may have been for long in possession of the view and even though his predecessors may have been in possession of the windows, nevertheless his neighbour may lawfully obscure the view from such windows by building opposite them or by placing anything on his own land as may seem to him most expedient, unless the person who has such windows can show any writing by reason of which his neighbour may not obstruct the view from the windows.

iv. In ancient times the greater part of the city was built of wood, and the houses were covered with straw, stubble, and the like. Hence it happened that when a single house had caught fire, the greater part of the city was destroyed by the conflagration – something which occurred in the first year of the reign of King Stephen [1135–36] when, by reason of a fire that broke out at London Bridge, the church of St Paul was burned, from where the blaze extended, destroying houses and buildings, as far as the church of St Clement Danes. After this many of the citizens, to the best of their ability to avoid such a peril, built stone houses on their foundations, roofed with thick tiles and thus protected against the fury of the flames. It has consequently often happened that, when a fire has broken out in the city, and has destroyed many buildings, upon reaching such houses it has been unable to do further damage, and has there been extinguished. In this way, by such a house as this the houses of the neighbours have been saved from being burned.

63. Harbour works at Bristol 1240

The expansion of the harbour was a major civic project for the mayor and commonalty of Bristol. Such an enterprise was a political no less than an engineering challenge. The two documents reproduced here illustrate the division of lordship and franchises which inevitably complicated grand designs for urban development. By (a) the mayor and council of Bristol obtained permission to build on land of the powerful abbey of St Augustine. The royal letter in (b) shows how the mayor obtained the king's intervention to require support for the project from the inhabitants of the suburban district of Redcliffe. Outside the city and therefore independent of its legal control, Redcliffe would continue during the Middle Ages to offer an attractive immunity to the wealthy shipowners, merchants, and others who lived there. The splendid local parish church of St Mary Redcliffe remains testimony to both the wealth and the local pride of the area.

D. Walker (ed.), *The Cartulary of St Augustine's Abbey, Bristol*, Bristol and Gloucestershire Archaeological Society, X, 1998, no. 588 (a); N. D. Harding (ed.), *Bristol Charters 1155–1373*, 1, Bristol: Bristol Records Society, 1930, pp. 18–19 (b). Latin, transl. by the editors.

(a) [24 March 1240.] This is the agreement made between William of Breadstone, abbot and the convent of St Augustine in Bristol and Richard Aillard, mayor with the whole community of Bristol. That is, that the said abbot and convent grant, for themselves and their successors in perpetuity, to the mayor and community of Bristol and their heirs all of that land in the marsh of St Augustine's, Bristol, which lies outside the ditch surrounding the canons' arable land and extends eastwards as far as the edge of the harbour on the Frome (*usque ad marginem portus Frome*), which ditch runs from the canons' grange to the Avon, saving to the abbot and convent the land next to the ditch which the commune has begun to dig, measuring 142 feet wide, 92 feet wide in the middle of the marsh, and at the outer part of the marsh towards the Avon, 60 feet wide. On the land thus measured the commune of Bristol is to have in perpetuity free access for its ships, as in the past; meanwhile the commune is to preserve the monastery's rights over the land, and is to maintain the watercourse if it deteriorates. The remainder of the marsh of St Augustine towards the Frome and towards the marsh of the town of Bristol, on the east and south sides of the said ditch, is to belong in perpetuity to the commune and its heirs, for them to make a ditch (*trencheam*), a gate or whatever suits them without any impediment or contradiction. For this concession and for their good faith, the mayor and commune of Bristol gave to the said abbot and convent £6 13*s* 4*d*.

(b) Henry, by the grace of God king of England … greetings to his men of Redcliffe in the suburb of Bristol.

Whereas our burgesses of Bristol, for the common utility of the whole town and suburb of Bristol (*pro communi utilitate tocius ville Bristollie similiter et suburbia*), have begun to dig a ditch in the marsh of St Augustine, in order that ships coming to our port of Bristol may more freely, and without impediment, enter and depart, which trench they cannot complete at their own charge, we direct you that, since the improvement of the port will be of great benefit not only to the citizens but to yourselves, who also enjoy the same liberties as are held by our burgesses in that town and are participants in scot and lot [i.e. are assessed for tax] with them, and the successful completion of this ditch could be of great utility and profit (*multum possit utilis et fructuosa*) in so far as it affects you along with our burgesses in the liberties of the county, you are to lend effective strength to their enterprise, lest the project, which we regard as our own, should be delayed for lack of your help. At Windsor, 27 April 1240.

64. A skinner commissions a new town house 1308

His profits from the trade in furs enabled this skinner to pay for an entirely new house on the edge of the site of his 'old chamber'. Favoured by wealthy townsmen, the type adapted the features of the typical hall house inhabited in rural contexts by the country gentry. The hall, two storeys high, was open to the roof. From one end of the hall, a door opened on to a cross-passage containing a pantry, on the other side of which was a ground-floor chamber with a chimney. The passage also gave access to a stair which led up to a bedroom, known as a solar, situated over the ground-floor chamber. The carpenter, in return for a lump sum paid by the skinner in the form of skins, undertook to oversee the entire work, from the procurement of the materials to the completion of the locks. The evidence is a contract recorded in the court of the mayor of London. This would give the patron recourse against the carpenter in the event that the work was not done to his satisfaction.

L. F. Salzman, *Building in England down to 1540*, Oxford: Clarendon Press, 1952, pp. 417–18. Latin, transl. by GR.

Simon de Canterbury, carpenter, came before the mayor and aldermen on Saturday after the feast of St Martin [11 November] 1308, and agreed to make at his own proper charges, down to the locks, for William de Hanigtone, skinner, by the following Easter, a hall and a room with a chimney, and a larder [for the storage of food] between the hall and the room; and one solar [upstairs bedroom] over the room and larder; also an oriel [space, here probably lit by a window] at the end of the hall beyond the high table; and outside the hall one step [flight of stairs] from the ground to the hall door with an oriel; and two spaces in the cellar, divided cross-wise, beneath the hall; and a room for a privy, with two pipes leading to the privy; and a stable, 12 feet wide, stretching between the hall and the old kitchen, with a solar above the stable, and a loft above the solar; and at one end of this solar there is to be a kitchen with a chimney; and there is to be an oriel [here meaning a porch or passage], 8 feet wide, between the said hall and the old chamber.

William de Hanigtone acknowledged that he was bound to pay to Simon for the work the sum of £9 *5s 4d*, 50 eastern marten-skins, fur for a woman's hood to the value of *5s*, and fur for a robe for Simon.

65. Houses and shops in Cambridge

Property deeds, of which examples are given here, are among the commonest form of surviving urban records from the Middle Ages. Individual examples can be informative regarding the scale and function of houses and shops. Where substantial concentrations of deeds survive, they can be used to reconstruct (if only in part), like a four-dimensional jigsaw puzzle, the evolving pattern of development of a city street. Two sites in Cambridge are described in the following late fourteenth-century grants. Although differing from one another in detail, both exemplify some common features of medieval urban building. The premium on space at the street frontage, for its commercial value, led to a pattern in which properties tended to be narrow on the street and to run back for a relatively long distance. Each of these cases exemplifies a house with a hall (of two storeys, open to the roof) set back from the street behind a solar (usually a bedroom) raised above cellars or shops. In the case of (a) a row of three tiny shops has encroached into the street in front of the solar block. In (b) there are three booths directly underneath the solar itself, two with doors opening outwards to receive customers approaching through the churchyard. In (b) the nuns grant the tenants a building lease on condition that the latter have built an additional house on the site. A great deal of urban property was leased, as in these cases, from communities of monks or nuns. Monastic landlords varied, amongst themselves and over time, in the degree to which they engaged actively in the development of real estate (see also [**66**]).

Jesus College, Cambridge, MS. Gray 141 (a); MS. Gray 250a–b (b). Latin, transl. by GR.

(a) This indenture* witnesses that Margaret, prioress of the nunnery of St Radegund in Cambridge, grants to John Berlee of Cambridge, carter, a tenement in the parish of St Andrew outside Barnwell Gate, between a tenement of Corpus Christi College on one side and a tenement formerly of John de Toft and a tenement of Robert de Parys on the other, abutting at one end on the king's highway and at the other on the king's ditch and on Pouches Croft of the prior and canons of the chapel of St Edmund of Canterbury ... for forty years, paying 18*s* per annum to the said prioress and her successors. [The property comprises] a hall, with a solar in front of the tenement, and two cellars and a door beneath the solar, under a roof. The hall is 21 feet long and 18 feet wide; the solar is 20¼ feet long and 14 feet wide. And there is a chamber at the west end of the hall beneath another roof, which chamber is 33 feet long and 20 feet wide. And there are three chambers joined in front of the said tenement, solar and cellars, under a separate roof. There is also a dovecote. John agrees to repair these as necessary at his own expense. Witnessed by John Morice, mayor of Cambridge, and others. Dated on Christmas Day, 1369.

(b) This indenture witnesses that Margery Clanvile, prioress of St Radegund's nunnery, has granted to Richard Milde, chaplain, John de Kelesseye, cooper, and Avisia his wife, a tenement in St Clement's parish, Cambridge, between the tenement of John Dunton and that belonging to the chantry of St Mary in St Clement's church, abutting on the churchyard of the same church at one end, for 7*s* per annum payable to the nunnery while Richard Milde lives, and after his death, 10*s* per annum. Witnessed by William Horwode, mayor of Cambridge, and others. Dated on Tuesday after the Beheading of John the Baptist (30 August) 1373.

This indenture witnesses that Margery Clanvile, prioress of St Radegund's nunnery in Cambridge, leases to John de Kelleseye and Avisia, his wife, a tenement in St Clement's parish between a tenement of John Dunton and another belonging to the chantry of St Mary in St Clement's church, abutting at one end on the churchyard, for their lifetimes and five years thereafter, paying to the nunnery 4*s* per annum. [The property comprises] a good hall on the north side of the tenement, with a solar joined above the same hall, of the same width as the whole tenement, towards the churchyard. Under the solar are three cellars, one of which has a door opening into the hall and two have doors opening into the churchyard. There is also a kitchen joined over the solar on the south side of the tenement, and two cellars beneath the same roof as the hall on the north side of the tenement. Within one year, John will build a new house of oak beams, 30 feet long by 12 feet wide, at the end of the same tenement on the south side, towards the east. Witnessed by John Cotton, mayor of Cambridge, and others. Dated on Sunday after the feast day of St Barnabas (14 June), 1377.

66. Building shops at Westminster 1362–63

The almoner, a monk and one of the officers of Westminster Abbey, here develops a commercial street within the monastic precinct. The source is an extract from the annual account roll of this official. The almoner's suppliers included other officers of the same monastery. The construction entailed making the wooden frames, which were laid out flat on the ground prior to being hauled upright and locked into position. Stone foundations are not mentioned. Once completed, the new shops were let for about 9*s* each per annum. The considerable investment was evidently made in an expectation of a continuing economic expansion, which demographic decline and consequently falling rents in the early fifteenth century would disappoint.

Westminster Abbey Muniments 18989. Latin, transl. by GR.

Expenses on new buildings

Carpentry work for seven shops newly built £6. The cost of lifting the same shops 8*s* 10*d*. Wood bought from the warden of St Mary's chapel 80*s*. Four carts hired to bring the wood from Claygate to Westminster 6*s*. The expense of the almoner's cart with two men and three horses fetching wood there on four occasions 4*s*. 7000 laths bought at Kingston 35*s*. For their carriage 3*s* 6*d*. Laths bought at Rosamund's [a nearby manor of the abbot] 5*s*. Elm boards 12*s*. 100 Eastland boards [imported from the Baltic] 23*s* 4*d*. 62 Eastland boards bought from Brother John Mordon 10*s* 4*d*. 21,000 roofnails 28*s*. 23,000 sprignails 26*s* 10*d* [... and other nails]. 350 sacks of powdered lime 36*s* 5½*d*. 2 casks for [holding] laths 3*s* 4*d*. 225 roof-tiles 20*s* 3*d*. 51,000 tile-pins 9*s* 6¾*d* ... 10 locks and keys bought for the doors of the shops and other doors in the Almonry 8*s* 4*d*. 7 hinges bought for the doors 4*s* 1*d*. 16 pairs of hinges 6*s* 8*d*. 8 door-handles for the doors with their attachments 2*s* 6*d*. The cost of roofing in total £6 3*s* 4*d*. For putting in the groundsills [wooden foundations] of the houses 4*s* 2*d*. The wage of a painter for lathing, plastering and painting the said houses in total 75*s* 6*d*. Total £38 8*s* 10¼*d*.

67. Ideas of public nuisance and private space in London

The London assize* of nuisance addressed issues of personal and public safety in the city, as had been provided in regulations of the twelfth century [**62**]. Its records survive from the very beginning of the fourteenth century. It allowed Londoners to express, and perhaps encouraged them to develop, a sense of propriety suitable to the dense living conditions of the town.

H. M. Chew and W. Kellaway (eds), *London Assize of Nuisance 1301–1431*, London Record Society, X, 1973, pp. 79, 160–1. Latin, transl. by the editors.

(a) 25 June 1333. Andrew de Aubrey and Joan his wife complain that whereas they possess an easement in the use of a cess-pit common to their tenement and those of Thomas Heyron and Joan relict of John de Armenters, and the same was enclosed by a party-wall and roofed with joists and boards, so that the seats of the privies of the plaintiffs and the others could not be seen, Joan de Armenters and William de Thorneye have removed the party-wall and roof so that the extremities of those sitting upon the seats can be seen, a thing which is abominable and altogether intolerable. Judgement, after the site has been viewed, that the defendants must roof and enclose the cess-pit as it was before, under the penalty described by the law and custom of the city in such cases.

As regards the aperture which the same Andrew and Joan his wife made in their room over the cellar of John de Armenters, now held by William de Thorneye, through which his private business (*secreta*) can be seen by those in the rooms above, and concerning which Joan de Armenters and the above-named William have made complaint, it is adjudged by the mayor and aldermen that it be blocked up.

(b) 19 March 1378. Thomas Yonge and Alice his wife complain by Richard Forster, their attorney, that Geoffrey Chadensfeld [rector of St Margaret Friday Street], Walter [Selsham, chaplain] and William [Whetele, citizen and tawyer], with Stephen atte Fryth, armourer, on Monday 5 October 1377 built a forge (*fabricam*) of earth and timber, 40 feet from the road, in the close of their tenement adjoining the plaintiffs' messuage* in the parish of St Augustine by Paul's Gate, on the south side of Watling Street, of which the chimney is lower by 12 feet than it should be, and not built of plaster and stone as the custom of the city requires; and the blows of the sledge-hammers when the great pieces of iron called 'Osmund'* are being wrought into breast-plates, *guysers* [*cuisses*, worn to protect the thighs], *jambers* [for the lower legs] and other pieces of armour, shake the stone and earthen party-walls of the plaintiffs' house so that they are in danger of collapsing, and disturb the rest of the plaintiffs and their servants, day and night, and spoil the wine and ale in their cellar, and the stench of the smoke from the sea-coal* used in the forge penetrates their hall and chambers, so that whereas formerly they could let the premises for £6 13s 4*d* a year, they are now worth only 40*s*. Andrew Pykeman and Nicholas Twyford, sheriffs, have testified elsewhere that the defendants have been summoned by John Little, tailor, and Andrew Cornewaille. They come in person but Stephen Fryth says that he has no interest in the tenement in dispute. Geoffrey, Walter and William answer as tenants. They deny the plaintiffs' contention that chimneys ought to be built of stone and plaster, and high enough to cause no nuisance to the neighbouring tenements, and declare that good and honest men of any craft, viz. goldsmiths, smiths, pewterers, goldbeaters, grocers, skinners, marshals* and armourers are at liberty to carry on their trade anywhere in the city, adapting their premises as is most convenient for their work, and that according to ancient custom any feoffor* may give, bequeath or lease his property as well to craftsmen using great hammers as to others. They add that they have let the premises against which the nuisance is alleged to Stephen Fryth for a term of years which has not yet expired, and that he has set up his anvil in what was formerly the kitchen at a sufficient distance from the plaintiffs' messuage, and strengthened the chimney with mortar and clay and raised it by six feet or more. They maintain that the plaintiffs cannot in any case complain of the chimney or of the noise of the hammers or the smoke, because their messuage was built as recently as 1349–50, and is much higher than the house it replaced, and has windows facing the forge, which its predecessor had not.

68. Clean water at Winchester

Streams ran down the middle of most of the streets of Winchester, providing water for various uses. Subordinate water-channels led from these into individual houses. Arguments concerning the communal interest in these streams evidently gave rise to an appeal through the sheriff for royal judgement, recorded in this writ transcribed in the court roll of the city for 1299. Such a case reveals the tensions which often arose in relation to communal resources in the city, and also the legal and diplomatic methods used in the attempt to resolve them.

J. S. Furley (ed.), *Town Life in the XIV Century, As Seen in the Court Rolls of Winchester City*, Winchester: Warren and Son, 1947, pp. 134–5. Latin, transl. by the editor, revised by GR.

[1299] Juliana atte Floude brought a writ of the king addressed to the mayor and bailiffs of Winchester in these words: Edward, by the grace of God king of England, lord of Ireland and duke of Aquitaine, to his mayor and bailiffs of the city of Winchester, greeting: Juliana atte Floude has represented to us that whereas a certain watercourse in the street called Shulworth Street is and ought to be common to herself and to each and every individual in the same city in such a way that she and all others of the town ought to have their convenience and easement in it when they wish, certain men of the city hinder the said Juliana from having her convenience and easement in the said water as she ought to have, and has been accustomed to have in times past, to her manifest loss; and therefore we bid you that, if this be so, you cause the said Juliana to have this convenience and easement in the water as she should and as she and her predecessors have had in the past, and that you in no way fail in this. Witness myself at Sheen 5 August 1299.

And thereupon the said Juliana makes plaint that certain men of the same city have hindered her from having her convenience and easement in the said water as she ought to have, and used to have in times past, for washing and cleaning her fine and coarse yarn, to her no small loss. And inquest was taken on this by the oath of John Botman [and twenty-three others], who say on their oath that John de Titinger and Henry de Colemere have hindered the same Juliana from washing and cleaning her cloths and having other conveniences to which she is entitled, to her damage of half a mark. And they say that the said water is common and ought, and in all times past has been accustomed, to be common to Juliana herself and to all and singular of the said city, except that they shall not put in the water the refuse of woad, called 'wodger', nor hides from tanning nor the dung of men or animals nor the guts of animals, nor shall they wash there children's clothes with their filth, nor have lavatories or drains over the said water. And the said John and Henry are forbidden to hinder Juliana or others from having any of their conveniences in the said water, save such as are above mentioned, in such a way that no further complaint about it shall reach our lord the king.

69. Water sold in the street

Access to a ready supply of running water was often limited, and townspeople in such cases were dependent on street vendors. Such suppliers were naturally poor, and lacking in the means to defend their interests before the law. From this record, it appears that the water-sellers of Nottingham had responded to the non-payment of one of their number by boycotting the customer concerned. This burgess, however, was able and willing to sue. The decision of the jury is not known.

W. H. Stevenson (ed.), *Records of the Borough of Nottingham*, 3 vols, London: Quaritch, 1882–85, i, pp. 115–17. Latin, transl. by the editor, revised by GR.

On 24 October 1330, Robert de Morewode brings a case against Henry le Waterleader on a plea of transgression: he complains that as Henry is a common servant (*communis serviens*) to carry water by bushels* to sell to all men of Nottingham wishing to have water by purchase, and on Monday before Michaelmas [29 September] last, in Nottingham, he [i.e. Robert] sent Alice, his servant, and very many times other servants of his, to Henry to request that he carry to Robert's house four horse-loads of water, and offered him a penny, according to his usual rate. But Henry would not carry any water to Robert, but altogether refused, and called Robert false and unfaithful, and alleged that he perforated his bushel and all the bushels of Nottingham with his knife, and further persuaded all his companions of the same calling that they should not carry water to Robert because Robert would not pay them their wage. So Robert had no water for five weeks, either from Henry or from any of his companions, by which he lost the meal of two quarters of malt [grinding malt into 'meal' was evidently Robert de Morewode's trade], of the value of 10*s*, to Robert's damage of 40*s*. Henry says that he is not guilty in any respect. Both appeal to a jury.

70. Water supply at King's Lynn 1378

As this record makes explicit, to endow the construction of a public water fountain was perceived as an act of Christian piety. A 'pious' burgess having provided the means to a convent of friars, the secular civic authorities collaborated with the monks to realise the project. The public provision of clean water was thus, for all parties – the mayor and town council, the Austin friars and the pious burgess – at once a practical and a religious duty.

D. M. Owen (ed.), *The Making of King's Lynn*, Records of Social and Economic History, new series, IX, Oxford: Oxford University Press for the British Academy, 1984, pp. 117–19. Latin, transl. by the editor. Reproduced by permission of the British Academy.

This is the agreement made between the mayor and community of the town of Lynn, on the one part, and the prior and convent of the Augustinian friars of Lynn, on the other, that is, that since the prior and convent have received £40 from one John Glower, formerly a burgess of Lynn, on condition that they should complete an aqueduct, not denying to any of the community the water flowing daily in it … the mayor and community, considering both the pious intention of the said John and the benevolence and the great diligence of the said prior and convent to complete the same aqueduct, grant for themselves and their successors that the religious may freely bring the said aqueduct beneath the wall and the ground of the town as far as their buildings without impediment from the mayor and community … and that they may inspect, repair or renew the aqueduct without contradiction … unless by chance the town should be in danger on account of war … And the said prior and convent will and concede for themselves and their successors that the said aqueduct shall flow continuously throughout the year for the free use of the community, from a cistern to be properly constructed in the street called Listersgate, through three pipes commonly called 'keys' (*claves*), the water to be available to anyone of the community from the sixth hour after midnight until the seventh hour after noon, between Easter and Michaelmas, unless any reasonable interruption of the flow should occur because of repairs or other impediment.

71. Public hygiene in Nottingham

The disposal of rubbish was both a practical problem and a catalyst of discussion concerning the values and amenities of community in the town.[9] The local court record reveals the twelve jurors reviewing a series of instances in which the collective interest and identity of the

9 See Introduction, p. 24.

town were seen to be compromised by the selfish behaviour of individual townspeople.

W. H. Stevenson (ed.), *Records of the Borough of Nottingham*, 3 vols, London: Quaritch, 1882–85, i, pp. 317–23. Latin, transl. by the editor, revised by GR.

[Borough court roll, April 1396] Presentments of the jurors, who say that a common lane is blocked up in Little Marsh, between the tenement of Ibot Barry and that of Richard Chilwell, and now it does not exist. Michael Brabayn and Henry Soothill have blocked up the end of Limering Lane with ordure, to the great detriment of the water of Lene and the loss of the town. Magota Ball blocks up Organ Lane with the weeds from her gardens. Margaret Salmon, Nicholas Alastre, and others, block up the common cave[10] of the town (*obturant antrum commune villae praedictae*) on the northern side with ordure, weeds and cinders. All who live in the street leading from John Whaplington to the chapel bar on either side of the street block up the common way with ordure and cinders, to the serious damage of all people passing there; they are pardoned because they are poor.

72. Animals in the town

Animals kept for a variety of practical purposes were a constant and at times intrusive presence in the medieval town. Domestic pets are not well documented, although we know from literary and testamentary records that cats, dogs and birds were kept – and even, in some social circles, monkeys.[11] The licence granted exceptionally to unleashed dogs of the aristocracy, who may have had such hounds running beside their horses or carriages, was a mark of class distinction.

H. T. Riley (ed.), *Liber Albus*, London: Richard Griffin, 1861, pp. 388–9 (a); W. H. Stevenson (ed.), *Records of the Borough of Nottingham*, 3 vols, London: Quaritch, 1882–85, i, pp. 356–9 (b); M. D. Harris (ed.), *The Coventry Leet Book*, 4 vols, Early English Text Society, London: Oxford University Press, 1907–13, p. 27 (c); M. Bateson (ed.), *Records of the*

10 The soft sandstone on which Nottingham stands has been excavated with caves since early times.

11 See Introduction, p. 2.

Borough of Leicester, ii, London: C. J. Clay, 1901, p. 292 (d). Latin, transl. by the editors, revised by GR (a), (b), (d); English, revised by GR (c).

(a) [London by-law, fourteenth century] To avoid the noise, damage and strife that this has caused in the past, it is forbidden that any person shall keep a dog accustomed to go at large and unleashed out of its own enclosure, by day or night, within the franchises* of the city, with the exception of the dogs of the nobility (*chiens gentilx*), on pain of a fine of 40*d* to the work of the chamber. And an equal fine for anyone making a plea on behalf of such an offender.

(b) [Nottingham borough court roll, 1398–99] John Blank makes plaint of Robert Hayward on a plea of trespass, that whereas the usage and custom of Nottingham is that every man having swine here in Nottingham should, by the proclamation of the mayor of the liberty of the town of Nottingham, keep his swine in his houses, or should have the aforesaid swine in a pig-sty, so that he should not cause damage to others through lack of proper custody, Robert's pigs, at the feast of the Nativity of St John the Baptist [24 June], worried and devoured a cock-chicken of the aforesaid John, worth 12*d*, and a mayse[12] of red herrings, worth 6*s* 8*d*. And this was Robert's fault, because the pigs were not guarded, so John is injured and has received damage to the sum of 10*s*, for which he enters suit. Robert comes in his own person, and defends the force and injury, and says that he is guilty of nothing that has been presented against him, and as to this he places himself upon the country [appeals to the judgement of a jury].

(c) [Proclamation of the mayor of Coventry, 1421.] That no man [may] have ducks going in the street, upon pain of forfeiture of the same ducks.

(d) [Leicester borough ordinances, October 1467.] That every horse, neat [cow] or any other beast of unfranchised persons that is found in the Cowhay [a field on the edge of the town] shall pay for each foot 1*d*, and that shall the chamberlains levy to the profit of the commons. And that no man have more than two neat going in the Cowhay, on pain of losing 12*d* for each beast.

12 Uncertain quantity.

Also that no ducks be let abroad in any street within the four gates of the town, on pain of forfeiture of ½*d* for every duck, that to be levied by the chamberlains to the use of the town.

73. Street-cleaning at Salisbury

Butchering was a recognised challenge to health in all towns, and all borough courts attempted to regulate it. The pressure of traffic on city streets was also general, but the civic officers of Salisbury faced particular difficulties. The streets of Salisbury had been laid out in the thirteenth century [**13**] in such a way that a wide stream ran along the middle of each (possibly in deliberate emulation of Winchester, see [**68**]), creating problems for large loads.

D. R. Carr (ed.), *The First General Entry Book of the City of Salisbury 1387–1452*, Wiltshire Record Society, LIV, 2001, pp. 117, 242–3. Latin, transl. by the editor.

[*c.*1450] That city butchers should not slaughter their animals in front of Butcher Row in the common street, but behind Butcher Row, because of the foulness of the rotting remains; that they should not render fat by day but in the night, and that they should not remove the filth or intestines of their animals by day but in the night.

[May 1452] Agreed: to elect certain persons both from the Twenty-Four and from other commoners to supervise the paving of the streets and the common privies, ditches, sewers, and gutters emitting their filth into the common ditches of the city, so that by their supervision the sewers and gutters may be stopped up or by the supervision and orders of the persons to be elected they may be cleansed and repaired, along with their banks, and so cleansed and repaired they may be kept in their state of well-being to the adornment of the city.

[May 1452] Also agreed and ordered: no carters or drivers of carts into the city to attach trailers to their carts or wagons, which so attached or joined are commonly called drays, [or] to drive them within 'lez barrys' or enclosures (*cepta*) of the city. Nor is anyone in future to bring within the said bars or enclosures of the city on the saddles or the backs of horses or pack-animals the long wooden packs which are commonly called trusses or draughts, on pain of forfeiting the drays, trusses or draughts, so that the pavements of the city's streets are not broken up as previously by drays, trusses or draughts of the kind, the banks of the common trenches are not destroyed, and the watercourses are not altered or blocked by the dragging of mud, as has happened. Advance notice of this matter is to be given by public proclamation.

74. Street furniture

The London mayoral ordinance in (a) shows civic authority regulating the competitive advertisements of taverns in the form of inn-signs which, in the attempt to attract custom, grew ever more elaborate, substantial, and dangerous to passers-by. The directive of the mayor of Coventry in (b), on the other hand, shows the city government taking advantage of innkeepers' desire to publicise themselves by regularising their lamps as public street-lighting.

H. T. Riley (ed.), *Memorials of London and London Life in the XIIIth, XIVth, and XVth Centuries*, London: Longmans, Green & Co., 1868, pp. 386–7 (a); M. D. Harris (ed.), *The Coventry Leet Book*, 4 vols, Early English Text Society, London: Oxford University Press, 1907–13, p. 234 (b). Latin, transl. by the editor, revised by GR (a); English, revised by GR (b).

(a) 21 September 1375. At the prayer of the commonalty [of the city of London], making plaint that the ale-stakes projecting in front of the taverns in Cheap, and elsewhere in the city, extended too far over the king's highway, so as to impede those riding there, and other persons, and, by reason of their excessive weight, did tend to the great deterioration of the houses in which they were placed – it was ordained and granted by the mayor and aldermen, as a befitting remedy for the same, and all the taverners of the city being summoned, orders were given to them, on pain of paying 40*d* to the chamber of the guildhall every time the said ordinance should be contravened, that in future no one should have an ale-stake bearing his sign or leaves [a bush] projecting or extending over the king's highway more than seven feet in length at the utmost.

(b) Ordinance of the mayor of Coventry 1448. All innkeepers are to have a lamp hanging before their doors until 9 o'clock at night, on pain of a fine of 6*s* 8*d*.

75. Town cattle

An unpaid debt provides a glimpse of the town's dependence on its rural resources. The woman's role appears in the legal record under the shadow of her husband. We may infer a significant social discrepancy between the man, Jonn Broxtowe, who held the civic office with responsibility for the town cattle, and the woman, Isabel Barrett, hired to drive the animals out to pasture each day from Easter to Midsummer.

W. H. Stevenson (ed.), *Records of the Borough of Nottingham*, 3 vols, London: Quaritch, 1882–85, ii, p. 133. Latin, transl. by the editor, revised by GR.

[Nottingham borough court roll, 30 October 1432] John Barrett of Nottingham makes a personal complaint of John Broxtowe in a plea of debt of 21*d*. And he says that whereas the said John Broxtowe engaged the said John's wife, Isabella, from the feast of Easter 1432 until the feast of the Nativity of St John the Baptist [24 June] then next following, to drive the cattle of the town of Nottingham to pasture for the time aforesaid for the aforesaid 21*d*, to be there paid to the said John Barrett at the feast of the Apostles Peter and Paul [29 June] then next following; which money the aforesaid John Broxtowe, although he has been often requested, has not yet paid to the aforesaid John Barrett, but refused, and still does refuse to pay him: whereby he says that he is injured to the value of 21*d*; and therefore he brings suit. And John Broxtowe says that he owes him nothing. Wherefore an inquest is appointed, and John Broxtowe is in mercy for licence [to agree].

76. Fuel

Every town's reliance upon its hinterland for the basic requirement of fuel was a perennial source of concern. In later medieval London the wood and charcoal supplied (as is described in this record) from neighbouring counties was supplemented by coal, brought from Newcastle by ship and consequently known as 'sea-coal'.* This record, a mayoral ordinance issued in response to a public complaint, gives a hint of the citizens' prejudice against the peasants who brought charcoal for sale from the woods of Kent and other counties adjacent to the metropolis.

H. T. Riley (ed.), *Memorials of London and London Life in the XIIIth, XIVth, and XVth Centuries*, London: Longmans, Green & Co., 1868, pp. 335–6. Latin, transl. by the editor, revised by GR.

The common people of the city of London have suffered great loss for a long time past, because foreigners, of diverse counties, have brought charcoal in carts and upon horses for sale in the said city, and given the common people to understand that every sack contained fully one quarter of charcoal. Therefore on 13 January 1368, James Andreu, mayor of the said city, caused diverse sacks, brought either by cart or by horse, containing charcoal for sale, to be assayed by the standard of the city. Of which sacks, one was found to be two bushels short, and another sack was deficient by one bushel and a half; and in all the other sacks fully one bushel was wanting. And for avoiding such damages and falsities, committed against the common people, it is ordained, by assent of the mayor, aldermen and good people of the commonalty, summoned to the guildhall on that date, that all those who shall be convicted of such deceit and falsity shall be put upon the pillory, and the sacks burnt beneath them.

77. The perception of decline: Winchester in the mid-fifteenth century

The pleas of towns for remission of royal taxation are, for obvious reasons, suspect evidence for urban decline in the fifteenth century. This example, however, shows how circumstantial such declarations could be; and at least some of its claims are borne out by archaeological evidence (some fifteen of Winchester's churches are, in fact, known to have become disused in the later Middle Ages: a figure close to that of seventeen lost churches claimed in the petition).[13] The despairing final phrase declares that, if Winchester cannot be helped by the king's remission of its tax burden, the mayor and other officers will be compelled to stand down and return the city into the direct control of the crown.

'A petition of the city of Winchester to King Henry VI', *Archaeologia*, I, London: Society of Antiquaries of London, 1770, pp. 91–5. English, revised by GR.

13 See Introduction, pp. 17–18; Keene, *Winchester*, i, pp. 86–105; *Calendar of Patent Rolls, 1436–41*, pp. 400, 507.

1 February 1452. To the king our sovereign lord. Beseech full humbly your humble true liege men, the mayor, bailiffs and commonalty of your poor city of Winchester, that whereas they have been charged to bear the fee farm of your said city, which amounts yearly to the sum of £75, and bear also to the master of the hospital of the Mary Magdalen beside Winchester £3; also when the 15th penny or tax is granted to your highness, it amounts to the sum of £51 10*s* 4*d* within the said city, the which when it is to be levied, some one man in the said city is assessed at £2 13*s* 4*d*, and some at £3 6*s* 8*d*, because your said city is desolate of people; also the expense of burgesses of the said city coming to your parliaments amounts to 4*s* a day. For the which said fee farm so to be paid, your bailiffs have little or nought of certainty to raise it but only of casualties [occasional levies], and yearly lose in payment of the said fee farm £40 or more. For which causes abovesaid, and also for the great charges and daily costs the which your said poor city bears about the enclosing and murage of your said city, it is become right desolate, in so much as many notable persons be withdrawn out of the said city for the causes abovesaid, and 997 houses which were wont to be occupied with people stand now void, and because of these withdrawing, 17 parish churches stand unused at this day, the which parishes and houses be more plainly expressed in a schedule hereto annexed. And where it pleased your highness in relieving of your said poor city, 24 May 1441, to grant unto your mayor and commonalty of the said city then being, in relief of all the charges above-said £26 13*s* 4*d*, to be taken yearly to them and to their successors unto the end of ... winters then next following of the feasts of Easter and Michaelmas by even portions, of the issues and profits coming of the ulnage* and subsidy of woollen cloths within the said city and suburbs and soke* of the same, and in all other places within your shire of Southampton by the hands of the collectors, farmers, receivers and other occupiers of the same, for the time being, as in your letters patent thereof to them made may appear more plainly: Which annuity is now void to them, and wholly returned to you, because of an act, made in your parliament, begun at Westminster and finished at Leicester.[14] And so now your said suppliants stand all utterly destitute of all manner of relief of their charges abovesaid, to the utterest undoing of your said city for ever, without your high and noble grace be showed to them in this behalf. That it please your said highness graciously to consider the charges abovesaid,

14 Henry VI, desperately short of funds, had secured an Act of Resumption in 1450 whereby he took back into his hands various rights and lands previously granted.

and, of your most abundant grace, to grant unto the mayor, bailiffs and commonalty of your said city *£26 13s 4d*, to be had and taken yearly to them, and to their successors, from the feast of Michaelmas [29 September] 1452, for evermore, of the ulnage and subsidy of woollen cloths to be sold within your said city, suburbs and soke of the same, and in other places within your shire of Southampton, by the hands of the collectors, farmers, receivers and occupiers of the said ulnage and subsidy for the time being, at the feasts of Easter and Michaelmas by even portions after the tenor and effect of another schedule to this bill annexed.

These be the streets that be fallen down in the city of Winchester within 80 years last past:

Jury Street, wherein were 80 householders, and now but 2.
Fleshmonger Street, wherein were 140 householders, and now but 2.
Fishmonger Street, wherein were 60 householders, and now but 4.
Coalbrook Street, wherein were 160 householders, and now be but 16.
Calpe Street, wherein were 100 householders, and now be but 6.
Gold Street, wherein were 140 householders, and now be but 8.
Burden Street, wherein were 60 householders, and now is never one.
Shulworth Street, wherein were 70 households, and now be but 4.
Buck Street, wherein were 40 households, and now be but 2.
Minster Street, wherein were 90 households, and now be but 4.
Gar Street, wherein were 100 households, and now is never one.

The number of households that be fallen 997, and apart from these be fallen within the same city, since the last parliament, 81 households.

The desolation of the said poor city is so great, and yearly falling, for there is such decay and unwin* that, without gracious comfort of the king our sovereign lord, the mayor and the bailiffs must of necessity cease and deliver up the city and the keys into the king's hands.

78. Paving the city streets

During the 1470s and 1480s a series of town councils petitioned the crown in parliament for permission to impose upon property owners the responsibility to make and repair the paving of the street in front of their houses. The cities concerned included Gloucester, Bristol,

Cirencester, and Winchester, together with Canterbury, whose successful petition of 1477 is reproduced here.[15] The case exemplifies the use of parliament by town councils to secure exceptional rights of taxation in order to fund substantial civic projects.

Rotuli parliamentorum, 6 vols, London, 1767–77, vi, pp. 177–9. English, revised by GR.

To the right wise and discreet commons in this present parliament assembled, shown unto your wisdoms, the mayor and commonalty of the city of Canterbury. For as much as the same city is one of the oldest cities of this realm, and therein is the principal see of the spiritual estate of the same realm, and which city also is most in sight of all strangers of the parts beyond the sea resorting into this realm and departing out of the same, and because of the glorious saints that there lie enshrined, is greatly renowned throughout Christendom, unto which city also is great repair [the flocking of multitudes] of much of the people of this realm, both of estates and others, by way of pilgrimage to visit the said saints. And it is so, that the same city is often times full foul, noisome and unhealthy, both to all the inhabitants and to all other persons resorting there, on account of which often times is spoken much disworship in diverse places, both beyond the sea and on this side of the sea, which cannot be remedied in any way, unless the said city may be paved. To this the greater part of the inhabitants of the same city, having burgages,* houses or tenements in the same, are right well willed and agreeable, provided that there be authority to compel others to contribute to the same.

Please it therefore your wisdoms … to enact that all and every persons, being seised* or possessed of any burgages, properties or tenements within or adjoining to the principal street of the said city, which begins at the gate called the Westgate … and extends eastward to Newingate, or in another street which begins at Burgate and extends westwards to a place called the Bullstake and to the gate of the Black Friars, or in another street, from the Bullstake southward to the church of St Andrew and southward from there to the iron cross in the parish of St Margaret, into which streets and places, commonly is more resort of both strangers and others, than to any other street or place within the city, after reasonable warning by the civic officers, as often as

15 For the others see *Rotuli parliamentorum*, vi, pp. 49, 180, 333, 390–1.

necessary, shall repair the pavement before each of the said burgages, properties and tenements ... up to the middle of the street before them.

Which petition being heard in the parliament, the response was: Let it be done as is requested.

VII. TENSIONS AND VIOLENCE

As the medieval town was defined by the diversity of its component elements, so it was condemned to the strains of tension and to periodic violence. Economic growth raised the stakes, leading to further differentiation of wealth and status and encouraging increased competition for control of taxation and access to markets. During the long thirteenth century, as the medieval European economy expanded to its limits, a series of clashes over municipal jurisdiction sprang from a clear economic motivation. A significant element in these conflicts was often resentment of the legal immunities enjoyed by the Church. At the beginning of that period, the leading cloth-workers and merchants of such a borough as Bury St Edmunds, which had grown up as a small market to service the monastic community, were already beginning to show signs of restlessness under the patriarchal aegis of the abbot, who reprimanded their disobedience as though they were unruly children [**79**]. At its end, the townsmen had organised themselves into a guild through which to orchestrate their commercial interests and political identity [**82**].[1] Monastic towns in general faced similar and usually immoveable ecclesiastical authority: only the royal act of Dissolution in the 1530s would remove the clerical yoke. But others in addition to Bury used a social and religious fraternity as a means to focus and express the concerns of the secular population [**87**]. Assaults by townsmen upon monastic communities, as occurred in Bury and Abingdon in 1327, seem in general to have been orchestrated through the formation of guilds which, if they did not at the time achieve the autonomy that was sought, none the less continued to function as surrogate communes for the articulation of collective identities and the undertaking of public works.[2] Such alternative vehicles of communal expression may go some way to explain the fact that such conflicts only rarely flared into open violence.[3]

1 M. D. Lobel, *The Borough of Bury St Edmund's: A Study in the Government and Development of a Monastic Town*, Oxford, 1935.

2 G. Rosser, *The Art of Solidarity in the Middle Ages. Guilds in England 1250–1550*, Oxford, 2015, esp. ch. 6.

3 N. M. Trenholme, *The English Monastic Boroughs*, Columbia, MI, 1927, is a useful account which, however, tends in general to exaggerate the violence of the conflicts.

The issue of ecclesiastical rights and franchises* could be no less potent a catalyst of political tension in other places, and especially in the cathedral towns, which on occasion witnessed dramatic scenes of a bishop blockaded within his palace (at Hereford in 1262) or a cathedral close in flames (at Norwich in 1272) [**5**]. Rifts at the level of the clerical and secular elites could open up debate to a larger political community, giving an effective voice to the unenfranchised, as rival authorities bid for popular support.[4] The legal immunity enjoyed by the clerical population of any town, in so far as it was subject to the ecclesiastical and not to the secular courts, created a particular atmosphere of intermittent tension in the university towns. In all towns, the clerical population represented a not insignificant 2 or 3 per cent of the total.[5] But in the cases of Oxford and Cambridge, that proportion was far higher because all students entered minor clerical orders (even if a decreasing number in the later Middle Ages eventually proceeded to become priests), and civic officers found themselves at times provoked beyond endurance by the snub to their dignity and authority. Even the deadly consequences of the St Scholastica's Day riot in Oxford in 1355 did not bring about a resolution of this jurisdictional conflict, which certainly went well beyond the apparently trivial incident in a tavern which set light to the city. The value of the students to the Crown as prospective bureaucrats and administrators was such that, to the mayor's exasperation, the king invariably upheld their academic privileges [**85**].[6] The university environment generated in peculiarly concentrated form a more widely encountered tendency of young men in towns to congregate socially, to drink, and on occasion to prove their developing masculinity in acts of collective violence.[7]

4 G. Rosser, 'Conflict and political community in the medieval town: disputes between clergy and laity in Hereford', in T. R. Slater and G. Rosser (eds), *The Church in the Medieval Town*, Aldershot, 1998, pp. 20–42; P. Maddern, 'Order and disorder', in C. Rawcliffe and R. Wilson (eds), *Medieval Norwich*, London, 2004, pp. 189–212.

5 R. N. Swanson, *Church and Society in Later Medieval England*, Oxford, 1989, pp. 30–6; N. Tanner, *The Church in Late Medieval Norwich 1370–1532*, Toronto, 1984, pp. 18–21.

6 For modern accounts of the disturbance of 1355, drawing on additional sources, see H. Rashdall, *The Universities of Europe in the Middle Ages*, ed. F. M. Powicke and A. B. Emden, 3 vols, Oxford, 1936, iii, pp. 96–102; W. Pantin, *Oxford Life in Oxford Archives*, Oxford, 1972, pp. 99–104; J. Catto (ed.), *The History of the University of Oxford*, i, *The Early Oxford Schools*, Oxford, 1984, pp. 146–7.

7 R. M. Karras, 'Sharing wine, women, and song: masculine identity formation in the medieval European universitites', in J. J. Cohen and B. Wheeler (eds), *Becoming Male in the Middle Ages*, New York, 1997, pp. 187–202; P. J. P. Goldberg, 'Masters and men in late medieval England', in D. M. Hadley (ed.), *Masculinity in Medieval Europe*, London, 1999, pp. 56–70, esp. pp. 64–8.

The secular population was itself, of course, divided by wealth, status and influence. Class also can be seen as a contributor to social conflict in the town. The large proportion of urban workers who did not own the premises or, probably, the tools of their trade but who worked for wages created tensions between shop-owners and this dependent labour force [**28**]. At times those tensions were manifest in an explicit challenge addressed to the masters by the journeymen of a craft, having been nurtured once again in the meetings of an unofficial fraternity [**90**]. However, in the course of a professional career, a working man or woman typically moved to and fro across this economic divide, complicating the image of a clear class distinction.[8] The group of townsmen in Oxford who in the middle of the thirteenth century identified themselves as 'the lesser burgesses' and who claimed to speak for the 'lower commune' of the city, catalogued a series of grievances which focused on the perceived corruption and manipulation of office on the part of a narrow group [**80**]. These were serious issues, but not in this case rooted in differences of class.

Xenophobia was the ostensible force behind a number of violent incidents, although, considering that these never amounted to a sustained persecution of foreigners, a more realistic interpretation of these attacks would seek the underlying cause elsewhere, and in particular in perceived economic threats. Intermittent assaults on Italian merchants in fourteenth-century London [**86**] need to be seen in this light, as does the attack on Flemings during the disturbances in London in June 1381.[9] The true causes of conflict are not always easy to determine. The particular role of urban populations in the Peasants' Revolt of 1381 continues to invite further analysis. While some studies have pointed to the class interests of dependent urban workers, others have noted the opportunism and lack of evident ideological motivation on the part of some of the townspeople subsequently charged with involvement in the uprising.[10] At Beverley, a dramatic overturning of the regime

8 See Section IV.

9 H. Bradley, 'The Italian community in London, *c.*1350–1450', Ph.D. thesis, University of London, 1992; M. Bratchel, 'Regulation and group-consciousness in the later history of London's Italian merchant colonies', *Journal of European Economic History*, IX, 1980, pp. 585–610; M. Carlin, *Medieval Southwark*, London, 1996, pp. 157–62.

10 R. H. Hilton, *Bond Men Made Free: Medieval Peasant Movements and the English Rising of 1381*, 2nd edn, with introduction by C. Dyer, London, 2003; A. F. Butcher, 'English urban society and the Revolt of 1381', in R. H. Hilton and T. H. Aston (eds), *The English Rising of 1381*, Cambridge, 1984, pp. 84–111; A. Prescott, 'London in the Peasants' Revolt: a portrait gallery', *London Journal*, VII, 1981, pp. 125–43.

coincided with the Revolt, with which some connection appears to be indicated, but the sources are enigmatic [**88**]. The most common catalyst of political awareness and activism among shopkeepers, artisans and merchants alike was a perceived inequity in the imposition of local taxes. Typical was the introduction in the late fifteenth century by the city elders of Coventry of a new toll on cloth, which precipitated disturbances by workers who drew on folk legend and used the media of rhyme and billboard publicity to maximise the impact of their protest [**91**].[11] At the end of our period widespread protest was occasioned concerning access to common pastures outside the towns. Civic officers who attempted to offset financial losses by leasing town fields to graziers provoked townspeople to appeal against this infringement of what were claimed (on little or no legal basis) to be their traditional 'liberties' and 'rights'. The significant outcome of such disputes was a heightened sense, amongst protesters, of their collective political identity.[12]

Official accounts and clerical histories which record such incidents tend to characterise their participants as irrational and chaotic.[13] The evidence, however, suggests that, on the relatively rare occasions when they revolted, townspeople tended to act with a deliberate purpose. The very emotionalism of their rhetoric and actions, which older historians overlooked or dismissed as insignificant, needs to be recognised as part of a conscious strategy.[14] Our sources often give no more than tantalising glimpses of the motives of those who caused disturbances, with the result that we risk underestimating the extent of rationally formulated protest.[15]

We should take care, therefore, in our interpretation of evidence of interpersonal violence in the medieval town: it is too easy to slip into lazy generalisation about the supposed absence of either jurisdictional

11 On such political use of popular culture see G. Rosser, 'Myth, image and social process in the English medieval town', *Urban History*, XXIII, 1996, pp. 5–25.

12 C. D. Liddy, 'Urban enclosure riots: risings of the commons in English towns, 1480–1525', *Past & Present*, CCXXVI, 2015, pp. 41–77.

13 See the monastic chroniclers on the Peasants' Revolt, excerpted in B. Dobson (ed.), *The Peasants' Revolt of 1381*, 2nd edn, London, 1983.

14 J. Haemers, 'A moody community? Emotion and ritual in late medieval urban revolts', in E. Lecuppre-Desjardin and A.-L. Van Bruaene (eds), *Emotions in the Heart of the City (14th–16th Centuries)*, Turnhout, 2005, pp. 63–81.

15 S. K. Cohn, *Popular Protest in Late Medieval English Towns*, Cambridge, 2013, catalogues many incidents, some, although not all, of which bear the mark of planning and co-ordination.

or emotional controls on aggressive behaviour [**83**], [**89**].[16] Every incident is a tiny window on to a larger world of social relationships and political debate. Crime is of course a function of law, no less than it is fostered by economic hardship and social exclusion. Like prostitution, which although condemned by canon law was additionally proscribed by the secular courts of the towns, occasional robbery was most frequently the recourse of those driven to desperate measures by poverty. Many would find it hard, having reached this level, to escape altogether from a world of crime in which some became hardened professionals [**81**], [**84**].[17] Most recorded incidents, however, had their origins in domestic arguments, generational conflicts, tensions in the workplace or, once again, the perceived corruption of justices or tax officials, each of which was fostered by the multiple inequalities of urban society.

79. Monastery and town: Bury St Edmunds 1197

A seemingly superficial incident in the ecclesiastical sanctuary proves to be the catalyst of a significant stand-off between an abbot and the burgesses of the surrounding town. The event is revealing of an underlying and persistent ambivalence concerning the relationship between monastic and urban communities. The monastic chronicler naturally tells the story from the perspective and in the sententious tone of the monks.

D. Greenway and J. Sayers (ed.), *Jocelin of Brakelond, Chronicle of the Abbey of Bury St Edmunds*, Oxford: Oxford University Press, 1989, pp. 82–3, reproduced by permission of Oxford University Press; with H. E. Butler (ed.), *The Chronicle of Jocelin of Brakelond*, London: T. Nelson, 1949, p. 92. Transl. by the editors, revised by GR.

On the day after Christmas Day [1197], there were gatherings in the cemetery, with contests and competitions (*colluctationes et concertationes*) between the abbot's servants and the townspeople, but matters

16 See the balanced discussion by H. Skoda, *Medieval Violence: Physical Brutality in Northern France, 1270–1330*, Oxford, 2013.

17 C. Hammer, 'Patterns of homicide in a medieval university town: fourteenth-century Oxford', *Past and Present*, LXXVIII, 1978, pp. 2–23; F. Rexroth, *Deviance and Power in Late Medieval London*, transl. P. Selwyn, Cambridge, 2007; B. Geremek, *The Margins of Society in Late Medieval Paris*, transl. J. Birrell, Cambridge, 1987.

escalated from words to blows, and then from punches to wounds and bloodshed. When the abbot heard about it, he asked some of those who had gone to the show, but had stood on the sidelines, to come and see him privately, and he commanded the names of the miscreants to be written down. He had all these summoned to appear before him in St Denis's chapel on the day after St Thomas [Becket]'s day [30 December]. In the interim he did not invite any of the townspeople to his table as in previous years he had normally done on the first five days of Christmas. On the appointed day, after the evidence on oath of sixteen sworn men had been heard, the abbot said, 'These wicked men obviously fall within the canon *sentenciae latae*, but because they are laymen from here and roundabout, and do not appreciate how outrageous it is to commit such sacrilege, I shall publicly excommunicate them by name,[18] so that others may be more fearful. I shall begin with my own household and servants to ensure that justice is done impartially.' This was carried out as soon as we had put on stoles and candles were lit. Then they all left the church, and after some discussion they undressed and, naked except for their underpants, prostrated themselves in front of the church door. When the abbot's assistants, monks and clerks, came and told him tearfully that over a hundred naked men were lying there, the abbot also wept. But in his words and in his face he displayed the severity of the law, hiding his inner compassion, for he wished to be urged by his advisers to absolve the penitents, knowing that mercy is exalted above judgement, and that the church receives all those who repent. Therefore, when they had all been severely beaten and absolved, they took an oath that they would accept the church's judgement regarding the sacrilege they had committed. The following day they were given penances according to canon law, and the abbot took them all back into complete unity. But he uttered terrible threats against anyone who, by word or deed, should create discord, and he publicly prohibited assemblies and shows in the cemetery. So, when everyone had been restored to the blessing of peace, it was with great rejoicing that on the following days the townspeople feasted with their lord the abbot.

18 For an anathema to have effect at this period, it needed to be addressed to named individuals.

80. Complaint of the lesser burgesses of Oxford 1253

This petition to the king was apparently supported by a group of Oxford burgesses, although it bears the seal only of one of these, Walter de Milton. The group he claimed to represent, and which he called the 'lesser commune', was evidently not made up of the humbler artisans, but comprised freemen who were not eligible to hold office in the town, or, in other words, the less important householders and burgesses, whom he distinguished from the 'magnate burgesses of the town'. According to the complaint (paragraph xxvii), many of this group had been deterred from putting their seals to the document by the threats of the 'greater burgesses'. The outcome of the petition is not known.

H. E. Salter (ed.), *Snappe's Formulary*, Oxford Historical Society, LXXX, Oxford: Oxford University Press, 1924, pp. 272–80, drawing also on *Calendar of Inquisitions Miscellaneous, 1219–1307*, London: HMSO, pp. 79–83. Latin, transl. by the editor, revised by GR.

The burgesses of the lesser commune of Oxford petition God and their lord the king of England against the magnate burgesses of the town:

i. Whenever the lord king demands a tallage* from the town of Oxford, by determination of the said magnates, the lesser burgesses are always assessed at a rate nearly double or more; because of which the latter are destroyed and, unless the king shortly make a great and stern enquiry, to establish the truth and enforce amendment by the council of the kingdom, they shall be forced by necessity and penury to leave their lands and houses. They will shortly be carrying the burdens of the entire town in tallages, gifts and all other misfortunes. And although the magnate burgesses declare themselves to be taxed, they always remain quit and indemnified, apart from three men, so that in four parishes there are not ten men left to bear tallage, they are so destroyed. And that this is true will appear clearly from the following articles.

ii. In the mayoralty of Geoffrey de Stokewell [1237–40], £40 were collected from the lesser commune by common counsel of him and the fifteen jurats [jurors] of Oxford in order to obtain from the papal court, it is said, the privilege that no layman should be forced to go to law either by a clerk or a layman outside the town of Oxford. This privilege has never been established, nor yet benefited any man; and this is clear, because the said Geoffrey is now bringing a case against certain laymen of Oxford at Hertford, which is against the said privilege.

iii. In the mayoralty of Nicholas de Stokewell [1247–49], a man of the household of Earl Richard [of Cornwall, brother of King Henry III] was crossing the High Street in winter and a man came up carrying a snowball, with which he struck the man so as to put out his eye. The lord earl, hearing of this, directed the mayor and bailiffs of Oxford to arrest the criminal and compel him to make amends; and because they would not arrest him, the earl caused the merchants of Oxford to be distrained, and their goods to be attached at fairs and markets on every side of Oxford; on account of which the mayor and bailiffs with the fifteen jurats gathered £40 and more from the lesser commune to satisfy the earl for the wrong done to his man.

iv. About the same time a man of the household of Sir Aymer the king's [half-]brother was coming one night from the mill under Oxford castle, leading a horse with a sack of flour to make bread for the said Aymer; and when he came into the parish of St Peter-le-Bailey, certain criminals assaulted him and beat him so that within three days he died. Upon this Aymer fell into a great anger, because this was shortly after his arrival in Oxford [in 1247], and he reported the matter to the king. The king ordered the mayor and bailiffs to arrest the criminals, who immediately after the deed went into hiding. So the mayor and bailiffs with the fifteen jurats gathered £20 and more from the lesser commune of Oxford, to recompense Sir Aymer for the death of his servant. But when Sir Aymer heard that the money had all been taken from the lesser commune, he was moved with pity, and at the suggestion of the masters of the university he directed the return to each man of what had been taken from him. But of those £20 neither the mayor nor the bailiffs ever made restitution to those who had paid them, but divided them amongst themselves.

v. In the mayoralty of Thomas under the Wall [1249–51], some of the greater burgesses beat a man of the household of Earl

Richard in Oxford, upon which the earl directed the mayor and bailiffs to make recompense; but because the criminals were of the magnates, the mayor and bailiffs would not compel them, with the result that the earl distrained and arrested the merchants and their goods at fairs and markets all around Oxford. Then the mayor and bailiffs with the fifteen jurats collected [blank] and more from the poor to satisfy the lord earl for the injury done to his man.

vi. It also happened that a knight named Anketin Malure came on the king's orders to Oxford, and laid on the burgesses a tallage of £200 of silver. Half of this was at once gathered from the lesser commune; but when the king demanded the remainder, £40 and more were again gathered from the lesser commune.

vii. In the mayoralty of Nicholas de Stokewell, the mayor and jurats were forbidden by the grace of the king to enter the houses of widows to levy taxes on them; but they devised amongst themselves a certain tax on alewives who were the wives of burgesses, thereby defrauding them of the king's grace granted to them; and from these they took £20 and more, not one penny of which went to the crown, but they divided it all among themselves.

viii. The said fifteen jurats chose the bailiffs each year from their own number. At the end of the year, the mayor comes and shows that the bailiffs are in arrears by £6 13*s* 4*d*, £10 or £13 6*s* 8*d*. These sums are then gathered by the mayor and jurats from the lesser commune; but the king gains no honour or profit, for the greater burgesses divide the money among themselves.

ix. When the bailiffs declare themselves to be in arrears by £6 13*s* 4*d* or £10, the mayor and the fifteen jurats by their common counsel gather £20 or £26 13*s* 4*d* from the lesser commune, of which the king has neither honour nor use.

x. When Adam Feteplace was mayor [for the second time, in 1251], William de Exemue, clerk, came to Oxford, and caused all the burgesses to meet in the guildhall where the king's pleas are heard, in order that an aid might be demanded of them for the king; whereupon the burgesses withdrew from the bench to consider what answer they should make. Meanwhile, the said William addressed those sitting and standing around: 'Sirs, I recently heard a surprising complaint made to the king in his court, that whenever tallages, amercements, or presents are paid to the king or queen or justices, the greater burgesses of Oxford take them entirely from the lesser commune and from the poorer townspeople, while they themselves never pay a penny but always remain quit, at which our lord the king was very angry.' Then nearly all the people answered with one voice: 'That is very true, and we are ready to say so to our lord the king whenever he will listen.'

xi. Also the said William de Exemue, on his return to Oxford from London, delivered the tallage rolls to the greater burgesses; and soon afterwards they demanded that poor persons liable to tallage should pay at twice the rates at which they had been assessed by their peers; but whether this was done by the will of William or the greater burgesses is unknown.

xii. At that time [1252], the town being in the sheriff's hand by order of the king, the mayor and jurats asked leave of the sheriff to have a gathering of money among the poor workmen of the town according to custom; and immediately they caused all the workmen of the said town, great and small, as many as were poor, to come together, giving as a reason, amongst others, that they would in no way allow them to dwell among them unless they were in their merchant guild, so that none could escape them, even by making the excuse of poverty, until he had satisfied them; nor did they permit questions as to how this was to be paid for, but they compelled them to enter their merchant guild, whether they wished to or not, which for the unfree was not even lawful. Neither that gathering of money, nor others, which are always held every third year, have yielded either honour or profit to the king and queen, but the greater burgesses have always divided the profit among themselves. And so by all kinds of device and deceit they crush the lesser people and the poor.

xiii. In the mayoralty of Adam de Feteplace, he and the jurats devised among them an ordinance for the confusion and destruction of the lesser burgesses and the poor, that if any man should act or speak against the mayor or any of the jurats in relation to any of their statutes or provisions, so that the fact could be proved by two or three men, then that man could be imprisoned and he should pay a fine of £5 to the mayor and £2 to each of the jurats.

xiv. Also in the time of the same Adam, the greater burgesses made an agreement with the king for £33 6*s* 8*d* to have the town in their own hands, to which end they gathered over £100 from the lesser commune; but of themselves only three contributed.

xv. Also in the time of the said Adam the mayor and jurats made provision that no man of the lesser commune should make woollen cloth that was not of 800 [threads] in width, and the warp corresponding to the woof; as a consequence of which no poor man who should support himself by this trade is able to get work at all or to earn a living. The jurats have six looms, besides the king's looms, on which they can make what cloth they like; and no poor man dares contradict them in these matters; but if any cloth is found in the lesser commune of less than 800 in width, it is confiscated into the hand of the greater burgesses, and he with whom it is found is fined. Thus through this ordinance most of the lesser commune are driven to beggary.

xvi. They make provision that no fishmonger should buy sea fish coming to Oxford in any market within ten leagues of Oxford, nor fresh fish within five leagues, nor until it has been two days in Oxford market. Also that no woman should buy butter or cheese or eggs or such wares before noon. And if anyone is convicted in such matters, he is to lose the wares and be subject to a fine.

xvii. Fishmongers used to have their stalls in the High Street on market days at a yearly charge of 2*d*; but now they pay half a mark [6*s* 8*d*], or 5*s*, or 12*d* at least.

xviii. They made provision that no cook should dare to boil or roast any food outside his door unless he first have paid 2*s* or 3*s* for his licence. Poor sellers of bread and beer, though they used to pay 6*d* or 12*d* at most, must now pay 4*s* or 5*s* or 12*d* at least. Despite paying these exactions the poor of the lesser commune are in arrears of £6 13*s* 4*d* or £9 every year, and are tallaged until the full farm of the town [the fee-farm rent of £63 0*s* 5*d* per annum] is paid to the king.

xix. Geoffrey de Stokewell stopped up a channel of the river Cherwell running into the Thames after the departure of the justices, to the destruction of the poor fishermen, and the damage of the whole town.

xx. Walter Bolled and Simon de Lundonia, who opposed that provision, had each to find sureties for a fine of £5 before he was released.

xxi. When the town is surveyed by the king's order, five or six jurats go through the streets, and cause two or three loyal men of the lesser commune to be called before them in each parish, to assess tallage on their neighbours together with the said jurats; but these poor men do not dare to tallage their neighbours according to their ability, but they are surveyed and plundered as it seems good to the said jurats.

xxii. In the time of Geoffrey de Stokewell, because one of the lesser commune bought half a last of herrings at Abingdon, all his herrings were taken from him and unjustly detained.

xxiii. In the time of Adam de Feteplace, the greater burgesses gathered money of the lesser commune, and with it bought three tuns of wine, and drank it together. At length it was said that one part had more wine than the other, and they fought, and pulled one another's hair: which was neither to the profit nor to the honour of our lord the king or his men. But the poor are always destroyed and reduced to nothing.

xxiv. When the king's bailiffs come to Oxford and make inquisition of ordinances and assizes* of buying and selling, whether they are kept in accordance with the custom of the realm, twelve of the jurats, to bring the poor under tallage by guile, swear falsely that the said ordinances have not been kept but broken. For this they make composition with the said bailiffs for ten or twelve marks, and then tallage the poor of the lesser commune for £13 6*s* 8*d* or £20, and divide the surplus among themselves.

xxv. When a man obtains a writ of right from the king's court concerning any injury done to him in respect of his possessions, and alleges his right either in person or by deputy, in the full court before the fifteen jurats, they meet in a secret place, and quash and overthrow the king's writ and the petitioner's claim. This was clear at the last coming of the justices, for many complaints were received before them.

xxvi. A man of the lesser commune made a chimney for the smoke to go out of his house, as is the custom of the whole town. Then came Adam Feteplace, because a little smoke came into his house, and wanted to block up the said chimney. And when the poor man tried to argue with him he beat him violently, and dangerously wounded his wife on the head. Nevertheless the poor man was condemned by the jurats to pay the said Adam £5, which are still unjustly kept from him.

xxvii. On Tuesday before St Peter Enthroned [apparently 18 February 1253], when the lesser burgesses were assembled at St Giles' church to fix their seals to this document, and to consider the best way of making their complaint, some of the greater burgesses came upon them and attacked them, calling them robbers, and saying that unless they dispersed, they would be deprived of all their goods. So they departed, and have not since dared to assemble and seal the document.

xxviii. On Friday in the week of St Matthew the Apostle [apparently 28 February 1253], the bailiffs of Oxford came by order of the mayor and jurats to the house of Walter de Middilton the bearer of this little book, who always defended the poor, and forcing their way into his house they took away most of his goods, and declared that he had forfeited all liberty of buying and selling by which he kept his household, and they have continued to detain his goods against gage and pledge. So the said Walter prays for mercy and aid from the king, seeing that unless he obtains it speedily, he will be destroyed, killed, and brought to nothing.

xxix. All the poor of the lesser commune beg the king that, for the love of God and the salvation of his soul, he should investigate these articles, together with all the men of Oxford, clergy and laity, except those whose names are here endorsed; command that the said Walter be treated peaceably; and have the inquisition taken before himself in person lest it should be overthrown by others.

[On the reverse of the scroll:]

These are the names of the greater burgesses of Oxford:

Adam Feteplace	Geoffrey Trutun	Henry Perle
Geoffrey de Stokewell	Thomas Mauger	Henry de Wycumbe
Nicholas de Stokewell	Roger Arconer	Walter Kepharm
Thomas under the wall	William the spicer	Henry Henge
Geoffrey the goldsmith	William de O.	William Wythe
Geoffrey de Heynkesey	Aufredus the spicer	William Boydon
John de Colleshell	John Halegod	Richard the mercer
John Cursy	Laurence Wyth	Robert the miller
John Pady	Thomas the spicer	Jaym Simeon
Adam under the wall	William junior, spicer	Henry de Camage
Walter de Kyngetona	Thomas de Elmeley	

81. Urban crime in the late thirteenth century

The range of criminal cases which could be judged by urban courts varied according to the privileges granted by the crown in civic charters. The most serious crimes, however, were reserved to the king: they were tried before itinerant royal justices or (increasingly over time) the county sheriff. Beyond naming the accused and their punishment, their records can shed light on the social context of crime. The first of the cases presented here shows how evidence produced in court can illuminate the surrounding environment of organised crafts and sociability. The second gives a glimpse of organised crime rings preying on urban trade.

R. B. Pugh (ed.), *Wiltshire Gaol Deliveries and Trailbaston Trials 1275–1306*, Wiltshire Record Society, XXXIII (1977), pp. 41, 62. Latin, transl. by the editor.

(a) [Delivery of Old Salisbury gaol, 29 May 1276] New Salisbury. Robert de Lym, Robert de Noneton and Philip the baker de Haghechereche taken and imprisoned for slaying Robert of

Winchester and John of Christchurch in New Salisbury, put themselves upon [a jury of] 12 of Salisbury. The jury say that on Tuesday before the Annunciation [24 March 1276] Robert of Winchester and John went to New Salisbury and were harboured in Robert atte Novene's house and there drank; and a boy was singing there about bakers. Walter de Taunton arrived, wishing to have sport, and heard the song. He returned, uttering threats, to Stephen de Harpeden's house and there found Robert de Noneton lying in bed and looked for a stick; and Walter went away without Robert de Noneton's knowledge or privity; and he beat Robert of Winchester and John so that they died on the fifth day. Afterwards he returned to Stephen de Harpeden's house and there with Robert [de Lym] and the others baked bread; and Robert de Lym and Philip did not know of the deed nor shared in it. So three are acquitted. Walter to be taken if he can be found.

(b) [Pleas before the royal justices at Wilton, 20 April 1281] John Allwyne, approver,* charges John of the forest of robbery and fellowship in robbery and says that on Sunday after Midsummer [20 June] 1280 he was in his fellowship at Bristol and that they there together stole cloth of Ireland, shoes and linen cloth, whereof he had 4*s* as his share, and on the Saturday following at Malmesbury where they stole cloth and shoes, of which he had 3*s* as his share, and that he was his fellow in thefts there and elsewhere, whereof he had 6*s* 8*d* and more as his share. Both offer to deraign* by their bodies as the court shall decide. So to battle. Gages offered. A day was given, Friday [ ]. John of the forest was vanquished, and so [condemned to death]. He had no chattels.

82. Dispute between the merchant guild and the abbot of Bury St Edmunds 1304

Here the king's justices attempt to resolve a dispute between the ancient and powerful Benedictine abbey of Bury St Edmunds and the wealthier burgesses of the expanding market town which had grown up at its gates. Economic growth and political experience gave rise to recurrent tensions of this nature in many such monastic towns. Their profits from trade in Suffolk wool and cloth lead the mercantile and manufacturing elite of Bury to claim the right to have a protective guild. The abbot, appealing to history (see also [**10**], [**79**]), denies the guild's pretensions. As a result of the quarrel, lesser traders and artisans find a political voice to protest against their exploitation. The merchants present a circumstantial case for the existence and legitimacy of their guild. The abbot denies that this is more than a social fraternity without legal rights (see [**95**] for a comparative instance of a fraternity with a substantial political role). The king's lawyers, in a judgement typical of such cases, uphold the rights of the monastic lords.

A. E. Bland, P. A. Brown and R. H. Tawney (eds), *English Economic History: Select Documents*, London: G. Bell & Sons, 1914, pp. 128–30. Latin, transl. by the editors.

Pleas at the town of Bury St Edmunds before William de Bereford, W. Howard and W. de Carleton, justices of the king, on Tuesday next after the feast of St Lucy the Virgin [13 December] 1305. Nicholas Fouk and others by conspiracy premeditated among them at the town aforesaid and by oath taken among them, making unlawful assemblies of their own authority on Monday next after the feast of the Nativity of the Blessed Virgin Mary [8 September] 1302, ordained and decreed that none should remain among them in the said town having chattels worth 20*s* who would not pay them 2*s* 1*d*, which payment they call among themselves hansing-silver, which money they took on that pretext respectively from Reynold del Blackhouse and Robert the Carpenter, men dwelling the town aforesaid, and also beyond this 12*d* of gersum* from each of the said Reynold and Robert. And likewise ... they decreed among themselves that every man of the same town having chattels to the value of £6 13*s* 4*d* should pay them 46*s* 8*d*, which by that authority they took from Robert Scot, a man dwelling in the aforesaid town. And also the same day and year they decreed among themselves that no man should stay in the aforesaid town beyond a year and a day without being distrained to take oath to maintain their aforesaid assemblies and ordinances ...

The aforesaid Nicholas Fouk and others readily acknowledge that the abbot is lord of the whole town aforesaid, and ought to appoint his bailiffs to hold his court in the same town. But as for the conspiracy aforesaid, etc., they make stout defence that they are not guilty. And as for the abbot's charge against them that they have made unlawful assemblies in the town, decreeing and ordaining that every man dwelling in the town having chattels to the value of 20*s* etc. as above, they say that the abbot makes plaint unjustly, for they say that they have an alderman and a guild merchant in the aforesaid town and are free burgesses, rendering judgments by their alderman of pleas pleaded* in the court of the same abbot before his bailiffs in the town aforesaid. And that without any trespasses or unlawful assemblies they meet at their guildhall in the same town, as often as need be, to treat of the common profit and advantage of the men and burgesses of the aforesaid town, as is quite lawful for them. And that they and their ancestors and predecessors, burgesses, etc., have used such a custom from time whereof no memory is, to wit, of taking 2*s* 1*d* from every man dwelling in the town, being in the tithing of the abbot of the place aforesaid, having chattels to the value of 20*s*, that he may trade among them and enjoy their market customs in the same town, and likewise of receiving 46*s* 8*d* from every man of the town aforesaid having chattels to the value of £6 13*s* 4*d* to keep [maintain] their guild merchant.* And that there is the following custom among them beyond this, to wit, that twelve burgesses of the aforesaid town have been accustomed to elect four men of the same town yearly to keep their guild merchant, each of whom shall have chattels to the value of £6 13*s* 4*d*...

The jurors say that the abbot must answer whether the aforesaid Nicholas Fouke and others have a guild merchant in the aforesaid town or not. The abbot says that they have not a guild merchant nor cognisance of pleas pertaining to a guild merchant, nor a commonalty nor a common seal nor a mayor; but they hold a guild at the feast of the Nativity of St John the Baptist [24 June] in a certain place to feast and drink together, there holding their unlawful assemblies and taking from every man dwelling in the said town the aforesaid 2*s* 1*d* and also 46*s* 8*d*, levying such money from the men aforesaid, that the payers thereof may be of their fellowship, by distraints made upon them; and he does not deny that the ancestors of the aforesaid Nicholas and others have been long accustomed to receive such extortions of 2*s* 1*d* and 46*s* 8*d*, but against the Law Merchant and against the will of the aforesaid payers and against the peace, and beyond the amount of a third part of their goods; and by such extortions and ransoms they claim to make burgesses within his liberty and lordship, which there pertains to the abbot himself and to no other.

A day is given ... It is awarded that the aforesaid abbot (recover) his damages of £199 13*s* 4*d* against the aforesaid Nicholas and others ... And let the same Nicholas and others be committed to gaol. Afterwards the same Nicholas and others came and made fine. And let certain others in the dispute be imprisoned for a month owing to their poverty. And the aforesaid Nicholas and others came before the justices and satisfied the lord abbot; therefore let them be delivered from prison.

83. Disturbance of the peace in Oxford 1306

It was the responsibility of the king's coroner to summon a local jury in a case of violent death. Coroners' rolls contain the juries' verdicts, sometimes including circumstantial detail as in the present case. This night-time altercation reveals the camaraderie of the artisans no less than the perennially latent violence of the town. St John the Baptist was the patron saint of tailors.

J. E. Thorold Rogers (ed.), *Oxford City Documents, Financial and Judicial, 1268–1665*, Oxford: Oxford University Press for the Oxford Historical Society, 1891, pp. 165–6. Latin, transl. by the editor, revised by GR.

On the Sunday after the feast of the Assumption [15 August], 1306, Gilbert de Foxlee, clerk, died at his lodgings in the parish of St Peter in the East in Oxford, at about midday. The following Monday, he was seen by Thomas Lisewys, the king's coroner for the town of Oxford. He had a wound in his left leg by the knee, about four inches long and an inch and a half deep. An inquisition was held. The jurors declare on their oath that on Thursday which was the eve of St John the Baptist's day [24 June], the tailors of Oxford, together with others of the town, made a festival all night in their shops, singing and making merry with harps, viols and other instruments as is customary there and in other places, in honour of that feast. After midnight, when they discovered no one else to be wandering in the streets, they left their shops and, with the others, led their dance into the High Street opposite the drapery. As they were playing there, Gilbert de Foxlee came up to them with a drawn sword in his hand and immediately started a fight, trying to break up their dance. Seeing this, some people there who knew him wanted him to go away with them, urging him not to hurt anybody. But Gilbert would not promise, and breaking away from them he returned to attack William de Cleydon, and would have cut his hand off with his sword as William went round in the dance had he not quickly withdrawn. Upon this Henry de Beaumont Cruisor, Thomas de Bloxham, William de Leye, servant to John de Leye, and William de Cleydon rushed at him, and Henry wounded him with a sword in his right arm, Thomas wounded him in the back with a dagger, and William de Cleydon wounded him on the head, so that he fell. Immediately afterwards William de Leye cut him in the left leg with an axe called a spar-axe, giving him the wound by the knee from which he died. He lived for eight weeks and two-and-a-half days, and he received the last rites.

84. Violence and crime in London 1311

These cases brought before the mayor of London yield glimpses of an urban world of taverns, gambling and latent violence. Criminal records need careful interpretation by the historian: by definition, they privilege crime; and the legal processes left poor offenders disadvantaged before their accuser (see also [**50**]). Such records, however, can provide an insight into the social values of jurors and witnesses called to testify.

H. T. Riley (ed.), *Memorials of London and London Life in the XIIIth, XIVth, and XVth Centuries*, London: Longmans, Green & Co., 1868, pp. 86–8. Latin, transl. by the editor, revised by GR.

(a) Process of inquisition and delivery, made in the time of Richer de Refham, mayor [1311], as to criminals, trespassers and nightwalkers in the City of London, against the peace of our lord the king

Elmer de Multone was attached* because he was indicted in the ward of Cheap for being a common nightwalker, and in the day is in the habit of enticing strangers and persons unknown to a tavern, and there deceiving them by using false dice. And also because he was indicted in Tower ward for being a bruiser and nightwalker, against the peace; as also, for being a common *rorere* [i.e. 'roarer']. And also because he was indicted in the ward of Cripplegate for playing at dice, and because he regularly entices men to a tavern and makes them play at dice there against their will. He appeared, and being asked how he would acquit himself, he said that he was not guilty, and put himself upon the country. And the jury came, by Adam Trugge and others on the panel; and they said upon their oath that he is guilty of all the trespasses aforesaid. He was therefore committed to prison.

(b) John de Rokeslee was attached because he was indicted in the ward of Vintry and divers other wards, being held suspected of evil and of beating men coming into the city, against the peace of our lord the king. And also because he was indicted in the ward of Cripplegate and diverse other wards for being a common nightwalker, against the peace, and unlawfully frequenting taverns in the city with prostitutes, against the custom of the City and the peace of our lord the king; and because he is well clothed, and yet has no business by which to support himself; nor has he any rental, as he pretends to have. Also because he is in the habit of beating men, against the peace of our lord the king; and he does much mischief in the city, and causes much mischief to be done, in the night-time. He appeared, and being asked how he would acquit himself, he said he was not guilty, and put himself upon the country. And the jury came, by Adam Trugge and others on the panel. The jurors said upon their oath, that the said John is guilty. He was therefore committed to prison.

(c) Master Roger le Skirmisour [i.e. 'the skirmisher'] was attached because he was indicted for keeping a fencing-school for divers men, and for enticing there the sons of respectable persons, so as to waste and spend the property of their fathers and mothers upon bad practices: the result being that they themselves became bad men. He appeared. And the jurors said that he is guilty of the trespasses. He was therefore committed to prison.

85. Students and townspeople at Oxford 1355

This was the most dramatic of many riots in Oxford, where the clerical immunity enjoyed by the scholars, students and masters alike created particular tensions with the secular administration of the mayor. Both sides appealed to the crown: reproduced here is the detailed complaint of the mayor. The king, appealed to by both sides, regularly defended the university, which provided clerks for royal government. He did so on this occasion.

H. E. Salter (ed.), *Munimenta Civitatis Oxonie*, Oxford Historical Society, LXXI, Oxford: Oxford University Press for the Oxford Historical Society, 1917, pp. 126–8. Latin, transl. by the editor, revised by GR.

These are the injuries done to the mayor, bailiffs and community of Oxford by the scholars of the University of Oxford.

First, on Tuesday before the feast of St Valentine last past [10 February 1355, the feast day of St Scholastica, patron saint of scholars], there came Walter Spryngheuse, Roger de Chesterfeld and other scholars to the tavern called 'Swindlestock' and there took a quart of wine and threw the said wine in the face of John Croidon, the tavern-keeper, and then with the said quart pot beat the said John without reason. The bailiffs came and prayed them amend and redress the same trespass in good manner. But they would not amend the trespass or redress it, but they issued forth from the tavern and at once they had bows and arrows and other arms ready for ill-doing at the Carfax,[19] and the bailiffs arrested the bows and arrows, and the scholars made great noise and great debate, for which reason the mayor, bailiffs and sergeants approached the Chancellor of the University and prayed him to have the malefactors arrested and to aid that the peace should be kept on his side. And when the mayor, bailiffs and sergeants returned from the Chancellor, he doing none of those things that they had prayed, there came two hundred and more of the scholars, armed in the manner of war, and beat and assaulted the mayor, bailiffs and sergeants, and wounded some of them, whereby there is despair of their lives, and then they slew a child of about fourteen years and threatened to set the town on fire. And further, the next morning, when the mayor, bailiffs and good folk of the town were gone to Woodstock to complain to the king of the said injuries, the said scholars came with royal power and took the wardens of the city and closed the gates and fought with shields and arms by plan and openly, and set the town on fire in diverse parts, and broke open and robbed diverse houses of lay folk, and wounded many people and killed many. Because of this alarm of fire and because of the fighting the common people arose in aid and defence of their town.

86. Attack on Italians in London 1359

Italian merchants in fourteenth-century London, even after the collapse of major Italian banks when the English crown failed to honour its debts in the 1320s, continued to enjoy royal privilege. The monarchs,

19 The central cross-roads of the town, where the Swindlestock tavern stood.

and particularly Richard II, spent huge sums on the silks and other luxury goods in which they traded. In consequence they periodically found themselves targeted by jealous Londoners.[20] Apart from the maintenance of peace, the mayor's concern in such a case was to bring such tensions involving foreigners to a peaceful solution, for the sake of trade no less than in the name of justice.

H. T. Riley (ed.), *Memorials of London and London Life in the XIIIth, XIVth, and XVth Centuries*, London: Longmans, Green & Co., 1868, pp. 302–3. Latin, transl. by the editor, revised by GR.

Inquisition taken before John Lovekyn, mayor of the city of London, and John de Chichestre and Simon de Benyngtone, sheriffs of the same city, on 18 October 1359, to enquire what malefactors and disturbers of the peace of our lord the king, with envious insolence and rancour, maliciously perpetrated a dreadful affray, in an attack made by certain mercers of the city upon some merchants of Lombardy in the same city dwelling, and beat, wounded and dreadfully maltreated Francisco Bochel and other Lombards* in the said city, being under the protection of our lord the king … upon the oath of Geoffrey Lovekyn and eleven others.

Who say upon their oath, that on Monday after the feast of St John the Baptist [probably the Decollation, 29 August] 1357, Henry Forester, mercer, Thomas de Meldone, mercer, and John Meleward, mercer, made a dreadful affray in the Old Jewry, in the ward of Colemanstreet, in London, and of malice aforethought by force and arms assaulted certain persons, namely, Francisco Bochel and Reymund Flamy, Lombards, and wounded, beat and maltreated them and, against the peace of our lord the king, committed other enormities against them. They say also that Richard Phelip, mercer, abetted the said persons in making this affray and trespass.

87. A guild at St Albans and the Revolt of 1381

The suspicious and hostile tone of the monastic chronicler is evident in this description of the activities of a town fraternity. The formation of links with such societies in other towns in the region is analogous

20 See also P. Strohm, 'Trade, treason, and the murder of Janus Imperial', *Journal of British Studies*, XXXV, 1996, pp. 1–23.

to the federations of guilds recorded in late medieval Germany and the Low Countries, although the relative strength of royal government in England limited the scope and effectiveness of such initiatives here. For the significance of politically influential fraternities in seigneurial towns (i.e. towns under the jurisdiction of ecclesiastical or secular lords), see also [**16**], [**79**], [**95**].

J. Taylor, W. R. Childs and L. Watkiss (eds), *The St Albans Chronicle: The* Chronica maiora *of Thomas Walsingham*, i, *1376–1394*, Oxford: Oxford University Press, 2003, pp. 122–5. Latin, transl. by the editors. Reproduced by permission of Oxford University Press.

On the day the king died [21 June 1377] a new community was formed in the town of St Albans in honour of St Alban, the protomartyr of the English. It marked the beginning of a very laudable and commendable expression of devotion. Indeed, it was decreed that whenever the martyr's image was carried in customary procession every single person who was not excused by the community should be present with his household; and that the stronger amongst them should, in honour of the martyr, carry in the procession around the image twelve torches, made at their own expense. But this expression of devotion did not last long, for soon when dissension occurred in the realm and the rebellion of the common people broke out, it was shown that they were not the brothers of St Alban but the synagogue of Satan.[21] This was made clear by their attitude and their entire behaviour during that period of time. In fact they rejected the lordship of the abbey, destroyed the dwellings and the cloisters, and in every way they could they threatened the destruction of the monastery. And they did not perpetrate these outrages alone, but invited the neighbouring towns to do the same, as, reader, you will be able to discover more fully in what follows.[22]

88. Revolt in Beverley 1381–82

A *coup d'état* in Beverley in 1381–82 replaced the town council of twelve burgesses with a broader government, headed by an alderman, two chamberlains and a council of twenty-four. The old regime was led by the richest families; the new by artisans. The old guard were the

21 Revelation 2.9.

22 A reference to the Peasants' Revolt in June 1381.

authors of the petition reproduced in (a), which secured the royal intervention recorded in (b). A statement by the leaders of the *coup* is lacking. The precise relationship between these events and the Peasants' Revolt of the summer of 1381 is unclear. The uprising was followed by conservative reaction.

C. T. Flower, 'The Beverley town riots', *Transactions of the Royal Historical Society*, 2nd series, XIX, 1905, pp. 93–4 (a); A. F. Leach (ed.), *Beverley Town Documents*, Selden Society, XIV, London: Quaritch, 1900, pp. 6–7 (b). French (a) and Latin (b), transl. by the editors, revised by GR.

(a) [Early 1382] May it please our excellent and redoubted lord the king and his wise council to grant and ordain in this present parliament that Adam Coppendale, Thomas de Beverley, John Gervays, William Dudhill, John de Erghum and other good people (*bones gentz*) of Beverley – exiled from the town of Beverley by barrators and rebels (*barettours et rebellours*) against our said lord the king in the same town, who have arrogated to themselves royal power, so that the good people have not dared to go near the town for a year and still do not, for fear of their lives – may be enabled safely to return to Beverley and to live there as loyal subjects. Let those guilty be compelled, on pain of losing their liberty. And may all the obligations imposed by the said rebels in charge of the town be annulled. And may the good people have their good old government, as it has been in use for fifty years, granted and confirmed by our said lord king and his ancestors. And may all the indictments, which were made maliciously before my lord John Bigot and his companions by the rebels against the good people at the time of the Revolt (*en temps de rumour*), which indictments have been brought to the King's Bench before my lord Robert Tresylyan, be pardoned if possible, and if they may be annulled that this be done. And that due pronouncement be made about the said rebels (*trespassours*), for the safety of the whole realm, for God and as a work of charity.

(b) 18 March 1382. Richard, by the grace of God king, etc., to all the good men and burgesses of Beverley, greeting. Through lack of good governance it often happens that contentions occur between the inhabitants and commons of cities and towns, evil and scandal arise and various dangers are created, and a life of peace is wickedly prevented; and it is well known that such contentions, evils and dangers have recently been more than usually common in the town of Beverley, above all through lack of good governance. For that town, in accordance with ancient and approved custom used there undisturbed for fifty years, has been accustomed to be peacefully ruled and governed by twelve good men (*probi homines*) of that town elected for that purpose on St Mark's day [25 April] with the common assent of the burgesses of the town at the guildhall. But by a sudden change of that custom, in place of the twelve good men, you have this year newly appointed and ordained an alderman and two chamberlains, and this order, which has not been seen in the town for fifty years or more, except twice or less – the better government of the town by the common assent of the burgesses being abolished – you intend to maintain and to continue, although the government of the twelve men is far better for the good rule of the town; and this order, if continued, will clearly lead, as we are informed, to the wasting of the town and the displacement of its burgesses.

We enjoin and command all of you that with one assent you come together peacefully as usual on St Mark's day at your guildhall and … after due deliberation, putting aside all quarrels and discussions, lay down and duly order such management, rule and government in the town that it and our people may be best and most quietly ordered and governed, our peace there kept, and friendship be maintained amongst you, now and in the future.

89. Interpersonal violence

The circumstances and details of these incidents being unrecorded, they are not easy to analyse. That the officers of the town of Nottingham reported forty-four such events, most involving bloodshed, in a single year is, however, suggestive of an urban society which took ready recourse to violence.[23] The instruments of attack were fists, trade tools or weapons such as knives, clubs and bows and arrows. One or two of the accused were described by the jurors as 'perturbed', apparently an indication that they were perceived as mentally unstable. In these

23 For what is known of the justice system of late medieval Nottingham, see T. Foulds, 'The medieval town', in J. Beckett (ed.), *A Centenary History of Nottingham*, Manchester, 1997, pp. 67–8.

instances, however, they were none the less held responsible for their actions and fined accordingly.[24] The imposition of a fine indicates the court's judgement of guilt; the record does not detail the defence, if any, submitted by the accused.

W. H. Stevenson (ed.), *Records of the Borough of Nottingham*, 3 vols, London: Quaritch, 1882–85, i, pp. 293–307. Latin, transl. by the editor, revised by GR.

Presentments of affrays before the mayor's court of Nottingham, 1395–96

The decennaries [tithingmen or ward representatives] present an affray made with blood by Henry Hickling upon John Pulter, the son of Anna, Henry's wife, because Henry drew his knife and struck John on the head: Henry comes and places himself upon the favour of the mayor, and pays 6*d* … An affray made with blood in which Stephen Wade beat Agnes Irish with his fists: Stephen comes, and pays 6*d* … Thomas Fox, draper, first drew his unsheathed axe, and afterwards went into his own house and took a club in his hand against John Hodings: Thomas comes, and pays 12*d* … Agnes, servant of William de Torlaton, came into the house of Robert Brinklow against his will, and there nearly strangled Robert's wife: Agnes comes, and pays 6*d* … Henry de Plumptre beat Joan Potter with a club: Henry comes, and pays 6*d* … Beatrice Matthew is a common scold* in the street of Houndsgate where she lives: Beatrice comes, and pays 6*d* … Thomas Fox, mason, was troubled (*perturbatus fuit*) and drew his axe against a stranger of the country whose name is not known: Thomas comes and agrees to pay 6*d*, Thomas Arnold standing pledge … Joan de Bawtry of Moothallgate was troubled (*perturbata fuit*) and threw Maud Donne down upon the pavement, causing blood to issue from her arm:

24 The term *perturbatus* in this context meant 'worked up' and perhaps also 'out of control'. *Dictionary of Medieval Latin from British Sources*, ed. R. E. Latham, Oxford, 1975–2013, s.v. 'perturbare', 1 b, c. On the medieval incidence of insanity and its recognition as a mitigating circumstance in criminal trials, see N. D. Hurnard, *The King's Pardon for Homicide before A.D. 1307*, Oxford, 1969, pp. 159–70; W. J. Turner, *Care and Custody of the Mentally Ill, Incompetent, and Disabled in Medieval England*, Turnhout, 2013, pp. 109–40. 'Perturbatus' is not one of the terms noted by Turner as occurring in contemporary discussions of crime on p. 78. On the issue of madness in the perspective of medieval urban law-courts, see W. J. Turner, 'A comparison of the treatment of the mentally disabled in late medieval English common law and chartered boroughs', in W. J. Turner (ed.), *Madness in Medieval Law and Custom*, Leiden, 2010, pp. 17–39.

Joan was imprisoned ... Thomas Briddam, tinker, slapped the face of a maid-servant of Joan de Crophill: Thomas comes, and pays 6*d* ... Thomas Fox, draper, lay in wait for, beat and wounded William Bunche, messenger of the sheriff of Nottingham: Thomas comes, and pays 6*s* 8*d* ... Margaret the wife of Hugh Spicer threw stones at the wife of William Spicer, Hugh's son, and Margaret also drew her knife against the same woman: Margaret comes, and pays 6*d* ... Margaret Gay took hold of William Leadenham violently with her *claunde* [meaning unclear], and threw William in her own house against a post, so that blood issued from his head, and afterwards she went out into the king's highway and made a hue and cry against him: Margaret comes, and pays 12*d* ... Randolph Daniell shot Gilbert Barber in the thigh with an arrow: Randolph comes, and pays 12*d* ... Thomas Benton, barber, seized Hugh Wymondslow in the common hall by his breast with one hand and took his own drawn knife in the other, and said malicious words to him, causing Hugh to despair of his life: Thomas comes, and pays 12*d* ... Joan, wife of Hugh Wymondslow, came into the common hall and there spoke malicious words to Thomas Benton, barber, and there slapped his face: Joan comes, and pays 12*d* ...

90. Subversive fraternity of journeymen saddlers of London 1396

Officially recognised crafts, in London and in other cities, comprised independent master craftsmen, in control of their own shops. But although less well documented, the qualified craftsmen without shops, the journeymen, and the servants to masters in the craft (in this text, the 'yeomen'), also regularly formed their own societies, guilds and fraternities whose existence tended to be looked on askance by the masters. The church of St Vedast was adjacent to the hall of the company of master saddlers. Here the masters seek and obtain a mayoral injunction against the association of the lesser craftsmen.

H. T. Riley (ed.), *Memorials of London and London Life in the XIIIth, XIVth, and XVth Centuries*, London: Longmans, Green & Co., 1868, pp. 542–4. Latin, transl. by the editor, revised by GR.

There had arisen much dissension and strife between the masters of the trade of saddlers of London, and the serving-men, called yeomen, in that trade; because the serving-men, against the consent, and without leave, of their masters, were accustomed to array themselves all in a new and common livery once in the year, and often held diverse meetings, at Stratford and elsewhere without the liberty of the said city, as well as in diverse places within the city; whereby many inconveniences and perils ensued to the said trade; and also very many losses might happen to it in the future, unless some quick and speedy remedy should be found by the rulers of the city. Therefore the masters of the trade, on 10 July 1396, made a strong complaint about it to the excellent men, William More, mayor, and the aldermen of the city, urgently entreating that, for the reasons mentioned, they would deign to send for Gilbert Dustone, William Gylowe, John Clay, John Hiltone, William Berigge and Nicholas Mason, the then governors of the said serving-men, to appear before them on 12 July next. On 10 July precept was given to John Parker, sergeant of the chamber, to give notice to the same persons to be here on 12 July. The governors of the serving-men appeared and, being interrogated about these matters, they said that time out of mind the serving-men of the trade had had a certain fraternity among themselves, and had been accustomed to array themselves in a common livery each year, and after meeting together at Stratford, on the feast of the Assumption of the Blessed Virgin Mary [15 August], to come from there to the church of St Vedast in London, there to hear mass on the same day, in honour of the glorious Virgin. But the masters of the trade asserted the contrary of all this, and said that the fraternity, and the being so arrayed in a common livery, among the serving-men, dated from only thirteen years back, and even then had been discontinued in recent years; and that, under a certain feigned colour of sanctity, many of the serving-men in the trade had influenced the journeymen among them, and had formed confederacies, with the object of raising their wages greatly in excess; to such an extent that whereas a master in the said trade could before have had a serving-man or journeyman* for £2 or £3 6s 8d a year, and his board, now such a man would not agree with his master for less than £5 13s 4d or £8 or even £10 a year; to the great deterioration of the trade.

And further, that the serving-men, according to an ordinance made among themselves, would often cause the journeymen of the said masters to be summoned by a bedel,* appointed to this end, to attend the vigils of dead members of the said fraternity, and at making offering for them on the morrow, levy a penalty on them for absence; whereby the said masters were very greatly aggrieved, and were injured through such absenting of themselves by the journeymen, so leaving their labours and duties, against their wish.

For amending and allaying these grievances and dissensions, the mayor and aldermen commanded that six of the said serving-men should attend in the name of the whole of the alleged fraternity, and communicate with six or eight of the master saddlers; both parties to be here, before the mayor and aldermen, on 19 July next, to make report to the court as to what was agreed between them. And further, the mayor and aldermen strictly forbade the said serving-men in any manner to hold any meeting thereafter at Stratford or elsewhere outside the liberty of the city, on pain of forfeiture, to our lord the king and to the city, of all that they might forfeit.

On 19 July there came here both the masters and the governors of the serving-men, and presented to the mayor and aldermen a certain petition, in these words: 'Gilbert Dustone, William Gylowe, John Clay, John Hiltone, William Berigge and Nicholas Mason do speak on behalf of all their fraternity, and do beg of the wardens of the saddlers, that they may have and use all the points which they have used hitherto.'

Which petition having been read and heard, and diverse reasons shown by the masters to the mayor and aldermen, it was determined that the serving-men should in future be under the governance and rule of the masters of the trade: just as serving-men in other trades in the same city are wont, and of right are bound, to be; and that in future they should have no fraternity, meetings, or covins [subversive assemblies], or other unlawful things. And that the said masters must properly treat and govern their serving-men in the trade, in such manner as the serving-men in like trades in the city have been wont to be properly treated and governed. And that if any serving-man should in future wish to make complaint to the mayor and aldermen, as to any grievance unduly inflicted upon him by the said masters, the mayor and aldermen would give him his due and speedy need of justice in that matter.

91. Rebellious weavers of Coventry appeal to the figure of Lady Godiva 1495

The verses here copied by an indignant clerk into the mayor's book of Coventry give a rare glimpse of a counterculture of resistance to the legislation of a city government perceived, at certain times more than others, to be unjust. Notable also is the invocation of the semi-mythical patroness of the city, Lady Godiva. She was the wife of Leofric, earl of Chester and lord of Coventy in the mid-eleventh century, at which time it is likely that the two granted certain liberties to the town. By the later Middle Ages the story of Godiva's naked ride, by which she persuaded her husband to free the townspeople from taxes, was sufficiently familiar to be invoked in justification of a protest movement. The commemorative Lammas ride was a popular civic ceremony in the city.

M. D. Harris (ed.), *The Coventry Leet Book*, 4 vols, Early English Text Society, original series, London: Oxford University Press, 1907–13, pp. 566–7. English, revised by GR.

Within eight days after Lammas [1 August] there was a bill set upon the north church door in St Michael's church by some evil disposed persons unknown, the tenour [tenor, i.e. substance] whereof hereafter ensues:

Be it known and understand
This city should be free and now is bond.

Dame Good Eve[25] made it free;
And now the custom for wool and the drapery.

Also it is made that no prentice shall be
But thirteen pennies paid should he.

That act did Robert Green,[26]
Therefore he had many a curse, I ween.

And now another rule you do make
That none shall ride at Lammas but they that you take.[27]

When our ale is tunned
You shall have drink to your cake.[28]

25 Lady Godiva.

26 When he was mayor, in 1494.

27 The restriction on participation in this civic procession had been justified because of the 'diverse riots and offences and great discords done and committed upon Lammas day caused by that that [*sic*] many in number undesired ride with the chamberlain.' *Coventry Leet Book*, p. 565.

28 An allusion to the wealth of the urban elite.

You have put one man[29] like a Scot to ransom:
That will be remembered when you have all ⌜been⌝ forgotten.

Beware!

29 Laurence Saunders, a thorn in the side of the political ruling group of Coventry and a hero to some of the artisans. Saunders had been imprisoned by the mayor.

VIII. ASSOCIATIONAL LIFE

As the sources in Section VII make clear, the diversity and economic hierarchy of the medieval town created a social environment in which there could be no natural community. These very conditions, however, go far to explain the deliberate creation, by townspeople themselves, of hundreds of voluntary associations. More diverse, flexible and indeed voluntary than the professional associations of craftsmen, the guilds or fraternities of the medieval town brought together men and women working in various crafts, to serve ends which included both mutual insurance and public charity.[1] That charity needs to be considered not merely for its significant yet limited impact on the actual needs of the poor, but also and more profoundly as an expression of mutual concern and common identity. The first two documents in the present section indicate the wide range of medieval guilds. The London Puy of *c.*1300 was an elite network dominated by wealthy Londoners with probable connections to the royal court. Their meetings focused on recitals of poetry and song written by the members and the award of prizes for the best compositions [**92**].[2] The contemporary 'penny brotherhood' at Nottingham, by contrast, exemplifies a much larger class of associations with less socially elevated memberships and whose solidarity was expressed on a more modest scale [**93**]. The relatively small contributions required by the majority of such institutions were within the financial reach of artisans and shopkeepers, and these – both men and women – comprised the greatest proportion of the memberships. Many guilds, however, attracted a social range of members, as diverse individuals and groups perceived advantage in fraternisation with significant others [**94**]. Their ostensible and primary declared purposes were religious, charitable and, in broad terms, ethical. The most common aim was to cultivate in the individual member a sense of

1 G. Rosser, *The Art of Solidarity in the Middle Ages. Guilds in England 1250–1550*, Oxford, 2015.

2 A. Sutton, 'Merchants, music and social harmony: the London Puy and its French and London contexts, circa 1300', *London Journal*, XVII, 1992, pp. 1–17; A. Sutton, 'The "Tumbling Bear" and its patrons: a venue for the London Puy and mercery', in J. Boffey and P. King (eds), *London and Europe in the Later Middle Ages*, London, 1995, pp. 85–110.

moral responsibility and openness to mutual charity in relations both with the brothers and sisters of the society, and with other townspeople. All of their practical undertakings followed from these principles.

The practical purposes of the guilds were very various, but participation in each case gave members an empowering sense of contributing to a larger goal. Their generally modest resources limited the scale of their operations, yet, in addition to the halls which numerous societies erected for their ritual meetings [**96**], many hostels, almshouses and schools were maintained by the late medieval guilds, and, if the need for assistance always outran the provision, none the less involvement in the setting up and running of these establishments helped to cultivate human connections both within and beyond the guild which were a potentially strong response to the fragmentation and alienation of life in the town. The guilds' potential to act as a catalyst in the larger urban society is seen in the public presentation by the York fraternity of the Pater Noster, or Our Father, of a play in which the meaning of the prayer was expounded through a series of dramatic encounters between Virtues and Vices [**97**]. The engagement of dozens of families in a collective project for the common good is exemplified in the construction of two new stone bridges over the Thames at Abingdon, a substantial civic work undertaken in the fifteenth century by the local guild of the Holy Cross [**98**].

Such works did not exhaust the range or significance of the guilds' activities. Their potential to channel political ambitions was especially manifest in a large number of small medieval towns whose constitutions were stifled by the presence of lay or ecclesiastical lords. In such places as Abingdon itself, Stratford-upon-Avon, Ludlow, King's Lynn, Boston and Maidstone, a prominent guild is recorded in each case as making a major contribution to the practical running of the town, or indeed as playing the role of *de facto* civic government. Another such instance is the cathedral town of Lichfield [**95**]. Between the late fourteenth and the early sixteenth century, the Lichfield guild's membership of between two hundred and a thousand men and women made it (allowing for a proportion of members drawn from the hinterland) a significant presence in a town of 1500 to 2500 inhabitants. The prevailing motif in the late fourteenth-century statutes is the proper organisation of religious services in the town chapel of St Mary in the marketplace: the text exemplifies the way in which a secular urban society not uncommonly took collective responsibility for the direction of its spiritual affairs, including the hiring and firing of suitable priests.

The immediate context of a national royal enquiry into the activities of the guilds, prompted by a petition in parliament originating in fears of subversion in the aftermath of the Peasants' Revolt, explains the under-statement, in this and other reports produced by the guilds themselves, of their political potential. Reading between the lines, however, it is possible to perceive that the scope of the guild's activities was by no means confined to the ordering of masses, important though these certainly were in the eyes of the membership. The references to the jurisdiction of the guild in disputes involving townspeople hint at an authority which emerges more explicitly in later ordinances of 1486. These show the master of the guild, together with a body called 'the forty-eight', effectivedly regulating local affairs, for all the world as though the guild of St Mary were the legitimate town council of Lichfield. In law, authority remained with the bishop until the incorporation of the borough in 1548. In practice, however, the guild acted – and probably did so from as early as the thirteenth century – as a surrogate government for the town.[3]

Guilds were not the sole context in which townsmen and women gathered and formed networks for survival and for collaboration in joint undertakings, and to build solidarity. Parishes, neighbourhoods and crafts, together with more informal friendship groups, each had a role. All of these manifested themselves in ritual and festive contexts which simultaneously offered a focus for holidays and dignified the events together with their participants. The mayor of Bristol's gifts of ale to the city's crafts which held a festival at Midsummer at once honoured the workers and presented the civic government in a benevolent and paternalistic light [**100**]. Keeping an eye on craftsmen on their days off became an increasing concern of magistrates towards the end of the Middle Ages. This anxiety, manifest in numerous by-laws, had several origins. The regulations were prompted by national legislation which, from the late fourteenth century onwards, attempted to limit activities deemed wasteful of time and money, and to focus the free time of craftsmen upon what were perceived by king and parliament as useful military exercises. Despite these efforts, the fifteenth century witnessed a marked commercialisation of leisure pursuits, in the forms, appearing on the edge of the metropolis and of all provincial towns, of archery butts, cock-fighting pits, gaming tables and tennis courts. Finally the authors of civic attempts to check these passions were inspired, with a

3 G. Rosser, 'The town and guild of Lichfield in the late Middle Ages', *Transactions of the South Staffordshire Archaeological and Historical Society*, XXVII, 1987, pp. 39–47.

zeal increasingly evident from the late fifteenth century, to impose regulation as a moral reform of what were identified as the less restrained elements of the urban population [**99**], [**113**].[4]

92. A society of poetry and song in London *c.*1300

The London citizens who comprised this religious, musical and social company embraced the courtly language and rituals of chivalry. The language used in these statutes – the 'prince' of the company, the 'royal feast' – speaks to its social aspirations. Given the many connections between the mercantile elite of the city and the royal court, some mingling of these social groups within the Pui is plausible and even likely. The precise derivation of the term, which is also found in northern France applied to similar singing societies, is unknown, although an original connection with the French town of Le Puy in the Auvergne is indicated. In general terms, the association closely resembles the religious and social fraternities which were so numerous in medieval towns [**93**], [**94**], [**95**], [**96**], [**97**]. Despite the refinement and solemnity of the dinner, the membership appears to have been socially varied.

H. T. Riley (ed.), *Liber Albus, Liber Custumarum, et Liber Horn*, 3 vols, Rolls Series, London: Oxford University Press, 1859–62, ii (1), pp. 216–28, ii (2), pp. 579–94. French, transl. by the editor, revised by GR.

In honour of God, Our Lady St Mary, and all Saints, both male and female; and in honour of our lord the king and all the barons of the country, and for the increasing of loyal love. And to the end that London may be renowned for all good things in all places; and to the end that mirthfulness, peace, honesty, joyousness, gaiety and good love, without end, may be maintained. And to the end that all blessings may be set before us, and all evils cast behind. The loving companions who dwell in and frequent the good city of London have ordained, confirmed, and established a festival that is called the *Pui*. And in order that this festival may be maintained in peace and in love, each one should bind himself on oath, firmly, as a reputable man, that so long as there shall be five companions, he shall be bound to the sixth, and shall be bound to obey all the commandments, good and lawful, of the *Pui*.

4 M. K. McIntosh, *Controlling Misbehaviour in England, 1370–1600*, Cambridge, 1998.

And each man ought to give, upon entering into the company, 6*d* for his entrance, by way of remembrance ... And after this, each companion, on the day of the sitting (*siege*), shall pay 12*d*; and as to him who shall have a new song, his song shall acquit him. And the Prince ought to provide the feast ... and if the Prince have need of assistance, he ought to take twelve of the companions, of the most prosperous men residing in the city, to aid him in advising about the day of the feast, and throughout the following year ... And on the day of the sitting, there ought to be no one in the company, to eat there, or to stay, or to hear the singing, if he be not of the company ... And at each sitting, they ought to have a new Prince; and the old Prince ought to appoint him, with the twelve companions, at most, chosen each year ... And when the old Prince and his companions have to make a new Prince, during the meal (*en plein manger*), the old Prince and his companions go through the room, from one end to the other, singing; and the old Prince must carry the crown of the *Pui* upon his head, and a gilt cup in his hands, full of wine. And when they have gone round, the old Prince must give to drink to him whom they have chosen, and must give him the crown; and that person shall be Prince.

And the old Prince and the new one ought to decide as to the songs, as also those of the companions who understand it best, to the number of fifteen at the most. And they ought to decide as to the best of the songs, to the utmost of their knowledge, upon their oath that they will not fail, for love, for hate, for gift, for promise, for neighbourhood, for kindred, or for any acquaintanceship, old or new; nor yet for anything. And the best of the songs ought to be crowned, and the crown ought to belong to him who shall be crowned...

And if there is any one of the companions who marries in the city of London or who becomes a priest, he ought to let the companions know about it, and each shall be there according to his oath, unless he has a proper excuse. And the married person ought to give them chaplets, all of one kind; and all the companions ought to go with the bridegroom to church, and to make an offering, and to return from the church to the house. And if there be any one of the companions of the brotherhood who departs this life and dies, all the companions ought to be there, and to carry the body to church, by leave of the kindred, and to make an offering.

And if there is any one who is unwilling to be obedient to the peace of God or to the peace of our lord the king – whom may God preserve – the community of the companions does not wish to have him or his fees, by whom the good company may be accused or defamed. And if there be any one of the companions who is evilly disposed in word or in deed, the Prince and his twelve companions ought to make peace to the utmost of their power, saving the rights of the king and the city of London.

...

And whereas the royal feast of the *Pui* is maintained and established principally for crowning a royal song (*chansoun reale*);[5] inasmuch as it is by song that the company is honoured and enhanced, all the gentle companions of the *Pui* by right reason are bound to exalt royal songs to the utmost of their power, and especially the one that is crowned by assent of the companions upon the day of the great feast of the *Pui*. Wherefore it is here provided as concerning such songs, that each new Prince, on the day that he shall wear the crown and shall govern the feast of the *Pui*, and so soon as he shall have had his coat of arms (*son blasoun de ces armes*) hung in the room where the feast of the *Pui* shall be held, shall forthwith cause to be set up beneath his arms the song that was crowned on the day that he was chosen as the new Prince, plainly and correctly written, without any error. For no singer by right ought to sing any royal song, or to offer it, at the feast of the *Pui*, until he shall have seen the song that was last crowned in the previous year honoured according to its right, in the manner described.

And that, for deciding as to the songs, there be chosen two or three who understand singing and music well, for the purpose of trying and examining the notes and the points of the song, as well as the character of the words set (*pur les notes et les poinz del chaunt trier et examiner, auxi bien com la nature de la reson enditee*). For without singing no one ought to call a composition of words a song, nor ought any royal song to be crowned without the sweet sounds of melody sung (*saunz doucour de melodies chaunte*).

And although the honest company of virtuous ladies is a rightful theme and a principal occasion for royal singing (*chaunt roiale*), and for composing and furnishing royal songs, nevertheless it is hereby provided that no lady or other woman ought to be at the great sitting of the *Pui*, for the reason that the members ought to take example, and due warning, to honour, cherish and commend all ladies, at all times and in all places, as much in their absence as in their presence. And this is required by breeding and propriety...

5 A ballad-royal was a poem or song written in stanzas of eight lines.

That he who shall be crowned for his song upon that day, may ride between the old Prince and new one in the procession on horseback which they shall make through the city after the feast …

As concerning the room where the feast of the *Pui* shall be served, it is agreed that from henceforth there shall be no cloth hanging of gold or of silk, nor shall the room be tapestried; save only that it shall be fairly decked with leaves, strewn with rushes, and dressed out with tapestry cushions, in such a way as pertains to a royal feast; save that the seat where the singers shall sing the royal songs shall be covered with a cloth of gold.

And that the crown of the *Pui* shall be found at the common cost, of the price of one mark [13*s* 4*d*], and not less.

And as to serving up the feast, it is also ordained, that all the companions shall be served amply, as well the poorest as the richest, in the following way: they shall be served with good bread, good ale and good wine; and then they shall be served with pottage, and with one course of solid meat; and then after that, with double roast in a dish, and cheese, and no more. And that after the companions shall all have eaten, neither of the Princes, the old one or the new, shall give a supper on that day, or a dinner on the next. But straight after they have given the crown to him who shall sing the best, they shall mount their horses and make their procession through the city, and shall then escort the new Prince to his house; and there they shall all alight, and shall have a dance there, by way of parting; and they shall then take one drink and depart, each to his own house, all on foot …

And whereas it has given a chapel, founded and begun in honour of God and of Our Lady, near the Guildhall, for all the company of the *Pui*, the which chapel cannot be completed without great assistance from the alms of good people; it is hereby ordained that each one of the company shall give of his means and do his almsdeeds for completing the work of this chapel; that is to say, the richest 1*d* every Saturday, and the others ½*d* each, or whatever each shall please to give, according to his affluence and his wealth …

And whereas the festival of the *Pui* is much honoured by the attendance of companions, and by far the majority of the company are merchants frequenting fairs, because of which they cannot come to the *Pui* on the fixed day appointed for the great feast at London, as that day falls during the fair of St Ives and other fairs; it is hereby agreed by the companions, that from henceforth the great feast of the *Pui* shall be held at London on the Sunday after the feast of the Holy Trinity [the Sunday after Pentecost, which is the fiftieth day after Easter]; and this for the convenience of the merchants of the company.

93. A penny brotherhood in Nottingham 1307

Religious fraternities were formed for mutual aid by townspeople at all social levels, including, in this case, that of the poorest urban workers. The case below exemplifies what was in all probability a very large class of such relatively informal associations. This one entered the record because members with a grievance took their case before the borough court. Although the primary ostensible purpose of the guild was to maintain a candle in front of an image of the Virgin Mary, evidently in the church of the Carmelite friars of Nottingham, the society also had a material purpose, the regulation of which is here referred not to the church court but to the secular justices of the town.

W. H. Stevenson (ed.), *Records of the Borough of Nottingham*, 3 vols, London: Quaritch, 1882–85, i, pp. 73–5. Latin, transl. by the editor, revised by GR.

Robert Mimot and John de Graham complain of John de Raisen, William de Wimeswold and William de Cossal, that the latter three have unjustly broken an agreement made between them, because it had been agreed amongst them on Friday, 25 March 1307, in the garden of the Carmelite friars of Nottingham, that each of them should give every week throughout the whole of the year next following, one penny to the light of the Blessed Mary, so that at the end of the year Robert, John de Graham, John de Raisen, William and William came and made account of this money, and found in each of their hands five shillings, whereupon it was then and there agreed between them that the said John de Raisen, William and William should have the aforesaid money in their merchandises, to the common profit of the light, and that Robert and John de Graham should audit every year the account of the money with the profit, and that they should ordain the money with the profit for the common profit of the light. And Robert and John de Graham on 25 April 1311 came to John de Raisen, William and William and desired them to come to account for the said money with the profit, in order that they might ordain the common profit to the light, and they would not, but unjustly broke the agreement made between them. John de Raisen, William and William say that no such agreement was made between them. They submit to a jury.

94. Guilds at Cambridge

There survive relatively few internally generated records of the medieval guilds or fraternities. The suppression of all the guilds in 1547 (with the exception of a very few London companies that were licensed to continue for commercial reasons), on account of their Catholic practice of prayers for souls in purgatory, explains this archival void. Records of these two Cambridge guilds survived in the archive of the academic college to which, by a deliberate decision, they gave rise. The Cambridge guild of St Mary was founded before 1298; that of Corpus Christi before 1350. In the early 1350s the two guilds joined forces, and in 1352 the brothers and sisters of the amalgamated guild used this society as the means to found a new academic college of the University of Cambridge. Guilds and individual burgesses not infrequently founded grammar schools; this was a more unusual enterprise. The foundation of Corpus Christi College was also a diplomatic bridge between the communities of the town and the University of Cambridge. The guild of St Mary evidently had a commercial interest in the sale of imported millstones. The enrolment as new members of a guild of individuals who were already deceased was sometimes secured by their descendants in order that their souls should benefit from the intercessory prayers of the company. On guild plays, referred to here, see also [**114**], [**115**], [**116**].

M. Bateson (ed.), *Cambridge Gild Records,* Cambridge Antiquarian Society, XXXIX, 1903, pp. 3–5, 8–9, 13, 26–7, 37–40, 47, 49, 51. Latin, transl. by the editor, revised by GR.

Records of the Guild of St Mary, Cambridge

30 December 1300. Roger Wollemonger and his wife entered the guild and fraternity on Friday after Christmas, for a fine of 2 quarters of malt payable at the feast of the Nativity of the Virgin Mary [8 September] with [an offering of] wax.

At a meeting of the brotherhood on this date it was established by the unanimous consent of all the brothers and sisters then present that each year thereafter, on the morrow of the feast of the Circumcision of Christ [1 January], all the brothers and sisters not legitimately impeded shall meet after the morning mass of the day at St Mary's church and there have a solemn mass celebrated for the deceased brothers and sisters of the guild, on pain of ½ lb of wax.

29 September 1303. The master of the Hospital of Shengay [of the Knights Hospitallers] gave the fraternity 3 quarters of corn to have the fraternity and he agreed to give the fraternity 1 quarter of corn each year and so was received into the fraternity.

Master Thomas of Halys [rector of Hardwick church] entered the fraternity for a fine of 2*s* of annual rent from his house in Cambridge.

30 April 1307. On Sunday before the Ascension 35 Edward [I] it was ordained by the common assent of all the brothers that the chaplains of the said guild shall celebrate two trentals [of 30 masses] specially for the soul of each brother [or sister] after his [or her] death; and if he should leave anything by will to his guild then, as the alderman shall ordain, the said chaplains shall celebrate additionally more or less according to the legacy.

20 July 1310. William Schurr entered by a fined of 6*s* 8*d* with wax, but this is remitted as he is to be the proctor of the guild in selling our millstones.

Henry de Foulburne, bedeman,* entered in return for his service in summoning the brothers of the guild whenever needed for his lifetime.

Joan the wife of John Culling entered by a fine of 1 comb* of malt with wax.

10 November 1319. True sum of 15 millstones sold £22 5s 4*d*.

Records of the guild of Corpus Christi, Cambridge

1350

John Appelby and Joan his wife entered the fraternity by a fine of 6*s* 8*d*.

Robert Herry and Sarah his wife both entered for 20*s* of which they paid 6*s* and Peter le Cok is pledge for the rest.

Matilda the wife of John de Impiton entered the fraternity for a fine of 5*s* with 6*d* for wax.

Richard Fouke, Alan le lattener,* Katherine his wife and Juliana Fouke entered the fraternity for a fine of 11*s* in all.

Alexander the vicar of St John's church in Cambridge became a brother and gave 40*d*.

Robert le Pipere and Alice his wife, John Pipere, Thomas Pipere and Imania his wife entered the fraternity for a fine of 13*s* 4*d* and wax.

In expenses for the procession 56*s* 10*d*. Item 9*d* paid to John Sekersteyn for masks [*visers*: for the guild play].

1351

Robert de Blaston, carpenter, and Alice his wife, and Adam de Newnham and Isabella his wife entered the fraternity and gave in alms 20*s* and wax. And the said Robert and Adam promised by their faith to serve the guild in the office of carpenters before anyone else, taking 1*d* per week less than others according to the current rate [*secundum comunem cursum*] of the town; provided they are not in service and are given sufficient notice.

Richard de Audele living and Thomas Audele, Richard Sombi and Alice Ribi, dead, entered the fraternity and gave 26*s* 8*d* in alms and 7*d* for wax.

Master Roger Attetownshend de Wilbi and John his elder brother, Walter and Alice his parents, John his younger brother and William, Roger's nephew, entered the fraternity and gave 40*s* in alms and 3*s* for wax which John Hardy, stationer of Cambridge University and proctor of the guild, received for making a breviary for the same.

1352–53

Alan Oxebourgh and Helen his wife and Geoffrey Forster entered the fraternity and gave all the vessels and utensils needed for brewing to the use of the master and scholars of the hall of Corpus Christi and the Blessed Virgin Mary of Cambridge, provided that they should be used for no other purpose.

John Clement of Tamworth and Alice his wife. Henry and Matilda, parents of the said John, entered the fraternity; and he was and is an excellent counsellor and helper of the guild or college (*Gilde seu collegio*) in all its negotiations in London; and John gave the college a chalice and a vestment.

Simon Francis citizen of London and Matilda his wife entered the fraternity.

Andrew Aubrey citizen of London entered the fraternity and gave, etc.

Henry de Lacy, servant of the said Andrew, entered the fraternity and gave 6*s* 8*d*.

Walter Neel and his wives, Alice [deceased] and Katherine, and John Doxenford entered the fraternity and [Walter] gave 20*s* to the proctor and promised in alms to the guild £40.

1353

William de Lenne, skinner and Isabella his wife entered the fraternity and gave in alms 13*s* 4*d* and 12*d* for wax and spent towards the play (*in ludo*) of the Children of Israel [the Massacre of the Innocents] 6*s* 8*d*.

95. Ordinances of a guild at Lichfield

In a few instances we can study surviving registers of members inscribed in particular guilds, into which supplementary records were sometimes entered. The regulations which follow were copied towards 1400 into the register of the guild of St Mary at Lichfield. This guild had acquired its first royal charter in 1387; however, its existence antedated that ratification, and it had probably been influencing civic affairs for some time. The register of the guild records a wide social and occupational range amongst the members. The ordinances hint at the extent of the guild's involvement in the secular life of the town. This text of 1388, however, is reticent about the scope of the guild's activities, of which the full extent appears more clearly in other records.[6] Regarding the religious and moral purposes of the guild, it is notable how far the secular members were in command of the team of priests employed to serve the society.

G. Rosser (ed.), 'The guild of St Mary and St John the Baptist, Lichfield: ordinances of the late fourteenth century', *Collections for a History of Staffordshire*, 4th series, XIII, 1988, pp. 19–26. Latin, transl. by the editor.

6 G. Rosser, *The Art of Solidarity in the Middle Ages. Guilds in England 1250–1550*, Oxford, 2015, pp. 205–7.

i. In 1387 the most illustrious King Richard II, vowed to God and wishing to promote more abundantly the divine cult and the devotion of the people, in the eleventh year of his reign, granted and gave his licence to Adomar de Lichefeld, Thomas Taverner, Simon de Lichefeld, Henry Broun, Robert Teyntrel, Richard Mortymer and David Brydd, to make a guild and fraternity in the vill* of Lichfield in honour of the glorious Virgin Mary, mother of God, as is more fully contained in the king's charter. And so by the licences obtained from the same king and from the reverend in Christ, father and lord, Richard, bishop of Coventry and Lichfield, the aforesaid guild was begun and founded in perpetuity. Many brothers and sisters began to flock into this guild, and they duly elected from amongst themselves a master and four wardens, according to the terms of the royal grant, and they made by common agreement various honest rules consonant with the law for the constitution and support of the guild, in the form following.

ii. First it is ordained that each year on the feast of the Conception of the Virgin Mary [8 December], or within the octave of that feast, a meeting of the brothers and sisters shall be held, and there the master and wardens shall be elected. No one, however, shall henceforth be elected to the office of master or warden who does not presently dwell in the town of Lichfield. And if any man is chosen master or warden, and refuse the office, then his name is to be cancelled from the register, and he is no more to be counted a brother. And if a man is particularly suitable as master or warden, he may be re-elected, although not compelled to take the office again. The election is to be made like this: On the day of the election, when the master, wardens and brothers of the guild are gathered at the common hall, the outgoing master shall name six of the brotherhood, who shall then choose another three, and these nine together with the four wardens shall choose one man to be master, whom they judge to be most suitable, and four wardens for the prosperity and rule of the guild. For the final determination of the election, the majority of the thirteen shall ratify and determine it.

iii. The master and wardens are obliged at the end of the year to make an account before the brothers of the guild, of all the benefits and profits received by the guild that year. And if the master or wardens together or severally lend any money from the common box, they shall answer for it at the accounts, and restore it and repay it to the wardens for the new year.

iv. It is ordained that the master and wardens shall make provision for the honourable distribution of the uniform livery towards the feast of the Virgin Mary's Nativity [8 September] and that each [member] shall pay for his own, so that on the feast day or within the octave there shall be a general gathering of the brothers and sisters of the guild, if the master and wardens consider it appropriate reverently to hold a solemn service and a feast in honour of the glorious Virgin Mary.

v. It is decreed that all the names of the brothers and sisters should be written in a register book with the gifts they make to the guild. And when any brother or sister leaves this life, the day of their obit is noted in the same book, so that the obit may be kept in perpetual memory.

vi. It is ordered that no brother or sister should be received unless by the discretion of the master and wardens, and that none should be admitted unless they be of honest conversation and good reputation, and make to the support of the guild whatever contribution is agreed with the master and wardens. And then they should make an oath on the Scripture at their reception in these words: 'I N. from this hour onwards will be faithful to the master and the brothers of the guild of the glorious Virgin Mary of Lichfield and to their successors in the future; I shall be obedient in all their lawful and honest doings; and the counsel which the master or wardens shall reveal I will not knowingly disclose to anyone. If it should come to my notice that the guild may be hurt or suffer grave loss then I will prevent it or cause it to be prevented so far as I am able. As a brother I shall faithfully observe the lawful ordinances made, and to be made in the future, by the master and wardens; may God and Scripture help me.'

vii. It is ordained that if any brother of the guild should be convicted of adultery or any other notable crime, then he shall be publicly defamed by the master and wardens of the guild; and if on the third warning he will not desist, repentant, from such crime, then he shall be removed from the guild, and on no account be readmitted, for it is written: 'Let the name of such a malefactor be blotted out of the book of the living, and not be written with the righteous' [Psalms 69.28]. And if any of the brotherhood be inclined to some error or vice which is not notorious, as the master and wardens may establish, they are earnestly to warn them about this failing, in accordance with the scriptural truth: 'If thy brother trespass against thee [go and tell him his fault between thee and him alone': Matthew 18.15], so that they may desist from such crimes.

viii. If discord should chance to arise between brothers of the guild, after regarding the level and nature of the quarrel the master and wardens should amend it if it can conveniently be done. And no brother should sue his brother in an ecclesiastical or secular court where peace should be restored by the fraternity; nor should anyone seek the maintenance of some foreign lord in prejudice to any member of the guild, on pain of loss of the benefits and suffrages of the guild.

ix. Goods and chattels given to the guild to augment divine service and charitable works shall be used according to the wish of the donors and in their perpetual memory. Anyone holding tenements by grant of the master and wardens of the guild shall first pay due service to the chief lords of the fee and afterwards to the master and the brotherhood, according to Scripture which says: 'Render therefore unto Caesar the things which are Caesar's, and unto God the things that are God's' [Matthew 22.21].

x. If any outsider should have a quarrel with someone of the guild, let him inform the master, wardens and brotherhood, and after due consideration of the facts of the case let them intervene to bring a good end to such discord.

xi. If any brother or sister should fall, without fault of their own, into poverty so that they have not enough to live on, then let them be helped by the discretion of the master and wardens, consideration being given to their previous state and the nature of their misfortune, according as God provides for the growth of the guild's resources.

xii. No chaplain shall be taken to serve the guild on the supplication of any individual, even of a member of the fraternity; but the admission of chaplains of the guild shall be done solely by the discretion of the master and wardens, together with as many of the more capable brothers of the guild as they deem expedient. And the chaplain to be admitted shall, before his admission, be duly examined by the other chaplains as to his ability. All the chaplains who should serve the guild must be of honest and good conversation, or else, after reasonable warning, they shall be removed from their office and others appointed in their place by the discretion of the master and wardens. The chaplains shall be assiduous each day in the saying of mass in the chapel of St Mary, so that with their help the parochial chaplains should be able to perform divine service more gloriously to the praise of God. One of the chaplains of the guild shall be chosen by the master and wardens to be clerk, and shall write down the income and expenses of the guild … for a salary of 6*s* 8*d* per annum in remuneration. All the chaplains of the guild shall be at the mass of the Virgin Mary and at the antiphon called 'Salve Regina' in the chapel of St Mary in the marketplace of Lichfield, unless prevented by reasonable cause. Since when the solitary falls he has not another to help him up [Ecclesiastes 4.10], and so that each should be a suitable witness to the honest conversation and grave morals of the other, it is ordained that all of the chaplains of the guild shall be sleeping and rising in rooms constructed next to the chapel of St Mary of Lichfield and shall dine together in a certain hall allocated by the master and wardens at the common cost, unless they should be prevented by reasonable cause or sickness of body previously intimated to their fellows. However, should it happen that any of the guild chaplains should dine or even live with someone else in the town of Lichfield for three, four or five days in the week or for a whole week together, he shall none the less pay his weekly contribution to the costs of his fellows.

xiii. It is ruled that the clerk who serves as deacon in the chapel should, from the voluntary gifts of parishioners and guild members, be faithful in observing the mass of the Virgin Mary and the antiphon called 'Salve Regina' each day, unless prevented by reasonable cause.

xiv. When Philip de Strethay, master of the guild, and Roger de Ridware, Thomas Wysse, Richard del Chambre and Richard Couper wardens, by common consent of the other members admitted William de Wilnehale, priest, to be perpetual chaplain, as is more fully declared in a writing sealed with the common seal of the guild, the same William was bound to undertake the office of listing and distributing the livery on the instructions of the wardens of the guild, and of keeping a list of the names of those receiving the livery, to be delivered to the wardens when required.

96. Building a guildhall in Canterbury 1438

The five men who commissioned this guildhall to be built were evidently the representatives of an unspecified fraternity in Canterbury. The agreement with the builders, of a kind which became standard from the fourteenth century, gave those named in the contract a lump sum to cover the full costs of materials and labour. The completed wooden structure was then to be handed over to plasterers for finishing.

L. F. Salzman, *Building in England down to 1540*, Oxford: Clarendon Press, 1952, pp. 510–12. English, revised by GR.

The indenture* made on 20 December 1438 between William Benet, John Sheldwich, Gilbert German, William Bryan and John Benet, citizens of the city of Canterbury of the one part, and Alan Echyngham of the parish of Woodchurch in the shire of Kent, yeoman, John Tuttewyf and Piers Colyn of the same of the same parish and Richard Wodeman, carpenters and Willliam Harlekyndenn of the same parish, yeoman and William Tuttwyf of Ivychurch in the same shire, yeoman, on the other part, bears witness that the said Alan, Richard, John Tuttewyf, Piers, Willliam Harlekyndenn and William Tuttewyf bind themselves … and undertake to make unto the said William Benet, John Sheldwich, Gilbert, William Bryan and John Benet in Canterbury aforesaid a hall called a guildhall (*an Ildhalle*), good and sufficient and well-timbered of heart oak, 41 feet and 10 inches long, well and cleanly made. That is to say, [having] three tie-beams (*myddylbemys*) 12 inches thick, and 18 inches broad in the middle, each supported by suitable pendants [vertical posts], 'enbowid' [bevelled] in the best way. It will have sufficient wall-plates [the horizontal beams supporting the roof] and the spandrels of the bays will be filled with mountants [vertical studs supporting the tie-beams at the centre], liernes [ribs], braces, rafters with ashlars [short vertical struts rising from the inner surface of the wall-plate to meet the rafters], 'footlaces or jowe pieces' [jopes or cornices] and soulaces [diagonal braces in the roof]. The rafters shall be 8 inches broad or better at the foot and 6½ inches at the top, and 5 inches and 4 inches respectively in thickness. The high dais at the high bench of the said hall [shall have] trimmed timber, 4 feet broad [meaning obscure]. [There shall be] windows and 4 *gapias* [? dormer windows] sufficient to give light into the said hall. And the said high bench with the two side benches will be of oak timber, duly made, and the stairs of sufficient breadth of oaken planks. And there will be two chambers on the south end of the said guildhall, 18 feet long beside the street, 'with double stage jettied' [with two stories, each projecting, above] according to [modelled on] the scantlings [timber-framing] of the new chambers of the Lion [a large inn in Canterbury] by the street, or better, in the most cleanly wise that may be. And at the north end of the said hall, a chamber with a stage jettied and of the [same] scantling as the chambers by the street. Also the said carpenters shall find all manner of timber, carriage, and all other manner of things that belong to timber-work in the stairs, boards, stanchions, laths, and all other things belonging to carpentry craft for the hall and chambers aforesaid. And the foresaid hall and chambers to be made and performed by the feast of St Peter ad Vincula [1 August] next ensuing; and to all these covenants performed according to the writing abovesaid, the said William Benet, John Sheldwich, Gilbert, William Bryan and John Benet shall pay or do to pay unto the said Alan, Richard, John Tuttewyf, Piers, William Harlekyndenn and William Tuttewyf £33 6*s* 8*d*, according to the obligations thereof made in full payment of [the total sum of] £43 6*s* 8*d*, both for all manner of timber and carriages for boards and laths and for their handiwork and workmanship of all the said work, provided that it be done well and cleanly and all ready to tile and to daub [plaster] by the said day of St Peter ad Vincula.

97. Guild of the Lord's Prayer, York

This is one of almost five hundred surviving returns to a royal enquiry into guilds of 1388–89. The enquiry had been demanded by parliament in 1388 because of fears of sedition within the guilds, a circumstance which will have encouraged those responsible to specify certain aspects of their activity, and not others. These ordinances therefore give an incomplete picture of the scope and influence of such associations. This guild, like the vast majority, included both male and female members.

The ordinances make clear the guild's ambition, through its various activities, to reach out to a wide public.

J. Toulmin Smith and L. Toulmin Smith (eds), *English Gilds*, Early English Text Society, original series, XL, London: N. Trübner, 1870, pp. 137–40. English, revised by GR.

i. As to the beginning of the said guild, be it known that a play, setting forth the benefit of the Lord's Prayer, was once played in the city of York, in which all manner of vices and sins were held up to scorn, and the virtues were held up to praise. This play met with so much favour that many said, 'If only this play could be kept up in the city, for the health of souls and for the comfort of citizens and neighbours.' Hence the keeping up of that play in times to come, for the health and amendment of the souls as well of the maintainers as of the hearers of it, became the whole and sole cause of the beginning and fellowship of this brotherhood. And so the main charge of the guild is to keep up this play, to the glory of God, the maker of the said prayer, and in order to hold up sins and vices to scorn.

ii. And because those who remain in their sins are unable to call God their father, therefore the brethren of the guild are, first of all, bound to shun company and business that are unworthy, and to keep themselves to good and worthy businesses. And they are bound to pray for the brothers and sisters of the guild, both alive and dead, that the living shall be able so to keep the guild that they may deserve to win God's fatherhood, and that the dead may have their torments lightened. Also they are bound to come to the burial services of the dead brothers and sisters of the guild. And if anyone does not leave enough to meet the cost of such services, the rest of the brethren shall bear that cost. And if any brother dies and is buried away from the city, the brethren shall hold services for him [or her] within the city of York.

iii. Also it is forbidden that any brother of the guild shall, in the belief that he will have help from his brethren, be forward in getting into any lawsuit or quarrel, or in upholding any wrongful cause whatever, on pain of losing all help and friendship, or any relief, from the guild.

iv. And because vain is the gathering of the faithful without some work of kindliness being done, therefore the brethren have made this ordinance: That if it happen that any of the brethren be robbed, or his goods or chattels happen to be burned, or he be imprisoned for any wrongful cause, or be brought to want through any visitation from God, the other brethren shall, for kindness' sake, help him according to his need, under the guidance of the wardens of the guild, so that he may not perish for lack of help.

v. Also they are bound to find one candle-holder, with seven lights, in token of the seven supplications in the Lord's Prayer. This shall hang in the cathedral of York, and be lighted on Sundays and feast days, to the glory and honour of God almighty, the maker of that prayer, of St Peter, of the glorious confessor St William, and of all saints.

vi. Also they are bound to make, and as often as need be to renew, a table showing the whole meaning and use of the Lord's Prayer, and to keep this hanging against a pillar in the said cathedral church near to the aforesaid candle-bearer.

vii. Also they are bound, as often as the play of the Lord's Prayer is played in the city of York, to ride with the players thereof through the chief streets of the city of York; and to distinguish themselves more becomingly while riding in this way, they must all be clad in the same suit. And to ensure order during the play, some of the brethren are bound to ride or to walk with the players until the play is wholly ended.

viii. And once in the year a feast shall be held, and fresh wardens shall be chosen by the guild, and a true account shall be given to the newly chosen wardens of all that has been done on behalf of the guild during the last year.

ix. Also it is ordained that no one shall be allowed to enter this guild until he has been questioned by the wardens of the guild as to whether he has bent his will to live rightly, and so to deal with the guild and its affairs that he may be at one with the wardens.

x. [By an additional clause] a chaplain shall, once a year, celebrate divine service before the guild, for the good of the brothers and sisters of the guild, alive and dead, and for that of all who help the guild. Moreover, the brethren are accustomed to meet together every six weeks, and to offer special prayers for the welfare of our lord the king and for the good governance of the kingdom of England, and for all the brothers and sisters of the guild, present and absent, alive and dead, and for all those who help the guild or its members.

xi. The guild has no rents or goods, apart from the properties needed in the playing of the play, which properties are of little worth for any other purpose. And the guild has one wooden chest, in which these properties are kept.

98. Building the Thames bridges at Abingdon

This poem was written in 1447–48 by an ironmonger of the small monastic town of Abingdon. John Formande was a member of the Holy Cross guild, which played a leading role in the major undertaking to construct, from 1416, two stone bridges across a bend of the river Thames (where there were two river crossings) and a causeway between them, thereby redirecting the main road between London and Gloucester. The verse, copied on vellum, is preserved in a unique fifteenth-century copy in the almshouse which was built by the guild at the same period.

L. T. Smith (ed.), *The Itinerary of John Leland in or about the years 1535–1543*, 5 vols, London: G. Bell, 1906–10, v, pp. 116–18. English, revised by GR.

Of all works in this world that ever were wrought
Holy church is chief, their children be chersid [Christened],
For by baptism these bairns to bliss be brought,
Through the grace of God, and fair refreshed.
Another blessed business is bridges to make,
There that the people may not pass after great showers.
Dole [grievous] it is to draw a dead body out of a lake
That was fulled in a font stone [baptised in the font] and a fellow of ours.
King Harry the Fifth in his fourth year
He hath found for his folk a bridge in Berkshire.
For carts with carriage may go and come clear,
That many winters before were marred in the mire.
And some out of their saddles fell to the ground,
Went forth in the water, whist no man where.

Five weeks after ere they were found,
Their kin and their knowledge [acquaintance] caught them up with care.
Then the commons of Abingdon cried on the king,
Upon dukes and lords that were in this land.
The king bade them begin upon God's blessing,
And make it as strong as they could with stone, lime or sand.
Upon the day of Saint Alban they began this game,
And John Huchyns laid the first stone in the king's name.
Sir Piers Besillis, knight, courteous and heend [kind],
For his father's soul and his friends' he did as he should.
He gave them stones enough unto the work's end,
As many as they needed, fetch them if they would.
Then crafty men for the quarry made crows of yre [iron],
Wedges, and weights, and many hard hoes,
Geoffrey Barbour bade pay them their hire.
Then must they have moulds to make on the bows [arch-stones].
They cocked [fought] for carts, and cast [dice] for their choosing.
They found out the fundament [foundation] and laid in large stones.
They raised up the arches by geometry in rising,
With eleven labourers laving [baling] at once.
There was water enough, stone, lime and gravel,
Workmen as wise as they could find any,
And ever bade the Barbour pay for their travail,
Till a thousand marks be spent each a penny.
Then the strength of the stream astonished them strong,
In labour and laving much money was lore [lost].
There loved them a lad, was a water-man long,
He helped stop the stream till the work were afore.
It was a solace to see in a summer season,
Three hundred I wisse [estimate] working at once.
Four and four, ruled by reason,
To wit who wrought best were set for the nonce.
The people proved their power with the pickoys [pickaxe].
The mattock was man-handled right well awhile.
With spades and shovels they made such a noise
That men might hear them thence a mile.
Wives went out to wit [learn] how they wrought:
Five score in a flock, it was a fair sight.
In board cloths [tablecloths] bright white bread they brought,
Cheese and chickens clearly adight [prepared].
Thus were the ditches dug in full hard ground,
And cast up to arear [make level] with the way,
Sithen [thereupon] they were set with a quick mound [a hedge]
To hold in the banks for ever and aye.
The good lord of Abingdon left of his land,
For the breadth of the bridge, eighty feet large.

It was a great succour of earth and of sand,
And yet he abated the rent of the barge.
A hundred and fifteen pounds were truly paid
By the hands of John Huchyns and Banbery also
For the way and the barge, thus it must be said.
Thereto witness all Abingdon, and many one more.
For now is Culham hithe [ferry landing-place] come to an end,
And all the country the better and no man the worse.
Few folk there were could that way wend,
But they waged a wed [left something as a pledge] or paid of their purse,
And if it were a beggar [who] had bread in his bag,
He should be right soon bid for to go about.
And of the poor pennyless the hireward [toll-man] would have
A hood or a girdle, and let them go without.
Many more mischiefs there were, I say:
Culham hithe has caused many a curse.
Blessed be our helpers, we have a better way,
Without any penny for cart and for horse.
Thus accorded the king and the convent
And the commons of Abingdon, as the abbot would.
Thus they were cessed [assessed] and set all in one assent,
That all the breakings of the bridge the town bear should.
This was proved act also in the Parliament,
In perpetual peace to have and to hold.
This tale is told in none other intent
But for mirth and in memory to young and to old.
Now every good body that goes on this bridge,
Bid [pray] for the barber, gentle Geoffrey,
That clothed many a poor man to bed and to rig [dress],
And hath help to rents to hold up [finance the upkeep of] this way,
The which rents right true men have taken in hand,
And graciously governed them now a good while:
Whoso have them hereafter with truth but he stand,
It shall be known openly he does himself beguile.
I council every creature to keep him from the curse.
For of this treatise will I no more tell.
And be not too covetous to your own purse,
For peril of the pains in the pit of hell.
Now God give us grace to follow truth even [evermore],
That we may have a place in the bliss of heaven. AMEN.

r. [i.e. rebus] A.B.I.N.D.O.N. R.F.I.

Take the first letter of your forefather, the worker of wax, and I and N, the colour of an ass; set them together, and tell me if you can what it is then. Richard Formande, ironmonger, has made this table and set it here in the year of King Harry the Sixth 26th [1447–48].

99. Regulation of games

A series of national statutes attempted to ban the playing of various games.[7] City governments translated these rules into civic ordinances, whose repetition is an indication of their limited effectiveness.

H. T. Riley (ed.), *Memorials of London and London Life in the XIIIth, XIVth, and XVth Centuries*, London: Longmans, Green & Co., 1868, p. 580 (a); M. Bateson (ed.), *Records of the Borough of Leicester*, ii, London: C. J. Clay, 1901, p. 290 (b). Latin, transl. by the editors, revised by GR.

(a) Proclamation made on Friday before the feast of St Bartholemew [24 August], 1411: That no manner of man or child, of whatever estate or condition he be, be so hardy as to wrestle, or make any wrestling, within the sanctuary or the bounds of [St] Paul's, nor in any other open place within the city of London, upon pain of imprisonment for forty days, and making fine to the chamber, after the direction of the mayor and aldermen.

(b) Borough ordinances of Leicester 1467. That no man of the town nor of the country play within the franchise* of this town for silver [i.e. for money] at no unlawful games that be defended [prohibited] by the statute and law and by the parliament, that is for to say at dice, cards, hazard, tennis, bowls, picking with arrows [blowing arrows through a hollow trunk at a target of numbers], quoits with horseshoes, penny prick [in which pieces of iron were thrown at a stick on which a penny was placed], football, nor checker in the mire [an unknown game], on pain of imprisonment. And the owners of the house, gardens or places where the games are practised, as often as it is so found, shall pay to the chamberlains 4*d*, and every player 6*d* to the same chamberlains, to the use of the commons.

7 12 Richard II c.6; 11 Henry IV c.4; 17 Edward IV c.3. There are references to games played by children in medieval towns in B. Hanawalt, *Growing Up in Medieval London: The Experience of Childhood in History*, Oxford, 1993; N. Orme, *Medieval Children*, New Haven and London, 2001.

100. Festivities of the crafts at Bristol

For craftsmen and women the feast day of their patron saint would be an annual holiday. In Bristol by the fifteenth century the various crafts had been grouped together for their collective celebrations on one of two nights in the year. The measure documented below appears to have been intended to contain the potential for disorder by discontinuing the gathered celebration of all the crafts together, the mayor instead sending gifts of wine to each of the companies for consumption in their respective halls. It was an arrangement which presented the mayor and his officials in a paternalistic light, while simultaneously attempting to limit the public revelries of the crafts, together, perhaps, with the perceived possibilities for political association on such occasions.

E. W. W. Veale (ed.), *The Great Red Book of Bristol*, 4 vols, Bristol Record Society, 1933–53, i, pp. 125–6. English, revised by GR.

Memorandum that on 20 May 1451 William Canynges, mayor of Bristol, Thomas Hore, sheriff [and others] with all the notable and worthy persons being assembled in the common council house of the town, having ordained, established and granted that the drinkings on St John's night [23 June] and St Peter's night [28 June] from this time forward shall utterly be left among persons of crafts going on those nights before the said mayor, sheriff and notable persons and their successors. And that the mayor for the time being shall ordain at his expense wine to be disposed to the said crafts to their halls on St John's day under the form that follows; and the sheriff for the time being on St Peter's day in like manner. Always provided that the said persons of crafts shall send their own servants and their own pots for the said wine.

To the weavers 10 gallons; fullers* 10 gal.; dyers 5 gal.; tailors 8 gal.; skinners 4 gal.; butchers 6 gal.; bakers 5 gal.; brewers 5 gal.; smiths, farriers, cutlers, locksmiths and cardmakers 4 gal.; masons 3 gal.; tillers [i.e. tilers] 3 gal.; carpenters 3 gal.; hoopers 3 gal.; barbers and wax-makers 4 gal.; corvesers* 8 gal.; tanners 4 gal.; whitetawyers* 4 gal.; bowyers and fletchers 2 gal.; wiredrawers 3 gal.; shearmen 5 gal.

IX. RELIGION AND CULTURE

The ruling officers of every medieval town invested the place with a religious identity, claiming on this basis the reverence of its subjects.[1] Devotion was recruited in this way to the service of ecclesiastical and political authority. The relics incorporated in the spire of St Paul's cathedral in London epitomised the distinction and pre-eminence claimed by the bishop [**104**]. The plays with religious themes put on in the streets of York were perceived to be 'for the honour and good of the city, the mayor and aldermen' [**114**]. The provision by households of bread for blessing and distribution after mass might be regulated, as at King's Lynn, by the civic council, which thus identified itself as a religious authority [**108**]. Striking, also, is the increasing extent to which town councils of the fifteenth and early sixteenth centuries took it upon themselves to legislate for the moral behaviour of the townspeople. Frequently trespassing in the spheres of responsibility of the church courts – perhaps, at times, encouraged by a sense that ecclesiastical regulation was relatively ineffective – urban rulers adopted the role of moral guardians of the town. There was in this attitude a degree of inconsistency and pragmatism. The regular condemnation of prostitutes by borough courts might appear expressive of complete intolerance; but symptomatic of a more widespread compromise is the evidence from London, whose governors attempted more realistically (albeit with only partial success) to concentrate the practice in a designated area [**111**], [**112**].[2] However, notwithstanding such accommodation to social realities, there is in the moral legislation of towns prior to the Protestant Reformation an evident desire, not merely for tighter policing of unruly social elements but for spiritual reform in the godly commonwealth [**113**].

Yet late medieval religious culture was too multivalent to be manipulated in the sole interest of bishops or magistrates. The secular

1 On the themes of this section see further G. Rosser, 'Urban culture and the Church 1300–1540', in *CUHB*, pp. 335–69, with bibliography.

2 See in general R. M. Karras, *Common Women: Prostitution and Sexuality in Medieval England*, Oxford, 1996. On the tendency to occupational zoning by sex workers see P. J. P. Goldberg, *Women, Work, and Life Cycle in a Medieval Economy: Women in York and Yorkshire c.1300–1520*, Oxford, 1992, pp. 151–2.

rulers of Salisbury who in the fifteenth century contributed to the lengthy, expensive and ultimately successful campaign to secure the papal canonisation of a local holy man, Osmund, deliberately aligned themselves with a pre-existing popular cult.[3] Nor were the cathedral chapter or the civic council of Norwich indifferent to the popular stories of miracles attributed to William, a local boy reputed to have been martyred by Jews. The veneration of the child saint brought honour both to the church and to the town which claimed him as their own [**101**]. Such instances exemplify a recurrent theme in the history of the Christian Church, which is the interpretation of a universal language in the dialect of a particular place and community. For all its possible utility to government, that dialect has the potential at times to appear heterodox or subversive. Religious localism can account not only for officially adopted cults but also for the rare incidences of heresy. The particular form taken by a local cult of the Virgin Mary at Coventry led to accusations of Lollardy there.[4] Official condemnation might in turn be disputed. In 1440 a priest named Richard Wyche was ordered to be burned at London for heresy. But the watching crowd took him for a martyr. They erected a cross at the site, and began to make offerings of money and wax *ex voto* images, until the city authorities dispersed them by casting about animals' dung as a preventative of 'further idolatry'.[5] Religious belief was not easily controlled or manipulated by authority.

A defining characteristic of the town, in contradistinction to other places, was the diversity of its religious institutions, and a consequent degree of choice open to men and women of the laity. The presence in the larger centres of mendicant friaries was largely welcomed by the secular community [**102**], although at times resented by more anciently founded Benedictine religious houses [**103**] and also by some parish priests who jealously complained of the evident appeal of the friars.[6] Fraternities, too, added to the texture of urban religious life, and further accentuated the scope for the agency and variety of lay religion.[7] Urban wills are eloquent of a creative range of both

3 A. R. Malden, *The Canonization of Saint Osmund*, Wiltshire Record Series, II, 1901.

4 J. Crompton, 'Leicestershire Lollards', *Transactions of the Leicestershire Archaeological and Historical Society*, XLIV, 1968–69, pp. 11–44, at pp. 29–30.

5 R. Flenley (ed.), *Six Town Chronicles of England*, Oxford, 1911, p. 101; J. A. F. Thomson, *The Later Lollards 1414–1520*, Oxford, 1965, pp. 148–50.

6 J. Röhrkasten, *The Mendicant Houses of Medieval London, 1221–1539*, Münster, 2004.

7 See Section VIII.

devotional and fraternal ties, forged over a lifetime as so many means to address the challenges of life in the late medieval town [**105**]. The collective memberships of both crafts and fraternities consolidated identities at once pious and civic by honouring the town's patron saints and through their promotion and performance of plays based on sacred subjects [**106**], [**114**], [**115**].[8] Those plays, some of whose texts we are fortunate to be able to read, were not (as has sometimes been imagined) bland and merely conventional *tableaux*, but were by turns funny, disturbing and provocative. Their potential to challenge and subvert social assumptions is illustrated by a passage from the Chester play of Christ among the Merchants [**116**]. The larger cycles, of which that from Chester is an instance, were at once an expression of religious ideals and a celebration of civic community. The town clerk of Chester in 1531–32, in the preamble to a public proclamation for the plays, declared that they would be performed 'not only for the augmentation and increase of the holy and Catholic faith of our Saviour Jesus Christ and to exhort the minds of the common people to good devotion and wholesome doctrine thereof, but also for the commonwealth and prosperity of this city'.[9]

That double potential was echoed in other fields of cultural production, including the iconography of urban church decoration. Although vastly depleted by Reformation and seventeenth-century iconoclasm, enough evidence survives to show how the fabric of a medieval city church functioned as a site for the construction of both social and religious identities, and for the negotiation of relationships between particular families and neighbourhood societies and a more inclusive vision of the town community.[10] The monumental inscriptions embedded in the walls of the church of Long Melford announce at once the pride of successful wool-merchants and their desire to be remembered as contributors to a common religious purpose [**110**]. A stained-glass window in a York church, which combines text and pictures in a visionary prayer on the end of the world, is a rare survivor of a much larger class of imagery which, like the plays, did not merely repeat familiar platitudes but engaged the senses and the minds of contemporary witnesses through arresting and potentially unsettling testimonies to

8 See in general R. Beadle and A. J. Fletcher (eds), *The Cambridge Companion to Medieval English Theatre*, 2nd edn, Cambridge, 2008; M. G. Briscoe and J. C. Coldewey (eds), *Contexts for Early English Drama*, Bloomington and Indiana, 1989.

9 D. Mills (ed.), *The Chester Mystery Cycle*, East Lansing, 1992, p. xii.

10 In general see R. Marks, *Image and Devotion in Late Medieval England*, Stroud, 2004.

another order of reality, close to and yet critically distinct from that which prevailed in the everyday world of the town [**109**].

In addition to the material and spiritual support offered to their own members, guilds or fraternities often provided charitable support to a wider community. The Boston fraternity of Our Lady made variable weekly distributions to particular paupers of that town, in addition to its management of a poor house for thirteen long-term residents, who were recruited after interview from towns throughout the region. Other community-run infirmaries specialised in caring for epileptics or the blind [**107**]. Such ventures were always insufficient to the need: the scale of sickness and indigence would always outstrip the capacity of largely modest and locally run charitable initiatives.[11] But it would be wrong to conclude from this that townspeople were hardened or indifferent to poverty. When making their last wills and testaments, few were in a financial position to be able to make a large material difference, and recorded bequests to the poor tended to have less of a practical than a symbolic value [**105**].[12] But the same evidence shows that the poor were kept in mind, and the collaborative efforts of parishioners and guild members during their lifetimes evince a clear sense not only of the material value of neighbourly assistance to those in need but of the social and spiritual benefit to the giver. Beyond its practical contribution to welfare, urban charity offered scope for participation, and consequently for a redeeming sense of personal contribution to the common good, to a wide range of townsmen and women.[13]

101. The fame of a city shrine: William of Norwich

In March 1144, the dead body of a boy was found in a wood outside Norwich. The truth cannot now be discovered, but the story began to circulate that a Norwich boy had been murdered by Jews of the city. It is also evident from the sources that the matter was disputed, and that many called the official ecclesiastical narrative into question. Thomas

11 C. Dyer, 'Poverty and its relief in late medieval England', *Past and Present*, CCXVI, 2012, pp. 41–78.

12 P. Maddern, 'A market for charitable performances? Bequests to the poor and their recipients in fifteenth-century Norwich wills', in A. M. Scott (ed.), *Experiences of Charity, 1250–1650*, Farnham, 2015, pp. 79–103.

13 G. Rosser, *The Art of Solidarity in the Middle Ages. Guilds in England 1250–1550*, Oxford, 2015, ch. 2.

of Monmouth, the author of the text from which these extracts are taken, was (from 1150) a monk in the cathedral priory where the shrine of 'St William' was displayed to pilgrims. As the sole source for the events described, Thomas cannot be relied upon for any of his information. His principal narrative is a melodramatic account of William's supposed murder, presented as the epitome of a larger clash between the Jewish community and the Christian population of the city of Norwich. The tale, like many another miracle story from the Middle Ages, presents an idealised image of innocent youth cut off in its prime which we would be ill-advised to read as a simple source for the history of childhood in the period.[14] But given the evident intention to use the material in sermons and teaching provided for the local population in the cathedral of Norwich, it can be taken that the miracle narratives, of which two are copied below, give at least a plausible account of the personalities involved and of their circumstances. The arrival at Norwich of pilgrims not only from Lynn, at the other end of the county, but also from as far afield as York, gives some indication of the circulation and impact of these narratives. The unique surviving manuscript of the text was made in a Cistercian monastery around 1200; earlier copies at the cathedral priory in Norwich will have been destroyed in a fire in 1272.

M. Rubin (ed.), *Thomas of Monmouth. The Life and Passion of William of Norwich*, London: Penguin, 2014, pp. 151–3, 179–80. Latin, transl. by the editor. Reproduced by permission of Penguin Random House.

At that time in King's Lynn, in the parish of St Edmund, there was a certain woman called Gilliva, daughter of Burcard the Carpenter. She lost her sight by some accident and was condemned to blindness of her eyes for three years. To add to the misfortune, so terrible a pain developed in her eyelids and oppressed her with suffering that for three whole years her eyes were always closed, as if stuck together with glue, as if she would never be able to open them again. When three years had passed, she decided to seek refuge in the haven of the blessed martyr William, as sole and singular remedy; and with greater confidence, since she had learned by common report that others similarly condemned to blindness had been cured at his tomb. Her young nephew walked before her, leading the way with a cord around her, and

14 For a review of sources and methods for the study of childhood in the medieval town, see P. J. P. Goldberg, 'The drowned child: an essay in medieval cultural history', *WerkstattGeschichte*, LXIII, 2013, pp. 7–23.

she finally arrived in Norwich at St William, thanks to that guide. And so, standing in front of the altar, she began to pray and, after saying a small part of the prayer, the rest was interrupted by a sudden attack of pain. Indeed, her head was troubled and both eyes were seized with a fiery heat; and she plucked at her forehead and cheeks with her nails. Wild with anguish, the wretch rolled on the ground and, as if in a fit of madness, she rolled on the pavement, filling and disturbing the whole church with immense and frightful cries. But among the pangs of pain she cried out with a clear voice, saying from time to time: 'Gentle boy! Martyr William! Have pity on me, a wretch! You who have so often had pity on others!'

A multitude of people had come to the church that day and they gathered round the spectacle. Seeing the violence of her pain, everyone shared her sorrow, and, inwardly moved to pity, they poured out both prayers and tears. It was such a miserable sight that men and women alike cried, made vows and wailed. For who could watch such things and be so stony-hearted as to keep their eyes from weeping? At last, after much suffering and torment, as we truly believe by the impulse of divine mercy and the interventions of the merits of the blessed martyr, gradually the pain began to abate. When she felt the coming of the celestial remedy she got up from the ground and stretched her hands to heaven; and the eyelids which before were closed and which for pain she could not open even a little, now she opened; and immediately something like a spurt of blood flowed out, bursting from both her eyes. Without delay, the night of her long-standing blindness was dispelled, as if by a dawn of new light reborn … she came closer to the tomb of the holy martyr, prayed and offered a candle, which was brought to her; and, turning to the people, she announced that she had received her eyesight.

Around that time a certain Thomas of York also came, a man feeble and disabled in his whole body, who guided his progress with two staffs, known commonly as crutches, sustaining his weak body. He set off from York as best he could to go to the holy martyr William to receive the grace of health, and, making little progress, his lengthy journey took up many days. Faith supported the weak traveller and hope drew on the disabled one. Being led by them, he finally came to the tomb of the holy martyr in Norwich, obtained the remedy of desired health and, as a sign, he left his crutches there.

102. The Franciscans come to English towns

The first arrival of the Franciscans in England in 1224, and their early efforts to establish bases in a series of English towns, are recounted by one of their number. While the mission of the two Mendicant Orders of Franciscans and Dominicans (both founded in 1216) was not confined to towns, their preaching and pastoral efforts were particularly targeted at the urban population, which was perceived by church leaders to be in particular need of such care as towns often outgrew their provision of parish churches and clergy. Brother Thomas was evidently concerned to underline at every stage the absolute poverty of the early friars. At the time of his writing, around 1250, controversy was growing in the new Order about its acquisition of buildings and other property. Thomas was at pains to emphasise that urban property was held by others for the 'use' of the friars. Even allowing, however, for the effect of this debate upon Thomas's text, he probably gives a fair impression of the dependence of the early Franciscans upon the support, amongst others, of the urban laity. While the monastic chronicler gave prominence in his account to the substantial gifts and beneficent influence of aristocrats and wealthy merchants, this should not be taken as evidence that the friars were not also popular with humbler townspeople, many of whom appear in slightly later records as members of guilds or fraternities attached to urban friaries [**93**].

Father Cuthbert (ed.), *The Chronicle of Thomas of Eccleston*, Edinburgh and London: Sands, 1909, pp. 25–9. Latin, transl. by the editor, revised by GR.

After this, the number of the brethren increasing and their sanctity becoming known, the devotion of the faithful towards them increased likewise, and they became anxious to provide the brethren with suitable dwellings. Therefore at Canterbury Alexander, master of the priests' hospice, made over to them a plot of ground and built them a chapel sufficiently becoming for the time; and because the brethren would receive nothing as their own, it was given to the city and the brethren were allowed to live there at the will of the citizens. Most especially, however, were the brethren cared for by Master Simon of Longton, archdeacon of Canterbury, and Master Henry of Sandwich, and by the noble countess, the Lady Inclusa de Baginton, who in all things cared for them even as a mother cares for her sons, diligently gaining for them the goodwill of princes and prelates, with whom she was held in favour beyond measure.

At London the brethren were befriended by Sir John Iwyn, who bought them a plot of ground and gave it to the city, but piously assigned the use and profit of it to the brethren at the will of the citizens. He himself afterwards entered the Order as a lay brother and left us examples of perfect penance and high devotion. Sir Joyce fitz Piers added to the ground. His own son, a man of good parts, afterwards devoutly entered the Order, and still more devoutly persevered to the end. The chapel was built by Sir William Joyner,[15] at his own cost; he also gave at various times upwards of £200 towards the other buildings, and until his death he continued unweariedly in spiritual friendship with the brethren, bestowing upon them frequent benefactions. For the building of the infirmary Sir Peter de Helyland left £100 at his death. To Sir Henry de Fowie, and a young man of good bearing, Salekin de Basing, was the aqueduct chiefly due, but their offerings were largely increased by the king's munificence. Many other and ever-increasing gifts have I seen in my own time in London, both as regards buildings and books and additions to the ground and for the relieving of other needs: gifts to be admired by mortal men, and provided for the brethren by the most sweet Jesus in order that they, more than others, should love and honour him who is the same now and for ever.

At Oxford the brethren were received by Robert le Mercer, who let them a house in which many learned bachelors and many nobles took the habit. Afterwards they rented a house from Richard le Mulliner, on the ground where they now are, but within a year he gave the ground and house to the city for the use of the brethren. The ground, however, was exceedingly narrow and of no great length.

At Cambridge the brethren were at first received by the burgesses, who made over to them an old synagogue near the prison. But as the neighbourhood of the prison was intolerable to the brethren since both they and the gaolers had to use the same entrance, our lord the king gave them £6 13*s* 4*d*, which was sufficient for them to buy out the lease from the court of the exchequer. Then they built a chapel so very poor that one carpenter built it in one day, and in one day set up fourteen bundles of planks. So on the feast of St Lawrence [10 August], though there were as yet but three clerical brethren, namely, Brother William of Ashby and Brother Hugh of Bugden and a novice named

15 Mayor in 1239.

Brother Elias, who was so lame that he had to be carried into the choir, they sang the office solemnly according to note, and the novice wept so much that the tears ran freely down his face as he sang. Now this novice afterwards, having died a most holy death at York, appeared to Brother William of Ashby at Northampton, and when Brother William asked how he was, he replied: 'I am well; pray for me.'

At Shrewsbury the king gave the brethren a plot of ground; but the church was built by a burgess, named Richard Pinde, and the other offices by a burgess named Lawrence. But Brother William, the minister,[16] in his zeal for poverty, ordered the stone walls in the dormitory to be removed and mud walls put up in their stead, which was done by the brethren with admirable devotion and meekness, and at great cost.

103. Franciscans arrive in Bury St Edmunds

The irony in this extract is characteristic of the jealousy and hostility encountered by the new friars in many towns, especially from members of the older Benedictine monasteries, such as the author of this passage.

A. Gransden (ed.), *The Chronicle of Bury St Edmunds 1212–1301*, London: Nelson, 1964, p. 22. Latin, transl. by the editor.

1257. On 22 June the Friars Minor entered the town of Bury St Edmunds by stealth. They celebrated mass in an audible voice in the house of Roger de Harbridge, knight, on the east side of the north gate, in the presence of all comers but unknown to the convent. Simon, the prior and at this time the abbot-elect, together with the sub-prior, the sacrist and many others representing the point of view of the abbot-elect, went to the king. But nevertheless, on the same day, when the above-mentioned knight and the friars had just begun their dinner, the friars' oratory and all the buildings belonging to the house were razed [by fire] to the ground.

16 William de Nottingham (d. 1254), minister in charge of the English province of the Franciscan Order.

104. Relics in St Paul's steeple, London

The construction of St Paul's, as of other medieval cathedrals, was a civic no less than an ecclesiastical project. The incorporation within the cross on the spire of sacred relics was perceived as offering protection not only to the church but to the urban population as a whole. The first of these records comes from a secular chronicle compiled in London, the second from a well-informed monastic writer based in York.

G. J. Aungier (ed.), *Chroniques de London*, Camden Society, XXVIII, 1844, p. 38 (a); W. Childs and J. Taylor (eds), *The Anominalle Chronicle 1307 to 1334*, Yorkshire Archaeological Society Record Series, CXLVII, 1991, p. 89 (b). French (a) and Latin (b), transl. by GR (a) and by the editors (b).

(a) In that year [1314] the cross of the bell-tower of St Paul's church was brought down to be repaired, and within the old cross were discovered relics, that is to say, a corporal for singing mass in, white and complete without any damage, inside which was found a part of the shaft of the Cross of Our Lord Jesus Christ, made into the form of a cross; a stone from Our Lord's tomb; another stone from the spot where God was when he ascended into heaven; and another stone from the mount of Calvary where Our Lord's Cross was set up. And there was found a purse, and in the purse a piece of fine red cloth wrapped around bones of the eleven thousand Virgin Martyrs together with other unidentified relics. These relics Master Robert de Clothale showed to the people when he preached on the Sunday before the feast of St Botolph [17 June]. Afterwards on St Francis' day [4 October] the same relics were put back into the cross with several new ones.

(b) At this time [1314] the cross was taken down from the steeple at St Paul's in London. In it were many relics; and it was repaired and put back up with these relics and others on St Francis's day after Michaelmas, and on that day there was chanting by various canons and vicars of the said church on staging forty feet higher than the cross; and at that time there was a great light from torches and various other music there, because of the great importance of the relics that were placed in the cross.

105. Urban wills

The wills and testaments of medieval townspeople survive in very large numbers. A small but significant proportion has been published (albeit in editions of varying degrees of completeness). Copies of wills were registered in diverse ecclesiastical courts, depending upon the wealth and distribution of property of the testator. The most socially elevated will-makers appear in the well-preserved registers of the court of the archbishop of Canterbury. Humbler people, whose wills were copied in local church courts, are more patchily represented in the surviving record. An individual's will and testament was influenced by the expectations of the clerk to whom it was dictated, and remains in any case no more than a partial guide to the testator's activities over a lifetime. But it remains a valuable trace of priorities at a particular moment. The social and religious loyalties recorded in these testaments are traces of the economic diversity and the range of spiritual choices which distinguished the medieval town from the countryside.

F. J. Furnivall (ed.), *The Fifty Earliest English Wills*, Early English Text Society, original series, LXXVIII, London: N. Trübner, 1882, pp. 112–15 (a); S. Flood (ed.), *St Albans Wills 1471–1500*, Hertfordshire Record Publications, IX, Hitchin: Hertfordshire Record Society, 1993, pp. 3–4 (b), 40 (c). Latin, transl. by the editors, revised by GR.

(a) 18 May 1439. I Nicholas Charleton, citizen and skinner of London, in whole and good mind being, thanked be almighty God, ordain and make my testament of my last will in this form that follows. First I bequeath my soul to almighty God, my maker, our lady Saint Mary, and to all saints of heaven, and my body to be buried in [St] Paul's great churchyard of London before the cross. And I bequeath to the new work of the same church 20*d.* And to the high altar of St Augustine's church where I am a parishioner, for my tithes and offerings negligently forgotten, 6*s* 8*d.* And I will and ordain that in all haste possible after my decease, that I have four trentals [of thirty] of masses sung for my soul in three houses of friars of London, that is to say, the Preachers [Dominicans], Whitefriars [Augustinians] and Greyfriars [Franciscans], and I bequeath therefore to each house of [the] three 40*d.* And I bequeath 1000 halfpenny loaves to be given to poor men by my executors within twelve months after my decease, that is to say, to every poor man that comes, a loaf.

Also I bequeath to the brotherhood of my craft of Corpus Christi, to the common box thereof, *6s 8d*; and to the common box of the brotherhood of Our Lady in my craft, *6s 8d.* Also I bequeath to every prisoner in the prison of Ludgate, and each of the two counters [additional prisons] of London, a loaf of 1 lb, to be delivered when corn is of reasonable price within a year after my death. Also I devise and ordain 100 lbs of wax to minister to the service of the Salve [Maria, i.e. 'Hail Mary'] of Our Lady's chapel in the said church of St Augustine, that is to say, two tapers of 1 lb weight there to be lit and burn at Salve time as long as the said 100 lbs weight of wax will last. And I will that Thomas Gloucester my brother, that is my executor, and the wardens of St Augustine's church aforesaid have the governance of the said wax and light as written above. Also I bequeath to each of my apprentices dwelling and standing with me in [the] manner of apprentices at [the] time of my dying *20s.* Also I bequeath to Thomas Bayle, my servant, *20s.* Also I bequeath to Thomas Dymmok, skinner, of Gloucester, my best gown of the livery of [the] skinners' craft, both fur and cloth, if he be alive. And to Watkyn Asshwell my second best fur and gown after the advice of Thomas Gloucester my brother. And if it so be that any of the said persons that I have made bequest to die before my decease, then I will that the same goods of him or them that so die be divided into two parts by my executors, that is to say, one part to the alms of the brotherhoods of Corpus Christi and Our Lady of my craft; the second part to the wardens of St Augustine's church, to the use of the same church. And the third part to be expended and given by Thomas Gloucester my brother and my executor to poor people of the parish of St Augustine abovesaid, and other parishes where there is need. Also I bequeath to the brotherhood of St Nicholas founded by parish clerks in London *3s 4d.* Also to the brotherhood of St John of the craft of tailors of London *3s 4d.* And the residue of all my other goods, chattels and debts that be not bequeathed above after my debts be paid, my burying also and funeral expenses done, and this testament fulfilled, I bequeath and will that it be divided by my executors into three parts, of which I bequeath two parts to my wife Joan, to have and to hold to her for ever more, in the name of her part and dower of my goods to her in any wise belonging; and the third part of the same residue, I bequeath to my executors, by them to be disposed in masses, alms and works of charity for my soul and all true Christian souls, as they hope best [to] please God's will. And of this testament I make my executors, that is to say, Thomas Gloucester, clerk, my brother, William Allard and Thomas Aston, citizens and skinners of London. And I bequeath to each of my said executors for his labour in this part to be had 100*s.* In witness of which thing, to this testament I have set my seal. Written at London the day and year abovesaid. Also, over and above these provisions, I, the said Nicholas Charleton, ordain, assign and bequeath by this testament to the said Joan, my wife, the terms and estate in the tenement with the appurtenances that I dwell in in Watling Street in the said parish of St Augustine, the which I hold to farm [on lease] of the master and convent of St Bartholemew's hospital beside West Smithfield of London, to have and to hold to the said Joan the said terms, estate and tenement with the appurtenances during her life, provided the terms of it last so long, she bearing, yielding, paying and supporting thereof the farm yearly, and other charges during her life, as I am bound to do by writing to the said master and convent. This testament was proved before Master John Lyndefeld commissary etc., 3 July 1439. And commission was made for the appointment of the executors named and for the administration of the goods.

(b) Will of John Felowe, barber, of St Albans, 25 June 1471. I leave my body to be buried next to my former wives Joan and Agnes in St Peter's churchyard. To the high altar of St Andrew's chapel within the precincts of St Alban's monastery for forgotten tithes 20d.[17] To the fabric of the new rood loft in the same chapel 20*d.* For repairs to the charnel chapel* in the said town 20*d.*[18] To the anchorite of St Peter 12*d* and the anchoress* of St Michael 12*d.* To Thomas Blythe 20*s* in ready money of such of my good utensils as his mother may choose. To John Blythe six of the better razors. All my other razors and scissors are to be equally divided between John Blythe, John Eynesham, my former servant, and Robert Overton, my servant. To the said John, John and Robert all my round basins and all things belonging to me in 'le Shavynger Shope' to be equally divided between them, except

17 The chapel of St Andrew was rebuilt *c.*1460 as a parochial church for the townspeople, thereby relieving the monks of the regular intrusion of laity within the monastery church of St Peter.

18 The charnel chapel was maintained by a fraternity of All Saints; it stood in the corner of the abbey churchyard.

the two larger and better round basins which belong to Joan my present wife. To Joan my wife, all the instruments belonging to the art of surgery and bloodletting. To Agnes my servant, two pairs of sheets ... I bequeath my tenement in Holywell Street to my wife Joan for the remainder of her life. After her death it is to be sold by my executors and the money used to pay a chaplain, at a competent salary, to celebrate mass for two years ... for the good of my soul, the souls of my parents and my former wives ... Provided that my wife Joan pays a priest [to celebrate] in the chapel of St Andrew for a whole year after my death ... out of her own goods mentioned above.

(c) Will of John Payes, fletcher,* of St Albans, 17 June 1478. I bequeath a twopenny wax candle to burn before St Erasmus on the day of my death. To my housekeeper, widow Idonia, for her good service to me I bequeath a gown edged with red, a murrey [purple] hood, a brass pot, another brass pint pot and a pair of sheets. To the wife of my brother William Pyes one red gown and a murrey hood. To the two sons of Matthew Clerk, fletcher, I leave all the tools of my trade to be equally divided between them. The residue of my goods I bequeath to Matthew Clerk, fletcher, and John Peerson of St Albans, draper, whom I appoint as my executors. Witnessed by Robert More, draper, and Edward Loryng of St Albans.

106. Craft patronage of civic religious ritual

The wiredrawers of Coventry were amongst the humblest crafts of the town. Their request to be given the honour of responsibility for a new canopy over the high altar of St Michael's church may have originated in their involvement in its manufacture. St Michael's and Holy Trinity were the two parish churches of the medieval town, and both had civic functions.

M. D. Harris (ed.), *The Coventry Leet Book*, 4 vols, London: Oxford University Press, 1907–13, pp. 131–2. English, revised by GR.

It is ordained that the craft of the wiredrawers shall keep the canopy over the high altar in [the church of] St Michael in Coventry, as it appears by indenture* made, the tenor of which follows in these words:

This indenture* witnesses that on 1 September 1430, John Sheldon, Thomas Eldbek, Henry Coton and Robert Burges, wardens of the wire-drawers of the city of Coventry, with John Stafford, John Rocheford, John Blakman, John Benett, William Deister, William Claybroke, Nicholas Jones, John Straunge and Thomas Stafford with other worthy men of the same craft in the name of all the persons of the craft, having their devotion to almighty God and to the blessed sacrament, the which is all Christian men's belief, and considering a devout thing called the new canopy over the altar in the church of St Michael of the said city in the which the blessed sacrament is worthily at this time kept, the which keeping must have cost and reparation, came before Thomas Paynell, then mayor of the said city, Laurence Cooke, Thomas Wildgryse ... & other more in St Mary's Hall, praying and desiring out of devotion that they have to the said sacrament, and worship to the said city, to have the keeping and the governance of the aforesaid canopy and all things belonging thereto. The which the mayor and other worthy men there being with him, considering their desire and holy devotion grant them their petition, thanking them of their desire and good will. And at request of the warden and other men of the said craft, this indenture is registered in a book called the mayor's register in St Mary's Hall, for perpetual remembrance to be had in time coming. And this indenture abides in Thomas Peynell's bag in St Mary's Hall.

107. Guild charity

Each of these guilds or fraternities was so prominent in its respective town as to have functioned, in the absence of a chartered corporation, as a surrogate town council. The membership of these bodies was in each case diverse: they comprised artisans and shopkeepers, professionals and merchants. They included both men and women. The focus of their charity ranged from individually identified recipients to guild-run almshouses. The rare and fragmentary survival of the internal accounts of medieval guilds means that we have only a partial impression of these communally supported forms of fraternal charity. The palmers'* guild of Ludlow evidently originated as a society of pilgrims, although by the later Middle Ages pilgrimage had ceased to be its principal *raison d'être.*

Shrewsbury, Shropshire County Record Office, MS. 356/321 (a); Norwich, Norfolk Record Office, King's Lynn MSS KL/C38/1–31 (b);

British Library, MS. Egerton 2886 (c); Wisbech Town Museum, MS Records of the Guild of Holy Trinity 1379–1547 (d). Latin, transl. by GR.

(a) The palmers' guild of Ludlow

[Rent-collectors' accounts, 1364–65] Cost of the hire of two horses going to Wyston [?] to bring the vestments of the guild for the burial of two sisters of the guild on two occasions on the order of the warden 3½*d*.

[Stewards' accounts, 1425–26] Given in alms for the relief of Reginald Draper de la Pole, a brother of the guild who was lately robbed by false thieves 8*d*.[19]

[Stewards' accounts 1426–27.] In alms given to several penniless brothers and sisters of the guild and to other poor people at Easter 2*s* 10*d*.

[Stewards' accounts, 1427–28] Given in alms to Henry ... of Chester to help him because he was robbed by false thieves 20*d* ... Given in alms at the burial of Agnes Nightingale 6*d*.

[Stewards' accounts 1533–34] Paid to the poor people in the [guild] almshouse at Christmas [sum illegible].

[Warden's accounts 1540–1] Received from Elizabeth Jonys for her admission as a sister of the almshouse 20*d*.

(b) The guild of Holy Trinity, King's Lynn

1343–44. Alms given to the anchoress* of South Lynn (20*s*), Clarice Sorel, a poor woman (6*s* 8*d*), Little John with the broken back (6*s* 8*d*), the hermit of the church of St Nicholas (5*s*) [and 21 others] £18 11*s* 0*d*.

1385–86. Alms paid to the hermit in the hermitage outside the south gate of Lynn 6*s* 8*d* for the year ... to Bliss of Hell from the same alms 6*s* 8*d* ... to the anchoress of All Saints church in South Lynn 20*s* ... [and 30 others] £18 14*s* 4*d*.

1406–7. Alms paid to ... Katherine, who was the anchoress's servant 6*s* 8*d* ... to Alice Stacy in Bolwerrowe 4*s*, to Katherine Taylour in Spynnerlane 2*s* ... to Richard Coke for half a year 2*s* 6*d* and then he died ... to Gilbert de Ketleston for half a year 10*s* and then he died, to Thomas Coke for a quarter of a year 2*s* 6*d*

19 Figure lost but calculated from other details on the account.

and then he died ... and granted to Robert Spycer of Norwich for the year 52*s*, and to Robert Paston of the same, for three quarters of the year, 5*s*, and then he died ... [50 individual recipients altogether named this year.] Total expenses on alms [the sum of four separate officers' sub-accounts] £22 2*s* 0*d*.

(c) The guild of St Mary, Boston

1514–15. In money distributed to thirteen poor people of both sexes in the almshouse or bedehouse* from 4 June to 27 May ... *viz.* for 51 weeks at 8*s* 8*d* per week £22 2*s* 0*d* ... For red cloth for [livery] clothing and for crowns [to sew on to the robes] for the poor people in the bedehouse £4 7*s* 2*d*.

1516–17. Alms given to Mr Downham for one whole year at 2*d* per week 8*s* 8*d*. To a certain woman coming from Ely to Boston to enter the bedehouse 6*s* 8*d*. To the widow of ... Lynwode 1*d* per week for one whole year 4*s* 4*d*. To the widow of Pavy, a pauper, 1*d* per week for 56 weeks 4*s* 8*d*. For food for one Hobchirche for eleven weeks 8*s* 3*d*. Paid into the hand of one called Fuller before his admission to the bedehouse 12*s*.

1517–18. Alms of the guild. Paid to Alexander ... at the tavern of the alms of the guild at 6*d* per week; to a person of Peterborough at 4*d* per week; to a certain old woman called ... Downeham at 2*d* per week; and to Mother Lynwode at 1*d* per week; all for 55 weeks this year (less 8*d* overall) 58*s* 11*d*. Paid to Mr Thomas Crawe for the purchase of a cloak provided for a man late of Peterborough out of the alms of the guild 6*s* 8*d*. The rents of John Lovell (13*s* 4*d*) and of Christopher Robson's wife (3*s* 4*d*) paid by the alms of the guild.

(d) The guild of Holy Trinity, Wisbech

1506. We ordain that the stewards in hall and servers at the kitchen board shall see every brother and sister honestly served in the hall upon Trinity Sunday next coming. And when the alderman and his brethren have dined we will that all the poor people then there present shall be sat at a table in the said hall, and served with such meat as shall be left [by] the said alderman and his brethren, by the aforesaid stewards.

1512. Agreed that Andrew Johnson and William Kyng shall have the rule and supervision of the almshouses, to select such persons as are most in need (*maxime debiles*) in the houses according to their discretion, with the counsel of the alderman and their other brothers of the guild.

108. Civic religion: blessed bread

From the early Middle Ages there developed throughout Christendom the custom, at the end of the weekly parish mass, of distributing to the congregation at the church door what was known as 'blessed bread'. Blessed (not consecrated) by the priest, the bread was provided by members of the parish in turn. Organisation of the responsibility to provide the bread which, once blessed, was then redistributed to the community, was most often undertaken by the parish, and in some continental instances by fraternities. Here, however, in an instance of the religious roles undertaken by secular urban governments, the arrangements are overseen by the civic council. The date of this record from King's Lynn is 1424–25.

D. M. Owen (ed.), *The Making of King's Lynn*, London: Oxford University Press for the British Academy, 1984, p. 142. Latin, transl. by GR. Reproduced by permission of the British Academy.

Each inhabited house in the town of Lynn worth 20*s* or more in annual rent shall give holy bread and a candle when required. And if the house is occupied in divided tenancy to a total value of more than 20*s* a year, then each shall give holy bread, sharing the cost according to the proportion of their rent, and one of them shall offer a candle. And if it should be several shops under a single roof to the total value of 20*s* per annum or more, they shall give the holy bread between them and share the cost according to the level of their rent. And if it should be a principal tenement which has diverse tenements annexed under the same roof and not divided, the principal tenement being worth 20*s* per annum or more and inhabited, that principal tenement shall give holy bread for all without any further contribution from the others. And if such a principal tenement should not be occupied, then the adjoining tenements, should their rents amount to 20*s* per annum or more and should one of them be rated at 6*s* 8*d* at least and in occupation, shall give the holy bread between them and shall contribute according to their rent. And should there be three separate tenements or shops together, each paying 6*s* 8*d* per annum rent, then they shall give the holy bread together. And if there should be two occupied tenements situated together, one paying 6*s* 8*d* and the other 3*s* 4*d* rent, they shall give the holy bread sharing according to their rent. Provided always that no tenement or shop paying 6*s* 8*d* in yearly rent by itself, nor those who live by begging, shall be constrained or compelled to make any contribution for holy bread.

109. Urban piety in stained glass: a parish church in York

In the church of All Saints, Pavement, in York, one of a series of early fifteenth-century (*c.*1410) windows contains a series of images to accompany texts loosely based upon a devotional work, 'The Prick of Conscience'.[20] This didactic poem circulated quite widely in later medieval England. The lines in question are apocalyptic, and the pictures associated with each couplet depict the impending end of the world. At the bottom, the lay donors were shown in prayer: Roger Henryson and his wife Cecilia, and Abel Hesyl and his wife Agnes. An adjacent window shows the Corporal Acts of Mercy. Its donors, a man and a woman, appear in the glass below.

E. A. Gee, 'The painted glass of All Saints' church, North Street, York', *Archaeologia*, CII, London: Society of Antiquaries of London, 1969, pp. 151–202; with S. Powell, 'All Saints' church, North Street, York: Text and image in the *Prick of Conscience* window', in N. Morgan (ed.), *Prophecy, Apocalypse and the Day of Doom*, Donington: Shaun Tyas, 2004, pp. 292–316. English, revised by GR.

The first day forty cubits certain
the sea shall rise up above every mountain.
The second day the sea shall be
so low as all men shall it see.
The third day it shall be plain
and stand as it was again.
The fourth day fishes shall make a roaring
that it shall be hideous to man's hearing.
The fifth day the sea shall burn
and all the waters that may run.
The sixth day shall spring on trees
with bloody drops great grisly bears.

20 For this text, see R. Hanna (ed.), *Richard Morris's Prick of Conscience: A Corrected and Amplified Reading Text*, Oxford, 2013.

The seventh day houses will fall,
castles and towers, and every wall.
The eighth day the rocks and stones
shall burn together all at once.
The ninth day a great dying shall be
generally in every country.
The tenth day for neven [?]
earth shall be plain and even.
The eleventh day shall men come out
of their holes and go about.
The twelfth day shall dead men's bones
be somen sett [? summonsed] and rise all at once.
The thirteenth day in truth shall
stars from the heaven fall.
The fourteenth day all that lives then
shall die, both child, man and woman.
The fifteenth day thus shall betide,
the world shall burn on every side.

110. The piety of merchants: inscriptions at Long Melford church

Long Melford grew rich on the backs of Suffolk sheep, whose wool was traded by local merchants including the Cloptons and others of Long Melford.[21] The parish church of Holy Trinity was all but completely rebuilt between *c.*1460 and *c.*1495. The series of inscriptions on the exterior and interior of the church functioned to advertise the distinctive combination of Christian piety and civic pride which motivated the generous gifts of the clothiers who funded this magnificent project. The inscriptions are still visible; the following texts include some details now lost.

N. Pevsner, *The Buildings of England: Suffolk*, 2nd edn, Harmondsworth: Penguin, 1974, pp. 343–7. English.

On the upper north side of the nave:
Pray for the souls of Robert Sparowe and Marion his wife, and for Thomas Cowper and Mabel his wife, of whose goods Master Giles

21 For a vivid case-study of a similar family in the adjacent county of Essex, see E. Power, 'Thomas Paycocke of Coggeshall, an Essex clothier in the days of Henry VII', in her *Medieval People*, 10th edn, London, 1963.

Dent, John Clopton, John Smyth and Roger Smyth, with the help of the well disposed men of this [town] did these seven arches new repair A.D. 14[81]. Pray for the soul of Master Giles Dent, late parson of Melford, of whose goods John Clopton, Mr Robert Coteler and Thomas Elys did this arch make and glass, and the roof over the porch A.D. 14[81].

On the upper south side of the nave:
Pray for the souls of Roger Moryell, Margaret and Kateryn his wives, of whose goods the said Kateryn, John Clopton, Mr William Qwaytis and John Smyth did these 6 arches new repair; and did make the table at the high altar A.D. 1481. Pray for the soule of Thomas Couper the which the 2nd arch did repair. Pray for the soul of Lawrence Martin and Marion his wife.

On the north porch:
Pray for the souls of William Clopton, Margery and Margery his wives, and for the soul of Alice Clopton and for John Clopton, and for all those souls that the said John is bound to pray for.

On the lower windows on the south side:
Pray for the soul of Roger Moriell of whose goods this arch was made. Pray for the soul of John Keche, and for his father and mother, of whose goods this arch was made. Pray for the soul of Thomas Elys and Joan his wife, and for the good speed of Joan Elys his wife. Pray for the soul of John Pie and Alice his wife, of whose goods this arch was made and these two windows glazed. Pray for the souls of John Distr' and Alice, and for the good speed of John Distr' and Christian his wife.

On the lower windows of the south chapel:
Pray for the souls of Lawrence Martyn and Marion his wife, Elizabeth Martin and Joan, and for the good estate of Richard Martyn and Roger Martyn and the wives and all the children of whose goods ... made A.D. 1484.

Around the Lady Chapel:
Pray for the soul of John Hyll, and for the soul of John Clopton Esquire, and pray for the soul of Richard Loveday, butler with John Clopton, of whose goods this chapel is embattled [i.e. the church walls were completed with battlements] by his executors. Pray for the souls of

William Clopton Esquire, Margery and Margery his wives, and for all their parents and children, and for the soul of Alice Clopton, and for John Clopton and for all his children and for all the souls that the said John is bound to pray for, which did this chapel new repair A.D. 1496. Christ be my witness that I have not done this to earn praise, but in order that my soul should be remembered.

111. Customary of the Southwark stews

The liberty of Southwark, on the south side of the river Thames, was in the Middle Ages under the jurisdiction of the bishop of Winchester, whose substantial London residence was located here. The franchise,* being part of London yet beyond the control of the mayor's officers, became a magnet for the prostitution which was banned within the city.[22] The officials of the bishop's jurisdiction oversaw the area designated for the 'stews', for which the following regulations were recorded in the fifteenth century. The rules were recorded in two separate, overlapping, lists, of which the longer and apparently older is printed (with minor omissions) below. Their precise date of origin is uncertain, but they were said at this time to be of great antiquity. Part of the motivation for the imposition of these regulations is hinted at in the allusion to the nearby gatherings of parliament and the royal court, just across the river Thames at Westminster.

J. B. Post, 'A fifteenth-century customary of the Southwark stews', *Journal of the Society of Archivists*, V, Abingdon: Carfax Publications, 1977, pp. 418–28. English, revised by GR.

i. First, that no stewholder that holds and keeps any stewhouse have nor keep any woman dwelling with him but his wife, and a washer, and a man (and no woman) as his osteler.

ii. That the women that be at common bordel be seen every day what they be; and a woman that lives by her body to come and go (provided she pays her dues as the old custom is, that is, 14*d* a week for her chamber) and at all times to have free licence and liberty, without any interruption of the stewholders.

22 M. Carlin, *Medieval Southwark*, London, 1996, pp. 213–19.

iii. If any of them that hold any stewhouse tarry any man against his will within his house as a prisoner for any debt that he owes to him, or for any other cause (but if the stewholder bring such persons to the lord's prison as the law wills . . .), he that otherwise does shall pay 20*s* at every time and as often as he breaks this ordinance.

iv. That no stewholder receive any woman of religious [life], nor any man's wife, if it be known ...

v. If any woman of the bordel let [stay] any man, but [and not] sit still at the door and let him go or come, choose whither they will, or if she draw any man by his gown or by his hood, or by any other thing, she shall make a fine to the lord of 20*s*.

vi. If there be any stewholder's wife that draws any man into her house without his will, her husband and she shall be amerced* to the lord in 40*s*.

vii. That no stewholder hold any woman that lives by her body to board, but that they should board wherever they like.

viii. That no woman be found within the lordship on holy days from Michaelmas [29 September] to Candlemas [2 February] after 8 o'clock in the morning until 12 noon, and that they be voided at one o'clock in the afternoon until 5 o'clock at night; and from Candlemas to Michaelmas, that they be not found there on holy days from 6 o'clock in the morning to 11 o'clock, and then be voided by one o'clock in the afternoon until 6 o'clock at night.

ix. If there be any woman that live by her body and keep a paramour, against the use and custom of the manor, she shall be three weeks in prison, and make a fine of 6*s* 8*d*, and then be set once on the cucking-stool,* and forswear the lordship ...

x. If any woman be found within the lordship after the sun is gone to rest, the king being at Westminster and holding there either parliament or council, until the sun be up upon the morrow, after the custom of the manor, she shall make a fine at every time she so does of 6*s* 8*d* ...

xi. If any woman take any money to lie with a man, but [unless] she lie with him till it be the morning time and then arise, she shall make a fine of 6*s* 8*d*.

xii. That no stewholder nor no tenant within the lordship receive any woman that lives by her body if she be known [to be] with child, after reasonable warning, upon the pain of paying to the lord 20*s*, and the woman to pay 6*s* 8*d*.

xiii. That no stewholder keep no woman within his house that has any sickness of burning [venereal disease], but that she be put out, upon the pain of making a fine to the lord of 20*s*.

112. Prostitution in London

As this record from the later fourteenth century illustrates, secular urban government became drawn into the regulation of moral behaviour – generally taken by canon lawyers to be the concern of the church courts – as an aspect of its concern for social order. However, the aspiration of civic governors that moral scandal could be eliminated or at least confined to particular areas was continually frustrated.

H. T. Riley (ed.), *Memorials of London and London Life in the XIIIth, XIVth, and XVth Centuries*, London: Longmans, Green & Co., 1868, pp. 484–6. Latin, transl. by the editor, revised by GR.

On 27 July 1385 Elizabeth, the wife of Henry Moring, was brought before Nicholas Brembre, knight, the mayor, the aldermen and the sheriffs of London, in the guildhall, because, on the information of diverse persons and on the confession of Joanna, her serving-woman, the mayor, aldermen and sheriffs were given to understand that Elizabeth, under colour of the craft of embroidery, which she pretended to follow, took in and retained this Joanna and diverse other women as her apprentices, and bound them to serve her in the manner of apprentices in that art; whereas the truth of the matter was that she did not follow that craft, but that, after so retaining them, she incited the same Joanna and the other women who were with her and in her service to lead a base life, and to consort with friars, chaplains and all other such men as desired to have their company, both in her own house, in the parish of All Hallows by the Wall in the ward of Broad

Street in London, and elsewhere; and used to hire them out to the same friars, chaplains and other men, for whatever sum they might agree upon, whether in her own house or elsewhere, she retaining in her own possession the fee thus agreed.

And in particular, on Thursday 4 May last, by the compassing and procuring of the said Elizabeth, and of a certain chaplain whose name is unknown, she sent the same Joanna, and ordered her to accompany the said chaplain at night, that she might carry a lantern before him to his chamber (but in what parish is again unknown); it being her intention that Joanna should stay the night there with the chaplain; while the said Joanna herself, as she says, knew nothing about it. Still, she remained there with the chaplain the whole of that night; and when she returned home to her mistress on the morrow, this Elizabeth asked her if she had brought anything with her for her work that night, to which she answered that she had not. Whereupon the same Elizabeth used words of reproof to her, and ordered her to go back again to the chaplain on the following night, and whatever she should be able to lay hold of, to take it for her labour, and bring it to her. Accordingly Joanna by her command went back on the following night to the said chaplain, at his chamber, and again passed the night there; and on the morrow she rose very early in the morning, and bearing in mind the words of her mistress, and being afraid to go back without carrying something to her, she took a breviary that belonged to the chaplain and carried it off, the chaplain himself knowing nothing about it; which breviary she delivered to Elizabeth, who took it, well knowing how and in what manner Joanna had come by it. And after this, Elizabeth pledged* this breviary for 8d to an unknown man.

And many other times this Elizabeth received similar base gains from the same Joanna and her other serving-women, and kept them for her own use, living thus abominably and damnably, and inciting other women to live in a similar way, she herself being a common prostitute and a procuress.

Whereupon, on the same day, the said Elizabeth was asked by the court how she would acquit herself of the charge; to which she made answer that she was in no way guilty, and put herself on the country [appealed to judgement by jury]. Therefore the sheriffs were instructed to summon twelve good men of the place to appear on 28 July, to make a jury, and the said Elizabeth was in the mean time committed to prison.

On which day the good men appeared: Robert Tawyere and eleven others, who declared upon their oath that the said Elizabeth was guilty of all the things imputed to her, and that she was a common prostitute and a common procuress. And because through such women and suchlike deeds many scandals had befallen the city, and great peril might arise through such transactions in future, it was therefore adjudged, according to the custom of the city of London in such cases and in order that other women might beware of doing the like, that the said Elizabeth should be taken from the guildhall to Cornhill, and be put upon the *thewe* [or cucking-stool*] there to remain for one hour of the day, the cause being publicly proclaimed. And afterwards she was to be taken to some gate of the city, and there to be made to forswear the city and the liberty, so that she would never enter it again, on pain of three years' imprisonment and the same punishment of the *thewe*, at the discretion of the mayor and aldermen.

113. Moral regulation by secular authority

During the later Middle Ages civic councils showed an increasing concern to regulate the moral behaviour of townspeople. As these records show, local inhabitants were on occasion prepared to cite their neighbours for such offences before the city courts. The imposition of social discipline required the participation of townspeople, no less than it did the willingness of the magistrates to take on the role of moral guardians.

R. W. Greaves (ed.), *The First Ledger Book of High Wycombe*, Buckinghamshire Record Society, XI, 1947, p. 42 (a); M. Bateson, *Records of the Borough of Leicester*, ii, London: J. C. Clay, 1901, p. 291 (b); L. C. Attreed (ed.), *The York House Books 1461–1490*, 2 vols, Stroud: Alan Sutton for Richard III and Yorkist History Trust, 1991, p. 723 (c); W. H. Stevenson (ed.), *Records of the Borough of Nottingham*, 3 vols, London: Quaritch, 1882–85, i, pp. 347–9 (d); P. M. Briers (ed.), *Henley Borough Records*, Oxfordshire Record Society, XLI, 1960, p. 109 (e). Latin, transl. by the editors, revised by GR.

(a) 4 April 1398. Memorandum: That on Maundy Thursday 1397, in the presence of the mayor and community of the town [of High Wycombe], it was ordered and agreed that no man of whatever condition dwelling within the borough of Wycombe is to go out wandering in the town after ten o'clock at night (*post decimam horam noctis*), unless he has some reasonable cause for his wandering; and if anybody should be found so wandering after the hour aforesaid, he is at once to be taken and imprisoned by the town officers, and kept in prison until he shall be released by the mayor or his deputy and the community.

Item: it was ordained the same day and year that nobody may play at dice in the town under pain of imprisonment; and also he who as host has received him shall pay to the community 40*d*.

(b) [Ordinances of the borough of Leicester, 1467] Also that no brothel be held within this town, or any prostitution or prostitute dwelling, but that the burgess living closest report them to the court. And that they are to be banished at the first warning on pain of imprisonment and fine and ransom to the king. Also concerning all manner of scolds* that are dwelling within this town, man or woman, that are found defective by sworn men before the mayor presented, that it shall be lawful to the mayor to punish them on a cucking-stool* before their door as long as he likes, and then to be carried forth to the four gates of the town.

(c) On 28 July 1483, a great many people from the parish of St Gregory in Micklegate [in York] came into the council chamber before the mayor and complained that Marjorie Gray, also known as 'Cherrylips' (*Cherilippis*), was of bad disposition and governance of her body, and also a scold with her neighbours, not for the first time causing serious harm to the neighbourhood. She was ordered by the mayor to remove herself beyond the boundaries of the city by evening of the following day and not to live in the same city again, under penalty of the tumbrel [or cucking-stool*] and imprisonment at the will of the mayor.

(d) Presentments of jurors before the mayor's court, Nottingham, September 1484. George Hoton, horner,* Richard Hardstrong, litster,* Thomas Hackett, mason, Thomas Duke, litster, John Bolton, junior, shoemaker, John Bilham, roper, Joan Porret, housewife, Henry Merill, cooper, Emma Annelsley, housewife, Margery Smith, widow, Catherine Stringer, housewife, John Marshall, shearman, Joan Saddler, housewife, Nicholas Wilson, labourer, John Isfeyth, labourer, Joan Sandiacre, housewife, and Christopher Tinkler, tinker commonly keep a brothel and disorderly conduct in their houses by days and by nights.

(e) 21 March 1493. It is agreed by the warden and the community of the burgesses [of Henley-on-Thames] that if John Archer ever comes drunk and rude to church and disturbs the parishioners in church during mass, then on every such occasion he shall pay a fine of *3s 4d* into the common box.

114. Civic drama at York

The precise origins of the religious play-cycles put on, at York and in other cities, from the fourteenth century until the sixteenth-century Reformation, are uncertain. But although the city government eventually (by the early fifteenth century) claimed oversight of these events, they were initiated (at an uncertain date prior to the 1380s) by the craftspeople by whom they were staged and performed. It seems likely that in their first form the scenes, focused on the story of Christ's Passion, were presented as *tableaux* on wagons, with costume and gesture but only minimal speech. Early in the fifteenth century we find the first clear evidence for written play texts. Each play was performed on a cart, which was drawn through the streets to a series of stations in the course of a day.[23] Here the organisers of the complex cycle of plays performed at various viewing places throughout the city ask for the mayor's approval for a revised itinerary. The reference to the plays being 'played in so many places' appears to indicate that diverse groups had developed the habit of performing their respective plays in a great variety of locations. The petition requests that these dramatic presentations be co-ordinated in a unitary celebration of the religious feast and of the city. Although undated, it is datable from its context to *c.*1395.

M. Sellers (ed.), *York Memorandum Book*, i, Surtees Society, CXX, Durham: Andrews & Company, 1911, pp. 50–2. French and Latin, transl. by R. Davies and revised by G. R.

The commons of York petition the honourable mayor and aldermen of the city, that whereas they are put to great expense regarding the performance of the pageants on the day of Corpus Christi, these pageants cannot be performed as has been customary because they are played

23 P. J. P. Goldberg, 'Craft guilds, the Corpus Christi play and civic government', in S. Rees Jones (ed.), *The Government of Medieval York*, York, 1997, pp. 141–63; P. J. P. Goldberg, 'From *tableaux* to text: the York Corpus Christi play ca. 1378–1428', *Viator*, XLIII, 2012, pp. 247–76.

in so many places, to the great loss of the commons and of strangers coming to the city on that day for this occasion. So they petition that in order that these pageants should be maintained and sustained by the commons and artificers of the same city, in honour and reverence of Our Lord Jesus Christ and to the honour and profit of the same city, the mayor and aldermen should ordain that the pageants should be played in those places delimited and assigned by those officers previously (which places are listed in a schedule attached to this petition), or in other places designated each year by the mayor and council of the chamber; and that anyone infringing these ordinances should pay a fine of 40*s* to the council chamber of the city. Also that, if any of the pageants should be delayed by the default or negligence of the jurors [of the various crafts], they should pay 6*s* 8*d* to the chamber ...

Places where the play of Corpus Christi will be played. First at the gates of Holy Trinity in Micklegate. Second at the door of Richard Harpham. Third at the door of John of Gyseburne. Fourth at Skeldergate-end and North Street end. Fifth at the end of Conyngstrete towards the Castle gate. Sixth at the end of Jewburygate. Seventh at the door of Henry Wyman in Coney Street. Eighth at the end of Coney Street next to the common hall. Ninth at the door of Adam del Brigg. Tenth at the gate of the monastery of St Peter. Eleventh at the end of Girdlergate in Petergate. Twelfth on the Pavement. And it is ordained that the banners of the play with the city arms should be delivered to the pageant of Corpus Christi by the mayor, to be set up in the places where the pageants are to be played; and that the same banners should be brought back each year on the morning after Corpus Christi to the chamber and delivered into the hands of the mayor and chamberlains of the city, to be kept there for the whole year following, on pain of a fine of 6*s* 8*d* payable to the community by any who fail to deliver them.

115. Plays for Corpus Christi at Beverley

As at York, so also in a number of other towns, the later fourteenth century saw cycles of pageants, mounted by artisans, become incorporated into the civic calendar.[24] The orchestration of these events, typically at the feast of Corpus Christi, was rendered complex by the emergence

24 L. M. Clopper, 'Lay and clerical impact on civic religious drama and ceremony', in M. G. Briscoe and J. C. Coldwey (eds), *Contexts for Early English Drama*, Bloomington, 1989, pp. 102–36.

of new groups and plays, and by occasional disputes over the burden of costs. These records of the borough government of Beverley in Yorkshire show the municipal officers being asked to adjudicate where tensions had arisen between the diverse crafts over their various roles.

A. F. Leach (ed.), *Beverley Town Documents*, Selden Society, XIV, London: Quaritch, 1900, pp. 32–7. Latin, transl. by the editor, revised by GR.

Orders for the Corpus Christi play and procession

It was ordered in 1390, by the whole community, that all the craftsmen of the town of Beverley, that is mercers and drapers, tanners, masons, skinners, tailors, goldsmiths, smiths, plumbers, bowlers (*bollers*), turners, girdlers, cutlers, latteners,* broochmakers, horners,* spooners, ladlers, furbishers,* weavers, fullers,* coverlet-makers, cartwrights, coopers, arrowmakers, bowyers, shoemakers, bakers, butchers, fishmongers, chandlers, barbers, vintners, saddlers, ropers, hairers,* shipmen, glovers, and workmen have their plays and pageants (*ludos et pagentes*) ready henceforth on every Corpus Christi day, in the fashion and form of the ancient custom of the town of Beverley, to play in honour of the body of Christ, under the penalty of every craft making default, of 40*s*.

On 3 April 1411, to the praise and honour of God and of the body of Christ, and for the peaceful union of the worthier and lesser commons of the town of Beverley (*pro pacifica unitate digniorum et minorum communium ville Beverlaci*), there was a short conference held between William Rolleston, merchant, Nicholas of Rise, Adam Tirwhitt, John of Holme, William Wilton, Adam Barker, and others, worshipful men of the worthier sort (*reverendis de dignioribus*), not having liveries every year like others of the other crafts of Beverley, and not playing in other plays, that the worthier sort should, though they have not hitherto been accustomed to do so, erect at their cost, maintain and cause to be played, in an honourable and becoming way, a pageant at the feast of Corpus Christi. Whereupon the said worthier sort for themselves and others of the worthier sort, so far as they were empowered, submitted themselves to the award and judgement of Richard Aglyon, Thomas Coppandale senior, William Dalton, William Melbourne, and their fellows, the twelve keepers of the community of the town of Beverley. Which twelve keepers gave judgement in this form, that the said worthier sort at the feast of Corpus Christi next, this present year, through four of them and under the supervision of the twelve keepers of the community, at the costs and expense of the said worthier sort, shall cause to be made a fit and proper stage (*pagendam*), and a proper play to be played on the same, under penalty of 40*s*.

And further that the honour of God and the reputation of the town of Beverley may be exalted with greater devotion and repute, most of the aldermen and stewards of the crafts in Beverley, that is mercers, clothworkers, tanners, weavers, tailors, shoemakers, watermen, dyers, fullers, saddlers, bakers, butchers, smiths, skinners, and others, for themselves and their crafts and for the whole community, so far as they were empowered, submitted themselves to the award of the twelve keepers, as well in respect of the erection of castles (*pro ereccione castellorum*) as for the maintenance of the Corpus Christi play. At which the said keepers gave their award as follows: that each and every craft, which was accustomed to have and set up wooden castles in honour of God and St John of Beverley, or in future shall have them, shall henceforth for ever set up and cover them in ornamental fashion, under a penalty of 6*s* 8*d* to be levied on every craft neglecting to do so for any cause whatever; and that every year for ever it shall play the scenes of the Corpus Christi play which it has been accustomed to play, and which shall be assigned to it at the discretion of the sworn governors of the town, upon reasonable notice given by the twelve keepers; and that the worthier sort of the town shall each year cause to be played, in the form declared above, a play on their stage, under a penalty of 40*s* to be levied for the use of the community from either the worthier sort or from lesser members of the community neglecting this.

Dissension having arisen between the aldermen and stewards of diverse crafts as to the carrying of wax lights or torches each year in the procession of the revered feast of Corpus Christi. Therefore by the assent and consent of the aldermen and stewards of all the crafts listed below, and of others assembled in the Guild Hall, in the time of Thomas Mayne, John Bewholme, and their fellows, the twelve keepers or governors of the town of Beverley, on 19 March 1430, it was ordered, and decreed to be perpetually observed, that every year in future on Corpus Christi day the stewards of each craft listed below shall pass with their light in the said procession in their order in the form underwritten, and no one else of their craft with them, under the penalty stated below; but each year to come with their aldermen shall hold, keep, and behave themselves in an honourable and decent way behind the most holy body of Christ, as the solemnity of that feast demands. And every man of the crafts listed who is found disobedient to this order shall forfeit to the community 40*s* without any pardon. Next to the priests of the guild of Corpus Christi [come] the guild of the Blessed Mary, the guild of St John of Beverley, the merchants, drapers,[25] butchers, bakers, carpenters, smiths, tailors, skinners, dyers, turners, weavers, shearmen, fullers, seamen, shoemakers, barbers, glovers, coopers, fishers, tilers, the guild of St Helen, the guild of Pater Noster, the guild of St John the Baptist, the guild of St John in May, and the guild of St Peter of Milan.

Penalty paid by the smiths for not playing their play on Corpus Christi day. Because Thomas Lorymer, Robert Marshall, John Lorymer by the Cuckstoolpit, John Lorymer over the smiths' row and their fellows failed in their play on Corpus Christi day 1392, it was therefore held by John Kelk, Stephen Coppandale, Richard Aglyon and their fellows, keepers of the town of Beverley, that they should pay to the community of the town of Beverley 40*s*, as was ordered by the whole community in ancient times. And thereupon, on Friday after 15 July in the said year came Thomas Lorymer, John Lorymer by the Cuckstoolpit, John Locksmith, Thomas Locksmith, as well for themselves as for their fellows, and offered to the twelve keepers 40*s*. which they had forfeited. And because they behaved obediently, therefore the said 40*s* were handed back to the said Thomas Lorymer and his said fellows, on this condition, that if the said Thomas or his fellows made default in their play, that is 'The Ascension of Our Lord', on any Corpus Christi day on which the other craftsmen of Beverley play, that then without delay they ought to pay to the community 100*s*. And for the due and faithful performance of this agreement, the said Thomas Lorymer and his fellows above written bind themselves collectively and individually to the said keepers and their successors in 100*s*, to be paid within twelve days after [any occasion when] they shall have made default in their said play.

On Friday after the Translation of St William of York, 1391, came John of Arras, hairer, in the Guild Hall before the twelve keepers of the town of Beverley, and undertook for himself and his fellows of the same craft to play a play called 'Paradise' every year on Corpus Christi day when the other craftsmen of the same town play, during the life of the said John Arras at his own proper cost, willing and granting that he will

25 Added in a later hand. The drapers did not become a distinctly organised craft until 1493.

pay to the community of the town of Beverley for every default [error] in the said play, 10*s*, Nicholas Falconer being his surety. And also he undertook to redeliver to the current twelve keepers of the town, at the end of his life, all the necessaries in his possession belonging to the said play, under penalty of 20*s*, that is: 1 car, 8 hasps, 18 staples, 2 visors, 2 angel's wings, 1 deal pole, 1 snake (*worme*), 2 pairs of linen stockings, 2 pairs of shirts, 1 sword.

116. 'Christ and the Merchants' from the Chester play cycle

The first reference to a public play in Chester at the feast of Corpus Christi dates from 1422, when it was clearly already well established. It is possible that the early performances were less extensive than is indicated by the eight surviving copies of the play texts dating from the sixteenth and very early seventeenth centuries. The particular play of which an extract is reproduced here was performed in the early sixteenth century, and in all probability in the preceding century also, by the shoemakers. This section of the drama illustrates the potential of the civic plays, not merely to teach or to entertain but to provoke both participants and audience to reflect critically on the prevailing values of urban society and on the part which they should play within it.

D. Mills (ed.), *The Chester Mystery Cycle*, East Lansing: Colleagues Press, 1992, pp. 245–7. English.

Then the boys shall go towards Jerusalem singing 'Hosanna!' with branches of palm-trees in their hands. And the citizens shall lay out their garments in his path: 'Hosanna, filio David! Benedictus qui venit in nomine Domini! Hosanna in excelsis!'[26]

Then Jesus, sitting upon the ass, seeing the city, shall weep and shall say:

Jesus: Ah, Jerusalem, holy city!
Unknown today it is to thee
that peace thou hast – thou canst not see –

26 'Hosanna to the son of David. Blessed is he that cometh in the name of the Lord; Hosanna in the highest'; Matthew 21.9: a Palm Sunday antiphon, evidently sung here by cathedral choristers.

but bale thou shalt abide.[27]
Much must thou dreigh yet some day — *suffer yet*
when woe shall fall on every way, — *everywhere*
and thou beguiled, sooth to say, — *deluded; truth*
with sorrow on all side –

destroyed, dolefully driven down. — *sadly cast down*
No stone with other in all this town
shall stand, for that they be unlieven — *unbelieving*
to keep Christ's come — *observe; coming*
and God's own visitation,
done for Mankind's salvation;
for they have no devotion, — *reverence*
ne dreaden not his doom — *nor fear; judgement*

Then Jesus shall ride towards the city and all the citizens shall lay down their garments in the way. And when he comes to the temple, he shall say to the merchants as he descends from the ass with a whip:

Do away, and use not this thing, — *stop*
for it is not my liking. — *pleasure*
You make my Father's wonning — *dwelling-place*
a place of merchandise. — *trade*

1st Merchant:
What freke is this that makes this fare[28]
and casteth down all our ware?
came no man hither full yare — *for very long*
that did us such annoys. — *harms*

2nd Merchant:
Out, out, woe is me!
My table with my money
is spread abroad, well I see, — *scattered*
and nought dare I say.
Now it seems well that he
would attain royalty; — *wants to become a king*

27 'You do not know what peace you have – you cannot see it – but you shall endure misery.'

28 'What fellow is this that creates this disturbance?'

else thus bold durst he not be *otherwise*
to make such array. *put on such a display*

1st Merchant:
It seems well he would be king
that casteth down thus our thing *belongings*
and says his father's wonning *dwelling*
in this temple is.
Say, Jesus, with thy jangling *idle talk*
what evidence or tokening *sign*
showest thou of thy reigning,
that thou darest do this?

2nd Merchant:
What signs now showest thou here
that preves such power *validates*
to shend our ware in such manner *destroy*
masterly, through thy main? *like a lord; power*

Jesus: This temple here I may destroy
and through my might and my mastery *power*
in days three it edify *build*
and build it up again.

1st Merchant:
Aha, Jesus! Wilt thou so?
This word, as ever mot I go, *may*
shall be rehearsed before moe. *repeated; more people*
Caiaphas I shall tell.

Then Jesus shall eject the buyers and sellers with his whip.

Jesus: Hie you fast this temple fro, *hasten; from*
for merchandise shall be here no moe. *trading; no more*
In this place, be you never so throw, *fierce*
shall you no longer dwell.

GLOSSARY

affer	horse
alum	aluminium sulphate, metallic salt mordant used to fix dyes in cloth
amerced	fined
anchoress	female hermit living in a walled enclosure
approver	one who gave king's evidence (in return for clemency)
assize	law or ordinance, commonly concerned with prices of food and drink
attach	in law, to seize the property of an accused person in order to bring them to court
bast	fibrous tree bark used for plaiting into screens and matting
bedehouse	almshouse where the inmates offered prayers (bedes) for their benefactors and others
bedel	officer who walks in front of dignitaries, bearing a mace or staff
bedeman of the town	town crier
bloodwite	fine imposed for drawing blood
brokage	fee for haulage of goods, the rate being dependent on the distance involved
burgage	rental property in a town
bushel	measure used for corn and other dry goods, equivalent to four pecks
butt	large cask of wine (or other goods)
card	comb with metal teeth for combing wool
cardmaker	one who makes cards*
carnival	annual festival in the period before Lent
carriage	toll on carts
chapman	merchant or trader
charnel chapel	mortuary chapel, for the bones of the dead
chirograph	indenture* on which a legal document is written in duplicate and the word 'chirographum' is written and cut through to demonstrate the authenticity of each part

comb	measure used for dry goods, equivalent to four bushels*
cordwainer	leather-worker
coroner	official representing the legal interest of the crown
corveser	cobbler
cucking-stool	chair to which a woman guilty of certain offences was bound for public humiliation
currier	tanner of leather
custumal	written collection of the customs of a city (or other body such as a village)
Cytherea	classical Greek goddess of love (also known as Aphrodite)
Danegeld	a tax for security of the realm
dauber	one who plasters walls with mud and straw
demesne	land attached to a manor
deraign	to maintain one's right by battle
distrain	constrain by sequestration of belongings
enthymeme	argument consisting of a single premise and conclusion as opposed to a syllogism made up of major and minor premises and conclusions
farm	rate of tax paid in lieu of diverse obligations
fealty	duty owed by a tenant
fell	the skin or hide of an animal
feoffor	one who transfers real property to another
fletcher	maker of arrows
folk-moot	periodic meeting of freemen of a town
forestaller	one who intercepts and buys goods before they come to market
franchise	liberty or privilege, attached in medieval towns to property of the Church and some secular lords
frankpledge	system of joint security to which all males over 12 years were required to be enrolled
fripperer	dealer in second-hand clothing
fuller	one who shrinks and thickens woollen cloth by dampening, heating and pressing it (originally by walking on it, hence walker*)
furbisher	one who removes rust from and burnishes armour and weapons
gersum	fine
girdler	maker of belts
guild merchant	association of leading traders of a town

haberdasher	seller of miscellaneous household goods and items of clothing
hairer	maker of hair cloth or hair shirts
Hansard	member of one of the international companies (Hanse) of German merchants
heriot	tribute paid to a lord out of the goods of a tenant who died
hide	area of land, usually about 120 acres
horner	worker of horn
huckster	normally female pedlar or hawker of petty goods
hundred	subdivision of a county (originally understood to comprise 100 hides*)
Husting court	premier judicial court and court of record in medieval London
implead	to sue (in court)
indenture	duplicate document separated by a zig-zag cut, so that the two parts can be matched
indulgence	partial remission of the penalty in purgatory due for sin
infangthief	the right to judge a thief caught red-handed
journeyman	qualified master of a trade working for hire (without a shop of his/her own)
kilderkin	cask containing approximately 16 gallons (half a barrel)
landgable	land tax or ground rent
lastage	toll on goods brought to fairs and markets
lattener	maker of articles in latten, a mixed metal like brass
litster	dyer
Lombard	a person (often a merchant or banker) from north Italy
lorimer	maker of horse's bridles and small ironware
madder	red plant dye
mark	sum of money: 6*s* 8*d*
marshal	horse-shoeing smith
marten	animal similar to a ferret, hunted in the Middle Ages for its skin
mazer	wooden drinking vessel
mercer	dealer in fine textile fabrics
merchet	payment for obtaining a lord's permission for a marriage
messuage	urban property

miskenning	fine for procedural irregularity in court
moneyer	minter of the king's coin
murder-fine	levy on a community where a Norman had been murdered
mystery	association of a craft
ora	money of account introduced in Anglo-Saxon England; equivalent to about *2s*
osculatory	pax, a tablet with an image of Christ, passed around and kissed in the mass
osmund	bar of (usually Swedish) iron
palmer	pilgrim
parmenter	furrier
passage	toll on travellers
pattens	overshoes or clogs
pavage	toll levied to defray the cost of maintaining roads
pentice	a sloping rainwater roof projecting from the side of a building over a door or window; also, a structure like a veranda connecting two buildings
perch	measure of length, about 10 feet
phial	small container with a stopper
pipe	large cask of wine (or other goods)
plead	submit or respond to a legal suit
pledge	pawn
pontage	bridge toll
potash	aluminium potassium sulphate, used in dyeing; see *alum*
potter	maker of brass pots and other brassware
reeve	sheriff
regrater	one who buys goods (especially food) before they come to market, in order to sell them on at a profit
scold	malicious gossip
scot	a land tax
scotale	collective drinking to raise funds, sometimes with pressure to attend
sea-coal	originally so-called because found washed up on the sea-shore, notably in the north-east of England; from *c.*1300 so designated, whether washed-up or mined in origin, because it was transported by sea
seised	having legal possession or seisin*
seisin	legal ownership

shearer	one who finished newly woven, washed and brushed cloth by cutting off loose threads
soke	area of independent jurisdiction
souter	cobbler
stallage	rental for keeping a stall in a market
staple	body of merchants holding by royal licence the exclusive right to handle the export of certain goods
stengesdint	fine imposed for striking another
sumpter	pack or baggage horse
tallage	tax on royal lands and towns
tawyer	one who prepares leather for working
thewe	cucking-stool*
timber	quantity (forty skins) of animal furs
train-oil	oil from the blubber of a whale, seal or walrus
tranter	hawker or trader of petty goods with a horse and cart
trencher	flat piece of wood for putting food on when eating
ulnage	levy imposed for the inspection of cloth
unwin	loss
vill	territorial unit, township
walker	fuller*
water-leader	one who carts water for sale
whitawyer	tanner of sheep and goat hides
woad	blue plant dye

SUGGESTIONS FOR FURTHER READING

Attreed, L., *The King's Towns: Identity and Survival in Late Medieval English Boroughs*, New York, 2001

Baker, N. and R. Holt, *Urban Growth and the Medieval Church: Gloucester and Worcester*, Aldershot, 2003

Barron, C. M., 'Chivalry, pageantry and merchant culture in medieval London', in P. Coss and M. Keen (eds), *Heraldry, Pageantry and Social Display in Medieval England*, Woodbridge, 2002, pp. 218–41

——, *London in the Later Middle Ages. Government and People 1200–1500*, Oxford, 2004

Barron, C. M. and A. Sutton (eds), *Medieval London Widows 1300–1500*, London, 1994

Beresford, M., *The New Towns of the Middle Ages*, Leicester, 1967

Bolton, J. L. (ed.), *The Alien Communities of London in the Fifteenth Century. The Subsidy Rolls of 1440 and 1483–4*, Stamford, 1998

Britnell, R. H., *Growth and Decline in Colchester, 1300–1525*, Cambridge, 1986

——, *The Commercialisation of English Society, 1000–1500*, 2nd edn, Manchester, 1996

——, 'Town life', in R. Horrox and M. Ormrod (eds), *A Social History of England 1200–1500*, Cambridge, 2006, pp. 134–78

Carlin, M., *Medieval Southwark*, London, 1996

Clark, J., *London 1100–1600: The Archaeology of the Capital City*, London, 2011

Cohn, S. K., *Popular Protest in Late Medieval English Towns*, Cambridge, 2013

Cullum, P. H. and P. J. P. Goldberg, 'Charitable provision in late medieval York: "To the praise of God and the use of the poor"', *Northern History*, XXIX, 1993, pp. 24–39

Dyer, C., *Standards of Living in the Later Middle Ages: Social Change in England c.1200–1520*, Cambridge, 1989

——, *Making a Living in the Middle Ages: The People of Britain 850–1520*, New Haven, 2002

——, *An Age of Transition? Economy and Society in England in the Later Middle Ages*, Oxford, 2005

Geremek, B., *The Margins of Society in Late Medieval Paris*, transl. J. Birrell, Cambridge, 1987

Goldberg, P. J. P., *Women, Work, and Life Cycle in a Medieval Economy: Women in York and Yorkshire c.1300–1520*, Oxford, 1992

Hilton, R. H., *English and French Towns in Feudal Society. A Comparative Study*, Cambridge, 1992

Holt, R. and G. Rosser (eds), *The Medieval Town 1200–1540. A Reader in English Urban History*, London, 1990

Horrox, R., 'The urban gentry in the fifteenth century', in J. A. F. Thomson (ed.), *Towns and Townspeople in the Fifteenth Century*, Gloucester, 1988, pp. 22–44

Keene, D., 'Rubbish in medieval towns', in A. R. Hall and H. K. Kenward (eds), *Environmental Archaeology in an Urban Context*, Council for British Archaeology Research Reports, 43, 1982, pp. 26–30

——, *Survey of Medieval Winchester*, Oxford, 1985

——, 'Shops and shopping in medieval London', in L. Grant (ed.), *Medieval Art, Architecture and Archaeology in London*, London, 1990, pp. 29–46

Kermode, J., *Medieval Merchants: York, Beverley and Hull in the Later Middle Ages*, Cambridge, 1998

Kowaleski, M., *Local Markets and Regional Trade in Medieval Exeter*, Cambridge, 1995

Lee, J. S., 'Piped water supplies managed by civic bodies in medieval English towns', *Urban History*, XLI, 2014, pp. 369–93

Liddy, C., *War, Politics and Finance in Late Medieval English Towns: Bristol, York and the Crown 1350–1400*, Woodbridge, 2005

Lobel, M. D. et al. (eds), *Atlas of Historic Towns*, London, 1969–

McClure, P., 'Patterns of migration in the late Middle Ages', *Economic History Review*, 2nd series, XXXII, 1979, pp. 167–82

Maitland, F. W., *Township and Borough*, Cambridge, 1898

Miller, E. and J. Hatcher, *Medieval England: Towns, Commerce and Crafts 1086–1348*, London, 1995

Palliser, D. M. (ed.), *The Cambridge Urban History of Britain*, i, *600–1540*, Cambridge, 2000

——, *Towns and Local Communities in Medieval and Early Modern England*, Aldershot, 2006

——, *Medieval York 600–1540*, Oxford, 2014

Phythian-Adams, C., *Desolation of a City: Coventry and the Urban Crisis of the Late Middle Ages*, Cambridge, 1979

Platt, C., *Medieval Southampton: The Port and Trading Community, AD 1000–1600*, London, 1973

Quiney, A., *Town Houses of Medieval Britain*, New Haven, 2003

Rawcliffe, C. and R. Wilson (eds), *Medieval Norwich*, London, 2004

Rees Jones, S., *York: The Making of a City 1086–1350*, Oxford, 2014

Rexroth, F., *Deviance and Power in Late Medieval London*, transl. P. Selwyn, Cambridge, 2007

Reynolds, S., 'The rulers of London in the twelfth century', *History*, LVII, 1972, pp. 337–57

——, *An Introduction to the History of English Medieval Towns*, Oxford, 1977

Rigby, S. H., *English Society in the Later Middle Ages: Class, Status and Gender*, Basingstoke, 1995

Rosser, G., *Medieval Westminster 1200–1540*, Oxford, 1989

——, 'Workers' associations in English medieval towns', in J.-P. Sosson (ed.), *Les métiers au moyen âge*, Louvain-la-Neuve, 1994, pp. 283–305

——, 'Myth, image and social process in the English medieval town', *Urban History*, XXIII, 1996, pp. 5–25

——, *The Art of Solidarity in the Middle Ages. Guilds in England 1250–1550*, Oxford, 2015

Schofield, J., *The Building of London from the Conquest to the Great Fire*, London, 1984

——, *Medieval London Houses*, New Haven, 1995

——, *London 1100–1600: The Archaeology of a Medieval Capital*, London, 2011

Skinner, P. (ed.), *Jews in Medieval Britain: Historical, Literary and Archaeological Perspectives*, Woodbridge, 2003

Slater, T. R. and G. Rosser (eds), *The Church in the Medieval Town*, Aldershot, 1998

Sutton, A., *The Mercery of London: Trade, Goods and People, 1130–1578*, Aldershot, 2005

Swanson, H., *Medieval Artisans: An Urban Class in Late Medieval England*, Oxford, 1989

Tanner, N. P., *The Church in Late Medieval Norwich 1370–1532*, Toronto, 1984

Thomson, J. A. F. (ed.), *Towns and Townspeople in the Fifteenth Century*, Gloucester, 1988

Thrupp, S., *The Merchant Class of Medieval London*, Chicago, 1948

Urry, W., *Canterbury under the Angevin Kings*, London, 1967

INDEX